ANGELS WITH DIRTY FACES

ANGELS WITH DIRTY FACES

HOW ARGENTINIAN SOCCER
DEFINED A NATION AND
CHANGED THE GAME FOREVER

JONATHAN WILSON

NATION
BOOKS
New York

Copyright © 2016 by Jonathan Wilson
Published by Nation Books, an imprint of Perseus Books, a division of PBG Publishing, LLC, a subsidiary of Hachette Book Group, Inc.
116 East 16th Street, 8th Floor
New York, NY 10003

Nation Books is a co-publishing venture of the Nation Institute and Perseus Books.

Books published by Nation Books are available at special discounts for bulk purchases in the United States by corporations, institutions, and other organizations. For more information, please contact the Special Markets Department at the Perseus Books Group, 2300 Chestnut Street, Suite 200, Philadelphia, PA 19103, or call (800) 810-4145, ext. 5000, or e-mail special.markets@perseusbooks.com.

Designed by Jack Lenzo

Library of Congress Cataloging-in-Publication Data

Names: Wilson, Jonathan, 1976– author.
Title: Angels with dirty faces : how Argentinian soccer defined a nation and changed the game forever / Jonathan Wilson.
Description: New York : Nation Books, [2016] | Includes bibliographical references and index.
Identifiers: LCCN 2016009501| ISBN 9781568585512 (pbk.) | ISBN 9781568585529 (e-book)
Subjects: LCSH: Soccer—Argentina—History. | Soccer players—Argentina.
Classification: LCC GV944.A7 W55 2016 | DDC 796.3340982—dc23
LC record available at http://lccn.loc.gov/2016009501

10 9 8 7 6 5 4 3 2 1

Una cigarrería sahumó coémo una rosa
el desierto. La tarde se había ahondado en ayeres,
los hombres compartieron un pasado ilusorio.
Sólo faltó una cosa: la vereda de enfrente.

—Jorge Luis Borges,
"Fundación mítica de Buenos Aires"

————

A cigar store perfumed the desert like a rose.
The afternoon had established its yesterdays,
The men shared an illusory past.
Only one thing was missing: the other side of the street.

CONTENTS

PROLOGUE

The game should never have been in the balance, but it was. Argentina had battered Brazil, had created chance after chance, had had shot after shot, yet it was with only three minutes to go that Humberto Maschio, the tough inside-right from Racing, finally made it 2–0. In the wave of relief that followed, the Independiente winger Osvaldo Cruz added a third, and Argentina, with a game to spare, were South American champions for 1957, their eleventh title. As the players celebrated on the field after the final whistle in the Estadio Nacional in Lima, a microphone was handed to River Plate defender Federico Vairo so he could address the crowd. Although a leader, he was a player whose gentle face suggested concern most of the time, and on this occasion his emotions overwhelmed him. He tried to compose himself, gripping the microphone more firmly, but when he began to speak, his voice was tremulous. "It's . . . ," he said uncertainly, "it's all thanks to these *caras sucias*, to these five *sinvergüenzas*."[1] His voice trailed away, and he handed the microphone back to the official who'd thrust it at him. He managed only one sentence, but in it he both gave that team the name by which history would know it and encapsulated the spirit of Argentinian soccer to that point.

Nobody had any doubt as to whom Vairo was referring. The forward line of Omar Orestes Corbatta, Humberto Maschio, Antonio Angelillo, Omar Sívori, and Osvaldo Cruz had been devastating throughout the tournament, playing skillful, fluent soccer that resonated with a sense of enjoyment. What better name for the five players who had inspired Argentina to the Campeonato Sudamericano than *los Ángeles con Caras Sucias*—the Angels with Dirty Faces—a nod to the 1938 film starring James Cagney and Humphrey Bogart and a recognition of both the impudence of their style and the carefree way in which they played, which extended to a less than rigorous attitude toward training. "Sívori drove [Coach Guillermo] Stábile mad," said left-half Ángel "Pocho" Schandlein. "If the bus left at eight for training, Sívori was always missing, and he'd show up at ten in a taxi. Sívori liked to sleep."

In time the *Carasucias*—as the nickname was abbreviated—came to stand for the great lost past of the Argentinian game, a golden age in which skill and cheek and fun held sway, before the age of responsibility and negativity. The image of the past may have been romanticized, but the sense of loss when it was gone was real enough, and in that nostalgia for an illusory past when the world was still being made and idealism had not been subjugated by cynicism is written the whole psychodrama of Argentinian soccer, perhaps of Argentina itself.

I n 1535 Don Pedro de Mendoza set off across the Atlantic from Sanlúcar de Barrameda, Cádiz, with thirteen ships and two thousand men, having been named governor of New Andalusia by Charles V, Holy Roman Emperor and king of Spain. Mendoza, and those at the imperial court who granted him half the treasure of any local chief conquered and nine-tenths of any ransom received, dreamed of a land of immense wealth. What he found was a vast prairie populated by hostile tribes whose culture seemed primitive when set against the sophisticated and wealthy empires of Mexico and Peru.

The whole expedition was a fiasco. Mendoza's fleet was scattered by a storm off Brazil, and then his lieutenant Juan de Osorio was assassinated; some say Mendoza ordered the murder because he suspected Osorio of disloyalty. Although Mendoza sailed up the Río de la Plata and, in 1536, founded Buenos Aires on an inlet known as the Riachuelo, any sense of accomplishment was short-lived. Mendoza was confined to bed for long periods by syphilis, while early cooperation with the local Querandíes turned to rancor. The three-foot adobe wall that surrounded the settlement was washed away every time it rained, and without the help of the local people, the early settlers struggled to find food and were reduced to eating rats, snakes, and their own boots before finally resorting to cannibalism. As the population dwindled, killed by the indigenous people, illness, or starvation, Mendoza decided to return to Spain to seek assistance from the court. He died on the voyage back across the Atlantic.

Help did finally arrive, but it was insufficient and too late. In 1541 the few survivors of Mendoza's mission abandoned Buenos Aires and headed north for Asunción. They did, though, leave behind seven horses and five mares, which, doubling their population roughly every three years, became an essential factor in the gaucho culture that dominated Argentina three centuries later.

From the very beginning, Argentina, the land of silver, was a myth, an ideal to which the reality could not possibly conform.

I used to live, on and off, in an apartment just off Avenida Pueyrredón, where the district of Recoleta starts to become Palermo. If I turned left out the door and walked past the hospital, carried on for four blocks, past the deli whose owner would loudly lament in English that only Europeans really understood cheese, and then turned right up the hill, I'd come to the cemetery where eighteen presidents, writers Leopoldo Lugones and Adolfo Bioy Casares, and Eva Perón—perhaps the greatest of all Argentinian myths—are buried.

Far more often, though, I'd turn right out of the apartment and follow Pueyrredón south. I'd cross the commercial busyness of Avenida Santa Fe and keep going, leaving the middle-class area behind. As I got toward Once—where touts tried to sell you coins for more than their face value because there was a shortage and you needed them for the bus—the Bolivian influence became more pronounced. It was there, if I needed it, that I'd go to buy coriander, herbs being weirdly difficult to find in Buenos Aires. Passing the bus station, I'd go on, following the length of Linea H of the Subte, through Balvanera to Parque Patricios, a down-at-the-heels barrio that was once noted for the blacksmiths celebrated in the tango "Sur." By then, Pueyrredón has changed names, first to Jujuy and then Colonia, and there, an hour's walk from the apartment, I'd find the Estadio Tomás Adolfo Ducó.

It may not be as feted as el Monumental or la Bombonera, but there is something striking about the home of Huracán. It opened in September 1947 and still feels authentically of the forties, with its red concrete seats and the tower that thrusts up from the main stand, seemingly in homage to the much larger tower at the Centenario in Montevideo, making it appear from the distance like an ancient cruise liner. With a capacity of almost fifty thousand, the stadium is far too large for Huracán, but the sense of faded grandeur captures the imagination. Certainly, it has attracted filmmakers. It's the Ducó that features in the famous tracking shot in Juan José Campanella's 2010 Oscar-winning film *La secreta en sus ojos* (The secret in their eyes). It begins with an image of Buenos Aires by night, slowly closing in on the brightly lit field, on which Huracán are playing Racing, before swooping over one of the goals to the *popular*, where one of the main characters stands looking for a murderer.[2] The stadium had also been used as a backdrop for scenes in Emilio Ariño's *Pasión dominguera* (Sunday passion, in 1971) and Luis Puenzo's *La peste* (The plague, 1992).

When I was spending a lot of time in Buenos Aires, Huracán often used to play on a Friday. It became a habit to wander down there and watch a game with friends before heading into Palermo or the Microcentro for something to eat. In red paint on a peeling white background along the top of the *platea* are written the names of Huracán legends: Carlos Babington, René Houseman, Alfio Basile, Miguel Ángel Brindisi . . . a reminder that this isn't just the shabbily beautiful ground of another failing Buenos Aires soccer team but that it was here, in 1973, that César Luis Menotti made manifest the counterrevolution against the *anti-fútbol* that had dominated the thinking since the 1958 World Cup. In that team lay the seeds of success in 1978 and of the clash between the opposing schools of *menottisme* and *bilardisme*, the debate between idealism and pragmatism, that has dominated the Argentinian game ever since.

I was fortunate that my spell of watching Huracán coincided with the Ángel Cappa era. Cappa preached a doctrine of skillful soccer that appealed to traditionalists. For him, soccer offers an opportunity for the poorest to climb the social ladder, a way out of poverty, both metaphorical, in the way a gifted player can achieve some kind of artistic transcendence irrespective of background, and literal in the way a good player can earn vast sums of money and gain general respect.

A disappointing subsequent spell with River Plate has tarnished Cappa's image, but in early 2009 this seemed stirringly old-fashioned, the attack on the corporate nature of modern soccer striking chords in an impoverished league. And, of course, it meant all the more because he was overseeing this thrilling soccer at Huracán, the most appropriate club for his romanticism. That Huracán team was tremendous fun to watch, beautiful in the buildup, wasteful in front of goal, and catastrophic at the back. They were never a side you would trust, but somehow they reeled on to go into the last game of the 2008–2009 *clausura* a point clear of Vélez Sarsfield, their opponents in that final round, at the top of the table.[3]

The title showdown was always going to be dramatic, but the game at el Fortín, Vélez's compact stadium in the western barrio of Liniers, soon took on an epic quality. Huracán forward Eduardo Domínguez had a goal wrongly ruled out for offside, and then, nineteen minutes in, came a hailstorm so ferocious that the game had to be stopped as fans fled to the concourses for cover. Cars parked in the streets around the ground were left with dented roofs and hoods, while the whole area wailed with alarms. Within ten minutes of play resuming an hour later, Domínguez hit the woodwork, and Gastón Monzón saved a penalty from Vélez's Rodrigo López. It was Huracán that remained on top, though, and they seemed relatively comfortable as Vélez became increasingly desperate in the second half. But with Huracán seven minutes from securing the draw that would have meant only their second league title, Monzón collided with Joaquín Larrivey as he came for a cross. Most thought it was a foul, but not the referee, and Maxi Moralez knocked the ball into an empty net—and was then sent off after collecting a second yellow card for removing his shirt in his celebration. The dream had been thwarted at the last moment, and, as is the way in Argentinian soccer these days, Huracán's best players were soon on their way to wealthier clubs. Two years later, they were relegated.

Even after falling out of the top flight, the symbolic appeal of the stadium is obvious. When Coca-Cola shot an advertisement there starring model Mariana Nannis, at the time the wife of striker Claudio Caniggia, creative director Maximiliano Anselmo explained that he had chosen it because it was a "universal stadium." The tower aside, it didn't have the individual characteristics of certain other grounds, but gave a sense of Buenos Aires in the forties. It gave a feeling, in other words, of a time when Argentina was still an optimistic country, when Juan Perón offered hope of a workers republic and people believed they were building a better future. In that sense, the Ducó works as a stage of rebirth on two levels: both in its physical construction and in the soccer it witnessed in the early seventies. It's no coincidence that it was there that Cristina Kirchner, as keen a judge of symbolism as any world leader, launched her campaign for reelection to the presidency in 2011 in her first official engagement following the death of her husband, former president Néstor Kirchner.

The sense of faded grandeur and disappointed hopes isn't limited to the Ducó. Nor is it limited to soccer. Argentina is a land of thwarted wish fulfillment: it's the utopian dream that never quite came to pass as it spiraled through one repressive regime after another to hyperinflation and, ultimately, the crash of 2002, which shattered living standards and added another layer of disillusionment to already significant deposits. But when the present is such a disappointment, there is always the past.

The whole of Buenos Aires has an air of wishing the past had never ended; the only question is which past it is. The stretch from affluent Belgrano southeast to the bohemian grubbiness of San Telmo is scattered with grand buildings, surprising plazas and parks, sudden boulevards in which it's easy to imagine men in fedoras promenading with an umbrella on one arm and a woman in a complicated hat on the other. Nowadays, many of even the most striking buildings are coated in grime and defaced with graffiti, while the pavements are in a dreadful state of repair, cracked and uneven and dotted with dog shit. On a bright spring day when the jacarandas are in bloom, Buenos Aires can be a city of remarkable beauty, but you're never far from thinking how much nicer it would be if only somebody would clean it up, re-lay the paving stones, and give it a lick of paint. Various mayors have promised to do just that, but once in office they invariably find that the budget has already been allocated to give a raise to teachers or garbage collectors or other public servants, and with strikes and protests a daily occurrence anyway, they soon give up the fight. I quickly came to the conclusion that the constant street demonstrations I had at first taken as an indication of an impressive level of political engagement are actually a sign of dysfunction. If there are people marching with placards every time you go to the Plaza de Mayo, if roads are regularly blocked by sit-ins, if the twenty-four-hour news channels constantly show one profession or another clashing with police,[4] it soon becomes little more than background noise, the specifics of each protest lost in a sea of dissent. Then again, in a country that has such traumatic recent memories of dissent being suppressed, perhaps the vigor with which the right to protest is exercised should be celebrated.

Nonetheless, a folk memory of the days of glamour seems to linger, and there is a clear nostalgia for the early part of the last century. Traditional red English mailboxes have survived, despite it all, in parts of Palermo, while the pride in what Buenos Aires used to be is seen in the preservation of the old-style cafés and the astonishing prevalence of sepia photographs of the city in the most unlikely places. In the otherwise unremarkable Coto supermarket on Calle French, for instance, two blocks southeast of Pueyrredón, the walls by the escalator up to the second floor are adorned not with advertisements and special offers but prints of old Buenos Aires. But nothing speaks so strongly of Buenos Aires's love affair with its own past as the ongoing obsession with the tango, a dance that originated in the city and in Montevideo in the 1890s, its popularity spread by its use in theaters and by street-side barrel organs.

The longing for the past is understandable. Around the turn of the twentieth century, Argentina was so buoyant that Nicaraguan poet Rúben Darío described Argentinians as "the Yankees of the south." In the 1920s Argentina was politically stable and economically prosperous, a thriving young nation often compared favorably to Canada or Australia. In 1928 its gross national product per capita was the eighth highest in the world. By 2012, according to the International Monetary Fund's (IMF) figures, it had fallen to sixtieth. In 1930 Argentina had enjoyed seventy years of unbroken civilian rule. Then came the first military coup. Over the following forty-six years, there would be a further thirteen governments that rose by either coup or less overt forms of military persuasion. A piece in the *New Statesman* in 1978 noted, "The failure of Argentina as a nation is the biggest political mystery of this century."

Yet it came so close to succeeding. After the massacres of its indigenous population throughout the nineteenth century, Argentina became, for theorists at least, a tabula rasa. That encouraged a utopianism, a sense that this was a land in which a new, better society could be created. Principles, though, always ran into reality and vested interests, and the most lasting effect of that utopianism was not to generate a better world but to encourage a mode of thought that sought always to establish ideals and absolutes and then, in response to the inevitable failure to live up to those ideals, an almost nihilistic belief that there can be nothing but pragmatism. Argentinian soccer, certainly, is populated by unusual numbers of both romantics and cynics, even some who seem almost to see a romanticism in extreme cynicism.

After the failure of Mendoza's expedition, others followed. In 1580 Juan de Garay refounded Buenos Aires. He, too, was seduced by mythical questing, spending much of the following two years hunting for the legendary City of the Caesars, a settlement of untold riches founded by, depending which version of the story you believe, survivors of a Spanish shipwreck, the last remaining Incas, ghosts, or giants, and supposedly lying somewhere in the Patagonian Andes. Garay died the following year, killed by a group of Querandíes on the banks of the Carcarañá River.

The early settlers found a land that resisted the schemes they had for it and, alienated from their homeland, began to construct a new identity based on that unease and the general lack of security: there were no state institutions, so everybody had to fend for themselves. Yet when those institutions did begin to emerge and national laws were imposed, they were seen as intrusive, as a curtailment of the freedom the New World was supposed to represent. As a result, the laws were never trusted, were never seen as a benign code that brought security, but rather were viewed as something to be gotten around. And because of that pervasive sense of instability, anybody with money or power or influence immediately sought to protect their position, the sense of insecurity only heightened by an army without an enemy.

Historian and intellectual José Luis Romero wrote that "the soul of Argentina is an enigma," arguing that the nation is a myth, a chimera, a land in which identity is there to be invented.[5] That search—and its almost inevitable lack of fulfillment—itself has consequences, as a number of Argentinian writers have articulated. In *La hipocresía Argentina*, for instance, essayist and economist Enrico Udenio argued, "Argentina is comprised of a neurotic society in which its inhabitants feel unfulfilled and compelled to act in a self-destructive manner. . . . It's a society that builds up dreams and, when they aren't realised, looks outside itself for explanations and to apportion blame."[6]

Udenio's is an extreme view, but it is true that a sense of what might have been hangs over Argentina, a frustration and a sadness that the glories that were expected never materialized. That perhaps explains why there is a higher incidence of Freudian psychoanalysis in Buenos Aires than in any other city in the world with the exception of New York. Virtually the only sphere in which Argentina has fulfilled its early promise is in soccer, which is perhaps the principal reason it has taken on such immense significance.

The sense of myth, of ideals of the past to be reinvoked, colors everything. Argentinians regularly lament that fans no longer know their history, and perhaps many don't, but in terms of the newspaper and television coverage, no other nation is so in awe of its own past. Before major games TV channels relentlessly screen past meetings between the sides.

And for a country of only 25 million, Argentina's is an almost incomparably rich history. They've won two World Cups and lost in three finals; they've won fourteen Copa Américas (six more than Brazil). Their clubs have lifted the Copa Libertadores twenty-four times (seven more than Brazil's). Argentina has produced, in Diego Maradona, one of the only two realistic candidates to be considered the greatest player there has ever been; in Lionel Messi, it may have produced a third, and few would place Alfredo Di Stéfano too far behind (and, this being Argentina, there is a whole list of candidates from the pretelevision age who have their advocates: Manuel Seoane, Antonio Sastre, Adolfo Pedernera, Omar Sívori . . .).

But it's not just about success or passion. No country so intellectualizes its soccer, so loves its theories and its myths. Soccer in Argentina is overtly cultural, overtly political. Presidents know its power and seek to harness it; the unscrupulous mobilize hooligan groups, the *barras bravas*, in their support. The philosophers, meanwhile, dismiss titles, whole generations of success, because they were won in the "wrong way." So while this is primarily a history of soccer, so entwined are the political and socioeconomic strands, so inextricably is soccer bound up with all public life, that this is also a book about Argentina.

PART ONE

THE BIRTH OF A NATION,
1863–1930

1

THIS ENGLISH GAME

Buenos Aires. Head northeast along Sarmiento from the statue of Garibaldi on Plaza Italia, bearing left across the patchy grass toward Plaza Holanda. The track around the lake in its center is marked off every hundred meters for the benefit of joggers, who chug around, dodging in-line skaters and any geese that aren't attacking paddleboats on the water. Skirt the path and head between the trees, and you reach Avenida Figueroa Alcorta. If you turned left and followed the road, you'd go past the rowing lake and the hippodrome before arriving at el Monumental. But if you cross Alcorta, onto the springier grass that surrounds the planetarium, you'll find, beside green wooden boards detailing cycling routes around the city, an unremarkable white-gray stone perhaps five feet in height. The sides are daubed with red paint. On the back, in blue, is scrawled "CMB 2011," and around that, in black paint, are other squiggles.

The front, though, is free of graffiti and bears an inscription proclaiming this to be a *lugar historico*—a historic site. There is another, much smaller, stone set at the base of the main one. If it ever carried any writing, it has long since been worn away. The monument was erected by the Comisión Nacional de Museos y Lugares Historicos: "Here was established the first sports ground of the Buenos Aires Cricket Club, 8 December 1864." Curiously, given the relative interest in the sports in Buenos Aires, it doesn't mention soccer at all, yet it was there, on June 20, 1867, that sixteen members of the city's business community—all from Britain apart from William Boschetti, who had been born in Saint Lucia—met to contest the first organized game of soccer ever played on Argentinian soil.

The Football Association's (FA) Laws of the Game, drawn up in December 1863, had arrived in Buenos Aires and been published in the English-language newspaper the *Standard* in early 1867. It served a population that, by 1880, had swelled to forty thousand, the largest British (or, rather, British and Irish, as the majority of that number were from what is now the Republic of Ireland) population in any country that was not part of the empire. So significant was the British influence that it could at times feel as though

Argentina *was* part of the empire, as a headline in the *Times* had declared it to be in 1806. The British ran the banking system, developed the railway, and exported hide, wool, and meat; at the time, Britain was by some margin Argentina's largest trading partner.

The British in Argentina had done what the British did everywhere, creating a miniature version of home, setting up schools, hospitals, churches, and—crucially—sporting clubs. Initially, those clubs tended to be focused on cricket, tennis, and, given the fine horses available, polo, but some of their members must have played soccer of a sort in high school or college. As early as 1840, meanwhile, British sailors had been playing some kind of soccer on the docks. It was a practice that seems to have provoked bewilderment among locals, as demonstrated by a report in *La Razón* that doubtfully explained that the pastime "consisted of running around after a ball."

To carry the game forward and begin its propagation required organization, and that came from Thomas—or Tomás—Hogg. His father had been the owner of a Yorkshire textile factory before moving to Buenos Aires, where he not only pursued his business interests but had also founded a British commercial center, a British library, a British college, and, in 1819, a cricket club. His son was no less active. He organized the Dreadnought Swimming Club, which staged its first competitions in 1863. He took up squash three years later and, with his brother James, established the Buenos Aires Athletic Society in 1867. At some point in the 1860s, he set up the first golf club on the continent. He was a pioneer in almost every sporting field, but it was his work in soccer that would gain the most traction, even though he soon abandoned the sport for rugby.

On May 6 Hogg placed a notice in the *Standard* under the heading "Foot Ball: A Preliminary Meeting." The first game had been scheduled for May 25 but had to be postponed for almost a month because of a waterlogged field at Boca Junction railway station. On that brisk June afternoon, after a brief delay while the propriety of wearing shorts in front of female spectators was debated, a team wearing red caps (los Colorados) and captained by Hogg played a team wearing white caps (los Blancos) and captained by Hogg's friend William Heald over two eight-a-side halves of fifty minutes. And so, in an area of central Buenos Aires farther from a soccer stadium than any other—as though today's clubs are too respectful to draw too close to the hallowed ground—soccer came to Argentina.

Heald seems not to have enjoyed the experience particularly. In his diary he writes of taking the ten o'clock train to Palermo with Hogg and marking out the field with flags before they "adjourned to the Confitería and had some bread and cheese and porter" while they waited for the rest of the players. The shortage of players made "the work very heavy," and by the end Heald was "utterly exhausted." That wasn't the only ill effect: "My back was very painful and indeed seemed to take away all my appetite as I could hardly touch a thing at dinner."[1]

Los Colorados won 4–0, and a second game was soon arranged, Heald being replaced as captain of los Blancos by H. J. Barge (Argentina has never had much patience with leaders held responsible for defeats—although by the sounds of it, Heald had little desire to play again). This time los Colorados won 3–0, and soccer had laid down tentative roots. Within three years *El Nacional*, a Spanish-language paper, was referring to "this English game" and predicting that "it will not be long before we get used to it."

Initially, soccer was just one game among the many played by the British community, but by the 1880s it was the predominant sport, spreading rapidly in part because of its simplicity—it required no equipment beyond a ball, which could be improvised from rags or tightly bound newspaper, and its laws were simple enough for anybody to grasp almost instantaneously—and in part because it was pushed through the British schools, which, following their counterparts back home, saw soccer as a way of promoting the muscular Christian virtues of discipline, strength, and endurance. Moreover, team sports were seen as a means of staving off the solipsism that could lead to that most debilitating of vices, masturbation—an obsession of Victorian schools.[2]

The greatest evangelist for soccer in Argentina was Alexander Watson Hutton. He was born in the Gorbals in 1852, the son of a grocer and his wife who had both died by the time he was five. He was brought up by his maternal grandmother and then at the Daniel Stewart Hospital School. Watson Hutton was also a keen soccer player, a photograph from around 1880 depicting him as a thin but athletic man with a high forehead and a luxuriant, if droopy, mustache.

In 1880 Watson Hutton was offered a job at St. Andrew's Scotch School in Buenos Aires. He completed a second-class degree in philosophy in 1881, and later that year he set sail from Liverpool to take up the position, although he didn't arrive in Argentina until February 25, 1882. For him, perhaps because he had lost two brothers to tuberculosis, soccer seems to have been rather more than a game: it was something that could improve physical fitness—and prolong life.

Few in the expat community would have disagreed with him, but their preference was for rugby, with one piece in the *Herald* dismissing soccer as an "animalistic game." The school board at St. Andrew's was equally skeptical, and there had been disagreements for some time over the prominence soccer should be given in the curriculum when Watson Hutton snapped, resigning after his request for a gymnasium and extended playing fields was rejected.

A man of lesser resolve may have repented or considered a return to Britain, but Watson Hutton was committed to his path and set up the English High School, which opened its doors on February 2, 1884. Within two years, with soccer central to the curriculum, he had fifty boarders and five hundred day pupils and had to move to larger premises. The British schools catered not only to the students of expat families but also to the Argentinian elite, and so the game began to spread among the local community.

Watson Hutton's roots in Edinburgh remained central to his life in Buenos Aires. In March 1885 he married a former teacher from the school at which he had worked, Margaret Budge, at St. Andrew's Presbyterian Church. The following year the first of their three children, Arnold, was born; he would himself have a major role to play in the early years of the Argentinian game. In July 1886 another old acquaintance reintroduced himself: William Waters, the son of Watson Hutton's landlady in Edinburgh. He arrived in Buenos Aires to take up a position at the English High School and brought with him a sack of leather soccer balls. Legend has it that the deflated balls baffled customs officers at the port, who initially thought they were wineskins or leather caps; eventually, they were noted as "items for the crazy English." Waters would later become a successful importer of sporting goods to South America, but his more immediate impact came on the field.

Just as Watson Hutton was placing soccer at the core of the curriculum and other schools were following his lead, an influx of railway workers from Britain who were already familiar with the game arrived. The combination of old hands and recent converts proved a potent mix, and soccer grew rapidly. In 1888 came Argentina's first attempt at international soccer, as a group of British expats in Buenos Aires arranged a game against counterparts from Montevideo to celebrate Queen Victoria's birthday. The event was repeated each year until 1894. By 1890 even Rosario, almost two hundred miles to the northwest of Buenos Aires, had two teams—Athletic for the management and Central for the workers.

The following year organized soccer in Argentina took a huge leap forward, as a group of immigrants led by Alec Lamont, a Scottish teacher at St. Andrews, brought together representatives from five teams—Old Caledonians, Buenos Aires and Rosario Railways, Buenos Aires Football Club, Belgrano Football Club, and St. Andrews Scotch Athletic Club—to found the Argentine Association Football League (AAFL). Waters captained and coached St. Andrews, which won the inaugural championship—the first soccer league contested anywhere outside of Britain. Waters's team was composed entirely of Scots, as was the side that finished second, Old

Caledonians, their side made up largely of employees from a British plumbing company, Bautaume & Peason, that had been engaged to install a sewage system in Buenos Aires.

The league collapsed the following year, undone by a lack of resources and leadership. Its salvation was Watson Hutton, who stepped in and relaunched it on February 21, 1893. An Argentinian championship has been contested every year since, and it is the body that oversaw it that is regarded as the oldest soccer federation in South America, the eighth oldest in the world. Watson Hutton remained AAFL president until 1896, refereeing the occasional game and continuing to supervise the English High School.

Five teams contested that 1893 championship, which was won by Lomas, a British institution set up by the old boys of Bedford School. A photograph of the first champions shows twelve players seated around A. Leslie, a benign-looking man with a gray mustache, dressed in a dark suit accessorized by a bow tie with a handkerchief spilling flamboyantly from his breast pocket. Of the thirteen, only one has a name that is not obviously British or Irish, F. Nobili.

According to a book published in 2006 that celebrates 115 years of the club, more than five hundred people turned up to watch Lomas play Flores in that first season, and a contemporary photograph shows spectators perched in trees peering over the heads of fans lined up three or four deep along the touchline. In another photograph, this one of the game against the English High School, it is the referee who catches the eye, the arc of his mustache reflected in the loop of his watch chain as he chases the play in jacket, waistcoat, broad white trousers, and flat cap.

Lomas remained dominant, winning five of the first six titles—their only failure coming when they were beaten by their own reserve side, Lomas Academicals. Decline, once begun, was rapid. When relegation was introduced in 1908, they avoided the drop by a single place, but the following season they slipped out of the top flight, an emblem of the waning power of the old British clubs as the game spread to other communities and an Argentinian consciousness began to emerge. By 1930 they'd given up soccer altogether, although the club still exists, focusing on rugby and wearing the green, scarlet, and gold colors settled upon in 1896.

The end of Lomas's hegemony came just as the rest of Argentinian soccer took another major leap forward: in April 1898 the Ministry of Justice and Public Education made physical education mandatory in all schools. Given the government's initial suspicion of soccer and the panic prompted earlier in the decade when a report was circulated claiming that more than four hundred deaths and injuries had been caused by the sport in Britain—insurance companies began to advertise specific policies for those taking part, while the *Standard* warned parents not to allow their children to play such a violent game—that was a significant sign that the game had gained acceptance.

Confirmed in his belief that soccer would take root in Argentina, Watson Hutton bought a sports field in northern Buenos Aires and founded the Club Atlético English High School for pupils, former students, and teachers. A year later they entered a team in the second division of the AAFL and finished a point behind the champions, Banfield. Under the name Alumni, adopted two years later after the implementation of a regulation banning the use of the names of educational establishments on the grounds that it was advertising, they would become the dominant force in Argentinian soccer in the first decade of the twentieth century, winning the first division ten times between 1900 and 1911.

Watson Hutton had long since retired from playing, but his son Arnoldo, as he became known, made his debut on the left wing for Alumni in 1902 at the age of fifteen. The real strength of Alumni, though, lay not in the progeny of Hutton, but in the offshoots of another Scottish family, albeit one that had left Britain much earlier and had far deeper roots in Argentina. James Brown was among more than two hundred Scots on the *Symmetry*, one of several ships that left Leith and Greenock for Buenos Aires in 1825, their passage paid by two Roxburghshire-born landowners, John and William Parish Robertson, who had received permission from the Argentinian government to establish an "experimental agricultural community" at Monte Grande, to the south of Buenos Aires.

Within four years it had become apparent that the experiment had failed, but few of the settlers returned home. Brown bought his own plot of land and became a successful farmer. His youngest son, also called James, had nine sons, seven of whom—Jorge Gibson, Ernesto, Eliseo, Alfredo, Carlos Carr, Tomás, and Diego Hope—played for Alumni.

Alumni were the last of the great Anglo-Argentinian sides, insisting that their aim was to uphold "British values" as much as it was to win and to "play well without passion." On one celebrated occasion against Estudiantes, Alumni players refused to take a penalty they had been awarded for handball. It would be misleading to suggest, though, that Alumni were popular only among the British community. They were champions, capable of superb soccer, and their appeal was near universal. As such, politicians made efforts to be seen with them; on one occasion, President José Figueroa Alcorta embraced Alfredo Brown, an event novelist Osvaldo Soriano suggested was "the first time that a president had used soccer for popular ends."

While Alumni were dominating, the landscape was changing. Buenos Aires was growing rapidly, in part because of urbanization as people from rural areas deserted the old ranches to take up jobs in the factories and industrial plants that were springing up in the metropolis and in part because of immigration from across the Atlantic, the majority from Italy and Spain, but also significant numbers of Jews from Poland and Russia as well as Germans, Britons, and *turcos*—the generic name given to anybody from the Middle East. By 1914, 80 percent of those born in Argentina were the descendants of immigrants who had arrived since 1860.

Soccer boomed as the city grew. A second division was added in 1895, a third in 1899—catering initially to under-17s who attended a full-day session at one of the schools—and a fourth by 1902; by then the game had long since ceased to be the preserve of British expats. Research by Julio Frydenberg shows that by 1907, there were at least three hundred clubs outside the official championship. Some represented specific professions or sections of society, but the majority represented specific barrios—a phenomenon that came into being only with mass urbanization and electrification; once houses could be lit and heated by electricity rather than gas, they could be built much higher, leading to the forests of apartment blocks that characterize Buenos Aires today. The teams can, in part, be seen as part of a general yearning for a sense of identity. As the old theory has it, all countries need an army, a bank, and a soccer team,[3] so the sporting club gave the people of a barrio something to rally behind, a projection of their area and by extension themselves in the wider world.

The first specifically Argentinian institution to field a soccer team was Gimnasia y Esgrima (Gymnastics and Fencing) of La Plata, a city thirty-five miles from the center of Buenos Aires. The club was founded in 1887 and adopted soccer in 1901, while each of the five *grandes* of the Argentinian game was founded in the first decade of the twentieth century: immigrants in the dock area founded River Plate in 1901 and Boca Juniors in 1905, French migrants from the factories of Avellaneda set up Racing Club in 1903,[4] while their neighbors Independiente were established by Spanish speakers from the British-run City of London Stores sports club in 1905, and in 1908 a priest in Almagro created San Lorenzo as a safe place for the local youth to play.

Proper international soccer began in May 1901, as a team made up largely of players from Lomas and Alumni went to Montevideo and beat Uruguay 3–2.[5] Uruguay won by the same scoreline in Buenos Aires the following year, and from their next meeting in 1905 there was a silver cup to play for, donated by Thomas Lipton, the tea magnate, who had been born a couple of streets from Watson Hutton in the Gorbals in 1848.

By 1905 the league had seventy-seven clubs that between them played more than five hundred matches a season. On June 1 that year, for example, fifty-two teams played, drawing a total attendance of more than five thousand. Soon, four-figure crowds became common, and English- and Spanish-language papers began reporting on the league regularly. So seriously was match reporting taken that, by 1912, the *Herald* was insisting that the press needed custom accommodations rather than just being given seats in the grandstand.

The biggest draws, though, were touring sides, the presence of which was itself a confirmation of the credibility of the Argentinian league. It was the Hippic Club, a sporting society for the social elite headed by Baron Antonio de Marchi, that arranged the first tour, inviting Southampton to visit in 1904. The president of the republic, Julio Roca, turned up for the first game, against Alumni, an indication of the social—if perhaps not yet the sporting—importance of the occasion. Southampton were fully professional, and although they still played in the Southern League, they had reached the FA Cup final in both 1900 and 1902. Comfortably the better side, they beat Alumni 3–0 and went on to win their four remaining games in Argentina by a combined score of 29–4 before heading across the River Plate and beating a Uruguayan XI 8–1. The clear superiority of Southampton confirmed to the British in Buenos Aires that the old country and the old values were still supreme, while they made such an impression that, even in 1923, the *Herald* was still eulogizing their "magnificent work with head and feet, their skilful blending of brains and boots."

Nottingham Forest followed in 1905, impressing so much that Independiente ditched their white shirts for Forest's red, although they stuck with their navy-blue shorts. Argentinian teams may at that stage have been unable to match even quite ordinary English sides (Forest had finished sixteenth of eighteen teams in Division I in 1905 and would be relegated the following season), but the 1906 tourists gave an indication of how Argentina compared to the rest of the world. The South Africa team that traveled to Argentina was amateur and featured in its party eight British players and seven who were born in South Africa—it was in no sense a national side—but it offered a glimpse of life outside soccer's motherland. The South Africans beat San Martín 6–0 and a student side 14–0 before a game that was arguably the most significant played in Argentina to that point.

The crowd at Sociedad Sportiva probably wasn't quite as big as the one that had seen Alumni hammered by Forest the previous year, but it wasn't far off, and this time it saw an Alumni side featuring Arnoldo Watson Hutton win 1–0, the first victory by an Argentinian club over a touring team. The *Herald*, with typical sobriety, noted that Alumni had been lucky, but that did little to stem the celebrations. The goal was greeted by spectators cheering "until they were hoarse; hats and sticks and papers were flung into the air; highly respectable, portly and usually sedate members of the community actually danced with joy." At the final whistle, the crowd poured onto the field and carried the Alumni players off. The South Africans went on to win their eight remaining fixtures in Argentina, but Alumni's victory had been a major breakthrough—even if the ease with which Everton and Tottenham dismissed Argentinian teams on their 1909 tours showed there was still a gulf separating them from the top-class English teams. Those games, particularly the ones against Tottenham, also showcased the growing divide in conceptions of how soccer should be played, with the local crowd antagonized by the English sides' use of the shoulder charge. It was a difference of interpretation that would go on to have serious consequences.

2

A SECOND BIRTH

The AAFL had been renamed the Argentine Football Association (AFA) in 1903 and, although it affiliated with the Football Association in London, decided that from then on, it would conduct meetings in Spanish, a sure sign of the *criollisation* of the game. In 1912 it changed its name again, this time to the Asociación Argentina de Football (AAF), and affiliated with the Fédération Internationale de Football Association (FIFA). By then, players with British heritage were very much in the minority: as a report in the *Standard* in June that year pointed out, Porteños, San Isodro, and River Plate had three Anglos each; Gimnasia y Esgrima (Buenos Aires) and Estudiantes (La Plata) each had one; and Racing didn't have any at all.

Further evidence of the growing strength of the local game on the field as well as off it came in 1910 as Argentinos beat Britanicos 5–1 in the final staging of what had been an annual exhibition game between the two communities. In part the match was discontinued because it was becoming one-sided, but the AFA also had bigger fish to fry. That year, to celebrate the centenary of Argentina's first autonomous government, the AFA tried to set up a four-team South American championship. Brazil declined the invitation, but Chile and Uruguay both sent teams for what was probably at the time the most significant international tournament played outside the British Home Championship.

The opening game saw Argentina face Chile. They won comfortably enough, 3–1, with a goal from Arnoldo Watson Hutton, but two other details are telling. First, the *Herald*'s report included the detail that Mrs. G. D. Ferguson had provided the teas—this was still, emphatically, a British social occasion. Second, Argentina missed a penalty: it had been controversially awarded, and there were shouts from the crowd urging the taker to kick the ball out of play. Whether the taker actually did miss on purpose is impossible to say, but even if he was trying to score, it says much for the prevailing mores that at least some at the game felt fair play demanded he should not.

That spirit of fair play was offended when the Uruguay side to face Chile was revealed and featured, in Buck and Harley, two players who had been born in the United Kingdom. However British the surnames in the home team may have appeared, all their side had been born in Argentina. The crowd, neighborly rivalry already setting it against Uruguay, was further riled by that and was notably supportive of Chile, howling in disgust as they had two goals ruled out. Uruguay won 3–1, but it was the Chilean goalkeeper who was chaired from the field.

The final, the *Herald* claimed in its preview, was the "most important association soccer match played in this country." Ten thousand paid to get in, and a further thousand or so watched from the embankment of the Central Argentinian Railway Company as Argentina swept to a 4–1 victory. Arnoldo Watson Hutton again scored, but the influence of his family and Anglo-Argentinians in general was waning.

When Alumni won their 1911 title, Alexander Watson Hutton was fifty-eight and tiring of the demands of running the club. Many of his players were aging, and the sense was growing that the old-boys teams couldn't compete in an era in which money was playing an increasing role as attendance swelled. Their self-conscious amateurism meant they hadn't developed their ground, often leasing fields from other teams, while what profits they did make tended to be donated to charity. Recognizing that Alumni couldn't realistically carry on and expect to be successful in that form, Watson Hutton decided to retire and disbanded the club. He continued to live in Buenos Aires and died there in 1936, being buried in the British Cemetery at Chacarita. His role is remembered, though: the library at the AFA's headquarters is named after him, and a 1950 film, *Escuela de campeones* (School of champions), told the story of Hutton and his Alumni side. He stands as the undoubted founding father of the Argentinian game.

After Alumni were wound up, the majority of their players moved to Quilmes, which, having finished at the bottom of the nine-team first division in 1911, won the title the following year.

The league was, in a sense, a victim of its own success. The tours by foreign clubs had proved highly lucrative to those deemed worthy of playing visiting teams; those who weren't not only missed out on those payments, but were also banned from playing matches on the same day as a tour game, so as not to draw away spectators. Money became an increasing motivation, and those clubs that hadn't developed their grounds early found themselves doubly disadvantaged: they were unable to accommodate the large crowds that brought significant revenues, and without those revenues they were unable to afford the costs of constructing a stadium, particularly as the price of land increased as the city expanded.

Financial gripes crystallized widespread disgruntlement, and in 1912 Richard Aldao, a lawyer, businessman, member of the International

Olympic Committee, and president of Gimnasia y Esgrima (of Buenos Aires), established a rival governing body, the Federación Argentina de Football (FAF). The result was a mess. The AAF championship was hit by withdrawals and annulments, and, by July, there were two championships being played. Quilmes won the six-team AAF title, while the FAF championship went ahead with eight teams. Independiente went into the final game of the rebel season needing to beat Argentino de Quilmes by more than a goal to pip Porteño to the title on goal average. As it was they won 5–0, but, recognizing that Argentino, which had little to play for in mid-table, had fielded a much-weakened team, Independiente offered Porteño a playoff for the title. Or—and it's difficult to tell at this remove—Porteño protested and, seeing the potential for a further money-spinning game at Gimnasia y Esgrima's stadium, the FAF pressured Independiente into playing the game.

Either way, it should have been possible to present the playoff as a noble gesture, one that confirmed that the best traditions of gentlemanliness hadn't died with Alumni and that a sense of justice and doing what was right prevailed, but it produced the most shameful scenes in Argentinian soccer history to that point. Pedro Rithner, the brother of the great goalkeeper Juan José Rithner, put Porteño ahead, but Bartolomé Lloveras leveled. Then, with three minutes remaining, Independiente believed they'd scored a winner, only for Carlos Aertz, the referee, to give a corner. Their protests were so ferocious that three players were sent off, at which the other eight decided they didn't want to play on. The FAF awarded the game and thus the title to Porteño.

In the midst of the chaos, Swindon Town had arrived for a tour, which at least gave locals some soccer to watch in June while the AAF and FAF squabbled. With no other soccer to watch, fans flocked to those games, with attendance twice topping twenty thousand. Swindon manager Sam Allen was taken aback by the enthusiasm for soccer. "Everywhere," he told the *Daily Chronicle*, "one sees the hold it has taken on the people. Boys in the streets, on the seashore, down alleys, soldiers on the barracks ground—all have the fever."

That only fueled flames that were already beginning to flicker. The schism was the result of a dispute over money, and players too were beginning to wonder why they weren't benefiting from the thousands of people who paid to watch them play. It was no great secret that for years inducements had been offered to players. As early as 1906 there had been complaints in the Buenos Aires newspapers about the number of Uruguayan imports, whom nobody believed were coming just for the love of the game. By 1913 *La Nación* was speaking explicitly of disguised professionalism.

That year was the first to produce a genuinely *criollo* champion, as both the AAF and the FAF titles were won by teams that had little to do with the British expat community. The FAF championship went to Estudiantes of La Plata, while the AAF, looking to build drama and interest, contrived a bewildering championship structure—and so began one of the great traditions of Argentinian soccer.

Racing faced San Isidro for the title three days after Christmas and won 2–0, the inside-right Alberto Ohaco, the son of one of the Spanish factory workers who had founded the club, scoring both goals. A glance at the line-ups says much about the changing makeup of the Argentinian game: of the twenty-two players who played in that final, only three—Wilson, Goodfellow, and Hulme of San Isidro—had British surnames.

For Racing, it was the start of a golden era in which they won seven successive championships. They dropped only a point in winning the AAF title (thankfully back to a straight round-robin schedule) in 1914, as Porteño took the FAF championship, and their dominance continued after the leagues were reunified into one twenty-five-team division, their neat, intelligent, progressive soccer earning them the nickname "la Academia." Ohaco, who always played in a white cap, was the league's top scorer four seasons in a row, 1912–1915, and by the time he retired at age thirty-nine in 1923, he had amassed 244 goals in 278 games for Racing, still the club record. Borocotó,[1] the editor of *El Gráfico*, later described him as a "one-man orchestra of Argentinian soccer in that he performed well in any position."

As the league developed, the AAF reached out to its neighbors. Games against Uruguay were already well established, and 1914 brought the first international against Brazil, a friendly Argentina won 3–0. In 1912 they met with delegates from the Rosarian league and the Uruguayan league to discuss the formation of a soccer federation of the River Plate. That was the beginning of a slow process that gained momentum in 1915 when Héctor R. Gómez, a Uruguayan teacher and member of parliament and the president of the Montevideo Wanderers, began campaigning for a South American confederation, arguing that it would help head off the sort of factionalism that had split the Argentinian game. The following year, as the AAF arranged a tournament to mark the centenary of Argentina's declaration of independence from Spain, Gómez made a decisive move. The Confederación Sudamericana de Fútbol (Conmebol) was founded on July 9, 1916, and boldly announced the schedule for four Campeonatos Sudamericanos, the first one having started seven days earlier.

It took only a week for Conmebol to face its first crisis. Argentina and Uruguay both hammered Chile, but Argentina could only draw with Brazil, while Uruguay beat them 2–1. That meant the final match, between Uruguay and Argentina, was effectively a decider, with Uruguay needing only a draw to lift the inaugural title.

The game was scheduled for July 16 at the Gimnasia y Esgrima stadium. More tickets were sold than there was space, though, and with the stands overwhelmed and crushes developing, the match was abandoned after five minutes. As the players left the field, fans reacted with fury. Some stole naphtha from the lights of cars parked near the ground and used it to set the stands on fire. The blaze burned for four hours, with only the central pavilion avoiding damage. The game was rearranged for the following day at Racing's ground in Avellaneda and ended, anticlimactically, in a goalless draw and Uruguayan glory.

Uruguay would go on to dominate the early years of the championship. On home soil in 1917, they beat Argentina in the final game to take the title ahead of them again, and, although the hosts Brazil won in 1919, in Valparaíso in 1920 the familiar order was restored: Uruguay first, Argentina second, Brazil third—with Argentina paying for their failure to beat the perennial fourth-placed side, Chile.

By then Argentinian soccer was undergoing another schism, this one growing from dissatisfaction at how the game was governed and how the regulations were implemented. The problems began toward the end of 1918 with a dispute over the eligibility of a player Columbian had fielded against Ferro Carril Oeste. At the same time in the Intermediate League, the second flight, Vélez were docked eight points for fielding a suspended player. They argued that they hadn't, that the player in question was actually the brother of the one who was suspended, an explanation the AAF accepted, restoring the points. A number of teams protested, leading the AAF to convene a special assembly, but that was undermined by a filibuster that came to seem like a concerted effort to highlight the body's failings.

What happened the following year was even more chaotic. With six of the nineteen sides suspended, the league was abandoned in July, with no team having played more than eight games. Although Boca, Estudiantes (La Plata), and Huracán remained loyal, thirteen clubs, including Racing, River Plate, San Lorenzo, and Independiente, broke away and were joined by Vélez in creating the Asociación Amateurs de Football (AAmF). Seemingly corroborating the rebel clubs' complaints about the AFA's ineptitude, the six-team championship it tried to institute dragged on into the following year and was eventually abandoned on January 21. The new AAmF championship, meanwhile, ran almost without a hitch and, despite some withdrawals in the final round of games, was completed on January 6, with every team having played (or had the governing body determine the result of) thirteen games. Racing, which had won six and drawn two in the AFA league before seceding, won thirteen out of thirteen, a fittingly perfect end to an extraordinary period in which they had won seven straight titles, four times going unbeaten through the season; in those seven years, they lost just five matches.

Both bodies declared a champion the following year. Racing's reign was ended by River Plate in the AAmF championship, while Boca retained their AAF title. Huracán and Boca went on to win three each of the next six AAF championships, while the AAF title was won twice each by San Lorenzo, Independiente, and Racing. Argentina's great sides were beginning to assert themselves.

3

THE GLOBAL STAGE

Uruguay went to the 1924 Olympics as unknowns; they left having redefined soccer. The final was almost a procession, as Uruguay, playing with a revolutionary fluency and verve, completed a simple 3–0 win over Switzerland to confirm the gold medals that had seemed ensured almost from their first game at the tournament. For South American soccer as a whole, it was the breakthrough moment. They had taken the game born on the mud and the cloisters of the English public schools to unimagined levels of refinement and sophistication, and the majority of Europe—Britain a notable exception—saluted their virtuosity. Remastered footage reveals a startling modernity to their play: the game was less frenetic then, but the one-touch passing and the fluidity generated by rolling the ball into space differ only in pace from the fundamentals of the twenty-first-century game. Gabriel Hanot, who would go on to edit *L'Équipe* but was then coming to the end of a distinguished playing career, wrote: "They have such a complete technique that they also have the necessary leisure to note the position of partners and team-mates. They do not stand still waiting for a pass. They are on the move, away from markers, to make it easy for their teammates."

Uruguay's story was a genuinely remarkable one. If the legend, as propagated by poet and political thinker Eduardo Galeano, is to be believed, theirs was a team of true amateurs, including in their squad a marble cutter, a grocer, and an ice salesman. There may be some poetic license involved in that description, but what is certainly true is that Uruguay had limited resources, traveling to Europe in steerage and paying for their board by playing a series of friendlies: they'd won nine games in Spain before even arriving in France after a thirty-hour train journey. Few seemed too excited when they did get there, with only around three thousand spectators turning out to see them play Yugoslavia in their first game.

"Game after game," wrote Galeano, "the crowd jostled to see those men, slippery as squirrels, who played chess with a ball. The English squad had perfected the long pass and the high ball, but these disinherited children from far-off America didn't walk in their father's footsteps. They chose to invent a game of close passes directly to the foot, with lightning changes in rhythm and high-speed dribbling."

Uruguay completed their success with a win over Switzerland and returned home to be greeted at the docks by celebrating crowds. "Millions of maps were sold in Paris to people who wanted to know exactly where that tiny nation that is the home of the soccer artists was," *El Gráfico* reported excitedly. "Soon there will be Argentinian and Uruguayan clubs going to Europe, just as the English were coming to South America to show us and teach us soccer. Argentinians and Uruguayans have enjoyed Uruguay's victory as if it was for both [nations]. There weren't many fans from South America, they were outnumbered by at least three to one, but they were so noisy that they cheered louder than the Europeans."

A national holiday was declared in Uruguay and commemorative stamps released. It was immediately recognized that this sporting success had greater ramifications: it was also a cultural success and proof that the New World could compete with the Old.

If the Uruguayans were delighted, though, the Argentinians were divided between respect and jealousy. As Uruguay were winning the Olympics, Argentina were entertaining Plymouth Argyle, which had just finished second in Division Three (South) and whose captain, Moses Russell, brought with him a bulldog, the team's mascot. The tourists began with a 1–0 win over an Argentina XI, a result that brought a weary response from *El Gráfico*. "Following our usual custom," it noted in a sentence that continues to be repeated with minor variations, "the *porteño selección* was nothing but a bunch of men who individually stand out in their respective clubs, but that have little knowledge between them and so lack a coordinated game that can only be achieved after a long practice with the same personnel."

The tour was deemed a success, although Plymouth's manager, Bob Jack, caused controversy with a comment about the lack of physicality of the Argentinian game. "The curious part," the report continued, "is that they [Jack and a director, a Mr. Waling] censure the excessive finesse of the style of our boys. . . . Is that a good or bad characteristic of *rioplatense* soccer? We respect the wise words of Mr Jack, but we prefer to continue with our school. For when it wins, their superiority is unchallenged; on the contrary it leaves unforgettable memories as happened with the Uruguayans in Paris. Science prevails without being escorted by harshness."

Everything looped back to the Olympics and the unspoken thought of what might have happened had there been more than one *rioplatense* team in Paris. "The Olympic matches that they've won in Paris have brought joy to Argentinians, because the impression is that their victories are also ours," said Boca Juniors goalkeeper Américo Tesoriere.

Others were less magnanimous, more partisan. If only Argentina had bothered to go to the Olympics, the attitude seemed to be, then of course they'd have won it—a self-confidence that conveniently ignored the fact that in six of the seven South American championships to that point, Uruguay had finished ahead of Argentina. So Argentina challenged Uruguay to a two-legged game to determine who was really the better side. Uruguay, seeing the financial possibilities of being Olympic champions and probably placing rather less emphasis on the game than their rivals, accepted.

Uruguay included nine of their gold medalists, but Argentina had the better of a 1–1 draw in the first leg in Montevideo. "The 1–1 scoreline reflects clearly there's no superiority as some people thought," said the report in *El Gráfico*. The second leg had been arranged for the ground of Sportivo Barracas in Buenos Aires the following week. There was great excitement, huge anticipation, a large crowd, and familiar problems. As fans encroached on the field, the players were forced off after five minutes. Police and conscripts drove fans back, but Uruguay refused to play on and the match was abandoned. "Rowdy elements," as the *Herald* put it, overturned ticket kiosks and tried to tear down the stadium. They were prevented from doing so, but before the rearranged game was played the following Thursday, a thirteen-foot-high wire fence was erected between the field and the stands—the first physical separation in South America between fans and the game. It would soon become accepted as a necessity across the continent.

Not that the fence did anything to calm the crowd. Around thirty-five thousand packed in for the rearranged match, with a further five thousand locked out—although *La Nación* suggested that as many as fifty-two thousand might have managed to squeeze into the stands. They saw a ferocious game, with both teams later protesting about the supposed roughness of the other and, after fifteen minutes, one of the most famous goals in Argentinian history. Cesáreo Onzari, a craggy left-winger from Huracán, whipped in a corner from the right. It evaded everybody and flashed into the net. The International Board had decided that goals could be scored direct from a corner only on June 14, and Uruguayan referee Ricardo Vallarino claimed official confirmation of the change hadn't been formally communicated to the Uruguayan federation: nonetheless, he gave the goal, and it was written into history as "*el gol olímpico*," even though its only connection with the Olympics was that Argentina wanted to emphasize that it was they who should have been gold medalists in Paris. As a consequence, all goals scored direct from corners are now known in Argentina as "Olympic goals."

Pedro Cea leveled just before the half hour, and as the game became increasingly frantic, Argentina right-back Adolfo Celli suffered a double fracture of his leg and was replaced by Ludovico Bidoglio (the regulations of friendlies in those days permitting each side one substitution for an injury if it occurred in the first half). Boca Juniors center-forward Domingo Tarasconi restored Argentina's lead eight minutes into the second half, prompting Uruguay to an even more aggressive approach. That riled the crowd, which began to pelt the away side with stones. The referee stopped the game, but Tesoriere, Argentina's captain, calmed the fans sufficiently for play to restart. When, with four minutes remaining, Vallarino failed to give a penalty as José Andrade, Uruguay's first black soccer hero, charged Onzari from behind, "a shower of pebbles," as the *Herald* put it, "fell on the offending darkie." The Uruguayan players returned fire, and when Vallarino told them not to, they walked off. They continued to throw stones into the crowd, leading police to intervene. Scarone kicked an officer and was arrested, although he was later released without charge. Argentina's players remained on the field, leaving Vallarino no option but to abandon the game. Argentina happily accepted the 2–1 victory—a 3–2 aggregate win—and insisted that proved they would have been Olympic champions had they turned up.

El Gráfico, though, saw little glory in the victory. "The scenes of guerrilla combats between the Olympic champions and the public, Scarone fighting against police officers," it wrote, "have no precedent in *rioplatense* matches. How can this happen? How did both sides and fans manage to create this?"

When Uruguay set sail for Montevideo the following day, a crowd gathered to see them off. There followed what the *Herald* termed "an exchange of coal" between ship and shore. But that wasn't the end of it: ten days later the South American championship began, held in Uruguay after Paraguay, which had been slated to stage the tournament, demurred on the grounds that they had insufficient infrastructure—although technically the tournament was still run by the Paraguayans. Argentina met Paraguay in the opening game in the Parque Central before a crowd that, while not huge, clearly supported the Paraguayans. After a goalless draw, they invaded the pitch and carried the Paraguayans in triumph from the field. Uruguay beat Paraguay 3–1, and, with both sides winning against Chile, a 0–0 draw when they met on November 2 secured Uruguay their fifth South American title.

That night a group of Argentinian fans gathered outside the Hotel Colón in Montevideo, where the Argentina team was staying. The players came out onto the balcony and were roundly cheered until a drunken Uruguayan in the street began to abuse them. The players responded by throwing bottles at him, and, as the mood turned ugly, another Uruguayan passer-by, Pedro Demby, took off his jacket and squared up to the Argentinians. It's alleged that an Argentinian in the crowd, José Pedro Lázaro Rodríguez, drew a gun and shot Demby in the neck and throat. He died the following day, the first fatality of Argentinian soccer violence. Rodríguez, a Boca fan and a friend of Onzari, escaped in the confusion of the night and, reportedly, the next day left on the same boat as the players, which departed an hour early to evade police. Two days later Uruguayan police identified Rodríguez from a photograph that appeared in the Argentinian newspaper *Crítica*, showing him dining with Argentinian players. Rodríguez was later arrested, but he was never extradited.

4

ARGENTINIDAD

A side from making the Argentinians jealous, the other major effect of the Paris Olympics was to generate a European demand for *rioplatense* soccer. In 1925 three South American teams toured Europe, including Boca Juniors, playing largely in Spain but also winning five matches in France and Germany. The games received widespread coverage in the Argentinian press; the sense of national pride that was felt in their achievements was palpable and reflected in the fact that the Argentinian national anthem was sung after games.

That sense of patriotism was part of a greater trend as Argentinian demographics were transformed. In fifty years *criollo* society went from being rural and agrarian to urban and industrial, while mass immigration from Europe created political pressures. In 1912 universal male suffrage was introduced, ending the hegemony of the conservative landowning elites. They contested elections but were overwhelmed by the weight of the urban middle- and working-class vote. At the same time, there was a clear shift in the attitude toward Britain. Where British capital had initially been regarded as encouraging liberalism and progress, it came to be seen as denying nationhood and autonomy.

In 1916 the general election was won by the populist Unión Cívica Radical (UCR), led by Hipólito Yrigoyen, who was nicknamed "the father of the poor" and had forced the reforms of 1912 by boycotting the election. He was a reformist and presided over a rise in living standards for the working class, but his power was still drawn from familiar sources: five of the eight ministers in his first cabinet were either cattle ranchers or connected to the export sector. Yrigoyen was a strange man, who seemed willfully to cultivate an air of mystery. For a long time he refused to give public speeches, instead having deputies read out texts he had prepared. He objected to having photographs taken of himself, claiming it offended his religious beliefs[1]—at least until the propaganda benefits of a nationwide poster campaign were explained to him in the run-up to the 1916 election. Yrigoyen was also wildly promiscuous, fathering at least a dozen children with a succession of mistresses, and prone to disappearing for hours at a time while entertaining young widows who had come to the parliament to claim state benefits.

With women and immigrants still disenfranchised and the economy in turmoil as the First World War came to an end, Yrigoyen faced significant opposition from those on the Left who felt he hadn't gone far enough. The discontent drove many to extremes: to anarchism, syndicalism, and radical unionism. A national general strike in 1918 drew widespread support. The UCR, tiring of the unrest, ordered the police and army to suppress dissent, which they did, often brutally. Socialism, though, was not easily to be erad- icated, and it became an increasing challenge for governments through the 1920s. The unrest was born of two sources: on the one hand, a sense of desperation among the very poorest and, on the other, the increasing self- confidence of the working class as the full implications of democracy and the power it gave them became evident. That in turn led to a vibrant culture at the heart of which lay soccer.

The major ideological conundrum facing the UCR was to try to find a way to pull its disparate support together, to find one theme that unified people across the class spectrum and so head off the attempts of the Far Left to outflank it. The obvious way was to use the one characteristic that united them all: a shared sense of national identity. That, though, wasn't easy to define.

There was the old Argentina of frontiersmen and gauchos, as charac- terized by Martín Fierro, the solitary hero immortalized in an epic poem by José Hernández, and that certainly had its adherents. It was Leopoldo Lugones, the preeminent poet of his day, who made the link explicit in a series of lectures given at the Odeon Theatre in 1913. "The gaucho," Lugones said, "was the country's most genuine actor when our sense of nationality was being shaped."

In the decade that followed, the sense of identification with the gaucho intensified. Jorge Luis Borges and other aesthetes published a magazine in the 1920s named after Fierro, while Italian immigrants set up gaucho clubs, dressed in *bombachos*,[2] and held *asados*[3] in an attempt to identify with the traditional embodiment of *argentinidad*. Tales of the gauchos were hugely popular. While some intellectuals eagerly propagated the cult of the gaucho and others, such as Borges, retained an amused interest, others were openly scornful. Novelist Adolfo Bioy Casares, for instance, argued that gauchos as they came to be portrayed had never really existed, pointing out that the costumes of many of the revivalist societies had more to do with the films of Rudolph Valentino than anything nineteenth-century men of the Pampas might have actually worn.

And even those who were devoted to the gaucho ideal had to accept that romantic ideals of the Pampas had little to do with the reality of life in a booming metropolis in the 1920s. There was a need both for more accessible, immediate heroes and for archetypes around which a new nationalism could be constructed. There was only one cultural mode with the general appeal to fill the breach: the space gauchos had occupied in the mid-nineteenth century came to be occupied by soccer players.

Those "organic intellectuals," who took *porteño* soccer and created from it an entire national myth, were largely journalists working for *El Gráfico*, which in the 1920s and 1930s was arguably the most influential soccer magazine there had ever been. It had been founded in 1919 as a general newsweekly for men, covering politics, crime, sports, and celebrity stories, but within two years it had decided to focus solely on sports, mainly soccer. By 1930 it was selling one hundred thousand copies a week, not only in Argentina but across Latin America.

Vitally, *El Gráfico*, under its Uruguayan editor Ricardo Lorenzo Rodríguez, better known by his pseudonym, Borocotó, didn't simply offer straight match reports or interviews. "Its tone," David Goldblatt wrote in *The Ball Is Round*, "was often moralistic, usually educative and self-consciously modern. Above all, it developed a model of sports journalism that was historical and comparative." It had an awareness of soccer history and shaped the discourse by examining where in the canon of great teams, players, and matches contemporary events should be placed. Whereas European publications still tended to regard soccer as "just" a sport, something to keep the masses entertained on a Saturday or Sunday afternoon, *El Gráfico* ensured that soccer was seen as a vibrant facet of culture; it treated players and games as literary magazines might have treated writers and their works.

Given that mind-set, it was inevitable that Borocotó should develop a theory of the historical development of *rioplatense* soccer. "It is logical," he wrote in 1928, "as the years have gone by that all Anglo-Saxon influence in soccer has been disappearing, giving way to the less phlegmatic and more restless spirit of the Latin. . . . [I]t is different from the British in that it is less monochrome, less disciplined and methodical, because it does not sacrifice individualism for the honor of collective values."

By the 1940s, with the great River Plate side that was known as la Máquina, the idea of soccer as a machine would have taken on far more positive connotations, but there is an irony anyway in Borocotó's theorizing in that it depicts British soccer as industrial and explicitly links *criollo* soccer to a preindustrial artistry. In an Argentinian context, that ties it to the ideals of the gaucho, a bond made concrete by the fact that the term *gambeta*, the style of dribbling so fetishized in Argentina, is derived from gaucho literature and refers to the running motion of an ostrich. As such, soccer's development had an inverse relationship to the development of society as a whole:

British influence waned with urbanization and industrialization, yet at the same time Argentinian soccer became less industrial and more concerned with the individual. Soccer's role in the Argentina of the twenties and thirties, perhaps, was analogous to that of Hollywood in the United States in offering a means of escape, its stadiums a venue of color and excitement in which dreams could be played out and individuals could be free of the suffocating routines of factory life.

An awareness of the difference between the Anglo and *criollo* approaches to soccer had been mounting through the first decade of the twentieth century. By 1929, when Chelsea toured Argentina, the differences in style were obvious. Their games, it soon became clear, would be far more even contests than those of previous tours. Before the fourth game, against a Capital XI, the *Herald* warned that Chelsea, which had just finished ninth in the second division, would be facing players who had "a sound knowledge of the intricacies of a non-intricate game." Chelsea lost 3–2, the game ending early amid "disorderly scenes" prompted by a tackle from Chelsea captain Andrew Wilson.[4] As fans invaded the field, one struck Wilson in the face. Again the shoulder charge had been booed, while Luis Monti had booted George Rodger in the testicles, leading him to be stretchered off. Chelsea director Charles Crisp subsequently claimed that a local player kicked through a pane of glass in the dressing-room door after the final whistle. The *Herald* was predictably outraged, railing against the lack of grace shown by the home fans and the cheers for the underhanded and violent sides of the game. It wasn't just the Anglo paper that thought things had gone too far, though: *La Nación*, *La Época*, and *El Diario* all criticized the Capital team. When Chelsea finally felt it safe to emerge from their dressing room, ninety minutes after the game had ended, they found the tires of their bus had been slashed. "*¡Que vergüenza!*" (Shame on you!), as *La Época* said.

Violence was an increasingly common occurrence at matches in Argentina. That same year, as rival supporters clashed after a second-division game between San Martín and Villa Bargano, two people were killed and an elderly woman injured in a subsequent gun battle.

The mood was very different when Ferencvarós toured a couple of months later. There was, of course, no historical reason for Argentinians to feel antipathy toward Hungarians, as many by then clearly did toward the British, but there seems also to have been an appreciation for how Ferencvarós played, the fluent, passing style of Hungarian soccer being far closer to the Argentinian model than the English one.

It wasn't just in style of play that the Anglo and *criollo* games diverged, though; there was also a huge difference in the approach to the game, something explored by historian Julio Frydenberg. "There was a model: the values of English sports . . . ," he wrote.

> The youth admired Alumni, and the *gentlemen*. However, in reality soccer was fashioned out of the practice of daily competition and there was a constant tension between the idea of a clean game and the explosion of rivalry with certain doses of violence. . . . While the new *soccer players* dyed their lives with the values of rivalry and enmity, the creators of *fair play* promoted the custom of "the third half," a moment of confraternity among the players once the game was over. In the practice of competition the popular groups had difficulty imagining friendly relations with the opponents when the game was over.

The British were unimpressed, both by the *criollo* way of playing and the *criollo* approach to playing. The *Standard* berated crowds who whistled at the Tottenham and Everton tourists, while in 1914 Arthur Chadwick, the manager of Exeter City, noted that locals were "clever in dribbling and fast, but their weak point is that they are individualist and try to shine each above their fellows. They will never achieve real success until they recognise that it takes seven men to score a goal."

For *El Gráfico*, Argentinian soccer effectively had two foundations. There was the British one, with its good manners, monotonous mechanicalness, sense of fair play, and teas provided by Mrs. Ferguson, and there was the *criollo* one, of passion, fury, trickery, and naphtha fires, ushered in by Racing's championship success of 1913.

Over the mid- to late twenties, Borocotó became increasingly strident in arguing for the merits of the *criollo* style. In a piece written in 1926, for instance, he was still careful to acknowledge the primacy of the British. "We are convinced," he wrote, "that our play is technically more proficient, quick and more precise. It perhaps lacks effectiveness due to the individual actions of our great players, but the soccer that the Argentinians and, by extension, the Uruguayans play is more beautiful, more artistic, more precise because approach work to the opposition penalty area is done not through long passes up field, which are over in an instant, but through a series of short, precise and collective actions; skillful dribbling and very delicate passes."

In 1928 he suggested that because *criollo* players learned to play in the *potreros*, on the uneven surfaces of the vacant lots of urban Buenos Aires, rather than on the playing fields at schools, their game was more rooted in tight technical skill and the cunning needed to survive in a game in which there was no space, than in the hard running required to keep up on a broad expanse of grass.

But there was a sense too that there was something innate about the *criollo* style of play. Chantecler, another writer for *El Gráfico*, also tackled the subject across a number of issues in 1928. For him, the dribbling ability of the *criollo* was born of the cunning needed to survive in the rougher parts of the city. The British, he insisted, were "a cold and mathematical people" who practiced "a learned rather than a spontaneous soccer," whereas the *criollo* played with greater warmth. There may be a certain truth to that, even if the distinction imputes to the British a love of theory and ignores the headless chickenness that so often overwhelms English soccer at its worst. More apposite was the distinction he drew between the Argentinian and Uruguayan styles, which picked up a point Hanot had made after watching Uruguay at the 1924 Olympics. Argentinians, Chantecler said, played with the heart—their soccer was about passion—whereas Uruguayans played with the head and were calmer.

Beneath the talk of national styles was an awkward question, one to which there was no simple answer and one that in some ways underlay the usefulness of soccer as a patriotic tool: what *was* an Argentinian? Why was the child of British immigrants any less of an Argentinian than the child of Italian immigrants? The term *criollo* covered some of the complication—but only some of it.

Up to a point, an Argentinian was best defined as somebody who supported Argentina at soccer. Borocotó may have acknowledged that, and by 1950, struggling to maintain his definition of Argentinian soccer as something unique, he had accepted the notion of Argentina as a melting pot and was insisting—not especially convincingly—that the distinguishing characteristics of Argentina soccer were environmental rather than innate. If that were not the case, he said, then why did Spaniards and Italians of Argentinian descent not play like Argentinians (or, it might equally have been asked, why would Argentinians of a huge array of descents play in the same way)? He concluded that what made Argentinians play like Argentinians was the *pampa*, *asado*, and *mate*.[5]

That sounds tenuous, but it does suggest just how much, by then, Argentinian self-identity had come to be identified with gaucho culture, which in turn was perceived—even if the historical truth was rather more complex—as being in opposition to British control. When the first issue of the children's magazine *Billiken* was published in 1919, it depicted, with the caption "This Season's Champion," not a neat, scholarly boy, which, as academic Mirta Varela outlines in her work on the magazine, remained the hegemoniacal image for years to come, but a disheveled *pibe* in soccer gear, an image designed to appeal to the growing urban working class.

Ultimately, the true heart of Argentinian soccer lay in *potreros* and the explosion of cultural self-confidence and creativity in the twenties that also inspired the rise of the tango, even if Martínez Estrada did describe it as "the dance of pessimism, of everyone's sorrow." As Galeano put it, what developed was "a home-grown way of playing soccer, like the home-grown way of dancing which was being invented in the *milonga* clubs. Dancers drew filigrees on a single floor tile, and soccer players created their own language in that tiny space where they chose to retain and possess the ball rather than kick it, as if their feet were hands braiding the leather. On the feet of the first *criollo* virtuosos, *el toque*, the touch, was born: the ball was strummed as if it were a guitar, a source of music."

Origins mattered, and it's telling that the most appealing practitioner of the *criollo* style in soccer was the player who was most obviously *criollo* of background. The soccer of the *potreros* was played best by those of the *potreros*, those who had learned the game in the rough and crowded alley games of myth. In 1928 Borocotó proposed raising a statue to the inventor of dribbling, saying it should depict

> a *pibe* with a dirty face, a mane of hair rebelling against the comb; with intelligent, roving, trickster and persuasive eyes and a sparkling gaze that seem to hint at a picaresque laugh that does not quite manage to form on his mouth, full of small teeth that might be worn down through eating yesterday's bread. His trousers are a few roughly sewn patches; his vest with Argentinian stripes, with a very low neck and with many holes eaten out by the invisible mice of use. A strip of material tied to his waist and crossing over his chest like a sash serves as braces. His knees covered with the scabs of wounds disinfected by fate; barefoot or with shoes whose holes in the toes suggest they have been made through too much shooting. His stance must be characteristic; it must seem as if he is dribbling with a rag ball. That is important: the ball cannot be any other. A rag ball and preferably bound by an old sock. If this monument is raised one day, there will be many of us who will take off our hat to it, as we do in church.

However dubious some of Borocotó's claims about nationality, that description seems to capture the essence of Argentinian soccer: at once the *pibe* is established as a liminal figure, the urchin who will make his way through life with a combination of charm and cunning. At the same time, soccer is established as an activity by which growing up can be deferred; it is the preserve of the urchin, and thus those who play it are absolved of responsibility, encouraged almost, never to mature into adulthood.

What is most stunning, of course, is that almost a half century before the greatest Argentinian (and the most "Argentinian") soccer player there has ever been made his debut, Borocotó drew, in extraordinary detail, a portrait of Diego Maradona.

5

THE COMING OF MONEY

As the soul and the style of Argentinian soccer were fought over, so too were its structures. In total, that third schism between the AAF and AAmF continued for eight seasons, with more and more clubs affiliating with the rebels until, in its final year, the unofficial league comprised an unwieldy twenty-six teams. In the end, only the personal intervention of the president of the republic, Marcelo Torcuato de Alvear, could reunify the two factions into the Asociación Amateur Argentina de Fútbol (AAAF), which decided that, to mark the new spirit of togetherness, the winners of the two leagues, Boca and Independiente, should play off to determine the 1926 championship. After an abandonment because of a field invasion and a goalless draw, it was decided it was probably best just to get on with 1927.

The first reunified championship featured thirty-four teams (with eighteen in the second), playing each other once. In the first example of the many attempts to keep certain favored sides in the top flight, it was determined that sides could be relegated only if they finished in the bottom four twice. It was unwieldy and perhaps illogical, but this was the beginning of the golden age: attacking soccer prevailed, and the virtuosos were adored.

British soccer had been transformed by the 1925 change in the offside law that meant a forward needed only two defenders (or the defender plus the goalkeeper) to play him onside rather than three, as had previously been the case. A number of teams experimented with withdrawing the center-half to become a third back, leading by the end of the decade to Herbert Chapman's development of the W-M at Arsenal. In South America, though, the change in the law had little immediate impact, and the majority of teams continued with the 2-3-5 that had been prevalent since the beginning of the league, albeit with the inside-forwards usually slightly withdrawn to create a shallow W shape.

There was, though, an intriguing variation, perhaps best seen at Independiente with the front five of Zoilo Canavery, Alberto Lalín, Luis Ravaschino, Manuel Seoane, and Raimundo Orsi, in which the wingers were the most advanced players, the inside-forwards slightly deeper than them, and the center-forward as a "*conductor*," creating the play from the back of a V-shaped forward line. His role seemed to symbolize the difference between the New World and Old World conceptions of the game: the British direct, looking to make directly for goal, the Argentinians favoring something more subtle, preferring to create patterns in midfield rather than simply getting the ball into the penalty area.

It is that Independiente team that features in Ernesto Sabato's novel *Sobre héroes y tumbas* as the character Julien d'Arcangelo tells the hero, Martín, of an incident involving Lalín and Seoane, who was nicknamed both "la Chancha" and "el Negro." "'I am going to share with you an illustrative anecdote,' D'Arcangelo says to Martín. 'One afternoon, at half-time, la Chancha was saying to Lalín: "Cross it to me, man, and I can go in and score." The second half starts, Lalín crosses and sure enough el Negro gets to it, goes in and scores. Seoane returns with his arms outstretched, running towards Lalín, shouting: 'See, Lalín, see?!' and Lalín answered, 'Yes, but I'm not having fun.' There you have, if you like, the whole problem of Argentinian soccer."

To modern eyes, Seoane looks a little round to be an athlete, the cords of his collar straining to contain his ample chest, a suggestive grin on his broad face. Looking at him, it's hard to imagine how in any partnership he could be the pragmatic one. Like so many of the early heroes of Argentinian soccer, he was loved not only for his abilities but because he seemed so representative of the club and its fans. Seoane's father was a smelter who emigrated from Galicia, living first in Rosario and then in Avellaneda. There's some confusion as to exactly when and where Seoane was born. Although the official record lists the Avellaneda district of Piñeyro in March 1902, Seoane himself said in an interview in the magazine *Imparcial* that he had been born in Rosario four months earlier. He was apprenticed to the Papini glassware factory and then employed at the Campomar textile factory, playing for their works team. In 1918 Seoane joined Club Progresista in the La Mosca district, where he began to develop a reputation for his dribbling, his powerful heading, and the sense of anticipation that compensated for his lack of natural athleticism.

Independiente signed him in December 1920, and in his first game, playing for the intermediate side against CA Students, he scored a hat trick that immediately cemented his place in the affections of the fans. He always had a tendency to put on weight, but he used that to his advantage: Seoane rarely outpaced anybody, but he could use his broad frame to hold off opponents, showing a remarkable capacity to wriggle through tight spaces. More than anything, he scored goals, a remarkable fifty-five in forty games as Independiente won the league in 1922–1923, more than anybody had ever scored in a season before and eight more than anybody has since. Arsenio

Erico, who followed Seoane to Independiente the following decade, is the only other player ever to have scored more than forty in a season.

A year later, as Independiente's title slipped away from them—they ended up three points adrift of the champions, San Lorenzo—Seoane was one of four Independiente players who attacked the referee during a home game against River Plate, forcing its abandonment. He was banned, during which time he played for El Porvenir in the AFA league and then for Boca Juniors on their 1925 European tour, before rejoining Independiente in 1926. He hit twenty-nine goals that season, as Independiente won the league again, dropping only four points.

By the time amateurism came to an end, Seoane had scored a record 207 goals. His weight, though, was beginning to count against him, and his fitness wasn't helped when, playing on a hot day in Concepción during a tour of Chile in 1931, he took a swig from a bottle of turpentine in the mistaken belief it was orange juice. For two days, it seemed he might not pull through. He did, but a bad injury suffered against Quilmes in 1932 further hampered him. He retired in 1933 and is still the fifth-highest goal scorer in Argentinian league history. His career over, he returned to the Campomar factory, where he worked as a wool sorter.

In the golden age, there was always a focus on style at least as much as substance, and the result is that discussion of the period—and to an extent of Argentinian soccer as a whole—tends to focus less on trophies won than on how a side played. The games that settled titles clearly mattered at the time, as the regularity of crowd trouble at those games suggests, but the details have faded quickly, and what is left is a general impression. The legacy of the golden age and the period that immediately preceded it was less the statistics of titles won and lost, of the tallies of goals scored and conceded, than an impressionistic folk memory by which clubs came to determine their identities.

Boca, having been founded by five Italian immigrants who had been taught to play by Paddy McCarthy, an Irish boxer who emigrated to Argentina in 1900, remained in the heart of the city and remained the team of the Italian community and the workers, the team of the masses, the 50 percent plus 1 that the club still boasts. It's easy these days to be seduced by the romance of La Boca, to think the brightly painted houses and the tango artists and Italian bars on the pedestrianized Caminito are somehow representative, but beyond the few blocks celebrating an idealized past for tourists, La Boca is largely rundown and petty crime a major problem.

The famed blue shirts with the horizontal yellow band were adopted in 1913 after seven years playing in blue with a yellow diagonal sash. When Boca were set up, though, they seem to have worn white shirts with a thin black stripe, changing to pale blue and then striped shirts again. The myth has it that, in 1906, they played a game against Nottingham de Almagro and discovered they wore almost identical colors. It was decided that the winner of the game would get to keep their shirts, with the losers changing. Defeated, Boca decided to adopt the colors of the flag of the first ship they saw enter the harbor: it was the freighter *Drottning Sophia*, a Swedish vessel bearing the yellow cross on a blue field.

River followed the aspirational route north away from the docks to Nuñez on the edge of the middle-class barrios of Palermo and Belgrano and came to be seen first as arrivistes and then the swaggering aristocrats, favoring style over the sweat and graft of Boca. Independiente remained rooted in the grime and industry of Avellaneda to the south, perhaps lacking the glamour of Racing, which came from a similar background but had their decade of dominance that allowed them to portray themselves as the fathers of the Argentinian game.

San Lorenzo's identity was more complex. A group of boys used to play soccer on the corner of México and Treinta y Tres Orientales, a block north of Avenida Independencia. A priest called Lorenzo Massa, seeing one of the boys almost knocked down by a streetcar as he played, feared for their safety as traffic increased and so offered them the use of the churchyard as a field, provided they all attended Mass on Sundays. In 1908 a meeting to establish a club was held in Almagro, a transitional area to the west of the city center in which working and middle classes mixed and tango halls rubbed alongside workshops. It was decided to name it San Lorenzo, in honor of the priest—although he tried to demur—of Saint Laurence and of the Battle of San Lorenzo, a key conflict in the independence struggle.

6

THE *RIOPLATENSE* SUPREMACY

The growth in the numbers playing and watching the game continued in the years following the First World War. As well as the official league (or, in the years of schism, leagues), there were countless smaller organizations catering to specific professions or political persuasions. Crowds would regularly exceed ten thousand, which meant even more money flowing into the game—which, at the same time, raised standards. "The men who compose our leading local teams," the *Herald* noted in May 1926, "are every bit as professional as the hardest-headed big leagues in England. Argentinian soccer players play the game winter and summer and train every day. . . . [N]ominally they are all engaged to work for gentlemen financially interested in the big teams."

Many of those gentlemen were also politically significant. From the very earliest tour matches, politicians had associated themselves with the game, but from the 1920s they began to get involved with the day-to-day running of clubs. Aldo Cantoni, for instance, was a senator for the western city of San Juan and the president of both the AFA and Huracán, while Pedro Bidegain was president of San Lorenzo and a leading figure in the UCR. That Alvear, the president of the republic, felt it necessary to intervene to end the schism said much for how politically significant soccer had become.

One of the two governing bodies may have included the word *amateur* in their name, but by the time of reunification, it was an obvious sham. In 1926 *El Gráfico* published a piece in which, without naming names, it made clear that a number of players were being paid. Money may not have changed hands, but players would be given gear, club membership, and suits. Without formal contracts, players had all the power and could change clubs at will. The *Buenos Aires Herald*, mounting its Anglo high horse, described the notion that Argentinian soccer was amateur as "a *criollo* joke."

European teams, which were overtly professional, were increasingly keen to flex their financial muscle, and had been alerted to the potential of *rioplatense* soccer by Uruguay's performance at the 1924 Olympics, soon began to take an interest. In 1925 Newell's Old Boys forward Julio Libonatti, a twenty-four-year-old with swept-back hair and a large, crooked nose, was spotted by Enrico Maroni, an Italian industrialist who owned both the Cinzano drinks company and the Torino soccer club, and was persuaded to become the first of the *oriundi*, the South Americans of Italian descent who returned to the old country. Libonatti had been an Argentina international, scoring eight times in fifteen appearances and being part of the side that won the Campeonato Sudamericano in 1921, but in Italy he enjoyed even greater success. He was cheerful and charismatic, noted for his silk shirts and generally flamboyant dress sense—so reckless was he in his expenditures that when he decided to return to Argentina in 1938, his then club, Libertas Rimini, had to pay for the boat ticket—and soon became a favorite in Turin, attracting the nickname "the Matador." Libonatti scored twenty-one goals in 1926–1927, as Torino won the title, only to have it revoked amid allegations that Juventus left-back Luigi Allemandi had been bribed to lose the Turin derby and was then top scorer the following season as Torino won the title for real.

Perhaps even more significantly, Libonatti was called up to the Italy national team in October 1926, having been given dual nationality to get around the Carta di Viareggio, a bill passed in 1926 that effectively outlawed foreign players.

After Libonatti, the doors were open. Italy offered high wages, a culture that wasn't particularly alien to Argentinians, and the possibility of international glory. Raimundo Orsi, after impressing at the 1928 Olympics, followed, enticed to Juventus by a salary of eight thousand lire a week, plus a signing bonus of one hundred thousand lire and a Fiat 509. The forward had won three Asociación Amateur titles with Independiente and claimed five *scudetti* with Juventus. He was also one of three Argentina-born players, alongside former Estudiantes forward Enrique Guaita and, crushingly for Argentina, their great captain and leader Luis Monti, who played on the Italy side that won the 1934 World Cup. Italy manager Vittorio Pozzo was criticized for selecting foreigners—or, as the Fascist government designated those of Italian descent who returned home, *rimpatriati*, the repatriated—but he argued that if they were subject to conscription, it was absurd they should not be eligible for the national team. "If they can die for Italy," he said, "they can play for Italy." Guaita, in fact, tried to move to France in 1936 with his fellow *oriundi* Alejandro Scopelli and Ángelo Sormani for fear they might be called up for Mussolini's Abyssinian campaign.

The exodus of a number of their players across the River Plate had done little to shake Uruguayan domination of the South American championship.

Four months after the Olympic success, on home soil, Uruguay won their fifth Campeonato Sudamericano, a goalless draw in their final match, against Argentina, securing the title. Still, Argentina did emerge from the tournament with a genuine hero in Boca Juniors goalkeeper Américo Tesoriere, who went unbeaten through the tournament and was chaired from the field by Uruguayan fans after that final game. The incident was depicted in the 1949 film *Con los mismos colores*, scripted by Borocotó and directed by Carlos Torres Ríos. As Pablo Alabarces points out in "Football and *Patria*," his portrayal in the film self-consciously created a national hero, even in the way the key scene was shot, "a three-quarter profile at medium distance, the hero . . . looking towards the future—the right."[1] More than two decades later, with Perón at the height of his power, Borocotó was looking to the twenties in his creation of the national myth.

Argentina won the Campeonato Sudamericano in Buenos Aires in 1925, but only after Uruguay and Chile had withdrawn to leave just three participants. In Santiago in 1926 it was back to the familiar pattern, with Uruguay winning the title and Argentina second, before, in 1927 in Lima, Argentina at last got the better of la Celeste, beating them 3–2 with an eighty-fifth-minute own goal to lift their third title. What they really wanted, though, was to match Uruguay's achievement in winning gold at the Olympics.

So desperate were Argentina to go to Amsterdam in 1928 with the strongest possible squad that the federation was prepared to overlook the occasional illegal payment or benefit in kind. The British nations, in which professionalism had been openly acknowledged for almost forty years, were rather keener that the Olympic Games should remain truly amateur. FIFA found itself cast as an awkward arbiter, wishing to appease Britain and the International Olympic Committee without alienating South American and continental European nations that saw the payments as essential to persuading players to commit to tournaments that required them to be away from their jobs for several weeks. Accordingly, it proposed to regulate "broken-time" payments, by which national federations could compensate players for the money they would have earned but missed out on by playing international soccer. The British nations, seeing that as professionalism through the back door, left FIFA in protest in February 1928.

Henri Delaunay, the president of the French Football Federation, had already recognized that the split was irreconcilable. "International football," he said at the FIFA Congress in 1926, "can no longer be held within the confines of the Olympics; and many countries where professionalism is now recognised and organised cannot any longer be represented there by their best players." Plans were put in place for a World Cup, organized by FIFA and so exempt from the Olympic movement's demand for amateurism, and, on May 26, 1928, a day before the first match at the 1928 Olympics, it was announced that the tournament would take place in 1930.

There were only seventeen participants at the 1928 Olympics, down five from the previous tournament, but the perception was that the quality was higher, with Italy and Spain expected to challenge Uruguay and Argentina. Yet for a time it had appeared Argentina wouldn't even make it to the Netherlands. The organization was chaotic, funding to stay in Amsterdam secured only in the week before the Games began. A pretournament tour had gone badly: a draw in Lisbon, a narrow win in Madrid, and a defeat in Barcelona, a game watched by the great tango singer Carlos Gardel.[2]

As they began to train amid the tranquillity of Bloemendaal, just outside Amsterdam, Argentina began to settle, and an easy opening game meant they hit their stride early. Argentina thrashed the United States 11–2, Domingo Tarasconi scoring four and Roberto Cerro three, with two each for Nolo Ferreira and Raimundo Orsi, four names that give some idea of Argentina's extraordinary attacking prowess. In Buenos Aires fans were agog, desperate for every scrap of information. Loudspeakers were set up outside newspaper offices to broadcast cables sent during games by correspondents in Amsterdam. During that first game, the correspondent for *La Prensa* filed ten thousand francs' worth of fifteen-word telegrams. If they had the quantity, though, *La Nación* claimed to have the speed, insisting one news flash took just fifty-two seconds to travel across the Atlantic from the Netherlands.

Uruguay began more sedately, although there were more than forty thousand packed in to see them beat the Dutch 2–0. In the quarter-final, Argentina met Belgium and raced into a 3–0 lead inside ten minutes, with two goals from Tarasconi and another from Ferreira. Belgium, perhaps capitalizing on Argentinian complacency, slowly fought back and drew level with a Jacques Moeschal goal eight minutes into the second half. Argentina, though, then pulled away again, Tarasconi scoring two more in a 6–3 win. Uruguay came through an ill-tempered quarter-final against Germany 4–1: Petrone scored a hat trick, while José Nasazzi and two Germans were sent off.

Argentina had by far the easier passage through the semifinals, Tarasconi scoring three and Ferreira two in a 6–0 demolition of Egypt. Uruguay, meanwhile, were involved in a classic, falling behind to Italy, which had beaten Spain earlier in the competition, before running out 3–2 victors. And so Amsterdam had the final it had expected and most neutrals had wanted: a clash between Uruguay and Argentina seven thousand miles from home. There were more than a quarter of a million applications for the forty thousand available tickets, while in Buenos Aires the crowd outside the offices of *La Prensa* stretched for two blocks in all directions.

Petrone gave Uruguay the lead midway through the first half, but Ferreira leveled five minutes after halftime, and it finished 1–1. They met again three days later. Again Uruguay took the lead, and again Argentina leveled. The *Albiceleste* seemed to have the better of it, but Nasazzi and Pedro Arispe were superb in the Uruguayan defense and goalkeeper Andrés Mazali inspired; with seventeen minutes remaining, Héctor Scarone scored the goal that won Uruguay their second successive Olympic gold medals. In Argentina there was a resigned sense of frustration.

There was at least some solace to be drawn at the Campeonato Sudamericano held in Buenos Aires the following year, the championship not having been staged in 1928 because of the Olympics. A 2–0 win over Uruguay gave them the title. They'd won successive continental championships, but Uruguay had won the one that really mattered, and it was clear that they would represent the greatest threat to Argentina's hopes of winning the inaugural World Cup.

From a soccer point of view, Uruguay was an entirely logical choice to host the tournament, but there were also sound economic reasons. Montevideo remained a prosperous city even after the Wall Street crash, while the celebrations of the centenary of independence offered sentimental cause to take the tournament to the north side of the River Plate. Perhaps most significantly, the Uruguayan government agreed to fund the construction of a stadium that could seat ninety-three thousand and guarantee the costs of every participating nation. That wasn't enough to tempt many of the realistic European challengers to take the boat across the Atlantic: Hungary, Austria, Italy, Germany, and Spain all stayed home, as did England and Scotland, still sulking after their defeat in the debate over definitions of amateurism.

In the end, only four sides bothered to make the trip from Europe. Romania went to fulfill a promise made by King Carol in 1928, although their team was largely made up of workers employed by British oil companies in Ploiesti, their release from their day jobs secured only by the personal intervention of the king's mistress. France were pressured into going by Rimet, but their coach, Gaston Barreau, and their leading striker, Manuel Anatol, stayed behind. FIFA's Belgian vice president, Rudolf Seedrayers, persuaded his national team to go, but they were weakened because their biggest name, Raymond Braine, was unavailable, having opened a café— something that breached the Belgian definition of amateurism.[3] Only Yugoslavia seemed to cross the Atlantic with anything approaching enthusiasm for the new competition. That supporting cast may not have been the strongest, but few doubted anyway that Argentina and Uruguay were the best two teams in the world and their meeting in the final seemed preordained almost from the moment of the draw.

Heavy rain delayed the construction of the Estadio Centenario, which was thrown up in just six months, and so Argentina played their first World Cup match not there as initially scheduled but in Parque Central, the home of Nacional. Bafflingly, they faced France, which had already played their first game of the tournament two days earlier, beating Mexico 4–1.

Given the lack of rest, France would perhaps have tired anyway, but their task was made even harder when Lucien Laurent, who had scored the first World Cup goal, was clattered early on by Monti and left limping with a serious ankle injury. France's goalkeeper Alexis Thépot had suffered an injury in that opening game that had led to right-half Augustin Chantrel taking over in goal for the final hour, and when he suffered a recurrence, France were down to just nine fit players for the final three-quarters of the game.

They battled hard, and with Argentina lacking a cutting edge as Nolo Ferreira struggled to come to terms with being asked to play as a more orthodox center-forward than normal and inside-left Roberto Cerro, usually such a dominant figure in the air, suffering a reaction to antianxiety medication, they held out until the eighty-first minute. Then Argentina were awarded a free kick just outside the box. France, rather than stationing a wall, lined up three players on the six-yard line, but they served only to obstruct the vision of Thépot, as Monti drilled in a straight shot. Three minutes later, Brazilian referee Gilberto de Almeida Rêgo blew for full-time, just as France mounted a desperate counterassault in search of an equalizer. He was eventually persuaded to restart the game and play out the final six minutes, but France's momentum had been lost and Argentina began the World Cup with a win that had been widely anticipated but one that was jeered by the many Uruguayans in the crowd of 23,409. So hostile was the reaction that Argentina threatened to withdraw from the tournament, agreeing to play on only after the president of the republic had given a personal guarantee of safety.

Ferreira had returned to Buenos Aires for a law exam, giving an opportunity at center-forward to Guillermo Stábile, a five-foot-six goal scorer from Huracán whose thin mustache and narrow-eyed gunslinger's stare gave the impression that he regarded the world with an air of amused and possibly lethal detachment. He scored twice in the first seventeen minutes, as Argentina raced into a 3–0 lead, and although Fernando Paternoster had a penalty saved by Oscar Bonfiglio, they went on to win 6–3, as Stábile completed the second World Cup hat trick, two days after the United States' Bert Patenaude had scored the first.

Stábile got two more, as Argentina made sure of their place in the semifinal with an ill-tempered 3–1 win over Chile. Photographs show at least thirty officials on the field in a massive brawl prompted by a clash between

Chile right-half Arturo Castro and Monti, the former reacting to a foul by the latter with a firm punch to the nose.

In front of thousands who had crossed the River Plate, the United States struggled to contain Argentina in the semifinal. Ralph Tracey missed two early chances, but once Monti had put Argentina ahead after twenty minutes, the result was never in doubt, particularly after two injury setbacks for the United States: Tracey was forced off with a wrenched knee at halftime, and goalkeeper Jim Douglas injured his leg in the second half. Alejandro Scopelli added a second after fifty-six minutes, and Stábile and Carlos Peucelle added two each against exhausted opponents who weren't helped when their physio, Jack Coll, dropped a bottle of chloroform to leave midfielder Andy Auld temporarily blinded. Jim Brown did steal one in the final minute, but 6–1 was a convincing victory.

Anything Argentina could do, though, Uruguay could at the very least match, beating Yugoslavia 6–1 in their semifinal to ensure the first World Cup had the final everybody had expected, the 111th *rioplatense* derby.

It was probably the biggest match there had ever been, and its result continues to reverberate. "If there is a game that I would not like to remember, it's Uruguay-Argentina in the World Cup final," Argentina inside-right Pancho Varallo said a few months before his death in 2010. "Yet it always come to my mind. It's in my mind. I'd do anything to go back there and play again." Varallo had a hugely successful career, winning three league titles with Boca Juniors, yet even at the age of one hundred, he was irritated by the clear sense that Argentina had been the better side. "The thing is," he said, "that we were winning comfortably, really, really, comfortably. At halftime, the score was 2–1 to us, but it could have been more. We were making them dance."

The postmaster general hired a cargo ship to take himself and his friends across the estuary, part of an exodus of around 15,000 Argentinians packing onto steamers and the transatlantic liners that stopped in Montevideo on their way to Europe. Adverse weather meant that many became fogbound and made it only the day after the final. Many thousands more lined the docks in Buenos Aires to see them off, chanting, *"Argentina, si! Uruguay, no!"* Offices closed for the afternoon, although many workers stayed behind to listen to the game on the radio. General Motors shut down their production lines, and the Chamber of Deputies abandoned its afternoon sitting. There was a parade of optimistic banners, while an estimated 50,000 gathered outside newspaper offices to listen to updates of the game being relayed by loudspeaker.

The day before the game Carlos Gardel visited the Argentina squad in the team's training camp. He preferred horse racing to soccer and, in public at least, maintained a scrupulous neutrality between the supposed land of his birth and the country whose citizenship he'd accepted, but there's little doubt that in private he wanted Argentina to win. "'Are you worried about the game?' Varallo said to him. 'Come, come and check out how passionate we are.' And I took him to a room where two of us were taking an afternoon nap. . . . [T]hey would sleep wearing the Argentinian jersey. When you say, 'I like that jersey so much that I even wear it when I sleep . . . ,' well, in our case it was true."

The official attendance for the final was 68,346, although in reality there were probably more than 80,000 there, with many more packing the streets around the Centenario. Fans were checked for weapons on their way in, while the referee, the experienced Belgian John Langenus, put in place an escape plan to enable him to reach his ship quickly after the game. He later spoke of having felt "genuine fear," while Monti received a death threat. Initially, he refused to play, which caused consternation in the Argentina squad, particularly given that experienced halfback Adolfo Zumelzú, who might conceivably have replaced him, had also been ruled out with injury. After all attempts to persuade Monti not to back out had failed, it was decided that Alberto Chividini, who had previously played only three times for his country, would step in, only for Monti to declare on the morning of the game that he was prepared to play after all. Morale, though, had been damaged, and, for once, the hard man was intimidated, something for which Varallo hadn't been able to forgive him, even eighty years later. "The Uruguayans beat us because they were sly," he said. "They took advantage of being the hosts. Some of my teammates were afraid of the consequences. Luis Monti was a great player, but that day he was totally pale. If a Uruguayan fell, he would go and try to assist him. He had received threatening letters, apparently, but I didn't care about anything. There was a Uruguayan defender that shouted at me, 'Let the ball loose because I will kill him.' And I didn't care. Then, another one approached and told me, 'Don't pay attention. He's nuts.'"

As Varallo described it, he would never have been so weak as Monti. "My cousin, who used to go to Uruguay quite a lot to set up games for Estudiantes and Gimnasia, traveled that day and visited the Uruguayan hotel before the game," he said. "When some of them saw them and asked him what he was doing there, 'I came to see my cousin, Varallo,' he answered. 'Oh, he's the first one we have to take out,' they said. The problem is that my cousin only told me this when we were back in Argentina! He didn't mention anything at the time. But I had character: I didn't care about intimidation."

Nor about a little pain. "As I was carrying an injury, I never thought I was going to play in that final match," he said.

But that morning I tried some shots in a henhouse near our hotel in Santa Lucía, and my knee responded pretty well. The most experienced team members then decided that I should be in the lineup. In those days, the oldest players made the decisions. We had a manager, true, but he wasn't important; I can't even remember his name.[4] I was eager to play; you can't imagine how badly I wanted to beat those Uruguayans. You know, the real derby of South America was Argentina-Uruguay. We had the best players, and facing Brazil was not really an issue at the time.

Legend has it that coach Francisco Olazar explained his tactics in the drying cement of the dressing-room wall and that the lines he etched can still be seen today. It's almost certainly not true, not least because it seems improbable Olazar would have issued any tactical instructions, but the widespread willingness to believe the tale says much for the legendary status that game has taken on either side of the estuary: just as grooves in rock formations or dips in the ground are claimed to have been scored by the tails of dragons or to be the footprints of giants, so there is a desire to see the game as leaving its mark on the environment.

Varallo was in no doubt of the magnitude of the game or of what his countrymen expected from the side. "We were in the dressing room before the game, and an assistant handed me a pile of telegrams, all wishing me luck for the match," he said. "They came from relatives, doctors, friends, and many people I didn't know in La Plata, my home city. Reading those lines was such a touching experience that it was difficult for most of us to hold back the tears and to keep focused."

Emotions were soon running even higher as referee Langenus, wearing his usual cap and plus-fours, led the teams out onto the field. "It was a special moment, seeing the immense crowd packing the terraces," said Varallo. "Most of them were Uruguayans insulting us, but there were some of our countrymen too, even though many ships hadn't been able to cross the River Plate because of the fog. My father was in the stands, and he had to leave the stadium disguised with a Uruguayan flag because some Uruguayans had discovered there was an Argentinian presence around and were trying to find the Argentinians to punch them. I will never forget the whole experience. From the best moment to the worst, everything happened that day."

The first moment of contention had come a couple of hours earlier, as both teams demanded to use a ball made in their own country. Langenus, showing his familiar authority and good sense, decreed that an Argentinian ball should be used in the first half and a Uruguayan one in the second.

Nonetheless, it was Uruguay that took the lead. When Paternoster blocked Scarone's shot after twelve minutes, the ball broke to Castro. He rolled the ball right, and Pablo Dorado hurtled in to crash the ball under the body of goalkeeper Juan Botasso, who had replaced Bossio after the group stage. The goal, strangely, seemed to settle Argentina, although not Monti, who, according to the report in *El Gráfico*, "was standing, literally, soulless, without being the great playmaker that in normal circumstances he would have been, in the middle of the park." A poise returned to Argentina's play, and they leveled eight minutes later. Eight minutes before the break, Argentina took the lead, as José Nasazzi, who had an otherwise exceptional tournament as a proto-sweeper, misjudged Monti's long pass, allowing Stábile in to score his eighth goal of the finals.

At halftime Argentina seemed in control, but the second half brought a Uruguayan surge, a manifestation of the *garra*—literally "claw," although the term is used to mean a combination of toughness, determination, and streetwiseness—they had always claimed as a key component of the national character, aided by the fact that, as well as Varallo, Botasso and Juan Evaristo had suffered knocks. Argentina had a chance to go two up: Stábile missed a presentable opportunity, and then came the moment at which Varallo saw history turn against him.

> I remember that I got the ball on a counterattack, took a shot, and saw how it went past the keeper, directly toward the top corner . . . and hit the angle of post and bar. . . . The stadium was silent. It hit the angle of crossbar and post, and then it went out. The worst part is that the shot was so fierce that I injured my knee properly. I kept playing crippled. That goal would have changed everything. From almost being 3–1, suddenly we were 2–2, and I couldn't play anymore. I moved to the wing and kept playing as winger, but actually, I should have left the field. The problem is that there were no substitutions. So I played with the pain. After that, it all became a hellish experience.

That equalizer came twelve minutes into the second half. Center-half Lorenzo Fernández, operating in a more advanced role after the break, played a free kick to Castro, who found Scarone with his back to the goal six yards out. He hooked the ball over his shoulder, and it looped beyond the two fullbacks, José Della Torre and Paternoster, for Cea to nudge in.

On the wing Varallo was overwhelmed by Ernesto Mascheroni, who dispossessed him after sixty-eight minutes, advanced, and slipped a pass to left-winger Santos Iriarte. His low shot seemed to take Botasso by surprise, and the ball was past him long before he dived. "In the second half," Varallo said, "we lost it because we lacked guts; we lacked courage. Some of our players really felt the intimidation and became chickens."

Yet courage can lead to misjudgment. Many later suggested that Varallo should never have started, given the risk of his knee giving way again. He had another chance later on that was cleared by José Andrade, but, in the final minute, the one-handed Castro made certain of Uruguay's victory, beating Della Torre to Pablo Dorado's cross and sending a looping header over Botasso and into the net.

Jules Rimet presented the trophy to Raúl Jude, the president of the Uruguayan soccer federation, and, as a national holiday was declared, Langenus made it safely to his ship. In his report for *El Gráfico*, Alfredo Rossi was unimpressed. "The Belgian referee Langenus let the Uruguayans go unpunished with violent challenges, while the Argentinians were doing what had been previously agreed, not to make violent fouls and use fair play," he insisted.

Back in Argentina the mood rapidly turned ugly. The Uruguayan Embassy was attacked, while the hopeful parade that had preceded the game was replicated with another march carrying only Argentinian flags, lowered as though in mourning. Two people were reportedly shot for refusing to salute as the parade went by, while a woman who foolishly waved a Uruguayan flag from a balcony overlooking the Plaza de Mayo was pelted with stones. Petulantly, the AAAF broke off relations with the Uruguayan federation.

An editorial in *La Nación* condemned the "ill-breeding" of those who had taken defeat so badly, while *La Prensa* turned its anger away from the Uruguayans toward those who, as it saw it, had let the nation down. "Argentina teams sent abroad to represent the prestige of the nation in any form of sport," it trumpeted, "should not be composed of men who have anything the matter with them. . . . We don't need men who fall at the first blow, who are in danger of fainting at the first onslaught even if they are clever in their footwork. . . . These 'lady-players' should be eliminated."

El Gráfico went even further, questioning the entire notion of international tournaments. "The World Cup is over," its editorial read. With a startling lack of self-awareness, given how often its own writers used soccer to create a notion of *argentinidad*, the editorial condemned those who saw soccer as a manifestation of national pride rather than just a game. "The poor sporting education of the soccer directors has created this attitude in the fans," it said. "It looked as though in these twenty-two men trying to kick the ball in the opposition goal lay the future of a nation, the progress of happiness of a barrio."

Eight of the players who had played in the final never played for Argentina again; Stábile's four games at the World Cup, in which he scored eight goals, were his only appearances for his country. Only part of that, though, was due to frustration at the result. There were other pressures; soccer was changing radically, demonstrated when Monti, who, however badly he had played in the final, was still one of Argentina's most iconic players, left San Lorenzo to move to Italy and join Juventus. Players were realizing their worth and recognizing the rewards on offer to soccer players elsewhere. That created pressure to increase revenues at home to prevent the talent drain, while an increasingly sprawling domestic structure generated further impetus for reform. Argentinian soccer would never be the same again.

PART TWO
THE GOLDEN AGE, 1930–1958

7

DAYS OF GLORY

There is no side in Argentinian history so revered as la Máquina, the River Plate team of the 1940s. To name their front five of Juan Carlos Muñoz, José Moreno, Adolfo Pedernera, Ángel Labruna, and Félix Loustau is to evoke a mystical past when beauty and flair were prized, when Argentinian fans had no doubt that their soccer was the best in the world. Even at the time, it seemed impossible to regard them with anything other than romantic wonder. "You play against la Máquina with the intention of winning," said Ernesto Lazzatti, the Boca Juniors center-half, "but as an admirer of soccer sometimes I'd rather stay in the stands and watch them play." Their legendary status went before them and defined them, the myth at times more potent than the reality, something hinted at by the fact that the fabled front five actually played together as a quintet only on nineteen occasions.

There was a sense of la Máquina not merely as the pinnacle of Argentinian soccer to that point, but as an embodiment of Argentinian culture as a whole. In la Máquina, the tango and soccer came together: they became a distillation of the *criollo* ideal. "The tango," Muñoz insisted, "is the best way to train. You maintain a rhythm then change it when you stride forward. You learn the profiles. You work your waist and your legs." And just as players practiced the tango, so musicians paid tribute to la Máquina, as in, for instance, Justo Pablo Bonora's tango "La Máquinita."[1]

The pure individualism of the twenties may have been tempered by the acknowledgment of a need for teamwork—and there was very definitely a passing, possession-based element to la Máquina's play—but this was still, at least as far as the rest of the world was concerned, an old-fashioned style of soccer, one based on skill and technique in which physicality and concerted defensive tactics had no part. Players had time on the ball and license to enjoy themselves on and off the field. "On Sundays at midday," Galeano wrote, "[Moreno] would devour a big bowl of chicken stew and drain several bottles of red wine. Those in charge at River ordered him to give up his rowdy ways. . . . He did his best. For a week he slept at night and drank nothing but milk. Then he played the worst game of his life. When he went

49

back to carousing, the team suspended him. His teammates went on strike in solidarity with that incorrigible bohemian." The story seems to be based on an incident that took place in October 1939, when Moreno was suspended after River had lost a vital game 3–2 to Independiente.

Embellished as the account may be, this was the essence of Argentinian soccer at the time: roguish, charming, brilliant, and, it eventually turned out, complacent. Between 1930 and 1958, no professional Argentinian player took part in the World Cup—at least not for Argentina. Nobody could pretend that the side Argentina sent to the 1934 World Cup was anything like a first team. Not only were all the players amateurs, but only two, left-half Arcadio López and center-forward and captain Alfredo Devincenzi, had been capped before. They twice took the lead in the first round against Sweden, but lost 3–2. Argentina were out after one game and would not return to the finals for twenty-four years.

They did, though, leave an image of their soccer. The scorer of their second goal, Alberto Galateo, with his long, mournful face and sad eyes, may not have been a classic *pibe*, but his demeanor and mastery of the *gambeta* (slalom dribbling) were typical of the more thoughtful school of Argentinian creativity and were cut through by a characteristic sense of tragedy. As a teenager, he played for San Lorenzo de Santa Fe, which functioned effectively as a feeder side for one of the city's two major clubs, Colón. With the coming of professionalism, though, he and his friend Antonio Rivarola were offered contracts by Colón's great rivals, Unión. That would have been controversial enough, but the situation was made even more sensitive by the fact that the girlfriends of Galateo and Rivarola were the daughters of a Señor Desimone, the founder of San Lorenzo de Santa Fe and a devoted Colón fan. As soon as he heard of what he saw as their treachery, Desimone cast the two players from his home. Rivarola returned the money he had received from Unión, stayed with Colón, and got engaged; Galateo did not.

Galateo became a local star and, after the World Cup, moved on to Nacional of Rosario before finally getting his chance in the Buenos Aires league with Huracán. He wasn't happy, though, and began to drink more and more. He joined Chacarita Juniors in 1937, playing alongside Ernesto Duchini, who later described him as the greatest dribbler he had ever seen. His alcoholism worsened, and, after he had retired, neighbors reported regularly hearing him arguing with his family. On February 26, 1961, he threatened his wife and daughter with a knife. His son, David, rushed to defend them, drawing a .38 caliber revolver. Three shots were fired, and Galateo fell dead.

Through the absence from World Cups, Argentina did continue to compete in the South American championships, which they dominated.

Essentially, Argentinian soccer grew in isolation, without natural predators, which led to the development of an idiosyncratic but vulnerable style of play, one based on individual technique and attacking and followed with a devotion that it's arguable no country has matched before or since. This was the golden age, when crowds were vast, *El Gráfico* was in its pomp, and the whole nation avidly followed the league as though it were a sporting soap opera. Remembering in 1954 a visit to Buenos Aires in the 1930s, Jules Rimet spoke of the "trams and buses, all sizes, overflowing with passengers hanging on the steps, the ledge at the back, in fact anywhere on which two feet can be planted, while some of the youngsters climb on the roof of the trams. Coming away from the games—not going—they sometimes disconnect the overhead tram guide wires causing chaos with the traffic, and the cacophony becomes deafening."

The boom was created by the convergence of a number of factors. From an economic point of view, the Wall Street crash of 1929 and the Great Depression—and rising nationalism—that followed diminished the European demand for Argentinian players, and that, along with professionalism and the financial rewards it made possible, meant the biggest stars remained at home. As financial conditions worsened with the collapse of the export market, soccer offered a form of escapism. Whatever else failed, soccer remained a constant.

But there were more practical reasons, too. Buenos Aires had sufficient neighborhoods with distinct-enough identities that there was support for the local side even from those who might not necessarily have been that keen on soccer. The first line of the underground network, the Subte, running from Plaza de Mayo west to Plaza Miserere, had been opened in 1913 and was extended through Almagro to Primera Junta the following year (what is now Línea A follows the same route and until 2013 retained the same carriage design). In 1930 a second line was opened, running west from Callao (part of the present Línea B), with further work through the thirties, including, most significantly for soccer, what is now Línea C, running from the rail station at Constitución, a couple of miles from la Boca, north to Diagonal Norte, and then, from February 1936, on to Retiro. There, was, in other words, a comprehensive public transport network that could easily ferry fans to games from most parts of the city. As games became events, planes would fly low over stadiums, dropping balloons advertising local products. Outside the grounds, salesmen jostled to hand out free samples of cigarettes and sweets.

And then there was radio, which, perhaps more than anything else, was responsible for the cultural domination of Buenos Aires over the burgeoning cities elsewhere in Argentina. By the thirties the network stretched from the subtropics of the North to the frozen southern tip to the Andes in the West, carrying with it broadcasts from the tango halls and the soccer stadiums, focusing the attention of the nation on the capital. So accepted did radio coverage become that it was common for matches to begin late, as journalists sought a final word with the players. Listeners from Tucumán to Tierra del Fuego were seduced by the tango bands of Héctor Varela and Osvaldo Pugliese and by the pioneering soccer commentary of Fioravanti, the name used by Joaquín Carballo Serantes. Born in Uruguay, he moved to Santa Fe as a child and became one of Argentina's most recognizable voices. The phrase "*Atento*, Fioravanti!"—as used by the studio anchor to interrupt the commentator if there'd been an incident in one of the other games— became one of the first great catchphrases of Argentinian radio. People in the provinces began supporting Buenos Aires teams as a result, while the allure of the metropolis led many to migrate there. The transatlantic influx of the turn of the century may have slowed to a trickle, but the process of urbanization begun by their arrival was completed by those from Argentina's rural backwaters.

8

THE COMING OF
PROFESSIONALISM

Hipólito Yrigoyen, having been constitutionally barred from standing for a second successive stint as president, was reelected by a huge majority when Marcelo Torcuato de Alvear's term came to an end in 1928. His first period in office had been characterized by a gradual expansion of workers' rights, the promotion of energy independence through the state-run oil company Yacimientos Petrolíferos Fiscales (YPF)—State Oil Fields—and a huge post–World War I boom, the gains of which were only moderately affected by high inflation. His second term was nowhere near as productive, undermined by rising social unrest almost from the start.

In December 1928, Yrigoyen was visited by US president-elect Herbert Hoover, who survived an assassination attempt when an anarchist who tried to plant a bomb by his rail carriage was arrested before it could be detonated. Yrigoyen traveled with Hoover from then on in an attempt to guarantee his safety, but it turned out the anarchist was only an extreme part of more general discontent. Yrigoyen was caught, hopelessly, between the radical Left and the conservative landowners, and his attempts to coerce the traditional power bases into compromise by encouraging mutinies in the armed forces only prepared the ground for his own overthrow.

By late 1929 Yrigoyen was desperately out of touch, the desire for privacy that had always been a feature of his personality leaving him insulated from what was actually going on. Yrigoyen's advisers censored reports to him and shielded him from newspaper and radio reports, so he had no comprehension of the full impact of the Wall Street crash. As the economic situation worsened, the middle class that had sustained the Radicals became disaffected, splintering into rival groups, some of whom took to the streets, initiating a cycle of political violence that it would take Argentina more than a half century to escape. Yrigoyen survived an assassination attempt on December 24, 1929, but there were continued plots against him, led by fascist and conservative elements of the army, as well as the Standard Oil company of New Jersey, which was opposed both to the YPF and to Yrigoyen's attempts to prevent oil smuggling between the northern province of Salta and Bolivia. On September 6, 1930, Yrigoyen was deposed by a military coup and General José Félix Uriburu installed as the new president.

Yrigoyen spent his final years under house arrest in Buenos Aires and in exile on the island of Martín García. He died in 1933. Uriburu left office in February 1932, having been diagnosed with stomach cancer, and died two months later. He was succeeded by Agustín Pedro Justo, a military officer and diplomat who had served as war minister under Alvear and who was at least nominally democratically elected, although there were allegations of electoral fraud. This was the beginning of the so-called *década infame*—the infamous decade—during which a coalition of conservative groups conspired in what was known as "patriotic fraud" to prevent radical elements from taking power.

Soccer had been part of the worker-led radicalism the conservatives had moved to suppress, the push for professionalism another part of the labor reforms of the twenties, although the final impetus for change seems to have been generated as much as anything else by a recognition that the championship had become impossibly unwieldy. By 1930 there were thirty-six teams in the top flight, and even with each team facing each of the other sides only once, that created concerns that the season was stretching into summer, forcing players to play when it was dangerously hot. The fears were tragically realized as the 1930 season went on until March 1931, and Héctor Arispe, the captain of Gimnasia La Plata, died of sunstroke after a match against Sportivo Barracas. That there was an enormous gulf in quality between top (Boca Juniors, which lost just three times and scored 133 goals in accumulating sixty-one points) and bottom (Argentino del Sud, which lost thirty-two of their thirty-five games and conceded 100 goals) could hardly be denied. There was a clear financial imperative to concentrate quality and generate more matches between the better teams.

The 1930 season finally finished on April 12, 1931, with the 1931 season scheduled to begin a month later. It soon became apparent, though, that it wasn't going to start, or at least not without major changes. A deputation of players, demanding freedom of contract—a tacit admission that they were professional—marched through Buenos Aires to present their case to the president of the republic, Uriburu. He passed the matter on to the mayor of Buenos Aires, José Guerrico, who pointed out what had long been obvious: the real issue was that of professionalism.

On May 9, a day before the 1931 season was due to start, twelve teams—Atlanta, Boca Juniors, Chacarita Juniors, Estudiantes, Ferro Carril Oeste, Gimnasia y Esgrima, Lanús, Platense, Racing, San Lorenzo, Talleres, and Tigre—dissociated from the Asociación Amateurs and declared themselves professional. The following day four of the seventeen scheduled fixtures weren't played, while Atlético Estudiantes and Sportivo Palermo declared their game a friendly. River Plate and Independiente quickly joined the professional clubs, and on May 31 an eighteen-team professional Liga Argentina de Football began, although it would take another six decades before players finally achieved the freedom of contract they had sought.

Not that the soccer establishment was in any sense opposed to the new regime. Rather, whatever the push for better wages or working conditions may have been among players, among the owners and administrators there was a pragmatic acceptance of the new circumstances. The tentacles of the coalition crept into all areas of life—and that included soccer. Many of the smaller and midsize clubs were, by the end of the thirties, still run by directors primarily motivated by local pride, but among the bigger clubs there was a clear nexus of political interest. Justo, for instance, openly supported Boca, and his daughter Otilia married Eduardo Sánchez Terrero, who went on to be president of the club from 1939 to 1946. It was under his leadership that Boca secured a favorable loan to build a stadium in 1940. It initially had two tiers; it was only when a third was completed in 1953 that it attracted the nickname la Bombonera—the Chocolate Box. When Ramón Castillo became president in 1942, his son Ramón Castillo Jr. had already been serving as AFA president for a year.[1] Soccer was recognized as a powerful social force and thus something politicians needed, if not necessarily to guide, then at least to be seen to be associated with.

It's a fair assumption too that, whether they realized it or not, the leaders during the *década infame* benefited from soccer's power as an opiate. As long as tens of thousands were going to watch matches every Sunday, and hundreds of thousands were listening avidly on the radio, the talk in the cafés and on the factory floor tended to be of soccer and so not of radical socialism or anarchy. Argentina wasn't affected as badly by the Depression as the United States or western Europe, but a drop in exports meant an inevitable rise in unemployment: official figures in 1932 suggest four hundred thousand were out of work, although the true figure could have been up to eight times greater. The general lack of disposable income can be seen in the way that the number of theater visits in Buenos Aires dropped from 6.9 million in 1925 to 3.4 million in 1935, a fall that can't be put down only to the coming of cinema. Soccer, though, rumbled on, remorselessly popular.

When Borges and Adolfo Bioy Casares collaborated on the short story "Esse est percipi" in 1967, it's no coincidence that it's to the soccer of thirty years earlier that they refer. When el Monumental disappears one day, the narrator of the story discovers that nobody actually plays soccer anymore, that there are no more players and no more matches. "The last time a soccer match was played in Buenos Aires," a club president tells him, "was on 24 June 1937. From that exact moment, soccer, along with the whole gamut of sports, belongs to the genre of drama, performed by a single man in a booth or by actors in jerseys before the TV cameras." The space race is revealed as a "Yankee-Soviet coproduction" to the same ends: "Mankind is at home, sitting back with ease, attentive to the screen or the sportscaster, if not the yellow press."

The most obvious change in the professional era was that it became much easier for clubs to sign players, enticing them with public offers of bigger salaries. The effect was to increase the domination of the *grandes*: Huracán had won the league in 1928 and Gimnasia y Esgrima (La Plata) in 1929, but after the birth of professionalism, it would be thirty-six years before the championship went to anybody outside the big five of Boca, River, Independiente, Racing, and San Lorenzo.

The first major transfer followed precisely that trend, as Pancho Varallo left Gimnasia y Esgrima to join Boca Juniors. Born in Los Hornos, a suburb of La Plata, Varallo was fourteen when he began playing for his local side, 12 de Octubre. "My uncles were in the team, too," he said. "I started as a defender. 'I will protect the goalkeeper,' I liked to say. The offside trap still did not exist for us. Then, as I progressed in the academy, one of my uncles put me as a number 8." He was an inside-forward, playing to the right of a central striker, and was so effective he soon gained the nickname "Cañoncito" (Little Cannon) for the ferocity of his shooting. At eighteen Varallo had a trial with Estudiantes, which wanted to sign him, but the directors of his club were fans of Gimnasia y Esgrima and insisted on his moving there instead. He won the league with them in 1929, and, the following year, he was called up to the national team, while Vélez borrowed him for a Pan-American tour on which he scored sixteen goals.

And then, at the beginning of 1931, came the bid from Boca. "They offered me 4,000 pesos," Varallo said. "You can't imagine how much that was. My father had never seen a 100-peso bill before. But the people of Gimnasia took it very badly. My house was attacked. They threw stones through the windows. I had to move [to Buenos Aires] because going back to La Plata was a nightmare. Once, they saw me getting off a train and ambushed me. They punched me, kicked me. I arrived home bleeding and crying." Varallo lived in the house he bought until his death eighty years later.

Boca's second game of the professional era was in La Plata against Gimnasia y Esgrima. They lost 3–2, which left them with just one point after two games. It didn't take long, though, for Varallo to form a formidable partnership with Roberto Cerro (or "Cherro," as it came to be spelled to reflect the Italian pronunciation), with whom he had played on the national team. "He saw me playing the World Cup in Montevideo," Varallo said, "and said to me, 'Come to Boca and you'll be a king.'" Between them they scored a flood of goals: Cherro got 221 in 305 official games and Varallo 181 in 210, making them, respectively, Boca's leading scorer and leading scorer in the professional era until Martín Palermo surpassed both records. It was only a matter of weeks after he had done so that Varallo died.

For Varallo, the heavy ball used at the time was an advantage. "It got the best out of Cañoncito," he said. "The best days were when the ball was wet. It absorbed the water so it was like a stone. 'Pancho, it's set up for you,' my teammates would say. Then I would strike it, and all the water would come out as the ball went into the net. Goalkeepers couldn't do much with those balls in these days. They had to be brave to put their hands in the way."

But frequent impact with a heavy ball also took its toll on Varallo. The knee trouble he suffered during the 1930 World Cup was a harbinger of problems to come, although he even used his reputation for injuries to his advantage. "The dog's limp, they called it," he explained. "You had to be smart. I would pretend that my knee was hurt, and I would walk with difficulty, so defenders wouldn't come too close to me. Then, when Cherro got the ball, I would suddenly start running as fast as I could, to get a slipped pass. When you're limping, defenders never expect you to react so quickly. Of all my goals, I think 150 were down to Cherro. He knew everything about me; he knew me better than my mother did."

At times, though, the limp was real enough, and Varallo had to be tricked into playing. "We had a coach called Mario Fortunato who was incredible," he remembered. "He would give me confidence even in the worst situations. Once, my cartilage was so badly injured that I couldn't walk very well. 'Boss, I think I won't be able to play,' I said to him. 'My right knee is in pain. I think it's the cartilage.' He said to me, 'Pancho, then there's nothing wrong with you, because you only have cartilage in the left knee.' Not only did I believe him, I played and I scored." By 1939, though, the pain had become intolerable. "I was only twenty-nine when I decided to quit," Varallo said.

Boca won the league again in 1934 and 1935, but what Varallo valued more than titles, he said, was "the sportsmanship that existed, the deep sense of being teammates, friends, and colleagues. I don't get why they kick opponents so much [in the modern game], the constant friction that is seen in every action, at corners or free kicks. It's a different soccer. . . . [T]hey run so much. Sometimes I wonder why they run so much and think so little. In the thirties and forties, every team had eight or nine great technical players. Now there are two or three." The lament is one heard commonly in Argentina: soccer was better then, in the days when technique and intelligence had room to prosper amid the hurly-burly.

It was a view shared by Cherro. "I liked soccer as it was before," he said shortly before his death from a heart attack in 1965, when he was fifty-eight, "with no boards or crosses, no circles or tactics. Soccer was art, theater, music, and those times had already gone by the time I retired." Cherro was born in Barracas, a barrio southwest of La Boca along the Riachuelo, in 1907. His brother Felipe took him to Sporting Barracas in 1922, and he began playing for their fifth team. Two years later he became a player simultaneously for Quilmes and Ferro Carril Oeste, which was permitted under the regulations at the time. It was after his move to Boca in 1926, though, that his career took off. He was talented and charismatic, earning the nicknames "Apilador" (Dribbler) and "Cabecita de Oro" (Little Golden Head), reflecting his technical ability and his soccer-playing intelligence. He was also powerful, with photographs showing his broad torso seemingly ready to burst out of his shirt, the dark curls of his chest hair spilling over the straining neck. His bulk aside, Cherro was a classic *pibe*, with his dark hair and his wide, wrinkled face always seemingly on the verge of breaking into a grin.

Soccer, for him, was never more than a game: he hugged opponents and teammates before and after games and in a match against Sporting Barracas insisted on being moved from inside-left to right-wing so he didn't have to play directly against his brother. "He existed on the border between two eras, the romantic era and the material era," said an obituary in *La Nación*. "He played at the time when soccer was played for the glory of love, and was also part of the time when soccer was played for the love of glory."

9

THE RISE OF RIVER

I t wasn't just Boca who used the new regulations to take advantage of their resources. River Plate were also building, as they had been since their foundation in 1901. If Boca's history was a tale of immigration, River's fans say, their own story reflects what happens next, as the immigrants try to improve themselves. The club was founded by the merger of two other clubs, Santa Rosa and La Rosales in Dársena Sur—literally South Dock—in Puerto Madero, which borders La Boca.

River's name supposedly derives from an incident when a club member saw construction workers at the Carboneras Wilson factory going off to play soccer and abandoning the crates they were supposed to be moving: on those crates were printed the words "River Plate." The club moved to La Boca, then to Sarandí on the other bank of the Riachuelo, near where Arsenal play today. There were teething problems. For the stadium to be sanctioned as fit for purpose by the AFA, it had to have running water, and River's new ground at first did not. It did, though, have the basic plumbing in place, so when the AFA inspector came to check the taps, a player, Alfredo Zanni, stood on the roof with buckets of water, tipping them down the pipes at a prearranged signal.

Then it was back to the port and La Boca. River's expansion was rapid. They played their first official game only in 1905.[1] In 1908 they had one hundred *socios* (members), but by 1911 that number had swollen to four thousand. The derby against Boca quickly became a ferociously contested affair.

River moved again in 1923, this time to well-to-do Recoleta, their new stadium designed by Bernardo Messina, who had been a creative midfielder and the club's first captain and president. To symbolize the link with the club's past, palm trees that grew by the Carboneras Wilson factory were planted by River's new home. That recognition of their history, though, did nothing to stanch the criticism of Boca fans, who saw River as ruthlessly upwardly mobile, determined to leave their immigrant origins far behind.

That impression was confirmed when they prepared for the first season of professionalism by signing right-winger Carlos Peucelle, a veteran of the

1929 Campeonato Sudamericano and 1930 World Cup campaigns, from Sportivo Buenos Aires for the seemingly huge sum of ten thousand pesos.

River finished fourth in 1931, six points behind Boca, and the next season broke the transfer record again, spending thirty-five thousand pesos to sign center-forward Bernabé Ferreyra from Tigre, a figure of such magnitude that it would be twenty years before any Argentinian club paid as much for a player again: the Millonarios nickname was born, and was well deserved. By then, River had more than fifteen thousand members.

Ferreyra was tough and explosive, with photographs suggesting an almost cartoonishly large chest, a perpetual scowl, and a broad, flat forehead under a mass of unruly, center-parted black hair. After the playmaking *conductors* of the twenties, he was a much more British style of center-forward, good in the air, powerful, and possessed of a ferocious shot, the product of endless practice as a child growing up in Rufino in the province of Santa Fe. "My brothers kept telling me I had to have strongest shot in town," he said. "They made me kick the ball from morning to afternoon, every day. They used to encourage me, shouting, 'Harder, even harder!'" The practice worked: he was soon nicknamed "el Mortero de Rufino" (the Mortar of Rufino) for the power of his shooting. In 1930 he was loaned to Vélez for a tour to Chile, Peru, Mexico, Cuba, and the United States. He scored thirty-eight goals in twenty-five games, but just as significant were the legends that grew up around him. In one friendly in Peru, for instance, he is said to have knocked out a goalkeeper with the power of his shot; visiting in the hospital afterward, the goalkeeper asked that if they ever met again, Ferreyra should warn him so he could get out of the way. Sure enough, on the way back south they did face each other once more. This time Ferreyra pointed to where he was going to shoot and scored, at which the keeper, having kept well out of the way, thanked him. On another occasion a referee made him retake a penalty three times. "Keep going," he's supposed to have said as the fourth kick followed the first three into the net. "I'll keep scoring for a whole week."

Ferreyra scored twice on his league debut for River, as they beat Chacarita 3–1. After the game, as Hugo Marini, a journalist for *Crítica*, left the field, he supposedly overheard a boy asking an old man what he thought of the new center-forward. "He's not a man," he replied. "He's a beast." And so was born the second of Ferreyra's nicknames, "Fiera" (Beast). He became a phenomenon, scoring every week, so that *Crítica* offered a reward for the first goalkeeper to keep Ferreyra out. Finally, after nineteen goals in twelve matches, Cándido de Nicola of Huracán took the prize, although his side still only drew 1–1.

Going into the final game of the 1932 season, River trailed Independiente by a point. At the time, results from other games were relayed to crowds at stadiums via large boards erected by the magazine *Alumni* and, although Independiente fell behind at home to Racing, their players knew that River had conceded against San Lorenzo. Thinking the title was theirs, they didn't overexert themselves in the search for an equalizer as the board continued to show San Lorenzo leading 1–0. The board's operator, though, was a River fan, and when River equalized, he delayed changing the score on the board until the final whistle had blown. As Independiente's players and fans celebrated, the awful truth dawned: they faced a playoff for the championship.

It was one leg only, played at the neutral ground of San Lorenzo, and was settled before halftime. Ferreyra and Peucelle, the two big signings, scored in the opening quarter before inside-left Ricardo Zatelli added a third after thirty-eight minutes. It finished 3–0, and River Plate had their first league title, with Ferreyra finishing as top scorer with forty-three goals, the club's investment thoroughly vindicated.

Like Varallo, Ferreyra was particularly effective when wet weather made the ball heavy. River, it was said, would stitch one casing inside another and then soak the resulting double ball in water for up to forty-eight hours before matches to try to make it as weighty as possible so as to take full advantage of the fearsomeness of his shooting. Goalkeepers in particular suffered: in 1932 Boca keeper Juan Yustrich fainted in conceding a goal against River, having taken a shot to the stomach, while in 1935 Independiente keeper Fernando Bello became the first player to save a Ferreyra penalty, but it came at the cost of a pair of broken wrists.

And, like Varallo, Ferreyra's physical exertions took a toll on his body as well. He was forced to retire in 1939 at the age of thirty, by which time he'd scored 187 goals in 185 games for River. He had been probably the first superstar of Argentinian soccer. When River toured the interior, for instance, the ticket price would vary according to whether he was playing. He was referred to in tangos and appeared in four films; after his death in 1972, streets in Rufino and Junín were named after him. "There's never going to be a hero like Bernabé," said tango star Aníbal Troilo. "It may be there have been better players, but there have been no idols like him."

For River, that was only the beginning.

10

MODERNITY AND THE BUDAPEST BUTCHER

The man who carried River and, more generally, Argentinian soccer into the modern age of tactics was, to use the name he seems to have been given at birth, Imre Hirschl. That was later Germanized to Emerich and then Hispanicized to Emérico, but his forename is the least of the mysteries that surround him.

Soccer had been changing in Europe since the 1925 amendment to the offside law that in England had prompted the development of the W-M. Central Europe was less enamored of the third-back as a stopper, but the center-half nonetheless dropped deeper as the twenties went on. And while he retained more creative responsibility than his English equivalent, by the early thirties a version of the M defense (confusingly often known as the W system) was common across the Continent. At the time the most sophisticated tactical debate was centered in the coffeehouses of Austria and Hungary, where intellectuals used the same analytical techniques they brought to the discussion of politics, music, and literature to dissect soccer. It was from the Danubian heartlands that a second wave of pioneers crossed the Atlantic to revolutionize the South American game, injecting the local interpretation of the sport left by the British with new tactical rigor. While the first wave had largely comprised young British men seeking adventure and economic opportunity, the second wave was largely Jewish and sought primarily to escape the growing anti-Semitism of home.

The man who introduced the M defense to Argentina was a Jewish Hungarian called Imre Hirschl, a mysterious figure who was appointed coach of Gimnasia y Esgrima of La Plata in 1932, despite having no background in top-level soccer. It has been widely assumed he had been part of the Ferencváros side that had toured Argentina to great acclaim in 1929, and various Argentinian sources confidently assert he made his debut for them in 1916, before retiring, aged twenty-nine, after that tour, but there is not a single reference to him in any document in the Ferencváros club museum;

he never played an official game for the club. Nor did Ferenc Rudas, who at ninety-two was the oldest surviving Ferencváros player when he was asked in 2014, have any recollection of him. Hirschl was a man from nowhere. If, as historian José Luis Romero argued, Argentina is a place in which men can invent a new identity for themselves, few have taken up that challenge quite as enthusiastically as Hirschl.

It does seem true that Hirschl was born in Apostag, a small town about sixty miles south of Budapest, on July 11, 1900, but almost everything else he allowed Argentinians to believe about him was a lie. He has a daughter, Gabriela, still working as a psychoanalyst in Buenos Aires. She said that her father rarely spoke about his past, but that he followed his brothers to Palestine during World War I, where he lied about his age and signed up with a unit under British command. He remained in Palestine after the war to fight with Jewish nationalists against the Ottoman Empire. A grenade attack left him with scars to his hip, and he also sustained a bullet wound to the wrist.

Gabriela says her father told her he played in Czechoslovakia, but the only club in whose records his name appears as a player was Húsos FC. That seems to corroborate the detail offered by Béla Guttmann[1]—another Hungarian Jew who would gain a lasting place in football history as an irascible but brilliant coach, the highlight of whose peripatetic career was winning two European Cups with Benfica—that Hirschl's main job was as a butcher. Gabriela, while acknowledging that her father knew how to take meat from a cow and was adept at making sausages, suggests that was common at the time and that her father was from a wealthy family rather than being a professional butcher.

In 1929 Hirschl, the story goes, had been in Paris trying to secure a visa to New York when by chance he met Count Materazzo, the richest man in Brazil and the president of Palestra Italia, the club that would become Palmeiras. Hirschl persuaded him to take him on as a coach.

It seems Hirschl approached Guttmann in São Paulo in late June or early July 1930 and said he was looking for work. Guttmann at the time was playing for Hakoah, which were touring the Americas as part of their remit to propagate the ideology of muscular Judaism. Hakoah took Hirschl on as a masseur, and he traveled with them for a month or so as they headed south to Argentina. Or at least that's Guttmann's story.

The problem is that Guttmann was a fabulist, somebody who was forever spinning yarns and, moreover, somebody who was forever falling out with people and allowing personal antipathy to color his anecdotes. "His original plan," Guttmann went on, "was to get himself sacked as soon as possible, get a golden handshake and use the money to pay for his wife and child to travel over from Budapest."[2] How can a coach get himself fired quickly? He decided to shuffle the team as much as he could. "He was hailed by the fans as a great coach," Guttmann said, "which made him change his mind and started to focus on soccer as a 'real coach.'"

Despite losing their first three games of the 1932 season—and winning just three of their first sixteen—Gimnasia went on to finish a highly respectable seventh. They took that momentum into the new season, winning their opening five games and leading the table at the midway point, with forward Arturo Naón in superb form. Hirschl seems initially to have kept himself to himself, something made easier by the press's habit of focusing on the *grandes* to the exclusion of everything else.

"The change at Gimnasia is astonishing," the profile noted. "The players can't just change so much by chance. His influence is evident." Hirschl, though, remained humble. "First things first: I do not teach soccer," he said. "It would be ridiculous to pretend to be teaching soccer in the country where the best soccer is played. Players like the Argentinians cannot be found anywhere else. The *criollos* have potential: everything I do is based on taking advantage of it."

According to the article, before taking the job Hirschl had watched the team play in three games, after which he'd told the board he could create a decent side, using the players who were already at the club without needing a budget for transfers. He promised that if they took him on, by 1933 Gimnasia would be challenging for the title. The board gave him the job, but there was soon friction, as Hirschl replaced a number of first teamers with players who'd been in the reserves. "The board," the profile said, "protested, because they thought that these players would be useless. . . . But his contract said he had carte blanche to make decisions, so these players remained."

Those "useless" players were Arturo Naón, a center-forward who remains Gimnasia's all-time leading scorer; inside-right Alberto Palomino; right-half Oscar Montañez; and goalkeeper Atilio Herrera, all of whom became regulars on a team known as "el Expreso." The star of the side, though, was José María "Pepe" Minella. He had started out as a center-forward, first catching the eye as a sixteen-year-old playing for a local league selection in Mar del Plata, the city of his birth, in their 1–0 victory over the crew of the HMS *Repulse*, a game staged to celebrate the visit of the Prince of Wales, later Edward VIII, to Argentina in 1925. Minella joined Gimnasia in 1928 and scored eleven goals in twenty-seven games on the club's lengthy postseason tour of 1930–1931 when he was called on to cover at number 5 because of an injury to Pedro Chalú. He never returned to the forward line and went on to redefine the role of a center-half. "History will be divided into the time before Minella and the time after Minella," wrote journalist Juvenal, the foremost tactical commentator of his day. With Montañez to his right and Ángel Miguens to the left, Minella was the heart of a midfield dubbed "*las tres M*s."

"I offered to become a friend of each one," Hirschl continued, "so we could work out our responsibilities better. There'd be no need to show my authority, as long as I saw that everything was going according to plan. . . . The *criollo*, for all his apparent lack of discipline, adapts himself easily to direction."

Having read what Guttmann said, it's impossible for doubts not to ring at every sentence Hirschl spoke: the line between the profundity of a genius and the platitudes of a spoofer is always narrow. He was certainly extraordinarily charismatic: in every photograph of him with a group of players, he is clearly the dominant figure, and not just because of his height—he was six foot five—and they hang on his words. Gabriela recalls that in banks, shops, or train stations, he could command attention and gather an audience simply by speaking.

Whatever Hirschl's motives when he took the job—and there is only Guttmann's word that they were anything other than noble—he soon became an inspirational coach. "My first task was to put the team together from a physical point of view," he said. "They had to be in good shape. To achieve that I had to think what kind of exercises each player needed and how much they had to practice them. You can't demand the same effort from eleven men, because for some it's a good level, for others it's not enough and for others excessive." He introduced "Swedish gymnastics and American gymnastics, combined," and insisted on a mix of sprints, long runs, basketball, and soccer in training. *El Gráfico* noted how in wins over Independiente and San Lorenzo, el Expreso had outlasted their opponents, beating them thanks to greater stamina.

Hirschl may have said all the right things about the *criollo* game and its virtuosity, but, as Guttmann would later do to great effect at São Paulo, he introduced a more direct approach with a greater emphasis on passing than individual skill.

Hirschl's other great innovation, and one that suggests his financial acuity while also seeming to indicate that he saw a longer-term future at Gimnasia than Guttmann would allow, was to put the entire team on the same salary, "so there was a common sense of sacrifice." On top of their basic wage, the first XI shared a percentage of the gate receipts. The result was that rather than earning between 120 and 300 pesos per month, all the first teamers—and Hirschl—took home more than 700.

Everything was going perfectly until the end of September, when Gimnasia went to Boca for the twenty-sixth round of the thirty-four-game championship, leading them by two points at the top of the table. At half-time they led 2–1, but the home side was then awarded a highly debatable penalty that was converted. A few minutes later, Boca added a third despite appeals for offside. Gimnasia were furious, and the league seemed to have sympathy, suspending the referee, although the result stood.

Gimnasia rallied to beat Independiente in their next game, but what happened at San Lorenzo the following week was even worse. Gimnasia were down 2–1 when they seemed to have won a penalty, only for referee Alberto Rojo Miró to decide the offense had taken place outside the box. Soon afterward, he awarded a goal to San Lorenzo when the Gimnasia goalkeeper seemed to have prevented its crossing the line. Distraught, the Gimnasia players staged a sit-down protest, as San Lorenzo walked in four further goals before the referee abandoned the game. Back-to-back defeats to River and Racing in their fifth- and fourth-last games of the season effectively ended Gimnasia's title chances. As Gimnasia saw it, they had been robbed of the title by two referees.

In that 1933 season, Gimnasia y Esgrima scored ninety goals, four more than the next-highest scorers, Boca, and drew praise for their attacking soccer (they also conceded fifty-five, a worse record than any other side in the top seven). There was widespread sympathy for them, with many accepting that the big five were too powerful, the size and vehemence of their crowds and their political clout intimidating referees into favoring them. That referees were often too scared to give big decisions was made clear the following year when only thirty-four penalties were awarded all season.

Guttmann, though, suggested that Hirschl and Gimnasia weren't exactly innocents, either. "He had a famous or infamous trick," Guttmann said.

> Hirschl made his players train with a heavy ball, similar to the ones used in England. At that time in South America, it was the custom to play the first half with the ball of the home team and then with the ball of the away team in the second. However, Hirschl came up with the idea of giving a barbed ring to his goalkeeper to puncture the ball at the right moment so they could use their special, heavy ball—which the team had already gotten used to at the training sessions. He was a real hustler, I'm telling you.

Could it be that it was this same heavy ball, soaked in water and with a double casing, that, after Hirschl had moved to River, became part of the myth of Bernabé Ferreyra?

River, attracted by Hirschl's attacking style, were looking for a specialist soccer coach as they continued their program of investment. Hirschl was appointed in 1934. He began slowly (or so he claimed—corroboratory evidence is hard to come by) to implement the M defense, withdrawing the center-half to play not as a pure defender, as he did in England, but as a very deep-lying midfielder, as was usual in the Danubian conception of the position, a player who defended but would also help create the play from deep. After a year he signed Minella from Gimnasia to fulfill the role.

Whether he began as a bluffer or not, Hirschl's success as a coach is beyond dispute. In 1936, as Argentinian soccer went through another of its bewildering restructurings, he led River to the Copa Campeonato (essentially the league, although teams played each other only once), winning thirteen of seventeen games and rattling in forty-nine goals as they did so.

Hirschl had great faith in youth, giving the great Adolfo Pedernera his debut as a sixteen-year-old in 1935 and making eighteen-year-old José Manuel Moreno a regular on the left of the forward line that same year. He would develop into an inside-forward equally comfortable on either side of the field. Moreno had grown up in La Boca, had supported Boca Juniors, and had been desperate to play for them, but he was rejected by them after a trial. He vowed he would make them regret the snub, and once a broken nose persuaded him to give up a promising boxing career he joined River. His big chance came on a tour of Brazil in 1934, when he demonstrated a preternatural confidence. "Relax, boys," he said before a game against Vasco da Gama. "We'll put five past this lot. Just look at the guy who's marking me. He's so ugly. I'm going to give him the run-around." Sure enough, River won 5–1.

Pedernera, having grown up in Avellaneda, was a Racing fan, but his father, who had first thrown him a ball when he was four, had played for River. He, like Moreno, learned a great deal from Ferreyra. In 1938, for instance, when he was still establishing himself on the side, Pedernera was allowed to take a free kick by the center-forward. He tried to curl it, but made poor contact, and the goalkeeper saved his shot easily. Ferreyra called him aside. "If I let you take a free kick," he said, "smash it properly, not like some fake bullet, okay?" "Of course, understood," said Pedernera. "Every time I stood by the ball for a free kick after that, I remembered Bernabé's advice."

Moreno formed a devastating partnership with Ferreyra. In 1936 Ferreyra was River's top scorer in the Campeonato, banging in 15 goals in seventeen games, but in the Copa de Honor it was Moreno who topped their scoring charts with 13. The following year, as the championship returned to a more orthodox format, Moreno hit 32 and Ferreyra 25 as River romped to the title, scoring 106 goals and losing just three of their thirty-four games to finish six points clear of a similarly free-scoring Independiente, which was inspired by the great Paraguayan forward Arsenio Erico. "No other team managed to walk on a field with the preparation that distinguished River," said *El Gráfico*, acknowledging Hirschl's role in their success. "No other team could match their fitness training."

With the title already confirmed, River faced Boca Juniors on the penultimate day of the season, having already lost to them in the league and in a friendly. There could be no easing back: River were desperate to end Boca's "fatherhood"—to use the term Argentinians employ when one team dominates another—over them. It was an ugly, fractious game that River won 3–2, violence simmering on the field and the terraces, despite being one of the first to be refereed by Isaac Caswell, an English official brought in precisely to try to prevent matches from getting out of hand.

The league may have turned professional in 1931, but the referees had not, and as the thirties went on officials were increasingly targeted. In 1932, for instance, when Vicente de Angelis disallowed a goal for Estudiantes when they were 1–0 down against table-topping River, enraged players charged at him, forcing him to flee to the dressing room. He reemerged to restart the game fifteen minutes later and awarded the goal, prompting rumors that he'd been threatened at gunpoint by the Estudiantes president. It became known as *el gol de la casilla*—the goal of the dressing room.

The AFA, demonstrating its familiar Anglophilia (or cultural cringe, depending on how you looked at it), decided the solution was to turn to Britain and brought over a British referee to set standards and train local officials. Caswell was a Labour councillor in Blackburn who had recently retired as a referee. He arrived in Buenos Aires in October 1937, undeterred by fellow passengers on the ship who warned him he "was undertaking a dangerous task," and spent his first three weeks visiting games, learning about conditions, and seeing how Argentinian referees went about their business.

The picture he painted was a troubling one:

> All the bigger enclosures are surrounded by a high wall. . . . Enclosing the playing pitch is a wire fence ten feet high . . . barbed at the top. Mounted police are on duty outside and, in some cases, inside the ground while foot police are held in reserve and, at times, the fire brigade as well. . . . There was rough play, incessant whistling by referees, frequent stoppages for injuries (accompanied often by about a dozen persons rushing on to the field to give the player water), constant arguing with the referee, fights on the field and interventions by police. Often there were free fights among spectators, some of whom waited after the match to threaten or throw missiles at the referee. For six months my work was heartbreaking.

Crowd trouble had been a problem from the earliest days of the Argentinian game. In 1905 a match between Belgrano and Quilmes had had to be called off after a field invasion. Five years later Boca fans forced the abandonment of a second-flight game against Ferro Carril Oeste after one of their players had attacked a linesman and another the referee. In 1923 in a game between a Combined Scottish XI and a Provincial selection, a Scottish player was forced to put a corner out of play for a goal kick, as fans, believing it had been erroneously awarded, lined up in front of him. But those incidents, disturbing as they sound, were essentially isolated. Things became much worse when fans began organizing and arming themselves. Caswell's fears about safety were borne out in 1939 when a policeman fired into the crowd as angry Boca fans threatened to invade the field as players scrapped in a game against Lanús. Two people were killed, the first victims of soccer violence in an Argentinian stadium.

Change, Caswell noted soberly, would take time. But there was a turning point, he believed, and it came in September 1938 in a game between Boca and Racing when he sent off Roberto Cherro for dissent. Although Caswell was stoned by fans at the end of the game, the player was banned for a month. "My firmness in this match," Caswell said, "and the fact that it showed I was out for discipline and was not to be deterred either by the fame of the player or by clubs, made an impression and changed the situation." Caswell returned home in 1940, seemingly widely respected.

River scored 105 goals in thirty-two games the following season, 1938, but it was not enough. Independiente, with Erico again supreme, racked up 115 and sealed the title on the final day of the season with an 8–2 victory over Lanús. Erico may have gotten the goals, but the real star of that side was Antonio Sastre, a player hailed by César Luis Menotti as the greatest he ever saw and in 1980 voted one of the five greatest Argentinian players of all time, capable of playing in a range of positions. That was part of what made him so dangerous: with the opposition concerned with Erico and his fellow striker Vicente de la Mata, Sastre would drift deep, breaking the traditional structures of the game to pick up the ball deep and create the play.

Born in Lomas de Zamora in 1911, Sastre, like so many others, came to prominence at Progresista in the Avellaneda barrio of La Mosca. He made his debut in 1931, replacing the injured Lalín at inside-left, seemingly at the instigation of Seoane, whose place he would eventually take. Tall and powerful, Sastre may have ended up playing as an orthodox center-forward, but he moved to the left after Independiente signed the great Uruguayan striker Roberto Porta, his versatility proving a key asset. In total, he played 340 games for Independiente, scoring 112 goals and winning the championship in 1938 and 1939, before moving to São Paulo in 1941. He helped them to three Paulista championships and had a statue erected in his honor. "If there was ever a Nobel Prize for soccer," the club president Décio Pacheco Pedroso said, "there's no doubt the whole of Brazil would vote for Sastre."

Hirschl left River at the end of the 1938 season after a second-place finish, returning briefly to Gimnasia before moving to Rosario Central. When they were beaten 6–0 at River in 1939, Hirschl recognized he had reaped the harvest he had sown. "I have come personally to gather the fruits of my teaching," he said. "Those six goals were scored by my boys."

He moved on to San Lorenzo, then Banfield, then San Lorenzo again, before, in 1944, his career in Argentina was abruptly ended. The minutes for the seventh issue of the agenda of AFA's disciplinary tribunal, held on January 13, note that Florencio Sola,[3] the president of Banfield, tried to bribe Ferro Carril Oeste goalkeeper Sebastián Gualco[4] before a game between Banfield and Ferro in September 1943 (it finished 1–1 and Gualco didn't play). Others are listed as having played a part in the conspiracy, including Hirschl, who had "intervened in the attempt to bribe the player Gualco with the sum of 2,000 pesos." Hirschl was one of nine men[5] convicted of *amoralidad deportiva*—sporting immorality—and permanently banned from any direct or indirect activity with the AFA or clubs affiliated with the AFA. The ban was overturned by the General Inspection of Justice on May 10 that year, although some stigma remained.

It would be dangerous to draw firm conclusions, but it's at the very least an intriguing coincidence that twenty years earlier Hirschl had left Hungary after Húsos were implicated in a match-fixing scandal. Suspended from working in Argentina, Hirschl went first to Brazil, where he managed Cruzeiro, and then to Uruguay, where he took Peñarol to two league titles and is credited with having instilled the tactical thinking that led to Uruguay's unexpected World Cup success in Brazil in 1950.

Yet for all that, there can be little disputing his genius or that, in the context of Argentinian soccer, he was years ahead of his time.

THE KNIGHTS OF ANGUISH

As they fiddled about unconvincingly with finding a replacement for Hirschl, River's next advance was the erection of el Monumental, the first modern stadium in Argentina, paid for, goalkeeper Amadeo Carrizo insisted, by the profits made from the increased attendance drawn by Ferreyra. Constructed of concrete and steel, it opened on May 25, 1938, in the presence of the president, Roberto María Ortiz, with a demolition of Peñarol. More significant, though, was what the stadium symbolized. In contained a school and a medical practice as well as facilities for *socios* (members) and so, it could be said, was ahead of its time in recognizing the potential ways in which a stadium could be used outside of game days.

Ángel Labruna, who would make his debut for the first team in 1939, was one of many *socios* who spent most of their free time there. He played soccer, table tennis, tennis, everything the club had to offer apart from swimming—because, he said, "I like to live." It was there that he met the woman who would become his wife. That social aspect was used to justify the incredibly generous terms of the loan River were granted by the government, but, really, this was simply another sign of the intermeshing of soccer and politics, of the open courting of fans by the elite.

Having finished second again in 1939—just the 100 goals scored this time, as Independiente, scoring 103, took the title by six points—River turned in 1940 to another Hungarian, former Barcelona goalkeeper Ferenc Plattkó. His attempts to introduce the M defense brought dismal results, and he was dismissed in July, with River having lost seven of their opening twelve games of the season, but his brief spell in charge probably represented a necessary period of transition.

Peucelle, though, acknowledged the importance of Plattkó's brief stint at the club in developing the ideas left by Hirschl. "He couldn't make it work, but he left the seed of change," Peucelle said. That seed would be nurtured by Renato Cesarini, who had been a key part of Hirschl's championship-winning sides of 1936 and 1937 but had begun his education in European tactics far earlier.

Cesarini had been born in Senigallia, near Ancona, on the east coast of Italy, in 1906, but his family emigrated to Argentina when he was a few months old. In 1929 Juventus persuaded him to leave Chacarita Juniors and join the exodus of *oriundi* (immigrants) back to Europe. He was hugely successful in Italy, winning five consecutive Serie A titles and developing such a knack of scoring late goals that even now in Italy, late winners are said to have been scored in the *zona Cesarini*. Cesarini was not just about goals, though; he also had a specific brief to man-mark the opposition's most creative player, an idea he brought back with him to Argentina in 1935, first with Chacarita and then with River, where he found Hirschl's theories chiming with what he had learned in Italy.

"He was a fundamental man for the River style," said Boca fullback Silvio Marzolini, who played under Cesarini with the national team. "And Cesarini took the players fishing. Fishing![1] He was very intelligent, always creating this special relationship with the players. But he was also very annoying because when he saw you making even one movement that wasn't what he wanted, he'd tell you."

Adapting the man-marking he had learned in Italy, Cesarini deployed Norberto Yácono as a very defensive right-half and ultimately effectively a right-back. That had a profound impact on which numbers became associated with which positions in Argentina. When shirt numbers had been introduced in the early thirties, it was still usual, following the British practice, to see a team lining up as a 2-3-5: numbering across the field, the goalkeeper was the 1, the right-back 2, left-back 3, right-half 4, center-half 5, left-half 6, right-wing 7, inside-right 8, center-forward 9, inside-left 10, and left-wing 11. By the time of la Máquina, Yácono had moved to right-back from right-half, who thus became the 4, and the two inside-forwards had fallen back toward the midfield, effectively creating a 3-2-2-3 (the same shape as Chapman's W-M in England) that was numbered, from right-back to left-wing, 4, 2, 3, 5, 6, 8, 10, 7, 9, 11. That's why a 5, even today, in Argentina is the holding midfielder, often the *caudillo*. In England, when the back three of the W-M had been created, it had been the 5, the center-half, who had slotted back between the fullbacks, which is why a 5 in England was traditionally a central defender and why *center-half* is often used in Britain as a synonym for *center-back*.

In retrospect, it can be seen that la Máquina was born on October 19, 1941, the penultimate day of the season. The previous week, Boca, the defending champions, had beaten San Lorenzo 2–1 to allow River, which beat Tigre 2–0, to open up a two-point lead at the top of the table. Boca had no chance of winning the title, but they went to el Monumental looking at least to disrupt their rivals. River were 3–0 up by halftime and went on to win 5–1. *El Gráfico* dedicated fourteen pages to the victory.

The following season they got even better. River had won six and drawn one of their opening seven games when they went to Chacarita Juniors on June 7. Boca beat Tigre 11–1 that day, but it was River's display in a 6–2 win that captured the imagination. Borocotó, the editor of *El Gráfico*, dubbed them "la Máquina," and this time the nickname stuck. In the twenties his magazine had criticized the mechanistic nature of the British game; now the machinelike was to be celebrated for its slickness, for the wonder of so many parts interlocking and working together. Fans seized on the beauty of the repetitions, chanting, "*Sale el sol, sale la luna, centro de Muñoz, gol de Labruna*" (The sun rises, the moon rises, center from Muñoz, goal from Labruna).

It had been Moreno who had been the star of the 5–1 win over Boca, and history probably judges him to have been the most technically gifted of that forward line. Certainly, he was representative of the era, sporting a raffish mustache and spending his nights in bars and *milonga* clubs, insisting, like Muñoz, that the tango was the best training a soccer player could have. The great Boca forward Pancho Varallo believed that if Moreno had trained properly and looked after himself, he might have surpassed even Maradona—and when a player is being considered more dissolute than Maradona, it's fair to say he must have enjoyed an extremely vibrant social life. His River teammate Loustau told a story of a game against Racing when Moreno, after a heavy night out, was warned by doctors that if he played twenty minutes he'd die; he didn't just play, of course, but was man of the match. Was the story true? Perhaps not strictly, but it encapsulated a greater truth, just like the story of a friendly played in Tucumán when the crowd was so large and security so tight that a mounted policeman got in Loustau's way as he made for goal. No matter, the story goes; he poked the ball through the horse's legs, ducked under its belly, and ran on to score. La Máquina were not just a great team but served as a mirror into which Argentinians saw reflected an idealized self-image: skillful and clever, impudent and daring, elegant and brilliant, unconventional and unrestrained to the point of irresponsibility.

There were toughness and aggression behind his artistry. In 1947, for instance, he confronted a group of Estudiantes fans who had run onto the field to remonstrate with the referee, raising his fists in a throwback to his days as a boxer. Later that year he was struck on the head by a stone thrown by fans of Tigre, but angrily dismissed River's medical staff when they raced over to help him. "Why should I accept treatment?" he raged. "So that lot can feel good and go around singing that they hit Moreno? No sir! The only time I get treatment on a field is when I have to be carried off."

The fabled front five was highly mobile, thanks largely to the fact that Ángel Labruna, the nominal center-forward, tended to operate to the left, creating spaces for the forward surges of Moreno from an inside-right position and for Muñoz to swoop in from the flank. "No *director técnico* produced that," said Peucelle. "The players made it happen." The son of a watchmaker who castigated his son for wasting so much time playing soccer, Labruna made his debut in 1939 when the first team went on strike in support of Moreno and remained on the first team for most of the following two decades, scoring a club record 315 goals. On the left was Félix Loustau, the *ventilador*—the "fan" whose running allowing the midfield to breathe and reduced the burden on Pedernera. "It's not modern soccer, it's the old soccer we're playing," Labruna insisted. "A team that has players ready for just carrying out one function can't go far."

La Máquina were winners, but they weren't relentless. They won the league in 1941 and 1942 but finished second behind Boca in 1943 and 1944, as the Xeneizes[2] benefited from their adoption of the M defense under the management of their former center-forward Alfredo Garasini, before taking the title again in 1945. "They called us the 'Knights of Anguish' because we didn't look for the goal," said Muñoz. "We never thought we couldn't score against our rivals. We went out on the field and played our way: take the ball, give it to me, a *gambeta*, this, that, and the goal came by itself."

Carrizo made his debut in 1945, although he remained very much the second choice behind Peruvian goalkeeper José Soriano, the last surviving member of la Máquina when he died at the age of ninety-three in 2011. His memory is of a side that, as far as possible, simply played. "The players listened to the manager with respect, because it's not that Moreno or Pedernera didn't listen, on the contrary," he said. "Sometimes there was a tactics board, and everybody paid attention. But when we arrived in the tunnel, some of them would always say, 'Okay, lads, let's do *la nuestra*:[3] *la nuestra* is the one that counts, eh?' It was an expression that was repeated often."

12

THE RISE OF JUAN PERÓN

The *década infame* could go on for only so long. Such inefficiency did it generate that at times, the government seemed almost to stop. In 1937, for instance, Congress passed only three motions, one that authorized it to spend more money and two that gave the president permission to leave Buenos Aires to go on vacation. By 1943 there was widespread discontent at the way the conservative hegemony was maintained, prompted largely by the disastrous attempts to rebuild the economy as the effects of the Great Depression destroyed the livelihoods of thousands of small landowners. It crystallized in a group of dissident army officers, the Grupo de Oficiales Unidos, who were frustrated by the inconsistency of Argentina's foreign policy during World War II and by the parochialism of the ruling powers.

The GOU contacted General Arturo Rawson, asking him to provide troops, and on June 4, 1943, he led ten thousand men through Buenos Aires to oust Ramón Castillo, who had served as acting president after Roberto Ortiz fell ill in August 1940, formally replacing him in June 1942. Congress was dissolved, politicians were forced out of the ministries, and political parties were banned. Rawson declared himself president and appointed a cabinet that would almost certainly have advocated backing the Allies in World War II. Other members of the GOU leadership, though, wanted to remain neutral and forced Rawson to resign on June 7. He was replaced by Pedro Pablo Ramírez.

Ramírez lasted eight and a half months before being succeeded by his vice president, Edelmiro Farrell. The most significant figure in the new government, though, turned out to be the labor minister, Juan Domingo Perón, who had been impressed by the possibilities of social democracy while studying mountain warfare in the Italian Alps in 1939. Over the course of two years he unleashed an extraordinary program of social and industrial reform and gained immense popularity as a result. Argentina was industrializing rapidly anyway, its economy becoming more urban.

Not only did the increase in literacy, allied to the disposable income released by a recovering economy, lead to the cultural boom of the early forties, but it meant there was a newly educated, politically active class waiting to be mobilized, and in Perón they found their leader, a man who could, for all his education and military training, trace his ancestry to an indigenous woman. When he graduated from a military academy, his father gave him three books, one of them *Martín Fierro*, "so that you will never forget that, above all other things, you are a *criollo*," as the inscription read.[1]

Senior officers were so worried by his personal magnetism that they had him arrested, but that only confirmed their fears as, on October 17, 1945, hundreds of thousands of protesters, the *decamisados*[2] (shirtless ones), poured across the Riachuelo from the industrial suburbs of the South and gathered in the Plaza de Mayo to demand his release. It was, novelist Ernesto Sábato wrote, as though "an enormous and silent force, almost subterranean, had been put in motion": the cult of Peronism, ill-defined as it was, was born.

In 1946, as democracy returned to Argentina, Perón was elected president with a majority of around 11 percent in the last election before the enfranchisement of women. The old liberal consensus had been swept away, as the working class took power for the first time, yet, as historian Robert D. Crassweller argues, Perón's accession was "a renunciation of spiritual kinship with Europe and a cry for the truly indigenous, for Creole reality and Creole myth, for the spirit of *Martín Fierro*."[3] It was the return of the *caudillo*.

Perón's style of leadership, meanwhile, also reshaped attitudes toward the presidency. Although he was democratically elected, his habit of wearing his military uniform perhaps helped to erode the notion of civilian democracy in Argentina, something that would have profound consequences in the three decades that followed.

At first, Perón's basic principles of social justice and economic independence allowed him to steer a middle path in the Cold War. The government tended to back the unions in strikes, leading to a leap in wages well above the rate of inflation, while prices for key consumables—and soccer—were kept low. The government also nationalized key industries, taking the railways from companies owned by the British, the docks from the French, and the telephone network from the United States. Control of exchange rates and exterior commerce meant that reserves could be used for redistributive projects. The gross industrial product rose 60 percent between 1941 and 1948, while Perón delivered on his promises of workers' rights. Paid holidays and Christmas bonuses were introduced and employees indemnified against dismissal. Salaries increased 50 percent in real terms between 1943 and 1951. Schools and hospitals were built, universities subsidized, and tuberculosis eradicated. So long as nobody asked what was actually funding the wave of construction and handouts, Argentina appeared a model of social welfare.

As Western Europe rebuilt after the war, the Argentinian economy boomed on the back of exports. The national debt was paid off, allowing Perón to claim that a state of economic independence had been achieved. It was, though, illusory: Argentinian neutrality during World War II and their rejection of pleas from the United States to break off relations with the Axis powers in the aftermath of Pearl Harbor had led to economic sanctions, which in turn prompted an attitude of isolationism. Argentina, successive leaders asserted, could and would go it alone.

Argentinian soccer, existing in its own beautiful bubble, found itself lulled into a similar false sense of well-being. Two weeks before Perón's election, Argentina had faced Brazil in the deciding game of the Campeonato Sudamericano (one of the extra editions that, while official, awarded no trophy). There was bad blood from the 1945 Copa Julio Roca, played in Brazil two months earlier. Although Argentina had won the first of three matches 4–3 in São Paulo, they were hammered 6–2 in Rio, with Heleno de Freitas[4] in his prime for the hosts. In the third and final game, three days later, Ademir broke José Pedro Batagliero's leg in the first half, and Brazil went on to win 3–1. It seems the incident was accidental, but when Argentina met Brazil in that Campeonato Sudamericano decider, their fans were bent on revenge, with street vendors selling unripe pears with which to pelt the Brazilians. Needing only a draw to retain the title they'd won in Chile the previous year, Argentina went 2–0 up inside twenty minutes, both goals coming from Norberto "Tucho" Méndez, the Huracán forward with the mass of greased-back hair and the dapper mustache who would become the tournament's record scorer.[5] Just before the half hour, though, Argentina's captain, José Salomón, went to block a shot from Jair. Their legs clashed, and Salomón collapsed, having fractured both his fibula and his tibia. His teammates attacked the Brazilians, at which fans invaded the field to take their retribution. Police waded in indiscriminately, and it was more than an hour before the game could be restarted. The referee, in what was more a symbolic gesture than anything else, sent off a player from each side—Chico and Vicente de la Mata—and the game was played out in an atmosphere of muted hostility. The 2–0 win gave Argentina the championship, but Salomón never played international soccer again. "You've broken the leg of Argentina's best defender," Argentina coach Guillermo Stábile said on seeing Jair after the game. "Nonsense," the forward is reputed to have replied. "The best Argentinian defenders are De Zorzi and Valussi."

Much has been said about the impact of national sporting success on elections—perhaps most notably the claim that Harold Wilson's shock defeat in the 1970 UK general election was partly caused by the dismay of England's defeat to West Germany in the World Cup quarter-final five days earlier—but little has ever been proved. Whether beating Brazil made any difference to Perón's victory is impossible to say, but it's certainly true that a feeling of patriotic well-being can't have hurt.

A year later, Argentina retained their title, a team that included Moreno, Méndez, Mario "el Atómico" Boyé, Loustau, and Di Stéfano, winning six and drawing one match in sweeping to success in a tournament that didn't include Brazil. It was an age, it seemed, of Argentinian self-confidence and pride, both in soccer and more generally, something reflected in the release in 1948 of the definitive film of the Argentinian game, coscripted by—who else?—Borocotó. *Ball of Rags* told the story of Eduardo Díaz, nicknamed "Comeuñas" (Nail-biter), a *pibe* who learns to play with a ball of rags on a *potrero* in his barrio. He becomes a top-class player and a hero of the terraces. At the key moment, though, just before an international final against Brazil—which had by then supplanted Uruguay as Argentina's main rivals—he is told that he has a chronic heart condition and that if he plays, he risks death. His manager urges him not to play, but the crowd insists, carrying him onto the field. At the moment of crisis, Comeuñas gazes at the Argentinian flag and resolves to play: "There are many ways to give your life for your country," he says, "and this is one of them." He pulls on the *Albiceleste* stripes and scores the winner.

Within a year, though, a real-life Comeuñas wouldn't have had the chance to risk death to play for his country. Argentina sent no team to the 1949 Campeonato Sudamericano or the 1950 World Cup, blaming bureaucratic difficulties. It took little imagination to see this as simply more protectionism: it was essential to Perón that the sense of Argentinian superiority could not be challenged. In Julio Cortazar's 1946 short story "House Taken Over," in which a bourgeois house is slowly overwhelmed by forces unknown and unexplained as its owners acquiesce grudgingly but without ever resisting—a fairly transparent metaphor for Peronist Argentina—the narrator speaks of traipsing around bookstores "uselessly asking if they had anything new in French literature. Nothing worthwhile had arrived in Argentina since 1939." The same, it could be argued, was true of Argentinian soccer: once the shutters of isolationism came down, the trade in ideas that might have saved Argentina from its complacency was stymied.

Sport hadn't just become a key strut in his creation of Argentina's self-confident, thrusting image; it was also part of Perón's own personal mystique. He merged the Argentinian Olympic Committee with the Confederation of Argentinian Sport, bringing them under state control and making himself president of the new body. It was launched with a campaign that proclaimed "Perón sponsors sports" and hailed him as "the First Sportsman." Perón himself preferred hunting and was an adept fencer, but he was well aware of soccer's role in nation building, and that meant the possibility of defeat could not be countenanced. Crucially, Perón differed from his predecessors in acknowledging sport as, to use Alabarces's phrase, "a new (and legitimate) patriotic symbol."

That did, though, mean some rewriting of the past. Ralph Pappier's 1950 biopic of Alexander Watson Hutton, *School of Champions*, seems troubled by the notion of soccer's British origins. Watson Hutton himself spends a lot of the film wearing a deerstalker, presumably on the logic that if Sherlock Holmes wore one, all British men of the era must have, but that cliché aside, it's significant that his all-conquering Alumni side is later, inaccurately, portrayed as a British team that turned Argentinian.

At the same time, there was an overprotectiveness toward soccer, the fear always lurking that Argentinian soccer was not so strong as it appeared. The big five had threatened to become a big two, but after six years of Boca and River sharing the title, their domination was finally broken in 1946 by San Lorenzo, which clinched the championship on the final day with a 3–1 win over Ferro Carril Oeste as Boca lost at Vélez Sarsfield.

The strength of the side was the *Terceto de Oro* (the Golden Trio): the inside-right Armando Farro, a spindly schemer who would drop deep to create the play; center-forward René Pontoni, with his carefully styled pale hair, his well-groomed mustache, and his eye for goal; and the swarthy and powerful inside-left Rinaldo Martino.

The team as a whole became known as *el Ciclón* (the Cyclone) and consecrated its legend on a tour of Spain and Portugal in December and January. Despite the "cold, snow and intense rainfall of that winter," *El País* said, San Lorenzo "caused a sensation."

Yet still the authorities remained timorous, particularly after seeing the crushing blow dealt Brazil in 1950 in the World Cup it hosted, as they faltered at the last to hand the title to Uruguay. Athletics, less popular and less liable to raise great passions, was perceived as safer. The government funded a large team to go to the 1948 Olympic Games in London, an event that was regarded as broadly successful, as Argentina finished thirteenth in the medals table, having claimed two golds in boxing and another in the men's marathon. Those who had been successful were awarded further medals by Perón at a ceremony at el Monumental in 1949. That same year Buenos Aires lost out by a single vote to Melbourne in the bidding to stage the 1956 Olympic Games.[6]

While the Peronist administration shied from international soccer, it did everything it could to dominate the domestic game. The appointments of Oscar Nicolini and Valentín Suárez as presidents of the AFA were made directly by Perón, while Huracán in 1947 and Vélez Sarsfield in 1951 followed River in having stadium construction projects effectively underwritten by the government. In return, the administration got control: each club had somewhere near its center of power a *padrino* (a "godfather") who linked them to Perón's web.

Soccer also played a significant role in Perón's social program, most notably through the Evita championship, named after his beloved wife, which began in 1950. Open to any team of children that presented itself to the offices of the Evita Perón Foundation, it served effectively as a welfare organization that supplied gear and submitted players to compulsory medicals, immunizations, and X-rays. The finals were held in Buenos Aires and were preceded by the national anthem and a march for Eva Perón, before she performed a ceremonial kickoff.

The tournaments were significant not only in themselves, the opportunities they gave talented young Argentinian players and in the use of soccer as a tool for social development, but because the celebration of childhood is significant to the whole self-image of Argentinian soccer. "In his notion of the *pibe*," the sociologist Sergio Levinsky wrote, "Borocotó not only pointed to his youth, but also to his freshness, spontaneity and liberty—values associated with childhood that often get lost in maturity with the assumption of responsibility."[7] In that regard, it seems telling that it should have been Eva Perón who fronted the children's tournament.

An actress who had arrived in Buenos Aires in the thirties, she married Perón in 1945[8] and effectively created for herself a new personality. She had documents relating to her birth falsified to make it look as though her parents had been married when she was born, and so Eva Ibarguren (her mother's surname), born 1919, became Eva Duarte (her father's surname), born 1922: Argentina was still a land in which anybody could reinvent themselves—and if it took a little *viveza* (cunning) to do so, so be it. Evita worked with prodigious energy, often sleeping only two or three hours a night, fronting many of Perón's social and charitable concerns, attracting the idolatry of the masses. There was, in the late 1940s, a youthful vitality about her, a freshness that, for good or ill, meant she occupied a similar liminal space between childhood and adulthood as the *pibe*. "In many ways," the British ambassador to Buenos Aires wrote, "Evita Perón was an ambitious, self-willed, self-seeking schoolgirl who had never grown up. Argentina . . . was still an adolescent country."

And she remained forever young. On January 9, 1950, Evita fainted in public. She had surgery three days later, and although it was announced she'd had an appendectomy, she had been diagnosed with cervical cancer. After Perón's reelection in 1952, she rode with her husband in a celebratory parade through Buenos Aires. By that stage she was too ill to stand, but was kept upright by a frame of wire and plaster under her fur coat, an act of considerable will that would come in time to seem a grotesque image of the state of the economy, a severely ailing body sustained by unseen and artificial supports. She died on July 26, 1952, prompting an extraordinary public outpouring of grief. When her body was moved on the morning after her death to the Ministry of Labor, eight people were killed in the crush and a further two thousand required hospital treatment, the first evidence of the cult of Evita that would survive long after her death.

13

EL DORADO

The advent of professionalism had deferred the problem, but it hadn't solved it: players across the continent were frustrated by poor wages and a lack of security. In 1939 José Nasazzi led a players' strike in Uruguay. Five years later the establishment of a professional league in Mexico attracted players from Uruguay and Argentina tired of conditions at home. That same year the first Argentinian players' union, Futbolistas Argentinos Agremiados, was founded. By 1948 it was demanding recognition from the authorities and seeking a minimum wage and freedom of contract. Initially, the clubs simply ignored the union, but when a strike was called for April 1948, they gave it official recognition. That postponed the dispute, but the underlying issues remained, and the strike was called again in July. Soccer, to general disbelief, came to a halt. The government intervened and set up a tribunal to arbitrate. That got soccer going again, but the tribunal's findings didn't satisfy the unions, and the players went on strike again in the November.

At another time the clubs might have held firm and the players might have capitulated, but the strike coincided with major events happening three thousand miles to the northwest in Colombia. At one o'clock on April 9 that year, lawyer Jorge Eliécer Gaitán, the leader of the Liberal Party and a staunch opponent of the use of violence in politics, left his office on Seventh Street in Bogotá. At two o'clock he had a meeting with an ambitious twenty-one-year-old Cuban lawyer named Fidel Castro, but first he wanted lunch. Arm in arm with his close friend Plinio Mendoza Neira, Gaitán set off for the Hotel Continental, five minutes' walk away. He never got there. An assassin approached, four shots rang out, and five minutes before he'd been scheduled to meet Castro, Gaitán was pronounced dead in a local hospital. Over the decade that followed, around three hundred thousand Colombians were killed in the aftershocks of the assassination.

The Colombian authorities could see the trouble coming and searched desperately for a solution. "Soccer was the only thing that the government could think of to control and calm the population after the death of Gaitán," Guillermo Ruiz Bonilla, Colombia's most respected soccer historian, told journalist Carl Worswick. "There was nothing else that came close."[1] The Argentinian authorities couldn't realistically have anticipated it, but the new league had a profound effect. El Dorado, as it was soon nicknamed, was a viable alternative to the domestic league and one that offered vast salaries and was recruiting players rapaciously.

As the relationship between the Colombian league and its own federation worsened, the league was disaffiliated. Far from being the blow it was intended to be, though, expulsion came as liberation. It meant the Colombian league was no longer part of FIFA, and that in turn meant its clubs had carte blanche to sign whomever they wanted because there was no authority to stop them. Early in 1949 Millonarios appointed former Platense and Quilmes defender Carlos "Cacho" Aldabe as their player-manager. Realizing he was a close friend of Pedernera—still one of the greatest players in the world at the time, although by then he had left River for Huracán—Senior sent Cacho to Buenos Aires to sign him.

Cacho boarded the plane with a suitcase stuffed with $5,000; Senior later admitted he was terrified he wouldn't come back. Cacho met Pedernera, who, at thirty and with the strike showing no signs of being resolved, was worried he might never play again. Pedernera named his price: a signing fee of $5,000, plus a monthly salary of $200. They were astronomical figures, and Cacho wasn't sure whether even Millonarios would be able to meet them. He sent a telegram to Senior and received an instant reply: "Bring him."

Nobody bothered even to tell Huracán, let alone consider compensating them. "It was like a bomb going off," Efraín "el Caimán" Sánchez, a Colombian goalkeeper who had joined San Lorenzo in 1948, told Worswick. "Argentinians considered their soccer to be the best in the world and so to lose their stars hurt a lot."

As Argentina fumed, hundreds of fans greeted Pedernera at El Dorado airport. The next day, Millonarios faced the Medellín side Atlético Municipal. Because of the strike, Pedernera was unfit and didn't play, but fifteen thousand turned up to welcome him anyway. Senior took $17,000 in gate receipts—and so covered Pedernera's annual salary in an afternoon. Pedernera made his debut against Deportes Caldas on June 26, 1949, running the game as Millonarios won 3–0. Soon, though, it became apparent that the relative lack of quality of his teammates was restricting him, so Senior sent Pedernera back to Argentina to recruit more disgruntled stars. He returned with Nestor Rossi and Alfredo Di Stéfano. Millonarios averaged almost four goals a game as they won the 1949 title.

For Di Stéfano, the move had profound ramifications. His paternal grandfather had emigrated to Argentina from Capri, while his mother was of French and Irish descent. He was born in the barrio of Barracas in 1926 and made his debut for River eleven days after his nineteenth birthday. Although his potential was obvious, that was the only game Di Stéfano played for River that season, and the following year he was loaned to Huracán. Back at River, he hit twenty-seven goals in thirty games, as River finished second behind Independiente, and scored six in six for the national side as they won the Campeonato Sudamericano in Ecuador. The probability is that had it not been for the strike, he would have established himself as one of the great stars of River and Argentina. As it was, he left for Colombia, where he was hugely successful. When Millonarios beat Real Madrid 4–2 in a friendly in 1952, he came to the attention of Spanish clubs and, after a legal squabble between Barcelona and Madrid, ended up joining Madrid in 1953. There "la Saeta Rubia" (the Blond Arrow) became recognized as one of the greatest players of all time, being one of only three players to play in all of Real Madrid's five successive European Cup triumphs at the end of the decade. He never played again in Argentina, and although he returned to manage both River and Boca, there was always a sense that his genius was played out at a remove.

The exodus from Argentina continued, and the fury of Argentinians increased. But as both the authorities and the union refused to back down, players could hardly be blamed for abandoning the strike to seek their fortunes in Colombia. Although the Argentinian championship limped on, by 1951 there were 133 Argentinians playing in Colombia, which had devastating consequences for the quality of the Argentinian league.

That year Pedernera was appointed as Millonarios' player-manager. He applied the lessons he had learned with la Máquina to his team of stars, and the results were stunning. Millonarios won twenty-eight of thirty-four games that season, but it was the style with which they did it, the blend of the technical and the artistic, that made them legendary. This was *el Ballet Azul*, the Blue Ballet, the apogee of the Argentinian aesthetic played out in Bogotá.

But 1951 was the beginning of the end for El Dorado. That August the league reached an agreement with FIFA: Colombia's suspension was lifted, but only on the condition that players either returned to their former clubs by 1954 or transfer fees were paid. A transfer embargo was imposed, and Millonarios went on to win the title in 1952 and 1953. As players began to leave, the league deflated, and, as it did, the civil war intensified. "It was terrible: without soccer, violence exploded," said historian Guillermo Ruiz.

As El Dorado declined and players returned home, so the Argentinian league began to return to normality and was able to slide back into its comfortable belief that it was the best in the world.

14

BACK HOME

As the threat of the 1948 players' strike escalated, rather than resolving the issue of wages the AFA concerned itself with refereeing. So successful had Isaac Caswell been—and by implication so low was the standard of Argentinian officiating—that in 1948 the AFA recruited eight British referees to take charge of all top-flight games, giving each of them an interpreter to help file their match reports.

Certainly, the British officials didn't always avoid controversy. After one gave a penalty to each side in the final five minutes of a game between Racing and Platense, he was stoned by the crowd and had to be smuggled away in a police van. "Get Out Mr Bob Turner and Bad Lucky [sic]," roared the headline of a local paper, moved to English in an attempt to get the message across.

Initially, the soccer the British referees presided over was conditioned largely by the strike. Amid the exodus to Colombia, the only club not to lose players was Racing, the team backed by Perón's finance minister Ramón Cereijo, the result of which was that they won the league title three years in a row, 1949–1951. It was even rumored that players were told any requests for a passport to emigrate would be denied.

Guillermo Stábile's reputation as a coach suffered serious damage at the 1958 World Cup, but in the decade before that he was hugely successful, creating an exciting, attacking Racing team based around the dribbling and finishing abilities of Norberto "Tucho" Méndez, who had joined the club from Huracán in 1947. "I have had three loves in my life," Méndez said after retiring. "Huracán was my girlfriend, Racing was my wife and Argentina was my passion."

If anything, Racing were even stronger the following season, when they moved into el Estadio Presidente Juan Domingo Perón, more popularly known as el Cilindro, the vast concrete bowl in Avellaneda that remains their stadium. Former Boca winger Mario Boyé returned from Genoa via Colombia to take up a place on the left, where he formed a highly effective partnership with the industrious Ernesto Gutiérrez. Racing still lost ten games, but they finished eight points clear of Boca, scoring eighty-six goals—nine more than San Lorenzo and seventeen more than anybody else than season.

The third title was the tightest, as Racing and Banfield finished level. The first leg of a playoff was drawn 0–0, the second won 1–0 by Racing with a goal from Mario Boyé. Those are the simple facts, but this is a case in which the simple facts are a fraction of the story.

Myths and rumors have grown up around the game. It was said that Evita, gravely ill with cancer at the time, was a fan of Banfield and was desperate for her team to win; she made her first public appearance after surgery the day before the second leg, walking around the presidential gardens, and two days after the game gave her first radio address after the treatment. Racing, of course, were supposedly the team of Perón, although there seems little evidence he cared much about soccer as a sport. It's been claimed that the rules were changed to deny Banfield the title, but the regulations were clear: if teams at the top of the table were level on points, they played off, as River Plate and Independiente had done in 1932. There were other stories, of Cereijo seeking favors for Racing, of cars being offered to opponents, but they seem to have emerged only later.

What is true is that most of the popular support was with Banfield. "A great vanquisher and a great vanquished," said the report in *Clarín*. "The *chico* that presumed to interfere with the prolonged monopoly of the *grandes* was already a champion after thirty-four match days. It was already consecrated and continues to be so despite its defeat yesterday."

Fifteen years later, with Evita dead and Perón in exile, Banfield defender Luis Bagnato began to hint that dark forces had been at work. "Can you imagine what was at stake?" he said in an interview with *El Gráfico*. "Our hopes ended and so did those of many who wanted to see a *chico* champion. . . . I prefer not to engage in controversies, but I can assure you that some things happened backstage. We were left with the satisfaction of being moral champions."

Evita may have supported Banfield, and it appears that presidential press secretary Raúl Apold visited Banfield as they prepared for the game and offered them each a car for victory, but there seems little evidence of actual conspiracy. In fact, it's probably telling that the rumors of manipulation emerged only in the midsixties, by which time the repeated coups and political turbulence had fostered a general atmosphere of paranoia: the talk of conspiracy came only after Argentinian society had been primed to see conspiracy everywhere by repeated conspiracies at the highest levels of government.

15

OUR WAY

In the 1950s, as the country began to emerge from isolation, Argentinian soccer's faith in its own superiority was bolstered by a string of fine international results. Most significant were a series of meetings with England, which remained, in the Argentinian imagination if not in fact, the ultimate test. Argentina were invited to play England in a friendly in 1951 as part of the Festival of Britain, the first time the two sides had met in an official international, with a reciprocal agreement for England to play in Buenos Aires two years later. A scan of the British press suggests it regarded the game as run-of-the-mill, just another tiny step on the road toward normalization after World War II. For Argentina, though, this was a chance to settle some quasi-colonial scores in the one cultural mode about which the whole nation cared. *El Gráfico* insisted Argentina had "been waiting fifty years for this."

In Buenos Aires newspaper coverage began weeks before the game and featured an extraordinary array of graphs and diagrams alongside in-depth dissections of training sessions and analyses of what the players were eating (beef, mostly). There was, *El Gráfico* made clear, a real urge to beat "those that boast of being the fathers and masters of our soccer; those that came to our soils to show us that one plays soccer like so." It's a very strange passage and one that says far more about Argentinian insecurities than about English arrogance. The idea that the English lorded it over Argentina in particular because they'd taught them the game is absurd: they'd taught everybody the game. The attitude and phraseology, rather, seem to recall the discourse of *El Gráfico* itself in the 1920s, as it created an identity for Argentinian soccer—and to an extent Argentina itself—in opposition to the British.

And while Argentina may not have gone into the game with any great sense of technical inferiority, there was something of the wide-eyed tourist about both them and media coverage of their visit to London. Players bought clothing, vacuum cleaners, and fridges to take home, while Santiago Vernazza, the River Plate forward who was on the bench that day, was struck by how green the grass was at Wembley by comparison with the dusty pitches of home.

England began the game much the better, Jackie Milburn drawing a fine save from Miguel Ángel Rugilo and Stan Mortensen heading just over before they won a corner after eighteen minutes. Rugilo came and neither caught nor punched it but missed the ball altogether. He was lucky, though: the ball was cleared at the back post and fell for Labruna, who turned inside Alf Ramsey and clipped a pass infield. Rubén Bravo flicked the ball on for Labruna, who took it around England keeper Bert Williams and chipped the ball across goal for Mario Boyé to head in. Boyé later described it as the greatest moment of his life. For a second he seemed overcome, disbelieving of what he'd done, before, as Geoffrey Green put it in the *Times*, "flushed with excitement, [he] ran back to the center as if he had conquered the world," skipping and jumping in unrestrained joy.

Slowly, Argentina were forced deeper and deeper. Rugilo, with his saturnine mustache and unusually short shorts, began to emerge as the hero, as he made a number of saves and delighted in playing to the crowd, swinging from his crossbar as shots flashed over and bowing after making saves. Twice Milburn hit the post before finally, with eleven minutes remaining, England leveled from their fourteenth corner of the game. There was no challenge on Harold Hassall as he met Tom Finney's delivery, nor on Mortensen as he stole in at the back post to divert the ball over the line. Rugilo, understandably, shrugged.

The aerial weakness Argentina had so feared had been exposed. Seven minutes later, Mortensen headed down for Milburn to stab the ball over the line. Rugilo was distraught.

It was a game that seemed to satisfy both sides, and the mutual respect was clear as the players left the field after the game. England had retained their unbeaten record at Wembley and, although they'd been behind until the seventy-ninth minute, could reasonably claim to have dominated the match, while Argentina went home with honor, having gotten to within eleven minutes of victory.

England's return trip was to involve two games, the first billed as a Buenos Aires League XI against an FA XI, the second a full international refereed by the renowned English official Arthur Ellis. Again there was a clear sense of cultural cringe, as *Clarín* described England as "giants from another world," but the cordiality that had marked Argentina's visit to London was a little strained. England were taken on the usual sightseeing trips, went to the San Isidro racetrack, laid a wreath at Eva Perón's grave, and attended a reception at the presidential residence, but Perón deliberately stoked nationalist sentiment, raising for the first time the issue of the Falklands.

Twice in the first half of the representative game, the home side struck the woodwork before their aerial vulnerability was exposed again, with Tommy Taylor heading in a Jack Froggatt corner four minutes before half-time. Within a minute, though, Argentina were level thanks to a strike that became known as "the Impossible Goal." Carlos Lacasia picked up the ball in midfield and laid it short to Carlos Cecconato, who sent it wide left to Ernesto Grillo. He beat Billy Wright on the outside, then twisted by Tommy Garrett, the fullback, before dumping Malcolm Barrass on the ground with a feint. As he cut into the box, Ted Ditchburn, the keeper, came to meet him, but went down too soon, allowing Grillo to smash the ball over him into the top corner. It remains such an iconic goal that a huge print of it hangs in the foyer of the players' union.

From then on, the Buenos Aires XI were unstoppable, with Rodolfo Micheli and a second from Grillo completing a 3–1 win. As England shrugged off a defeat in what was to them only a warm-up, Perón declared that the anniversary of the success, May 14, would thereafter be known as Footballers' Day.[1] "We say it's the day soccer was born," said Micheli.

Three days later, on the Sunday, came the full international, for which England, highlighting the differing level of seriousness with which they took the two games, made seven changes. Argentina merely left out the injured Cecconato for Norberto Méndez. The day dawned warm and dry, leading Billy Wright to comment that he would love a drop of rain. By 1:25 p.m., he had his wish. By 2:00 the skies were black as a torrential thunderstorm raged. By the time the game started at 3:00, there were puddles across the pitch, and at 3:22 Ellis decided to take the players off. A little more than ten minutes later, he officially abandoned the match. The crowd, having approached the game with such anticipation, was furious and pelted officials and players from both teams with oranges.

In their frustration Argentina returned to the first game, elevating that to the status of full international, although FIFA sided with England in recognizing only the second fixture. Official or not, it was a victory of huge symbolic importance for Argentina. "We won the match with a demonstration of quality," said *Clarín*. "The *criollo* style can always overcome the English method. We know how to beat European tactics; our way is best for our character. We don't need foreign ideas: the Argentinian supporter wants virtuosity, beauty and glamour."

16

THE ZENITH AND BEYOND

For all the positivity around Argentinian soccer in the early fifties, the AFA didn't send a team to the 1954 World Cup. Officially, the AFA was in dispute with FIFA, but there were suggestions that Perón had vetoed entry when the AFA hierarchy admitted it couldn't be sure of success. Given the devastation Brazil had suffered when they failed to win the 1950 World Cup on home soil—reports of mass suicides may be fanciful, but the psychological trauma of the defeat to Uruguay in the final game was real enough; as playwright Nelson Rodríguez described it, the *Maracanazo* was Brazil's first great national tragedy—Perón's caution was perhaps understandable, but in hindsight it looks like an opportunity missed.

Attendance numbers reached a peak in 1954 to which they would never return, while Perón lost control of the economy. Once the country's reserves were exhausted, his redistributive program had to slow down. Agricultural production was falling, not helped by a series of bouts of bad weather between 1950 and 1952 that destroyed significant quantities of crops. In response, Ramón Cereijo refocused the economy on exports. In 1952 a National Austerity Plan was introduced to try to recoup capital, but that process was hindered by a clause in the 1949 constitution that prohibited the reexport of profit. By 1953 inflation was on the rise, but salaries were not.

Meanwhile, Perón's reformist zeal had begun to strike at the pillars of the Argentinian establishment. In 1953 a Peronist mob burned down the Argentinian Jockey Club, an attack on the social hub of the upper classes, destroying numerous paintings and an estimated fifty thousand books. When somebody called the fire department, they replied, "We have no instructions to put out a fire at the Jockey Club." The following year Perón turned his attention to the Catholic Church,[1] which had withdrawn its support, ignoring its opposition to legalized divorce and bringing religious schools under state control. Again, the extremist fringes of his support turned to arson, setting fire to cathedrals. The pope responded by excommunicating Perón and his cabinet.

By 1954 Perón was exhausted. He was approaching sixty, had developed a nervous tic in his right eye, and had taken a fourteen-year-old companion, Nelly Rivas.[2] More than ever, he was courting the unions, and wages were increasing rapidly. The consequence was rising inflation, and that, combined with the attacks on the church, proved too much. In June 1955 Admiral Samuel Toranzo Calderón mounted a coup attempt, but bad weather delayed his attempt to bomb the Casa Rosada,[3] so Perón had left by the time the attack was launched. As navy soldiers fought in the street, around two hundred people were killed. Perón addressed crowds of supporters gathered in the Plaza de Mayo with words that would become only more chilling in retrospect, with the knowledge of what the twenty-five years that followed would bring. "To violence," he said, "we will reply with a greater violence. With our excessive tolerance, we have won the right to suppress them violently. . . . [A]ny person who in any place tries to disturb the public order in opposition to the constituted authorities, or contrary to the law or the constitution, may be killed by any Argentinian. . . . [W]hen one of ours falls, five of theirs will fall."

But the forces arrayed against him were too strong, and on September 20 a conservative core of the military and industrial leaders issued Perón with an ultimatum: resign or face a coup. There were those who urged Perón to rally the unions and make a stand, but, fearing a bloodbath, he fled into exile in Paraguay. Perón was replaced first by the Catholic nationalist general Eduardo Lonardi, who insisted he was leading a "Liberating Revolution" against a "tyrant"—slogan: "Christ overcomes"—but within two months, his health failing, he had been deposed and replaced by hardliner General Pedro Aramburu. When, in 1956, Peronist loyalists within the military launched a counterrevolution, Aramburu authorized the illegal detention and execution of dissidents. The Peronist party was banned, and it was made an offense even to mention the names of Juan Perón or Evita as part of a process of concerted de-Peronization. For soccer, used to soft loans, *padrinos*, and a cautious outlook when it came to international competition, that meant profound changes.

Perón's growing confidence had led to increased international contact—of which the games against England were the most obvious sign—and, having skipped the 1949 and 1953 Campeonatos Sudamericanos, Argentina returned to the competition in Chile in 1955. It did nothing to dispel their sense of superiority. Only Peru could so much as take a point off them, as they won their tenth title and made it four in a row of tournaments they'd entered. They put six past Uruguay and rattled in a total of eighteen goals in five games; their victory was crushingly emphatic. Which raises an obvious question: given that Argentina were so good, so transparently better than everybody else on the continent, what was Perón so afraid of? It's almost as though Argentina had become so used to winning that the prospect of defeat was more alarming than the potential rewards of victory: better to allow superiority to be assumed than to let it loose in the world to be tested.

Argentina's run of success did come to an end in Uruguay a year later. They began the Sudamericano with three wins before meeting Brazil for the first time since Salomón's career had been ended in the final game of the 1946 tournament. It turned out to be vital, Luizinho scoring the only goal with two minutes remaining to secure Brazil's first victory over Argentina in the tournament since 1922. Victory over the hosts in their final would still have secured Argentina the title, but again they lost 1–0. There was perhaps evidence there that Argentina's hegemony was not so secure as it had been.

In a sense, the narrow failure made what happened next all the sweeter, as Argentina regained the crown in Peru. The victory of the *carasucias*, the dirty faces, was the apotheosis of *la nuestra*, not just another championship but a perfect demonstration of the ideals of Argentinian soccer, as Omar Orestes Corbatta dazzled on the flank and the *Trío de la Muerte* of Humberto Maschio, Antonio Angelillo, and Omar Sívori scored goal after goal. Sívori of River Plate was twenty-one, an explosive dribbler with a large head—its size earned him the nickname "El Cabezón"—a mop of black hair, gaps between his teeth, and a lopsided smile: he was the image of the *pibe*, the self-schooled urchin Argentina lionized as the perfect exemplar of how it played the game. Angelillo of Boca Juniors, the center-forward, was nineteen and sported a slim mustache and neatly combed, swept-back hair. Maschio of Racing, nicknamed "Bocha," was the oldest of the trio at twenty-four, his hair severely parted, his gaze stern. Together, they were irresistible.

It wasn't just the Trio, though, something Maschio was keen to make clear. There was his Racing teammate Omar Orestes Corbatta, a brilliant dribbler, his life as yet untainted by the alcohol that would later overwhelm him, and on the other flank Osvaldo Cruz of Independiente, who came onto the side when Antonio Garabal left Ferro Carril Oeste to move to Spain with Atlético de Madrid. And in the center, perhaps most important of all, was Néstor "Pipo" Rossi, the great *caudillo*.[4]

The mystique of the *carasucias* grew because their exploits existed largely in the public's imagination: they became a myth, a distant, half-dreamed ideal. "No one in Argentina had the chance to see that team," Maschio said. "There was no television. They could only hear us on the radio. The only opportunity people had to see us was in three friendly matches [before the tournament], and they were very flattering. We beat a selection from the interior 8–1, then we beat Huracán 3–1, and then we beat another team from the interior 6–0, so that helped create an impression."

It was in those games that the manager, Guillermo Stábile, who had been the top scorer at the 1930 World Cup, first began to realize something special was beginning to form. "In the practice games we had the feeling that we were looking at an exceptional attacking lineup," he told *El Gráfico* eight years later. "They understood each other as if they had always played together. Their strength was the combination: old virtues with a modern rhythm. And behind them they had an experienced and efficient defensive block. . . . [T]he axis of the team, sweating quality and injecting soccer, was the Voice, Pipo Rossi: 'Run, Bocha, don't stay. Zurdo, raise your head, don't show off too much. Enrique, pass it, the others can also play. Corbatita, who are you marking? Mark someone, do you want me dead?'"

Stábile wasn't just focused on soccer, though, something that became apparent in Peru. "He used to take the girls off us," said Maschio, whose interest in women was legendary. "Sívori started dating the telephone operator in the hotel, and I was going out with one of her friends. And when the girls called, he said to us, 'Give me the phone; I want to talk to her.' He always tried to steal our conquests. He was really good-looking. We didn't have a chance."

The form Argentina had shown in the buildup was continued in Lima, where they began with an 8–2 win over Colombia. They followed that up by beating Ecuador 3–0 and Uruguay 4–0.

A 6–2 victory over Chile meant that a win over Brazil in their penultimate game would secure the title. Brazil were the pretournament favorites and had racked up twenty-three goals in their first five games thanks to the creativity of Didi and the finishing of Evaristo.

Angelillo put Argentina ahead midway through the first half. Then, the report in *El Gráfico* said, "Brazil showed their claws trying to equalize. Argentina entrenched behind the screaming of its commander Rossi. Corbatta kept running and distracted Didi. Sívori kept dribbling and Maschio's coldness awaited for a deadly counterattack." And finally, after numerous chances to settle the game, came those two goals in the final three minutes. The reaction in Brazil was savage. "The team didn't do anything," said playwright and soccer journalist Nelson Rodrigues. "Absolutely nothing. Terrible technically, tactically and psychologically, we escaped, without doubt, an astronomical thrashing."

There was still one game to play—in fact, as it turned out, two. "The Argentinian ambassador in Peru was called General [Roberto Tomás] Dalton," said Maschio.

When we beat Brazil 3–0 we'd already won the championship, but we still had the last match against Peru on the Saturday. On the Thursday,

Stábile told us that we had the days before that game free. The whole team went out celebrating, apart from [Pedro] Dellacha, Angelillo and me. We shared a room. Dellacha was like a father to us: he took care of us and wouldn't let us go. He just introduced us to some female friends on the beach. We lost 2–1 to Peru and Dalton was furious. He thought that because we were champions it was impossible for us to be beaten, so he arranged a rematch. Stabile said that those who wanted to go away were free to do so, but the rest of us lived like we were in cloisters. We had breakfast at the hotel, practiced at El Revolver Club, then lunch, then we trained again in the afternoon. After that we had dinner and went to bed. We won the second game 4–1.

Brilliant as they'd been—Pedro Escartín, the Spanish referee and journalist, hailed Argentina as the favorites for the 1958 World Cup—Argentina didn't return home to any great reception. "I remember a few people were there to welcome us in the airport," said Maschio. "There was nothing like there would have been nowadays, nothing to compare with the number of people that came when we won the Intercontinental Cup with Racing. It was not really special. There were only a few fans, journalists and our families."

It soon became special, though: in retrospect, the victory of the Angels with Dirty Faces in Peru was the last great flowering of *la nuestra*, the elaborate, free-flowing attacking style of play that Argentinian soccer came to see as characteristic of its golden age. Within a year it was over, humiliation against Czechoslovakia in the World Cup in Helsingborg tipping Argentina into a spiral of self-reflection from which it has never really escaped. The ideal of *la nuestra*, like so many Argentinian dreams, couldn't withstand the reality.

Argentinian soccer may, like the country itself, be a world of impossible and illusory ideals, but this was an occasion when the reality didn't fall far short. This was technically proficient, attacking soccer played by a group of players who spent each match with half an eye on their evening entertainment, and it swept aside the best the rest of the continent had to offer. Argentinian soccer would never be so good—or at least not as good while remaining true to the bohemian ideals of the golden age—again.

17

THE LAST OF THE ANGELS

Humberto Maschio was eighty when I met him in a café amid the industrial sprawl of Avellaneda. He'd suggested meeting at 10:30, but, worried about the traffic, I got there at around 9:45. He was already sitting at a table, a basket of *medialunas,* a smaller, sweeter variant of the croissant, before him. The waiters and other customers clearly knew him, and I got the impression he spent a lot of his time there, holding court and flirting. As I stood on the pavement, having finally left hours later trying to work out which bus I needed to get back into Buenos Aires, a waiter came dashing out. Maschio, he said, wanted me to go back in and meet somebody; it turned out Juan Carlos Rulli, his Racing teammate, had just arrived. Sitting in cafés, talking about soccer, is his life. "After every match in Avellaneda, we all come to eat pizza in this bar," he said. Given the level Racing achieved when Maschio was in his prime, there's something poignant about the way he and his circle of friends still care so much when they—and the Argentinian domestic game in general—have suffered such obvious decline. Still, they are far from atypical.

Maschio could have left Avellaneda. He grew up there, but when he went to play in Italy, it would have been easy enough to make the break; on his return, newly wealthy, few could have blamed him had he chosen to live in Buenos Aires itself. But he didn't. "I couldn't have moved from here," he said. "I only leave when I go to Córdoba to visit my family." Avellaneda is ingrained in him.

"I was born here," he said, gesturing through the window as a squally wind buffeted the lines of cars.

> But, you know, I am here as a result of a miracle. My grandfather had already arrived in Argentina [from Italy], and my father had to bring his sisters to Buenos Aires so that they didn't have to take the ship by themselves. But because he was playing soccer for Sampdoria, he sent a friend of his to take the girls to the *Mafalda*, which sank. Two of the girls were saved, but the youngest died from a heart attack by the

Brazilian coast. My father came later, so it's really a miracle for me to be here.

And I started playing soccer in the streets. Back in that era, there was no traffic. The streetcar was the only transport here. My house was like a dressing room for me and my friends, and there was a *potrero* nearby with four or five fields. At night we'd play *a cabeza* [head-to-head] under the lampposts.

Maschio joined Racing in 1954, but the bulk of the side that had won the three straight championships between 1949 and 1951 was still there, so he initially found it difficult to break through. Within a year, though, after Juan José Pizzuti had left for Boca, he had made himself a regular.

When Pizzuti returned after a year as Angelillo went to Boca, becoming even at twenty-six the father of the side, they established a formidable partnership, Maschio probing from an attacking midfield role, picking out the runs of the older forward. "I remember Corbatta: he was really generous to everyone and had a really good heart. Unfortunately, many people took advantage of him, and he got lost in alcohol."

Corbatta's was a tragic and sadly typical tale. What's worst about it is that there was no one freakish event that precipitated the misery, no car crash or murder, no one betrayal or moment of catastrophic bad fortune: he was just a man with a majestic talent that propelled him into a sphere in which he was ill-equipped to cope. At soccer he was a genius, at life a disaster.

Born in Daireaux, a small town in the Pampas a little less than three hundred miles to the southwest of Buenos Aires, he moved with his family to La Plata at an early age following the death of his father. He never learned to read or write, a fact of which he was ashamed: later in life he spoke of how humiliated he would feel when teammates discussed something they'd read in a newspaper or a magazine, but at the time he disguised his illiteracy by keeping a newspaper beside him whenever he was interviewed. Dellacha eventually taught him how to scrawl a signature.

Corbatta started out at Estudiantes, but was released at the age of fourteen after injuring his ankle and picked up by Juverlandia de Chascomús, where his dribbling ability and powerful shot persuaded Racing to sign him in 1955. Even as he became famous—it's said fans of other clubs became *socios* of Racing just to watch Corbatta play—he remained painfully shy, particularly around women. Taking pity on him, his teammates introduced him to a blonde woman who was crudely described as "a girl who did the street," expecting them to have a brief fling that would build up Corbatta's confidence. Unexpectedly, he fell in love with her, and they married, moving to a house in Banfield. But one day in 1959, Corbatta returned home to find she'd gone, and the house had been stripped. "There weren't even any spiders left," he said.

He had, at least, overcome his shyness with women. Tita Mattiussi, the legendary manager of Racing's youth hostel, told the story of Corbatta climbing over the wall of the *concentración*[1] at six o'clock one morning after a hectic night out. Mattiussi dunked him in a cold bath three times, but still heard Corbatta telling teammates not to pass to him because he felt so dizzy he wasn't sure he could stand up. "But when he woke up," Mattiussi said, "he played like a beast and scored two goals."

On one occasion, in a *clásico* against Independiente, Corbatta found himself man-marked by Alcides Silveira and, followed everywhere, couldn't get into the game, so he dashed off the field and hid briefly behind the police who lined the front of the stands. In a game for the national team against Uruguay in 1956, he'd so exasperated Pepe Sasía with his showmanship that the forward waited for him to be fouled, ran over, and kicked him in the face. Corbatta lost two teeth; he never had them replaced.

Corbatta became noted as a penalty specialist, famed for his knack of sending the goalkeeper the wrong way. Of sixty-eight he took in his career, he scored sixty-four. "At penalties," he said in an interview with *El Gráfico*, "I stood near the ball so the keeper could not react. I never stood directly behind the ball—always to the side. I struck it with the inside of the right foot in the middle, always with a sharp blow. And I would duck my head so the goalkeeper didn't know which way I was going to shoot, and I would change when I saw what he did. And when he moved, he was a dead man."

Boca bought Corbatta for 12 million pesos in 1963, a payment that Racing invested in expanding their stadium and developing their training base. Already, though, drink was beginning to take its toll. On a tour of Europe, defender Carmelo Simeone was assigned to keep an eye on Corbatta. He was sure he'd succeeded until one day he looked under his bed and found a pile of empty beer bottles.

Corbatta played in only eighteen league games for Boca before leaving for Independiente Medellín in the dying days of the El Dorado league. In Colombia his second wife left him, he ran out of money, and he became ever more dependent on alcohol.

When he returned to Argentina at the age of thirty-four, he was a relic of the player he had been, playing for San Telmo in the second division and then Italia Unidos and Tiro Federal de Río Negro in the lower leagues, the need for money and his lack of other skills forcing him to put off retirement as long as possible. "There are no friends in soccer," he said, "especially when you're in a bad way. They all disappear." Many would say he didn't want to be helped. His money gone, he took to living in a bar near the

Fiorito Hospital, sleeping beneath the counter in two drawers that had been knocked together. "My sister came to get me," he said, "but I didn't want to go back to La Plata. At night I'd get a magazine, look at the pictures and that would distract me a little so I could sleep. I spent everything I had. I gave a lot away without looking who I was giving it to."

At thirty-eight, when he finally retired from the professional game, he moved to Benito Juárez, a small town just south of the capital, where he lived in a shack, playing occasionally for two local sides. Drunk, homeless, and penniless, with four marriages behind him, Corbatta ended up sleeping in a changing room at el Cilindro, paying his board by working with the youth teams, his example a devastating reminder of the transitory nature of soccer-playing glory. He died, at the age of fifty-five, in 1991. Two years later, the street leading to the stadium was named after him.

Racing finished as runners-up to River in 1955 and were fourth in 1956, four points off the top, as River again took the title. Maschio by then was a bona fide star and an international, an aggressive creator who worked hard and scored goals; that season there was talk of his being signed by Juventus. "I was the best player in Argentinian soccer," he said.

Maschio stayed at Racing for another year, but by early 1957 Italian scouts were sniffing again, and he, Angelillo, and Sívori decided that they would leave after the Campeonato Sudamericano. Club president Santiago Saccol told Maschio in March that negotiations were at an advanced stage and that he would be joining Bologna. "The president's assistant, who'd been born in Uruguay, told me that I was going to like it," Maschio said. "It was a city that had been destroyed in the war, but the people were very friendly. They were happy, and the men only talked about three things: politics, soccer, and women. The women there were a little curvier, but really pretty."

As Maschio went to Bologna, Angelillo joined Inter and Sívori went to Juventus. Maschio found the first year "tough" playing as a striker alongside the great Yugoslav forward Bernard Vukas and after two seasons moved to Atalanta. "I arrived there for preseason and had to train a lot, before lunch and in the afternoon. I felt I was dying. After dinner, the coach gave us a spare hour, and my teammates went out. I just slept." In that there was warning of what would happen to Argentina at the World Cup the following year. "And I was a slower player and they man-marked me. Then Ferruccio Valcareggi [the Atalanta coach who was manager of Italy from 1966 to 1974] told me I should change my way of playing to improve. I played in the goalmouth, and he told me to play farther away, so I could read the movements of other players more easily. I became a better player. I was all over and could decide where to go. I was not any faster but could avoid my markers, like Riquelme. I was named their best player of all time."

Maschio wasn't the only Angel to struggle at first. "Sívori had a rough time in Italy at the beginning," Maschio said. "He missed home a lot, as I did, so Umberto Agnelli, the president of Juventus, surprised him with a special dinner, with an orchestra that was playing tangos. The place was full of Argentinians."

Angelillo, meanwhile, scored thirty-three goals in the 1958–1959 season, a tally that has not been surpassed in Serie A since. Inter still finished only third that season, though, and as time went by, frustration grew at his inconsistency. His lifestyle, as for so many Argentinians of his generation, meant he was never fully dedicated to soccer. "Angelillo tailed off a little bit toward the end of his time at Inter," Maschio said, "because he started dating a girl ten years older than him." Others blamed an affair with a high-profile Italian singer. Either way, his womanizing was never likely to find favor with the puritanical Helenio Herrera, who took charge of Inter in 1960. In the summer of 1961, Angelillo was sold to Roma, where he spent four years, before his career dwindled into retirement via two spells at AC Milan, a season at Lecce, and a final flourish at Genoa. He ended his playing career in 1969 and spent the next two decades coaching in the lower leagues in Italy and then in Morocco, never able to return home because he hadn't fulfilled his military service.

As Maschio rediscovered his form at Atalanta, he began to settle down. He even ended up playing for Italy, as the three Angels, abandoned by Argentina, sought international soccer by other means. Angelillo and Sívori had played for Italy in the qualifiers for the 1962 World Cup, and when Giampiero Boniperti was injured shortly before the tournament, Maschio was called up. He didn't play in Italy's first game, a 0–0 draw against West Germany, but was selected for the second match, against Chile, the notorious Battle of Santiago. "I really got it," said Maschio. "They broke my nose in the first twenty minutes, and then they kicked my ankle. I played the entire match completely incapacitated, as there were no substitutions." Chile won 2–0, and although Italy then beat Switzerland, they were out.

After two successful seasons with Atalanta, Maschio was sold to Inter in 1962, then managed by Herrera, who had been born in Buenos Aires to Spanish parents before moving to Casablanca while still a child. Maschio never warmed to him, and although Inter won the *scudetto* in his first season, he was sold to Fiorentina. He spent three years there before finally, in 1966, at the age of thirty-three, going back to Argentina and Racing. The world to which Maschio returned was very different from the one he had left, Argentinian soccer's sense of its superiority shattered in the aftermath of the 1958 World Cup.

PART THREE
AFTER THE FALL,
1958–1973

18

THE DEATH OF INNOCENCE

Argentina's glorious victory in the 1957 Campeonato Sudamericano in Peru bolstered a self-confidence that was never in much need of reinforcement. They went to the World Cup in Sweden the following year with a blithe expectation of success, but the warning signs had been there if anybody had cared to look for them.

The most obvious blow came with the departure of the *Trío de la Muerte* for Italy—which meant none would be considered for the national side. Guillermo Stábile knew immediately what a setback that was. "For a few million pesos we'd lost everything that had been acquired in Lima," the coach said.

The qualifiers for the 1958 World Cup, the first one in which they'd played since 1934, did little to dampen general Argentinian self-belief. Three of the *carasucias* had gone, but the magic remained, even if they did start with a 2–0 defeat against Bolivia in La Paz. The altitude always offered an excuse, and when goals from Norberto Menéndez and Norberto Conde gave Argentina a 2–0 win away to Chile, Argentina were back on track. At home they thrashed Chile 4–0, Corbatta scoring twice, his second one of the most celebrated goals in Argentinian history. Argentina already led 2–0 when Corbatta beat his marker, took the ball around the goalkeeper, waited for another Chilean to approach, dribbled past him, and then, as the crowd urged him to finish the move off, with the goalkeeper and two other defenders charging back, dummied to shoot, leaving all three on the ground before finally stroking the ball over the line. *El Gráfico* called it "the most impossible piece of play ever." A 4–0 home win over Bolivia, with Corbatta and Menéndez again on the score sheet, confirmed Argentina's qualification for Sweden.

The public in Argentina, conditioned by the apparent strength of their league and by propaganda telling them this was the best soccer in the world, generally believed they went to the World Cup as favorites. They played in the opening game of the tournament in front of thirty-one thousand in Malmö and took the lead against West Germany, the defending champions, after three minutes. But West Germany's greater quality and physicality soon began to tell. Helmut Rahn, the hero of the final four years earlier, had been recalled only after cutting down his consumption of beer, and in that detail there seemed a lesson for Argentina. He equalized after thirty-two minutes with a right-foot drive from twenty-five yards and then rounded off a 3–1 win with a curling left-footed effort from just outside the box. "We are not used to such violent soccer," Stábile said, his comment seeming to relate to the pace of the game as much as any overt aggression on the part of the Germans.

Stábile's response to that violence was to recall Ángel Labruna, by then thirty-nine, at inside-left for the second game, against Northern Ireland in Halmstad. Midfielder Jimmy McIlroy described the Argentina team as "a lot of little fat men with stomachs, smiling at us and pointing and waving at girls in the crowd," while there seems to have been general bewilderment about Argentina's relaxed approach as they whistled and sang before kickoff. Northern Ireland took the lead, with Danny Blanchflower's backheel releasing Billy Bingham to cross for Peter McParland to head in.

Slowly, Argentina began to come back into the game, but there was an element of fortune about their equalizer after thirty-seven minutes, as Ludovico Avio's cross cannoned off Dick Keith's thigh onto his hand. Swedish referee Sten Ahlner gave a penalty, which Corbatta converted. Still Northern Ireland had their chances, and they should have regained the lead when Wilbur Cush dummied McIlroy's center to leave Fay Coyle free six yards out, but he fluffed his shot, the first of three bad misses in what turned out to be his final international. Menéndez capitalized on an Avio through-ball to take Argentina ahead, and Avio headed a third to give an impression of such comfort that by the end Argentina's players were taking the ball from each other to perform party pieces, "taking the mickey," as McIlroy put it. But the truth was, it had been far from easy, and the gulf between the sides many Argentinians had anticipated simply hadn't been there.

Weaknesses in the Argentinian game had been apparent in the El Dorado league in Colombia. When Neil Franklin returned to Britain after his unhappy time at Independiente Santa Fe, he insisted he had been ostracized by a clique of Argentinians who feared a British invasion. "They became insanely jealous," he said, "because they realized the British players would train and train hard. Training was not quite the strong point of the Argentinians. They were very good ball players, very good exhibitionists, but they were incredibly lazy in the training sessions."

The warning was ignored, and the golden age of Argentinian soccer came to a bitter, shocking end in Helsingborg against a Czechoslovakia side that would lose a playoff against Northern Ireland and fail even to progress from the group. "We were used to playing really slowly, and they were fast," said José Ramos Delgado, who was on the squad for the tournament but didn't play. "We hadn't played international soccer for a long time, so when we went out there we thought we were really talented, but we found we hadn't followed the pace of the rest of the world. We had been left behind. The European teams played simply. They were precise. Argentina were good on the ball, but we didn't go forward."

What happened in Sweden was so crushing as to be almost incomprehensible. There was shock and there was anger as, three years after the coup against Perón, another of life's great certainties was swept away, the complacent belief in Argentina's superiority shattered. It's far too simplistic, of course, to say that one game changed the whole course of Argentinian soccer, but at the time it certainly felt like it. After the 6–1 against Czechoslovakia, nothing could ever be the same again. "It's a pity," noted *El Gráfico*, "that the Brazil that was swept from the field [in Lima] by the *Albiceleste* storm, would be resurrected and win the World Cup in Sweden, while we, put forward as strong contenders, started to disassemble the team right after the victory, ran out of *carasucias*, lost the joy for a soccer that was loved in the stands and fell into the night of history."

The reaction in Argentina was predictably ferocious. Argentina had suffered exactly the sort of humiliation Perón had feared, the very policy that had been designed to hold it off—that of sporting isolationism—helping to foster the complacency and stagnation that were ultimately a huge contributory factor in its coming to pass. And because it was so unexpected, of course, the shock and fury were that much greater. The players were pelted with fruit and coins at Ezeiza, Stábile was sacked, and the nation began to question every soccer-playing principle it had held dear. If *la nuestra* wasn't the answer, what was? And if a belief in Argentina's superiority was a lie, what else was?

The assumption was that the Argentinian league was so strong, Argentina so rich in talented players, that it could afford to spurn those who had left, and it was a similar mentality that led to a belief that Argentina could simply play their game without needing to worry too much about opponents. Scouting was, at best, rudimentary.

Beyond the initial anger and pain at Argentina's exit, there was a deeper issue. Since the 1920s, Argentina had consciously equated their way of playing soccer with the national character: the country's identity and prestige were bound up with the results of the national team. If Argentina the team was humiliated, if their style was exposed as inadequate, what did that mean for Argentina the country?

Peronism may have stored up problems for the future, but generally it had been good for soccer. The new regime stopped the practice of giving clubs favorable loans, ending what had effectively been a state subsidy for soccer. At the same time, the growth of the middle class—itself a result of Peronist economic policy—and the broadcast of soccer on television led to a drop in the number of people going to watch games at the stadium, something that was exacerbated by the sense of disillusionment that followed Helsingborg. With revenue reduced, the financial stakes were raised, and the game increasingly became less about spectacle than about winning. The focus on beauty, on doing things the right way, was gone, and Argentina found once again, as it had in so many contexts, that when the dream withered, cynicism sprouted in its place. After the golden age came the age of *anti-fútbol*, ushered in partly by disgust at what had happened in Sweden and an accompanying self-doubt and partly by economics. "It was then that European discipline appeared," said philosopher Tomás Abraham. "That was the way that modernity, which implies discipline, physical training, hygiene, health, professionalism, sacrifice, all the Fordism entered Argentinian soccer. There came these methods for physical preparation that gave importance to defense—and who had cared about defense before? It's a strange thing that it should come then, in parallel with the Brazilian triumph, which really should be an argument for our own local soccer."

19

THE CONTRARIAN AND THE
GROWTH OF *ANTI-FÚTBOL*

Of course, nothing is born of nothing: *anti-fútbol* did not spring fully formed from the shock of Helsingborg. Rather, that defeat raised questions about prevailing preconceptions—just as other areas of Argentinian society were beginning to question what had gone before—and led the game's leaders to look for ways of playing that weren't all about skill and tricks and didn't share the attacking emphasis of *la nuestra*.

There had always been a contrarian streak in Argentinian soccer, and one of its main proponents, Victorio Spinetto, was appointed alongside José Della Torre and José Barreiro in the aftermath of the 1958 World Cup to see the national side through the 1959 Campeonato Sudamericano. On home soil there was a bristling desire to put right what had gone wrong in Sweden. Of the team that had lost to Czechoslovakia, only Corbatta and Independiente midfielder José Varacka survived to play in the opening game against Chile. In front of seventy thousand at el Monumental, Argentina won 6–1, Pedro Manfredini and the experienced Juan José Pizzuti both scoring twice. Bolivia, Peru, and Paraguay were dismissed by two-goal margins before a meeting with Uruguay, which had gone into the tournament regarded as one of three favorites. This was a Uruguay side in chaos, though, at war with itself and the world, and they were dismissed 4–1.

That meant a point against Brazil in the final game would secure the title: Pizzuti gave Argentina the lead before Pelé, still only eighteen, leveled with his eighth goal of the tournament, but the hosts got the draw they needed. Argentina were champions, which eased the pain of Helsingborg to an extent but did not eradicate it, and there was still an awareness that, stylistically, all was not well.

Spinetto has been painted as an archpragmatist, but in his own way he was as romantic as anybody in Argentinian soccer; it was just that his romanticism took a different form from that of most of his contemporaries. He didn't care about the spectacle, didn't regard soccer as some sort of test of artistic or aesthetic merit; he just cared about his Vélez—and about winning. He questioned the values of *la nuestra* and was accused of playing *anti-fútbol* as a result, but his conception of the game was far less violent and far less cynical than that of the teams the term was later applied to.

Taking charge in 1941 after their relegation, Spinetto reestablished Vélez as a top-flight side and, in 1953, made them the first side from outside the five traditional *grandes* to break into the top two. In a sense, though, his fourteen years in charge were less about league position than about defining the Vélez style and giving them an identity distinct from that of the other Buenos Aires clubs. The legendary club president José Amalfitani, a construction magnate and sports journalist, moved the club west from Floresta, a commercial barrio whose rough edges and down-at-the-heels atmosphere fitted the image of the club perfectly: they were scrappers and fighters, born without the advantages of the *grandes* but prepared to take them on anyway. Spinetto gave Vélez a sense of self-esteem and imbued them with *garra*—or, to use the term he preferred, *fibra*, literally "fiber," but in his usage suggesting toughness, stamina, and determination. Six decades later, they'd be a side of similar stature to Racing and San Lorenzo, differentiated from them by tradition rather than anything more concrete.

The toughness for which Vélez became reowned came straight from the manager. Spinetto lived the game as no coach in Argentina ever had before, standing in his tracksuit—or, later, a blue jacket with a *T* for *tecnico* marked in tape on the pocket—with a towel draped over his shoulder, right leg raised, foot on the edge of the dugout, right elbow resting on right knee to create a support for his head.

Although the term *anti-fútbol* came to be associated with the violence and on-field skullduggery of Estudiantes in particular, when it was applied to Spinetto, it was more about the fact that he focused on team spirit and commitment rather than individual skill. "He was a man who worked a lot with the players on psychology, because a player has to be a little bit aggressive," said attacking midfielder Norberto Conde.

Spinetto's legacy reached far beyond Vélez. It would perhaps be overstating the case to call him a tactical revolutionary, for his theories were nowhere near as radical as those being experimented with and implemented in Brazil and Europe at the same time, but the very fact he thought about tactics and challenged the tenets of *la nuestra* made him unusual in Argentina.

Perhaps most heretically of all, Spinetto wouldn't simply leave forwards to attack. He demanded they play an all-round game. His greatest success came with Osvaldo Zubeldía, a number 10 who was prepared to push the boundaries of the role. In 1953, when Vélez finished as runners-up, Spinetto had him tracking back, working the length of the field like a modern midfielder. Whether that was Spinetto's idea or Zubeldía's is impossible at this remove to know; better perhaps to see it as a symbiosis between the intelligence of the player and the willingness of the coach to try something different. As a coach Zubeldía would become recognized globally as the high priest of *anti-fútbol*.

20

THE MOUSE'S NEST

I met José Sanfilippo in a café in Caballito, the geographical center of Buenos Aires, but he refused a coffee, insisting on orange juice. "I only drink coffee before noon," he said, his tone making clear this was a moral as much as a medical decision. Keeping in shape was an obsession for him, and he was scathing of soccer players who drink or smoke. "I don't eat pastries," he said. "I take care of my liver. For me, diet was important when I was a player, but nobody listened to me. I'm a self-programmed man, I do the same things every day. I'm like an Englishman . . . like the English buses.[1] . . . And it's got to be that way. My teammates wouldn't understand that. After training sessions, they'd disappear, and I'd stay."

Sanfilippo has a reputation as a difficult, awkward man, a television pundit who pulls no punches. It's fair to say that he places a high value on his opinions. As we were sitting down, he asked how long I'd been working as a soccer writer and professed outrage that didn't seem entirely feigned when I told him. "Fourteen years trying to understand the history of soccer, and you only come to see me now?" he protested.

He would argue that he simply demands high standards from everybody, from nobody more than himself, his commitment to self-improvement having made him the fifth-most prolific striker in Argentinian history, scoring 200 goals in 260 appearances for San Lorenzo and 21 in 29 for the national side. "I invented the Sanfigol," he said, "a big cage with a wall the size of a goal that I'd use for practicing, divided into squares of eighty centimeters [thirty inches] by eighty centimeters. The most important corners were the lower ones, *la ratonera*, the mouse's nest. Practicing every day was fundamental. Hitting the lower corners is safer than the upper corners, but you need to hone your precision because you're giving twenty-one feet to the goalkeeper. So I'd need to know how to aim and hit those lower corners, from every position."

He was seventy-nine when I met him and clearly proud of the fact that he can pass for much younger. At one point he jokingly strangled me, and as his hands closed around my windpipe and didn't immediately release, I had a momentary panic that he might just keep squeezing and that, if he did, I probably wouldn't be able to fight him off. With his obviously dyed hair and signet ring on with his initials marked out with diamonds, he had the air of an aging don from a Scorsese film. The most remarkable aspect of his appearance, though, was his fingernails, which were highly polished, the tips long, white, and square at the corners. The fashion is not uncommon among Argentinians of his generation who come from a working-class background but have made good: having manicured nails shows they no longer have to labor with their hands.

Sanfilippo grew up twenty-two blocks from San Lorenzo's stadium in Boedo, a working-class area noted for its influence over the tango and, in the 1920s, the home of a group of left-wing Argentinian and Uruguayan writers. He was a fan and dreamed of playing for the team, although for him glory was only a partial consideration. "I had humble origins," he said. "I knew that I was the only one who could drag my family away from that, and I needed to get better in order to do it." And so he practiced relentlessly, even before inventing his Sanfigol. "When you don't have an impressive physique, you must develop other skills. I started practicing with a ball a little bigger than a tennis ball, made of plastic and rubber. And I'd use the curb to practice one-twos. I started when I was six, and I did it until I was twenty." He demands similar dedication today from those around him. One of his sons, he said proudly, had qualified as a plastic surgeon, the other was an accountant, while his wife had just passed her law exams. "In the house of Sanfilippo," he said, "nobody rests."

He was eighteen when he signed his first professional contract with San Lorenzo in 1953, but he'd been training at the club for several years before that. The days of *el Ciclón* may have passed, but they were still a team that finished regularly in the top six. "San Lorenzo had an established style," Sanfilippo said. "And I did what many people don't. When I was sixteen, I played with the seniors."

Even before the disgrace of Helsingborg, Sanfilippo was preaching a doctrine of abstinence and self-improvement quite out of keeping with the bohemian ideals of the golden age. "Of all the managers I had, nobody taught me anything," he insisted. "I learned everything by myself. I only needed the ball on the ground. That was my only condition: crosses or passes, but don't send me high balls—I knew where my strength lay."

At first San Lorenzo weren't a side that challenged for titles, but by the late fifties they were improving. Sanfilippo finished top scorer in the Primera four seasons in a row between 1958 and 1961, and, after finishing second in 1957 and 1958, San Lorenzo finally won the title for their fourth time in the professional era in 1959, Sanfilippo scoring thirty-one times.

By then he'd pared his game back to the essentials. "Many wondered why I never picked up injuries," he said. "It's because I'd never get the ball and try to go past you. My business was shooting, receiving the ball in space, and knowing in advance what I had to do. I would always have two different ways of resolving a situation in mind so I didn't have to think. Dribbling is only necessary when you feel that you're surrounded."

21

THE OPEN MARKET

The 1958 elections were won by Arturo Frondizi. He had stood as a vice presidential candidate on Ricardo Balbín's ticket against Perón in 1951, but after being defeated had split with Balbín to form an "intransigent" wing of the Unión Cívica Radical. The Radicals were thus split in two, but so too were the Socialists, while the Conservatives were split in three. Factionalism and chaos reigned. In the buildup to the 1958 elections, though, Frondizi secured Perón's endorsement through his closest backer, businessman Rogelio Frigerio, and took power with the support of those banned Peronists who did not simply spoil their ballot papers. But Frondizi's mandate was flimsy, and he was hampered throughout his presidency by the continuing influence of conservative forces. In 1959, with inflation soaring, he was forced to impose unpopular austerity measures, which cost him Perón's support.

Banning people from saying Perón's name could not eradicate Peronism, and the unions became a de facto Peronist party, keeping his ideals alive. The military, determined to avert a reformation of the working-class coalition that had sustained Peronism and that they recognized might perhaps pave the way for his return, became increasingly visible both on the streets and in political circles.

After Perón the preeminence of the working class declined, and there emerged in its place a new urban middle class, many employed in the growing service and cultural sectors. "This was the time," historian John King wrote of the period between 1958 and 1965, "in which considerable sums were spent on advertising, visits to the psychoanalyst became an integral part of middle-class Buenos Aires life, people flocked to the films of Ingmar Bergman and helped to create a boom in Latin American fiction by buying fictional works in tens of thousands."

Argentinian soccer, meanwhile, became less self-consciously an art form. Modernization in industry and economics was reflected in soccer as scientific, and technocratic theories took hold: the sport became less about the performance and more about the result, as theories of *anti-fútbol* became more prevalent. At the same time, Argentinians, at least in comparison to what had gone before, began to live a less public life. Bergman may have been acclaimed, but television supplanted the cinema as the most popular form of entertainment; there were 5,000 television sets in Argentina in 1953, 800,000 in 1960, and 3.7 million in 1973. Perhaps more significantly, as soccer was televised for the first time from the midsixties, many Argentinians came to prefer watching at home to going to the stadium. In the decade from 1954, the average attendance at Argentinian league matches fell by 40 percent.

The decline in attendance would in itself have been bad enough for Argentinian soccer, but, having lost state support, it also began to be challenged in a global market. As the clubs struggled to make ends meet, Boca and River in particular sought to draw the crowds back with exoticism, bringing in players and coaches from Uruguay, Peru, and Brazil. In 1961, for instance, Boca appointed as coach Vicente Feola, the man who had led Brazil to the World Cup in 1958. Little more than an average player, he had taken São Paulo to the Paulista championship in 1949, and after standing down as coach he had served as assistant to the great Hungarian Béla Guttmann. Feola was a barrel of a man with stocky little legs, an unrepentant bon vivant who, it was rumored, would doze off on the bench during matches.

Unprepossessing as he may have appeared, Feola was a tactical revolutionary. He had seen the efficacy of the back four as it developed in Brazil in the fifties, and it was his use of that system that had brought the *selecão* success in Sweden. Naturally enough, he wanted to play that way at Boca, employing two central defenders and so encouraging the fullbacks to attack. Yet there is a paradox here, one that is not easy to untangle. If, as philosopher Tomás Abraham said, the effect of Helsingborg had been to turn Argentinian soccer away from a "traditional" South American style just at the time when Brazil's success seemed to have validated that way of playing, what were Boca, a team that had historically prided itself on its *garra*, doing appointing the architect of the Brazilian victory? The most convincing answer is, perhaps, that there was simply confusion: what had happened in Helsingborg had shattered the consensus on how soccer should be played without offering any clear answers as to what should take its place.

After a disappointing 1960 season in which they'd finished fifth under José D'Amico, four points behind the champions Independiente, Boca were desperate for success and saw the manager who had just won the World Cup as the man to bring it, without giving a huge amount of thought to how he would set about doing it. "He didn't talk much, but what he said made complete sense," said the great left-back Marzolini. "He created a team; he gave us team spirit. He established the modern Boca, a strong team based on a tight defense so that when we scored once, the game ended."

Boca finished fifth again, this time twelve points behind the champions, Racing. Feola went back to Brazil, and D'Amico was reinstated. "Feola was unlucky," the midfielder Antonio Rattin insisted. "Under him we kept hitting the post or missing penalties, and then D'Amico won the championship with the same team."

As well as winning the title, that Boca side also produced the first real celebrity of Argentinian soccer. Silvio Marzolini was the heartthrob of his day, the first Argentinian soccer player really to exploit his commercial potential, and after our interview he insisted on signing one of his original advertising photos for me (and for the grandmother of one of the journalists who'd come with me, who had been quite overcome to learn her granddaughter would be meeting him). It showed Marzolini in Argentina uniform, blond hair neatly parted, blue eyes smoldering at the camera, the only actual advertising a small red and blue logo in the bottom-left corner for a company that sold espadrilles. Marzolini still has the blue eyes, and his hair, though graying, retains some of its golden luster. He is rather fuller of figure now, but there is still an easy charm about him, a generosity of spirit. When I met him he had just sent back the shirt he had swapped with Bobby Charlton after the 1966 World Cup quarter-final—and worn as a pajama top—so it could be displayed in a museum, and two days after I'd spoken to him for an hour and a half at his apartment in Belgrano, he turned up at my interview with Rattin at la Bombonera, tossing in anecdotes and gently teasing the man who had been his captain both at Boca and with the national team.

Marzolini was born in October 1940 in Barracas, a barrio in the southeast of Buenos Aires that had been the home of many wealthy families in the nineteenth century but by the mid-twentieth century had become a working-class area dominated by factories and favored by Italian immigrants. He began playing for Deportivo Italiano, a local side set up by the Italian community and, with them, won one of the Evita tournaments in 1952. Marzolini still has a trophy from that success on a shelf in his living room.

In his midteens Marzolini got a job working in the port as a draftsman for a company that was subcontracted by Fiat while playing for the academy of Ferro Carril Oeste, which he'd joined in 1955.

Marzolini played for Fiat in a tournament for Italians in Argentina, and when his side won he was invited to join Juventus's academy. Ferro, though, refused to let him go and suspended him for three years. That was quickly forgotten when it became apparent that, having just been promoted back to the top flight, the first team was in desperate need of a left-back.

Marzolini's performances were good enough that he was called up to the Argentina squad for the Pan-American Championship in Costa Rica in 1960, and when Argentina won that he was signed by Boca. The change to a back four under Feola encouraged Marzolini to push forward, but it was after the signing of Alberto González in 1962 that his role really changed. "They bought him because they needed a number 11," Marzolini said.

> Argentina was still suffering from the disaster of 1958 in Sweden, and Atlanta, where González was playing, were a very hard team, all running, working as a complete tactical unit. González had the number 11 on his back, but, in truth, he was a midfielder. So when he started playing for Boca, he didn't play as a real 11, and I found the left corridor always open, without anyone there. That encouraged me to go forward even more often. In Chile in 1962 and in England in 1966, I played like that, thanks to Juan Carlos Lorenzo, who was a very important manager in my career.

The other major influence on Marzolini as he developed into one of the era's great trio of attacking left-backs—along with Nílton Santos of Brazil and Giacinto Facchetti of Italy (like Facchetti at Internazionale, he was liberated by playing on a team that prioritized defense)—was Bernardo Gandulla, who had served as Boca's head coach in 1957 and 1958 and stayed on the staff through the sixties. "I remember I made a mistake that nobody else knew about," Marzolini said. "If the winger outran me, I'd stay standing there, thinking, 'Oh shit, now he crosses and they'll score.' But Gandulla told me, 'You don't have to be a witness: if you're out of the action, you have to run into the area and see if you can get the loose ball.' And he was right: mistakes are there to be corrected."

22

THE CONSECRATION
OF PRAGMATISM

With winning an economic imperative and the consequences of failure dire, in the 1960s Argentinian soccer became tougher and more
cynical, the outlook more defensive. After the days of Sastre and Erico, who
left the club in 1941 and 1942, respectively, Independiente had settled into a
familiar routine. Their role, it seemed, was to float around the upper reaches
of the table, occasionally registering a major victory but rarely winning anything. It was after Manuel Giúdice had replaced Armando Renganeschi as
coach that the revolution began.

Even as a player Giúdice had a reputation as a deep thinker about the
game, and he accumulated a vast library of books and articles about tactical
and technical theory as he moved into coaching. His career as a manager
took him first to Peru, where he won a league title with Centro Iqueño, and
then to Uruguay, where he worked with Roberto Scarone as Peñarol won
a hat trick of championships and two Copa Libertadores, before returning to Argentina with Independiente in 1963. By then his style was well
established and very different from the attacking passing rhythms of la
Máquina: his teams sat deep, packed men behind the ball, and looked to
spring forward on the counterattack, an Argentinian version of *catenaccio*.[1]
"The player must adapt to the team and not the team to the player," he said
in an interview with *El Gráfico* in 1964: not such a remarkable idea to modern eyes, perhaps, but in the context of the Argentina of the time a radical
manifesto. He spoke of aiming for "an associated soccer." "From this style
there is one truth: that nobody works for himself. Respecting this soccer of
togetherness, the modality of the team would be of course with the characteristics of the different players who form the squad, respecting, for sure, the
individual inspiration of each one."

Giúdice's sides were always physically extremely well prepared, thanks
largely to the groundbreaking work of Horacio González García, a fitness
coach who pioneered sports science in Argentina. They were also a team

with a ferocious spirit, symbolized by their habit of walking out before games and raising their arms in unison to the crowd, a gesture conceived by their captain Jorge Alberto Maldonado, a tough holding midfielder nicknamed "Chivita" (Little Goat), because of his goatee beard.

Independiente conceded just twenty-five goals in twenty-six games in winning the title in 1963, passing unbeaten through the second half of the season. On a postseason tour they thrashed Santos 5–1 and Peñarol 5–0 and in the following season extended their unbeaten run to forty matches before going down to the eventual champions, Boca Juniors. By then, though, it was clear that the Copa Libertadores had become the priority.

The tournament had begun in 1960 and rapidly gained in credibility. There had been attempts to set up an international club competition in South America since 1913, when Estudiantes, champions of the dissident Federación Argentina de Football, were supposed to meet the Uruguayan champions, River Plate of Montevideo. Whether that game was ever played is unclear, and the trophy was contested only irregularly, the final edition coming in 1955, eight years after the previous staging, when River Plate beat Nacional to match their tally of six victories.

In 1948 there came an attempt to spread the competition with the Copa de Campeones, one side from each of Argentina, Bolivia, Brazil, Chile, Ecuador, Peru, and Uruguay gathering in Santiago to play a round-robin over the course of six weeks. The experiment, though, was never repeated.

Finally, in 1959, plans for the Copa Libertadores were passed by Conmebol, with only Uruguay—which feared the impact international club soccer might have on the Campeonato Sudamericano—voting against. The Libertadores did not immediately capture the imagination of the Argentinian public. When Peñarol arrived in Buenos Aires for the second leg of their semifinal against San Lorenzo, having drawn 1–1 in the first, they found a city largely unaware the game was being played at all. Only fifteen thousand turned up to watch a goalless draw that necessitated a playoff in Montevideo that Peñarol won 2–1. They defended their crown the following year, as Argentina's representative, Independiente, fell to Palmeiras in the quarter-final.

It's great champions that breathe life into a tournament, though, and however talented and obdurate Peñarol had been, they had nothing like the glamour of the team that took the title in 1962. The Santos of Pelé, Gilmar, Zito, and Coutinho were on their way to becoming the most famous club in the world—so feted that in 1967 a two-day cease-fire was declared in the Biafran War so both sides could watch them play in a friendly as they toured Nigeria—and they swaggered through the group stage, scoring twenty goals in their four matches.

It was only in the Libertadores' fourth year that an Argentinian club really committed to the tournament. Boca's president, Alberto Armando, was determined his side should become the first from Argentina to win it. "He set [the Libertadores] as a priority," Marzolini said, "so in 1963 we practically didn't play the league because we were traveling for the Libertadores. We didn't have a large squad to tackle both competitions."

They had signed José Sanfilippo from San Lorenzo, despite already having a goal scorer in the hugely popular Paulo Valentim. That meant Sanfilippo playing a little deeper than he had, he and Norberto Menéndez acting as creators for the Brazilian. As a result, he managed just seven goals in twenty league games, as Boca finished third in 1963. He did, though, score the winner against River in the penultimate game of the season, a 1–0 win that handed the championship to Independiente.

His league form may have been disappointing, but Sanfilippo thrived in the continental competition, scoring a hat trick away to Universidad de Chile to see them through the group and netting again in the home leg of the semifinal, as Boca ousted Peñarol.

In the final Boca met the defending champions, Santos, which had crushed Botafogo 1–0 and 4–1 in their semifinal. "We were going to lose it anyway because they were the best team of the moment," said Marzolini, "and it was like the Maracanã was 200 meters long and 100 meters wide. It was the best against the best, and the best among the best was Pelé's Santos." Sanfilippo's sharpness brought him three goals over the two legs, but it was not enough, Santos winning 3–2 in São Paulo and 2–1 at la Bombonera.

Boca ended that season joint third, and there had been signs, in the Libertadores in particular, that Sanfilippo was beginning to come to terms with his role on the side. His time at the club, though, was drawing to a close. In March 1964 Boca faced San Lorenzo in the Copa Jorge Newbury, a preseason tournament. Sanfilippo, understandably, was desperate to play against his former club, but he was left on the bench by the coach, Aristóbulo Deambrossi, a forward on River's la Máquina side. The regulations stipulated that substitutions could be made, but only in the first half in the event of an injury (which was easy enough to feign if required). "I was the goal scorer," said Sanfilippo, "the one who'd scored against all the big teams in the Libertadores. San Lorenzo were one point ahead at the top of the table, so if we beat them, we'd be champions."

He felt he should have been on the field, and shortly before halftime, realizing that if he was going to come on it would have to be soon, Sanfilippo asked Deambrossi how long there was to go. "'Four minutes,' he says. And I was thinking, 'Fuck this guy.' The whole stadium was singing my name." Sanfilippo still thought he was coming on. "Nothing. End of the first half, nothing. He starts going to the center of the field, and I run in his direction, chasing him. 'Why did you do that?' I asked. 'Because managers can do whatever they like.' And that was it. Pim! I knocked him down. And while he was on the floor, I said to him, 'You'll be able to say that you didn't bring on the great goal scorer Sanfilippo, but you'll also have to talk about that punch.' And that's why I had to leave for Nacional of Montevideo."

It wasn't only that. He also abused Adolfo Pedernera, then Deambrossi's assistant, and condemned the decision to leave him off the side as "a whim." Few of his teammates were disappointed when Armando backed the coaching staff and decided Sanfilippo had to be sold. "In the history of soccer," said the usually genial Marzolini, "there have been three truly great players—Pelé, Maradona, and Messi—but only one great *hijo da puta*: Sanfilippo."

However good a finisher he was, it can hardly be denied that Boca prospered without Sanfilippo. Boca won the title in 1964, conceding just fifteen goals in thirty games—only six in their final twenty-five—and scoring a mere thirty-five. A year later, playing in a slightly more adventurous way—fifty-five scored, thirty conceded—they retained their crown.

That May Argentina played Peru at the Estadio Nacional in Lima in the qualifying tournament for the Olympic Games later that year. The hosts appeared to have scored a late equalizer, but it was disallowed, at which two fans climbed the perimeter fence, seemingly with the intention of attacking the referee. They were caught by police and severely beaten, igniting a riot on the terraces. As bonfires were lit and bricks were hurled onto the field, police fired tear gas into the stands. The result was panic, as fans raced to exit gates only to find them locked. In total, 312 fans were killed and more than 500 injured, most of them crushed on the stairwells. As the riot spread outside the stadium, three policemen were murdered.

With all soccer suspended in Peru, Independiente's away game against Alianza was switched to Avellaneda. A dispute between Conmebol and the Colombian federation meant they didn't have to play away to Millonarios either, and so they qualified for the semifinal without playing a game outside their home ground, la Doble Visera.[2] In the semifinal Independiente faced the sternest of challenges: Santos, which were on course for a hat trick of titles.

At the Maracaná, Santos swept into a two-goal lead inside thirty-four minutes. But four minutes later, Mario Rodríguez headed in a cross from Raúl Savoy, and a minute before halftime, with Santos wilting against far fitter opponents, Raúl Bernao scored with a shot from the right flank that might have been a cross. Santos came again at the beginning of the second half, but Independiente had the physical advantage, and, knowing a draw gave them control of the tie, they could sit back, absorb pressure, and strike on the break—their preferred mode of play anyway. But they ended up with more than a draw. In the final minute Savoy sent in another dangerous cross, and this time Luis Suárez converted it, making Independiente the first foreign side ever to win at the Maracanã. There was still anxiety ahead of the second leg, but Independiente were much the better team.

In the final, they met Nacional of Montevideo in a tie that came to be seen as the apotheosis of Giúdice's conception of soccer. Independiente went to the Centenario and forced a goalless draw. Back at la Doble Visera, where eighty thousand packed in, they won 1–0 with a performance of immaculate defensive discipline, the only goal Rodríguez's smart lob ten minutes before halftime. Argentina had their first Libertadores champion. Independiente defended their crown the following year: significantly, they'd won playing in what was coming to be recognized as the modern Argentinian style.

23

BACK ON THE HORSE

Giúdice was one pioneer of what might loosely be termed the Italian style in Argentinian soccer; the other was a coach whose links with Italy were far more overt—Juan Carlos "Toto" Lorenzo. As a player Lorenzo had been a gifted midfielder and forward, first for Chacarita and then for Boca. He joined Sampdoria in 1947, when he was twenty-four, before moving to Nancy, Atlético Madrid, Rayo Vallecano, and Mallorca. He brought his playing career to an end in 1958, when he was appointed coach of Mallorca, then in the Spanish third flight. Lorenzo was strongly influenced by the ideas of Helenio Herrera. The Herrera of the late fifties was perhaps not as cautious as he would become, but his style would still have been perceived in Argentina as *anti-fútbol*. It was an approach that Lorenzo embraced, leading Mallorca to back-to-back promotions. He returned to Argentina with San Lorenzo in 1961 and, the following year, was appointed national coach. "Lorenzo made us understand what was happening in the world," said Marzolini, who played under him with the national side and later Boca. "Not just what we could read in the papers about players that were good, but descriptions of how they played and why they played in one way or another way, based on some strategy."

He represented a dose of modernity many felt was desperately needed. As Argentina approached the 1962 World Cup, the sense of self-mortification had continued. They'd qualified easily enough, beating Ecuador 6–3 and 5–0 in December 1960, but that year they'd also played Brazil five times. Although Argentina had won twice, they'd been hammered 5–1 in the last of those fixtures. In an interview with *El Gráfico* the following January, Pelé was unusually candid in his assessment of Argentina. "There is much slowness," he said, "an excess of lateral passes, and they don't have any depth. . . . To use a slow central midfielder and to play 'lateral' is already a tactical error, and especially when he is expected to mark a quick player." In another era his remarks might have provoked a furor; as it was, they merely chimed with what was being said in Argentina anyway.

In June 1961 in preparation for the World Cup, Argentina went on a tour of Europe. They beat Portugal 2–0 in Lisbon, but then lost 2–0 to

Spain, the second goal scored by the naturalized Alfredo Di Stéfano. A 4–1 defeat to Italy and draws against Czechoslovakia followed.

There was a wariness about the squad that went to the 1962 World Cup. The hurt of 1958 was still fresh, and that meant an approach that was consciously more pragmatic and more risk averse than what had gone before. That Argentina had developed a hard edge since the embarrassment of Helsingborg became clear even from their first game at the tournament, against Bulgaria in Rancagua, when Lorenzo selected a side that averaged over six feet in height. Mystifyingly, he announced in the week before the game that Rattín would play only if conditions were dry; it rained, and so he left him out, an indication of the tension between them that would undermine Argentinian morale. Rattín was scathing of Lorenzo and later claimed the 1962 side was the worst team he ever played for.

Marzolini got forward in the fourth minute to send in a cross that Marcelo Pagani touched on for Héctor Facundo to score, after which Argentina settled back to absorb pressure, to spoil, and to foul. Ivan Kolev, Bulgaria's left-winger, was hacked down repeatedly, while Hristo Iliev and Todor Diev suffered injuries so severe they were unable to play again for the rest of the tournament. "A triumph like this," noted a disgruntled *El Gráfico*, "leaves a bitter taste."

England, who had begun the tournament with a defeat to Hungary, saw the physicality of Argentina's approach and decided to meet fire with fire. Walter Winterbottom, a studious, schoolmasterly figure told his team to "bite in." Rattín returned as Lorenzo adopted a strange 4-2-2-2 formation in which none of the players seemed comfortable. The idea was for Rattín to mark Johnny Haynes and for Vladislao Cap to mark Charlton, but the plan unraveled and England soon got on top, winning 3–1. *Clarín* put the defeat down to the "strength and speed" of England, an indication, perhaps, that Argentinian soccer felt it had to move even further in that direction.

That meant that if Argentina were to progress to the second phase, they had to achieve a better result against Hungary in their final group game than England got against Bulgaria. Hungary rested three forwards and were effectively left with ten men when János Göröcs was left hobbling by another rough Argentinian challenge, but Argentina struggled to break them down. It finished goalless, and when England also drew 0–0 in what Bobby Moore described as "one of the worst international matches ever," Argentina were out, protesting vainly that they'd been undone by a European conspiracy and that Bulgaria had let England go through.

24

EL CAUDILLO

These days, even in his midseventies, Rattin sells insurance, which seems an oddly prosaic profession for a man who remains one of the great idols of Boca and who, for England fans of a certain age, embodied the dark face of Argentinian soccer. Both he and Marzolini relay the story that Bobby Charlton once told them of English mothers frightening their children into eating their greens by telling them that if they didn't, Rattin would come for them. Charlton, perhaps, was using some poetic license, but with his stooping gait and broad saturnine features, there is something of the bogeyman about Rattin. That, though, is only a fraction of the story of a player who for a time was probably the best defensive midfielder in the world.

Rattin was born in May 1937 in Tigre, a small town built on an island in the Paraná delta seventeen miles north of Buenos Aires. Rattin's father was a ferryman. "My old man never went to the stadium to see me play," he said. "He'd say that soccer was for lazy people. He wanted me to study. It didn't matter what; he just wanted me to study."

His heart, though, was set on playing for Boca, although his idol was the River number 5 Pipo Rossi. Rossi lived in Beccar, not far from Tigre, so Rattin would see him relatively often, although he never dared try to engage him in conversation. Rattin said:

> One Saturday, the day I made my debut for Boca's fifth team, I was on the train, on the back seat, and at the Beccar station he gets in the same car. As soon as I saw him, I stood up and approached, not to talk to him, but to be closer to him. I sat behind him. We reached the Retiro station, and we both changed for the Subte. He left at Avenida de Mayo, I continued to Lanús, where the game was being played, the first time I'd ever wear the Boca jersey in my life. But it was great, because I could see him, check how tall he was,[1] look at how he walked, everything.

When he arrived, it turned out the equipment manager had no boots in Rattin's size, and so he made his debut for Boca wearing his everyday shoes.

Rattin's great break came in September 1956 when he was called up to the first team to face River Plate. That meant going to the Hindú Club,[2] in the satellite town of Don Torcuato, where Boca held their *concentración*. The club president, Miguel de Riglos, gave him a lift. "We stopped at my house so I could get my gear bag and clothes," Rattin recalled. "The problem was that the president asked to go the bathroom. To do that, he had to go through a narrow corridor, all in wood. The bathroom had walls, because we had just finished them, but it still had no proper plumbing or anything else. When he came back, he said to me, 'Get a budget for how much you need for the bathroom installation.' 'Okay, sir.' Twenty days later, I gave him the budget: thirty-two thousand pesos. He paid for the tiling, hot water, a bathtub, bidet. . . . I played for a whole season for that."

River were on their way to the championship, but Rattin was determined not to be intimidated. Before kickoff he went up to Rossi and asked if he could have a photograph taken with him. "I still have it," he said. "I really wanted that. Pipo became my manager later on. He was my idol, a real idol. He had this thick and sharp voice, and on the field it was like a match commentator, yelling and barking orders all the time."

Once the game had started, a tackle on Ángel Labruna set the tone—not just for the rest of the game but for Rattin's career. "In the fifth minute, I kicked *el Feo* [the Ugly One] incredibly hard, a fucking harsh tackle. He was lying on the floor, and from there he says, '*Pibe*, take it easy: this isn't going to be the only game you play in the Primera.' And I answered [adopting a high-pitched, faux-apologetic voice], 'Nooooo, I'm so sorry, Ángel. I didn't mean to do that.'" Boca went on to win 2–1. "For that game," Rattin said, "they gave me four *lucas* [four thousand pesos]. They gave me two thousand in cash and two thousand directly to the bank account. Just for beating River."

The first real sense of the new style having a positive effect at national level came in 1964 as Argentina, managed by Spinetto and with Rattin at its heart, went to Brazil for the Taça das Nações, a tournament to celebrate the fiftieth anniversary of the Brazilian soccer federation. Brazil thrashed England 5–1 in their opening game in the Maracanã.

England had allowed Pelé space, but Argentina closed him down, using José Mesiano as a man-marker. Although he can hardly have been unused to the tactic, Pelé reacted badly, becoming so frustrated that, after a half hour, he head-butted Mesiano, breaking the Argentinian's nose. The referee missed the incident and Pelé escaped dismissal, but he seemed so distressed by what he'd done that he was barely involved for the hour that remained.

I told Spinetto, "Bring [Roberto] Telch on, and I'll grab Pelé." So Telch was eating a hot dog and didn't have his boots on. He gave the hot dog to somebody else and came on. Straightaway there was a corner kick. I approached Pelé, and he said to me, "Rattin, with the ball, yes; without the ball, no."

"No problem," I said. "If I kick you, I'll kick you with the ball. You just play." I marked him one-on-one all over the pitch. Telch scored two goals. And we made them dance after that: it was so embarrassing that the Brazilian fans were all chanting, "Olé, olé, olé," when we were passing the ball to one another. It was a humiliation, and they were really harsh on their own side. Pelé? He closed his eyes and never opened them again. He probably felt bad for what he'd done to Mesiano.

Defending deep, Argentina scored three times with quick counterattacks. The teams returned to Rio. Argentina, knowing a draw would be enough for them to be champions, sat men behind the ball, content to spoil, hold possession, and let time run out. England, like "a bunch of yokels trying to puzzle their way out of a maze," as Desmond Hackett put it in the *Daily Express*, were nonplused.

The days of *la nuestra* were long since departed, not that anybody on the Argentina team cared. "The next day, we were invited to this gala dinner," said Rattin. "Each of the Brazilians received a gold watch. And we, we who've won the bloody tournament, received miserable pens bearing a Taça das Nações inscription. *Hijos da puta!*"

25

THE MORAL VICTORY

For all his struggles with the economy, Frondizi's downfall as president, in the end, was foreign policy, as, after a meeting with Che Guevara, he tried to negotiate between John F. Kennedy and Fidel Castro. That, allied to his decision to lift the ban on Peronist parties ahead of the 1962 midterm elections, alarmed the military. On March 29 the army chief of staff, General Raúl Poggi, ordered a coup. The senate president, José María Guido, was nominated as Frondizi's successor. He initially refused the role, citing loyalty to the former president, but accepted when Frondizi asked him to, thus becoming the only civilian in Argentina's history to ascend to the presidency by way of military coup.

Guido's time in office was characterized by a power struggle within the military between the moderates (the Blues), led by Poggi, and the hard-liners (the Reds), led by the commander of the cavalry corps, General Enrique Rauch. It culminated in April 1963 when the navy, supported by factions of the army and air force, mounted a coup to try to prevent elections scheduled for that July. It was defeated after two days of fighting that left twenty-four dead.

Arturo Illia of the UCR won the elections that July, and for three years he charted a difficult and uncertain course between the generals and industrialists on the Right and the unions and the vestiges of Peronism on the Left. Illia's presidency was troubled from the start, the factionalized nature of the government illustrated by the way his majority in the senate contrasted with a lack of support in the lower house.

The military, though, remained suspicious, while the price controls, particularly those in the pharmaceutical industry, set business leaders against him. Initially, the unions were supportive of Illia's economic expansionism, but as covert plans for Perón to return from exile became more defined, the unions began to turn against him. A general strike was called as early as May 1964, and, the following year, leaders of the General Confederation of Labor began to hint that they would be in favor of a coup. That they could contemplate such a step barely eighteen months after democratic elections—and with the economy apparently resurgent—suggests just how broken the institution of democracy in Argentina had become.

The newsmagazine *Confirmado* openly called for a coup, printing an opinion poll that supposedly showed public support for it. The military rarely needed much persuading. General Julio Alsogaray, the commander of the First Division of the army, backed by the military, sections of the media, and numerous politicians, among them Frondizi, presented himself in Illia's office at 5:00 a.m. on June 28, 1966, and invited him to resign. Illia initially refused, but as armed officers took over his office, he gave in at 7:20. The following day General Onganía was named as the new president.

This, though, wasn't just another coup. Whereas previous military take-overs had been short-term measures to stabilize the country before restoring civilian control, the coup of 1966 aimed at something rather more permanent. Onganía suspended political parties and imposed a system of *participacionismo* under which he was advised by committees representing various interest groups—which he had, of course, appointed himself. His intellectuals, the message was, were a positive force; others were to be regarded with suspicion. In July 1966 the directors of all universities were dismissed. Resistance at the University of Buenos Aires led to the Night of the Long Sticks, as police armed with batons cleared demonstrators in faculty buildings, followed by the persecution of scientists and academics. Many fled the country.

When the coup happened, the national team was already in Europe, preparing for the World Cup, which began on July 11. Irrespective of the political background, preparations had been chaotic. To Rattin's disgust, Lorenzo was reinstalled as coach six weeks before the tournament began, even though Argentina had lost just one of thirteen games under José María Minella in 1964 and 1965. Lorenzo, having seen the effectiveness of *catenaccio* while coaching Lazio and Roma in Italy, wanted to employ a sweeper, but his attempts to explain the system in training provoked only confusion, even after he had the *libero* wear a different-colored shirt. The players, understandably, complained at being asked to adopt a radically new system on the eve of a tournament. "When we played before the World Cup, we thought we were playing with a replica of the ball that was going to be used," Marzolini recalled. "An Argentinian had made it. But when we arrived there, the ball was completely different, far better." A warm-up tour of Italy could hardly have gone worse. The organization was poor, players fought with delegates—of whom there were, as several Argentinian papers noted, a vast number—delegates fought with the coaching staff, and Rattin punched reserve midfielder José Pastoriza. "When we were in Turin," said Rattin, "we asked the AFA to send us a different coach, and they said no."

The stories of mutiny were worrying enough for Valentin Suárez, the AFA's president, to fly to Europe to try to smooth things over, and when the Argentina squad arrived in England, Rattin insisted everything had been patched up and that he was content. He was never, though, entirely happy outside of Buenos Aires and had brought a recording of his wife and two children speaking to try to help him over his homesickness. "If I could draw up my own contract for soccer at this level," he said in an interview with *La Razón*, "I assure you I would put in a clause that said I would only have to play in Buenos Aires and would never leave my country again." The sensitivity seems incongruous alongside Rattin's image, but that unease, coupled with his disgruntlement at the AFA's disorganization, perhaps explains why, during that World Cup, his fuse always seemed so short.

Preparations were little better once they'd gotten to England. The Argentina squad was based near Birmingham and tried to conduct a secret training session at Lilleshall. The bus got lost on the way there, taking two hours to cover the thirty or so miles, and once they had arrived it turned out nobody had packed the gear, forcing the players to scrounge what they could from a local gym. According to Marzolini—although Rattin claims not to remember the incident—the captain led the squad in singing offensive songs about Lorenzo on the way back. Perhaps the greatest dereliction by AFA officials, though, came shortly before the quarter-final.

Argentina had battled their way through their group. The *Mirror* approvingly noted that they were of a "warrior race" after a 2–1 win over Spain, a game that Spanish playmaker Luis Suárez finished hobbling about ineffectually. That was later used in evidence against Argentina, but it seems he suffered a recurrence of a preexisting injury rather than being the victim of any skullduggery.

It was in the second game, against West Germany at Villa Park, that perspective began to change. It was an aggressive, tense match that finished 0–0 and was chiefly memorable for the incident twenty minutes into the second half that resulted in Rafael Albrecht being sent off by Yugoslav referee Konstantin Zečević for a clattering foul on Wolfgang Weber. There's no doubt it warranted expulsion, and the delay before Albrecht finally went, following a melee as medical and coaching staff entered the field, did little to encourage sympathy, but equally it's understandable that Argentina should ask why that foul in particular was penalized in a game that was littered with them. And why was nothing done about Albrecht apparently being kicked as he lay on the ground after the foul? "Why are Argentina being singled out?"

Lorenzo asked. "Why are we being made scapegoats?" The largely English crowd reacted by booing, while FIFA warned Argentina about their "unethical" play.

So tarnished was Argentina's reputation in England that they were booed onto the field at Hillsborough for their final-group game, a 2–0 win over Switzerland in which every foul, every backpass, and everything that could be construed as time wasting were jeered.

Yet Argentina committed fewer fouls than England in the group stage, statistics that were published without comment in a number of newspapers. That only riled Argentina more: why were they the ones seen as a dirty team? What of Nobby Stiles, who had been censured by the Football Association after a particularly bad foul on France's Jacky Simon? It could only be, the conclusion seems to have been, that northern Europeans were out to get them. Perhaps in a world in which the political intrigue never stopped, in which you were never more than a couple of years from a coup, a certain paranoia was understandable.

The doubts about the referee and a possible fix were inflated by the choice of official. FIFA held a meeting at the Royal Gardens Hotel in Kensington to discuss which referees and linesmen would be used in the quarter-finals and reached their decision before the two Argentina delegates had arrived. Marzolini suggested they simply arrived late, while Juan Santiago, the head of the AFA delegation, insisted he had been told the wrong start time. FIFA's allocation of referees was probably ill-conceived rather than sinister, but it's easy to see why a country should spy conspiracy in a German, Rudolf Kreitlein, being appointed for England's game against Argentina, while an Englishman, Jim Finney, was put in charge of West Germany against Uruguay. And even if there were no suspicion of overt collusion, a European referee, more inclined to let physical play go unpunished, was an advantage for a European team. The differing interpretations of the rules had been a persistent source of friction between European and South American teams throughout the tournament.

Argentina's sense that everything was stacked against them was enhanced the day before the game when stadium officials at Wembley refused to allow them the twenty minutes of practice to which they were entitled on the grounds it would have interfered with the evening's greyhound racing. Given there were more than two hours between the scheduled end of training and the first race, that seems both baffling and outrageous—if that is what happened; so utter was Argentina's sense of victimhood by then that it's easy to imagine the slightest misunderstanding escalating into acrimony.

The match itself was scrappy and stop-start, largely due to Kreitlein's fussiness, but it never degenerated into the sort of violence of, say, Argentina's group game against West Germany; it was not the pitched battle of legend. The incident for which the game is notorious occurred after thirty-five minutes, when Rattin was sent off, although quite what he had done was far from clear. He had been booked a few minutes earlier for clipping Bobby Charlton's heels, and the anxious look he shot Kreitlein after catching Geoff Hurst a few minutes later suggested he realized he was on thin ice, but the dismissal itself, after the ball had drifted innocuously out of play for a goal kick, was shocking.

"Suddenly," wrote Geoffrey Green in the *Times*, "it was seen that Rattin, far from the actual play at that moment, but adjacent to the German referee, was being ordered off the field." Even having had an entire Sunday to work out what had gone on, in other words, one of Britain's leading soccer writers was at a loss. In the *Sunday Telegraph*, David Miller insisted Rattin had been "sent off for persistent arguing and obstruction of the course of the game," which is probably true, but, watching the video, there's little to explain why Kreitlein reacted the way he did.

Rattin was, without question, one of the great moaners of the sixties, forever pleading with referees, hands pinched before his chest, usually stooping to bring his eyes level with officials who were invariably shorter than him, but on this occasion, unless his complaining was done largely off camera, he seems to have been relatively restrained. Even when he was dismissed, his reaction seemed one of disbelief. Rafael Albrecht, Roberto Perfumo, and Ermindo Onega all raged at the referee, Perfumo at one point grabbing his arm, but Rattin simply stood, hands on hips, looking bemused, shaking his head slowly. As his teammates protested, he walked over to Lorenzo on the bench, seemingly seeking his advice. "In the chat before the match," he said, "I was told that if a problem arose, as captain, I had the right to ask for an interpreter and that's what I did. But the referee interpreted my attitude badly. The first time I asked him he pretended to be deaf, and the second time he just showed the way to the changing rooms." That excuse has been widely ridiculed by British histories—and to modern ears it does sound absurd—but it is consistent with his actions. "They wanted me to leave the field and I refused," Rattin said. "What the fuck did they want? I didn't insult anyone, I didn't kick anyone, so why the fuck should I leave the pitch? Just because I've requested a translator to be able to speak to that German *concha*? Because it was arranged, oh yes, a German here and an Englishman there."

As Rattin refused to leave the field, Ken Aston, the head of the referees committee, came to the touchline to give his support to Kreitlein. That night, as he drove home, Aston stopped at a set of traffic lights and had a flash of inspiration, coming up with the idea of red and yellow cards to aid communication between officials and players. It wouldn't have helped in this case, though: Rattin was well aware he'd been sent off; he simply couldn't believe it. Strange though it sounds, the most likely explanation for his behavior is a sincerely held, if misguided, sense of grievance: distrusting his own soccer federation, but convinced there was a conspiracy against Argentina, his overanxiety to ensure his side wasn't cheated led him to antagonize the one authority who could have done something about it, who then, of course, himself became, to Rattin's mind, implicated in the plot.

Briefly, it seemed Lorenzo might insist all his players leave the field, but eight minutes after he'd been sent off, Rattin set off on his long walk back to the tunnel, in those days opposite the royal box rather than behind the goal. The official film of the tournament, *Goal!*, follows his trudge, the game out of focus in the foreground, the Fellini-inspired score investing his departure with a weird dignity. As he passed the corner flag, a miniature of the Union Jack flag with a World Cup logo at its center, Rattin took it up in his right hand and ran his fingers briefly over it. The incident has attracted various interpretations, some saying he was wiping his hand on the cloth, symbolically muddying the emblem of the British state, others that he was signaling that this was a British World Cup and that therefore a British winner must be expected.

For a moment Rattin stopped, put his hands on his hips, and contemplated the field, perhaps pondering some other gesture of protest or simply considering the shattering of his dreams. As Rattin reached the tunnel, the Argentinian official who had accompanied him began shaking his fist in the air, seemingly reacting to jeers from English fans. Rattin seemed oblivious. As he went down the tunnel, he passed a small pony, a regimental mascot draped a in a maroon coat marked with a gold emblem. He didn't so much as glance at it before disappearing into the darkness. Asked about it now, he is bemused: in his emotional state, the pony didn't register. "The game was suspended for twentysomething minutes," Rattin said. "I talked to our board members, and they finally told me, 'This can't go on. You have to leave.' 'But I didn't do anything.'"

Bobby Charlton was certain the sending-off had been the right decision. "In my opinion, there was no question that eventually his only option was to send off Rattin . . . ," he wrote in his autobiography. "Twice in a few minutes Rattin fouled me, on the second occasion stopping me with a quite blatant trip. I was close to Rattin when he was cautioned and I could see by the expression on his face that he was near to erupting, which he duly did when his team-mate Alberto González followed him into the referee's book. At that point, it seemed Rattin lost all interest in the flow of the game."

Part of the problem was that nobody really knew what Rattin had been sent off for. Kreitlein wasn't much help when, the day after the game, journalists tracked him down to a deck chair in Kensington Gardens. "The look on Rattin's face was quite enough to tell me what he was saying and meaning," he said. "I do not speak Spanish but the look told me everything. He followed me all over the pitch and I got angry. I had no choice but to send him off." Rattin himself, at least if a photograph in the *Mirror* was to be believed, spent the day after his disgrace sightseeing, cheerily taking snapshots of a guardsman outside Buckingham Palace. He remembers going to Harrods. "The taxi driver from the hotel didn't charge me," he said. "And in Harrods, people were asking me for autographs and saying that they were sorry. I didn't understand shit about what they were saying, unfortunately, but you could sense that they were embarrassed about what had happened."

Once the game had restarted, Argentina regrouped and defended well, sitting deep and frustrating England as they had in Rio two years earlier, before eventually being undone by Hurst's seventy-eighth-minute header from a Ray Wilson cross. The mechanics of the game, though, are not what dominate the memory. "Not once had I played in a game that so thoroughly debased the true meaning of soccer . . . ," said Bobby Charlton. "I had been obstructed, tripped, kicked and spat upon but never before had I experienced so much foul practice applied so intensely and so relentlessly."

In his finest hour, Ramsey committed his gravest mistake. In victory he could have been gracious, but instead, for once, he allowed his emotions, his irritation at Argentina's attitude, to take over. First, he tried to prevent his players from swapping shirts with Argentina's, an act that looked churlish and ruined what would at least have been a symbolic moment of sportsmanship after all the unpleasantness. In the famous photograph of him tugging at Cohen's shirt as the fullback tries to hand it to González, he looks petty, even a little childish. "When the famous picture at full-time was taken I was about to change shirts with this guy," Cohen said. "He was insisting on having it. Alf saw what was happening and he rushed over. He said, 'You're not changing shirts with him.' Or words to that effect. By which time the sleeve of that shirt must have been about three feet long." And Ramsey couldn't be everywhere, so shirts were exchanged, which is how Marzolini ended up with Bobby Charlton's.

From Ramsey, worse was to follow, as he allowed himself to be needled during a television interview by a question about England's supposed negativity. "Our best soccer," he said, "will come against the right type of opposition—a team who come to play soccer, and not act as animals." It was a stupid and discourteous thing to say, and Ramsey's well-known discomfort behind a microphone is no excuse; then again, one loose comment should never have been allowed—as it subsequently was by Argentinian officials and journalists—to attempt to justify retroactively what had gone before, nor as the basis for decades of acrimony.

Ramsey wasn't the only one to lose control after the final whistle. Memories have faded and the accounts are far from clear, but it seems a group of Argentina players and officials berated Kreitlein as he left the field. One—although nobody seems clear who—tried to manhandle him and was restrained by police, while Harry Cavan, the Northern Irish FIFA delegate, claimed to have been spat at. There were uncorroborated reports of an Argentinian player urinating in the tunnel, while damage was certainly done to Argentina's dressing-room door.

The newspapers were—predictably—split on national lines. England, *Clarín* concluded, had been "sunk in the mud of indecency by its soccer manager, a seller of lies, a terrorized individual who will lose his job if his team doesn't become champions. The country recognizes this and England celebrated its victory timidly. . . . [T]he true England is in shame, the public celebrate with a bitter taste." The newspaper sent a plane to one of the outlying Falkland Islands where their journalist symbolically planted a flag.

Argentina returned home to be greeted by cheering crowds at Ezeiza. Rattin was draped in the flag, a globe was brandished to symbolize some sort of moral victory, and the team was rushed to a reception with Onganía, who praised "your brilliant performance, your courage and your fighting spirit." And perhaps, in Argentina's spirit there was encouragement to be drawn, a positive development from 1958. "This team," Juan Sasturain wrote in his history of Argentina at the World Cup, "unlike those before it, resisted, like a pilot resists in the rain, as Uruguay played to resist for decades, halting the rhythm, hiding the ball."

Almost five decades later, Rattin remains in no doubt that the 1966 World Cup was fixed. "You have to understand when you talk about World Cups there are World Cups before satellite television and World Cups after satellite," he said.

> Before satellite the host nation always did well, because the only way FIFA made money was from selling tickets to the games. I remember in that game in '66 there was not a single ad in the stadium [in this he is quite right; the stands were fronted by plain white walls]. So the host team had to do well. Until 1970, the country that organized the World Cup either won it or made it into the final. Sweden played the final.

Who the fuck are Sweden in soccer? Chile earned a third place. Italy, champions. Everything was different, no substitutions, no TV, nothing. Empty stadiums, unless the hosts were playing. After satellites they could make money from TV, so it was not so important.

Or maybe hosts did better in the past because travel used to be far more arduous than it is now, and away sides felt less at ease.

26

A PECULIAR GLORY

Almost unnoticed, Racing had been improving, finishing fifth in 1965, going unbeaten through their final fourteen games of the season. That year Juan José Pizzuti, having retired as a player in 1963, returned to the club as a manager, and before the start of the 1966 season, Humberto Maschio also went back, having spent three seasons at Fiorentina after his falling-out with Herrera at Inter. He found Argentinian soccer much more similar in style to the Italian game than the sport he had left nine years earlier. "I noticed a huge change in the physicality, not in the tactics," he said.

Maschio had his doubts about playing for a manager who had once been his teammate, but they were soon dispelled. "He had a very joined-up way of thinking," he said. "As we say here, he married no one. He was my friend, but he treated me as if I was a regular soccer player. He was strict. I don't know if he could apply the same rules now. For example, he fined us if we cursed or insulted anybody."

Most assumed Maschio, by then thirty-three, was going home for a sentimental final season or two before retiring, but it soon became apparent that, five years after their previous title, something special was stirring in Avellaneda. "At first, they completely wrote us off," said forward Juan Carlos Cárdenas, who was twenty at the start of the 1966 season. "We were seen as a mix of old guys with young guys who were not going to win anything. At the time, when you turned thirty you became a dinosaur. They said we were the leftovers, that Racing were finished. You just had to accept it, because in the end Racing were old and experienced. Rulli had played for Boca, Rodríguez for Nacional, Maschio came from Europe . . . The kids were me, Díaz, Basile, Cejas and Perfumo."

These days Cárdenas runs a real estate business from an office in the central barrio of Floresta, once the home of radio in Argentina, five minutes or so from the stadium of All Boys, whom he once managed. Like many from the North, he was nicknamed "Chango," and it's by that name that he is still widely known. His hair is gray now, the face lined, and there's a weariness about him, but the memory of those early days under Pizzuti raises a chuckle. "When we saw Maschio, a great guy, we would take the piss out of him: 'Run, old man, run.' We were all eighteen, nineteen . . . so we were confident that we'd have more stamina than him. We started running round the pitch, five laps at full speed: one, okay, two, still possible, three, four, we were so exhausted, and the creepy old man kept running. We couldn't take it; we just stopped and yelled at him: 'You, old man! Get a girl! You haven't seen a girl in years.'" He broke off, laughing, the thought of Maschio without a woman too ridiculous to contemplate.

Racing beat Atlanta 2–0 on the opening day of the season, then drew away at Vélez Sarsfield before beating Newell's and Quilmes. When they won 1–0 at Chacarita Juniors, their run without defeat stretched to twenty games. "We just started playing and winning, and suddenly we had this unbeaten record," said Cárdenas. "Neutrals and soccer fans in general became more and more curious about Racing, about José's team. 'What is it with these guys? How is it that they don't lose?' So we had supporters from other clubs: today that would be impossible."

The main reason for the success was Pizzuti. "He could see every single attribute of a player and he was right," said Maschio. "That team revolutionized soccer in Argentina," said Cárdenas.

> We had a manager who played a leading role, who had experience at Boca and River and had already won tournaments with Racing. So he had no fear and he wanted us to be the protagonists. I want this kind of team, he told us. At the time, there were teams with great names, but the reigning concept was, "Don't take too many risks."
>
> So he drew a completely new tactical scheme compared to what was normal in those days. Boca won the league in 1965 with all 1–0s and 0–0s: nobody could score against them, but it was rather boring. Then we showed up. I was the number 9, the typical center-forward inside the box with the mentality of "if I've scored I've played well, if I haven't scored, I've played badly." But Pizzuti pulled me out of that position and made me roam all round the front line with no fixed position. "I don't want to see you anymore waiting inside the area," he said. And that was one of the key aspects of the team. The number 7 or number 11 could end up in the area. The three forwards rotated a lot and that was a surprise.

The bohemian age, the years of players staggering onto the field after a couple of bottles of wine, may have gone, and the 1967 Intercontinental final showed Racing could be as tough and pragmatic as anybody on their day, but Maschio insisted some of the old spirit remained. "We went thirty-nine games unbeaten and then lost against River," he said. "We never thought about results. We had more fun. The only time we were thinking about the upcoming result was against River and we lost. We had a little fear and we played really badly."

That game, though, came in the twenty-sixth round of the season, by which time Racing were already clear at the top of the table. They sealed the title with a goalless draw, but the overall statistics tell the story: that season Racing scored seventy goals in thirty-eight games; the previous season Boca had won the league with fifty-five goals in thirty-four games and the season before that with thirty-five in thirty. Racing had begun the process of restoring an attacking edge to Argentinian soccer.

The following season brought the first major change to the structure of the championship since 1937. Onganía's attempts to balance the books had led to a reduction in subsidies, which had hit the provinces far harder than Buenos Aires. In Tucumán, for instance, the sugar plantations collapsed. That brought unemployment and discontent, which in turn led Onganía to ask the AFA to incorporate the regions—for there was no greater opiate than soccer. A program of two championships was instituted: the Metropolitano for clubs from Buenos Aires, La Plata, Santa Fe, and Rosario, which in its first iteration featured two groups of eleven sides with the top two progressing to semifinals, and the Nacional, a sixteen-team league in which everybody played each other once that incorporated sides from the rest of the country.

For Racing, the season began well. They topped their Metropolitano group and beat Independiente in the semifinal before losing to the emerging might of Estudiantes in the final. In the Libertadores, Racing surged through the first round, winning eight and losing only one of their ten matches to go through to a semifinal group that also included River Plate and the two Chilean sides, Colo-Colo and Universitario. By then, wise to the tricks of the Libertadores, Pizzuti had started taking forty boxers with the squad for security. "When we got to Chile," said Cárdenas, chuckling at the absurdity of it all, "José introduced them as photographers but none of them had their noses in the right place, their necks were thick and their faces were massive. As we were getting off the plane, a journalist ran up to ask a question and BAM! A punch in the face. 'I didn't mean to do anything wrong . . . ' he said. 'Sorry,' the photographer replied. 'I got carried away.' It was chaotic, but that's what it was like: you were expecting the worst."

Racing reached the final after beating Universitario of Lima in a playoff in Santiago after they'd finished joint top of their semifinal group. That set up a final against Nacional of Montevideo. The first leg, in el Cilindro, finished goalless. The atmosphere in the Centenario for the return was tense. "When we went onto the pitch against Nacional, [Oscar] Martín, who was the captain, and the rest of us were carrying a big Uruguayan flag and they took a picture of us," said Maschio. "After that, the flag fell on the floor. A policeman told Martín to pick it up, but he didn't want to. The policeman hit him with a truncheon, and Martín ran at that policeman." He was eventually placated, but the game was an ugly affair.

Racing were quite happy to get out with a 0–0 draw, meaning yet another playoff in Santiago. This time there were goals. João Cardoso stooped to divert in a low-near-post free kick from a deft back-header after fourteen minutes, and Norberto Raffo, after jinking by Montero Castillo, drilled in a second just before halftime. Milton Vieira pulled one back with eleven minutes remaining, and there was further violence as Roberto Sosa threw a punch at Rubén Díaz when the defender tried to prevent him from grabbing the ball out of the net to get the game restarted quickly, but Racing held out for the win.

With fatigue setting in, Racing paid almost no attention to the Nacional and ended up winning only two of their fifteen games. Their whole focus was directed at the Intercontinental Cup final against the European champions Celtic and becoming the first Argentinian side to win a world title.

Celtic were at home for the first leg, played in October. Racing flew to Rio de Janeiro, refueled, and then crossed the Atlantic before changing planes in London. "There, on the plane, appeared Sean Connery, James Bond himself," said Cárdenas. "As a Rangers fan, he didn't want to see Celtic win so he supported us." Connery wasn't the only British celebrity to come out as a temporary Racing fan, although the other is more surprising. John Lennon rarely showed much interest in soccer, but it is an often-repeated fact in Argentina that he wanted Racing to win that game. "I remember that John Lennon was interviewed and he said that the goal he celebrated the most was Racing's," said Cárdenas, "because that meant the Scots weren't the champions."

Given what subsequently occurred, the atmosphere seems to have been very relaxed, far removed from the tension and paranoia that surrounded Copa Libertadores games, at which it had long been a basic rule never to drink from an open bottle in case it had been spiked. "It was a different culture," said Cárdenas. "It wasn't just the Libertadores. You'd travel to Santa Fe even for the Argentinian league and people at the airport would give out *alfajores*[1] and then maybe you'd get diarrhea because the *hijos de puta* had put in a laxative."

Celtic had much the better of the game and took the lead after sixty-nine minutes. "They beat us in the collective game and they beat us well," said Cárdenas. Having scored, McNeill rubbed it in with a few words to Basile, an indication of how irritated he already was by Racing's approach. Bertie Auld—whom Cárdenas, with his low brow and glasses, has come to resemble—had already taken a back-header in the nose from Martín, whose guilty scuttle away from the incident suggested it had been no accident, while Johnstone was the victim of a horrendous foul by Rulli.

Two weeks later at el Cilindro, the atmosphere was far tenser, exacerbated by the presence in the stadium of Uruguayan fans. The incident that ignited the unpleasantness came before kickoff, as Celtic goalkeeper Ronnie Simpson was struck by a missile. Exactly what it was remains unclear—Argentinian histories usually refer to the projectile as a coin, while Sir Robert Kelly, in his 1971 history of Celtic, described it as "a flat iron bar" and suggested it had been fired from a catapult rather than simply thrown.

Back at home Racing could return to their natural, more attacking game. "It was like playing like a mirror," said Cárdenas, "two winning teams, two teams that enjoyed attacking more than defending." Midway through the first half, Celtic even took the lead, Johnstone felled by Cejas as he ran into the left side of the box and Tommy Gemmell firing the penalty just inside the post. "It was terrible," said Cárdenas. "And the fans did their part: it was like they were injecting you with the idea of, 'This is possible, let's win this.'" Ten minutes before halftime Norberto Raffo got behind the Celtic back four to head a cross from the right past Fallon. McNeill was adamant he was offside, but video footage is inconclusive.

Three minutes after the break, Cárdenas was slipped through and finished neatly across Fallon, and Racing had the lead. "When we were winning they hit the post," said Cárdenas. "If that had gone in it would have been the end. But it didn't. We deserved to win here; they deserved to win there." And so the tie, as three of the previous finals had, went to a playoff, to be held three days later at the Centenario in Montevideo.

As the Celtic team had left el Cilindro, fans had surrounded their bus and, as police watched, begun rocking it from side to side. Craig remembered a voice from the back of bus—he wasn't sure whose—shouting, "Boss, for God's sake, give 'em the cup." Johnstone agreed: if they wanted it that badly, he said, he was happy to let them have it. Celtic's board, it seems, seriously considered forfeiting the game, fearing just the kind of violence that did eventually ensue, but Stein was adamant: he wanted the game played, and he wanted Celtic to be the first British side to win the Intercontinental Cup.

Yet Racing also approached the playoff with an air of apprehension, fearing the reception they would get in Uruguay; Celtic's players seem to have been as oblivious to that rivalry as Racing's were to the distinctions between English and Scots. When Racing arrived in Montevideo, those anxieties were realized as they were greeted by Uruguayan fans playing a *candombe*.[2] "The Uruguayans brought fireworks to the hotel at 2:00 a.m. and stayed there the whole night, so we had to move to the upper floors. But I guess they made a huge mistake and they were betrayed by the atmosphere. Out of 80,000 fans there were only 20 or 25,000 for us and the rest for them. But rather than trying to play like they usually do they just went to take us out. They came onto the pitch having decided not to play but to make sure we couldn't play; and at that game, they lost."

After a series of early tangles, Paraguayan referee Rodolfo Osorio, feeling the game slipping away from him, told the two captains that at the next incident he would send off Basile and Lennox, seemingly irrespective of who was involved. Basile was combative, but why he picked Lennox, a fairly placid inside-forward, was a mystery. Nonetheless, when a Basile foul prompted a fracas in the center circle, Osorio sent both off. Lennox, bewildered, walked off, only for Stein to push him back on. Osorio sent him off again, and Stein again shoved him back onto the field. Osorio sent him off for a third time, and, on this occasion, a policeman with a drawn sword prevented him from returning.

Jimmy Johnstone soon followed, swinging an arm after his shirt had been grabbed. Then center-forward John Hughes went for attacking Agustín Cejas. "The crazy thing is," Hughes said, "when I got up close to the goal-keeper, there were 80,000 there and television cameras, but what came into my head was, 'If I hit this guy, nobody will see me.'" Having hit him, he then kneed him. "Big Jock [Stein] came up to me afterwards and said, 'What were you thinking?'" Hughes went on, "And I was stupid enough to repeat it to him. You can imagine what he said."

Gemmell was extremely fortunate not to go off after kicking Maschio "in the goolies" in another melee—he said after being spat on—but eventually Auld and Rulli were both sent off as well, although Auld managed to stay on for the rest of the game, simply by refusing to leave the field. As he subsequently pointed out, that was a sign of just how far the game had slipped out of Osorio's control. "At halftime we were convinced that we had them," Cárdenas said. "Pizzuti always told me about my accuracy. 'You have to take shots,' he would say. 'You're very precise.' I'd already missed two chances and I believe the only way anybody was going to score in that game was with a long-range shot."

And then came the goal that defined Cárdenas's career, that overshadowed everything else he did in sixteen years as a player and, you suspect, since his retirement in 1976. Cárdenas's office is spartan, but he has arranged it so that when he looks up from his desk he sees a painting of his most famous moment. Alongside it on the wall are two other framed cuttings. One is an article from *El Gráfico* discussing the goal and its significance, illustrated with a diagram showing the move that led up to it. The other is a photograph from *El Tiempo* magazine of Argentina's People of the Year 1967. In it, Cárdenas sits awkwardly on a chair in his Racing gear.

When he describes the goal, it feels as though he's on autopilot, slipping into a very familiar routine. "It started with a throw-in, and it was absolutely spontaneous that I decided to take the shot," Cárdenas said. He advanced through the Celtic half, the ball bobbling awkwardly on a dry surface before, thirty yards out, sitting perfectly for a left-foot shot. "I had a passing option, but as the defender kept going back, thinking that I was going to make a pass, I decided to take the shot. I aimed at the top corner." And he hit the top corner, the ball arcing away from Fallon's right hand to flash just under the bar and just inside the post. "It was a dream goal," said Cárdenas, "the most beautiful thing that ever happened to me."

It was a strange kind of beauty, though. Racing's lap of honor was curtailed when fans hurling missiles forced them to retreat to the center of the field. Fans clustered around the exit to the dressing room, and only after police charges could the Racing players get out. Fighting continued between Uruguayans and Argentinians in the park around the stadium.

"It took so many years to win something again," Cárdenas said, "that people started to tell me that if all Racing fans kept watching my goal, there was a risk that the shot would finally hit the post." It never has, though, and as barren year succeeded barren year, Cárdenas's winner became more and more significant. As Racing celebrated, fans of Independiente broke into their stadium and cursed the club, burying seven black cats. Racing lost a three-way playoff for the Nacional title to Giúdice's Vélez Sarsfield in 1968 and were beaten by Chacarita Juniors in the Metropolitano semifinal in 1969, but the decline had begun.

Pizzuti, after a stint of four years and four months in charge—still the longest reign of any Racing coach—left in 1969, and the fact that four different coaches were tried in 1970 and a further three in 1971 is indicative of the turmoil that followed him. There was one final flail against mediocrity in 1972 as Racing finished second behind San Lorenzo in the Metropolitano, after which Cárdenas left for the Mexican side Puebla. As the drought went on, and even took in a humiliating relegation, Racing became increasingly desperate. They staged an exorcism to try to lift the curse and dug up the field in a search for the skeletons of the cats, but only six were found. It wouldn't be until 2001, when the stadium was redeveloped, that the seventh skeleton was uncovered. That season, thirty-four years after their previous trophy, Racing won the league.

Cárdenas returned from Mexico in 1976 and played one final season for Racing before turning to management. He did win the fourth division with General Lamadrid and also led Deportivo Armenio and All Boys, but he soon drifted out of soccer and into real estate. For Racing fans, though, he will always be the man who beat Celtic.

27

SCORNING THE
PATH OF ROSES

When, in 1965, former Vélez forward Osvaldo Zubeldía arrived at the flat, windswept field outside La Plata that Estudiantes used as a training base, he was thirty-eight, his reputation uncertain. Although he had impressed as manager at Atlanta, whom he'd led to fourth, seventh, and fifth in the Primera between 1961 and 1963, a spell in charge of the Argentina national team had been a failure. At Atlanta Zubeldía had become noted for the hard work he demanded, the double training sessions, the relentless practice of set-plays, the offside trap and pressing, but nobody was quite sure whether those methods could successfully be applied with better players. It's no exaggeration to say that if Zubeldía had failed with Estudiantes, his career might never have recovered.

It's easy, given the reputation his side eventually earned, to imagine Zubeldía as a cynic, a man who placed winning above all else, and perhaps in time that is what he became, his all-consuming love for soccer being corrupted into a need for victory, but at the beginning, he was as wide-eyed and excited by soccer as anybody. Zubeldía was born in Junín, 160 miles west of Buenos Aires, in June 1927. From childhood he dreamed of being a soccer player, and when his mother saved up to buy him a pair of boots, he insisted on wearing them in bed. He was a fan of River Plate, but, after being called to the club for a trial, he panicked on seeing Moreno, Pedernera, and Loustau, turned around, and went straight home. He ended up joining Vélez, where he flourished under Victorio Spinetto as a hardworking inside-forward, the highlight coming in September 1949 when he scored a hat trick in a 5–3 win over his beloved River.

Zubeldía was industrious and diligent, but his greatest gift was his ability to see possibilities. "He was capable of tying a goalkeeper's bootlaces together to distract him," Marzolini said. If there was an advantage to be gained, Zubeldía would look for it.

Estudiantes had finished third-bottom in 1964, and when Zubeldía arrived the priority was simply to avoid relegation. "He came to the club a month before starting," said Juan Ramón Verón, Juan Sebastián's father, who is widely recognized as having been the most naturally gifted player in that Estudiantes side—"he is for us what Pelé is for Santos," Zubeldía once said. There is a quiet dignity about Verón, a gentleness that is hard to square with the reputation of the Estudiantes team with which he played.

"Zubeldía looked at the first team," Verón said, "and he looked at the third team and he saw the third team was playing better, and asked himself what was the point of keeping the old players." So he got rid of all but four of them, reasoning that young minds would be more malleable to his methods and ideas.

In Zubeldía's first season, Estudiantes finished sixth. In his second they came in seventh. "The fans here were more patient, so Zubeldía could work here for three years without having to win championships, which he would not have been able to do at, for instance, Boca," Verón said. "We were really young and didn't really notice what was happening. Things just started growing, and we realized one day that we had a great team."

The following year, 1967, as the championship split, they finished the group stage of the Metropolitano second on goal difference behind Racing and so reached the semifinal.

They trained harder and more meticulously than any Argentinian side ever had before. "All the possibilities afforded by the game were foreseen and practiced," said midfielder Carlos Bilardo. "Corners, free kicks, throw-ins were used to our best advantage and we also had secret signs and language which we used to make our opponents fall into the trap." For Zubeldía, humility and industry went hand-in-hand. "Few of us had cars," said midfielder Carlos Pachamé. "We all took the train to go the practice sessions. But when Zubeldía wanted to motivate us, he would take us all to Retiro train station at 6:00 a.m. to watch the commuters. 'You believe you are workers,' he would tell us. 'You are not. They are! Don't ever forget that.' And he was right."

The real tactical innovation was the use of an aggressive offside trap, something virtually unknown in the Argentinian game at the time. Verón was sketchy on the details, but remembered the notion of pressing being explained by a video of "some Eastern European team." It's hard to be absolutely certain, but it seems likely this was the Dynamo Kyiv of Viktor Maslov. The precise details are less relevant than the fact that Zubeldía would go so far in search of an advantage that he was studying teams from across the world, even those behind the Iron Curtain. "They were the first to use it and not just on set pieces," said Juan Carlos Rulli. "Besides, referees weren't used to it, so they gave them free-kicks all the time, even if they'd timed it badly and the player was still onside: the benefit of the doubt was always in their favor."

Estudiantes came from 3–0 down in the Metropolitano semifinal to beat Platense 4–3, setting up a final against Racing at San Lorenzo's Viejo Gasómetro stadium. In front of almost sixty thousand fans, three goals in twenty second-half minutes, from Raúl Madero, Verón, and Felipe Ribaudo, made Estudiantes the first side from outside Buenos Aires to win an Argentinian title.

It wasn't difficult to see the political parallels: the militarism of the Onganía government reflected in the effort of Estudiantes, the sense of a new—pragmatic—world taking shape. Traditionalists may have been skeptical, but there was nothing sinister about the shift in focus to spirit and cohesion, nor about the way Zubeldía pioneered pressing and the high offside line in Argentina. But there was a darker side, and it was that that gave *anti-fútbol* a bad name. It wasn't so much the physicality and occasional violence of their play, shocking as they may have been to the European opponents they faced in the Intercontinental Cup—an inversion of the usual argument that South Americans struggled to deal with the muscularity that was accepted in the European game—as the willingness not merely to countenance but to encourage dirty tricks. "You don't," Zubeldía said, "arrive at glory through a path of roses."

That may be true, but neither do you have to prick your opponents deliberately with the thorns. It was alleged that Bilardo, and perhaps others, would carry pins onto the field with them to jab opponents as they were marking them. Verón insisted that was "a myth," but Bilardo seemed to admit it in an advertising campaign in 2011. Rattin was certain it was true, although he admitted he had never himself seen Bilardo stab anybody.

Verón, understandably, was coy about exactly what Zubeldía allowed or told his players to do, but he did acknowledge that Estudiantes "tried to find out everything possible about [their] rivals individually, their habits, their characters, their weaknesses, and even about their private lives so we could goad them on the field, get them to react and risk being sent off."

"They used psychology in the worst possible way," said historian Juan Presta. "There was a player from Independiente who had accidentally killed a friend on a hunting trip—when he played Estudiantes, all game long they chanted 'murderer' at him. Or there was a goalkeeper for Racing who had a really close relationship with his mother. She didn't want him to marry, but eventually he did, and six months later his mother died. Bilardo walked up to him and said, 'Congratulations, finally you've killed your mother.'"

It was even said that Bilardo, who as well as being a professional player was a qualified gynecologist (and for a time ran his parents' furniture business), drew on his contacts in the medical profession. Racing's Roberto Perfumo, for instance, was sent off for kicking Bilardo in the stomach, supposedly because Bilardo had taunted him about a cyst his wife had recently had removed from a particularly sensitive area.

"We knew the Laws of the Game by heart, right up to the last comma, and we knew how to take advantage of them," said defender Ramón Aguirre Suárez, who was voted the most violent player in Argentinian history in one Internet poll. "We used to hire a referee to give us lectures. The offside trap, for example, was seen as 'anti-fútbol' by the Argentinian press. Later, everybody copied it."

So unsavory were their antics that even now, many of those who played against that Estudiantes team cannot forgive them. Rulli was tenacious in the extreme, not afraid of leaving his foot in a challenge or chipping away verbally at an opponent, but even he felt that Estudiantes went too far—and that despite the fact he had once been an Estudiantes player. "Insults, knocks, kicks, punches . . . that's all accepted," he said. "But certain things are not. I'm still in touch with the players I played with at Estudiantes but not that lot."

Given how notorious they became for their unpalatable methods, it's easy to ignore the fact that Estudiantes could actually play. "They were really well constructed," said Delgado, who played against them after his move to Santos. "Aside from marking, they knew how to play. Verón was the key player. He gave them a flow. The two central midfielders—Pachamé and Bilardo—were not really talented. Pachamé was really defensive and Bilardo was not talented but really, really smart. Bilardo was the least talented of them all."

Victory over Palmeiras in a playoff in the final made Estudiantes the third Argentinian side to win the Libertadores. It was during that run that the term anti-fútbol first began to be used to describe Estudiantes, while El Gráfico, although largely supportive, noted that the way they played was "more solid than beautiful." A few weeks later, the magazine ran a feature imagining a game between Estudiantes and River's la Máquina side, deciding la Máquina would have won. The legend of la nuestra clearly still held some sway.

The Intercontinental final against Manchester United later that year picked up where Racing's clash with Celtic had left off. Zubeldía was even more meticulous than usual, confining his players in concentración at the club's headquarters at City Bell for fifteen days before the game. Always keen to set an example, he stayed with them. Players were restricted to one phone call per day, and even then Zubeldía had banned their wives from telling them about day-to-day problems. "My players can't know if their son's caught a fever or if the electricity bill has gone up," he said. "All these matters worry them unnecessarily, as they have to be focused, not with their bodies in City Bell and their minds somewhere else."

The first leg was played not in La Plata but at la Bombonera and, despite seemingly genuine efforts from both sides to rebuild relations, quickly degenerated. In total there were fifty-three fouls, thirty-six of them committed by Estudiantes. Denis Law complained of having his hair pulled, George Best was punched in the stomach, and Bobby Charlton needed stitches following a foul by Bilardo. It was Nobby Stiles, though, who was the focus of the violence. He was responsible for ten of the seventeen fouls United committed, eight of them on Bilardo. Stiles had been a bête noire since the 1966 World Cup, and any chance his reputation might have been forgotten was removed by an interview in the program with Benfica's Brazilian coach Otto Glória in which he referred to the midfielder as "an assassin" and described him as "brutal, ill-intentioned, and a bad sportsman."

Having been goaded all game and suffering a cut eye from a head butt, Stiles snapped with eleven minutes remaining, flicked a V sign at the referee, and, having already been booked for a foul on Bilardo, was sent off. "In Buenos Aires, Stiles and I had a real go at each other," said Bilardo. "In one incident, I turned my back and he kicked me up the arse. One of many kicks. But my philosophy was always that sometimes you give and sometimes you receive. If it was tough, you put up with it. Never speak after the game, never cry to referees. In one of the incidents, he fell and later said that he had lost a contact lens, that he was half-blind."

The only goal had come after twenty-six minutes, as Marcos Conigliaro headed in a Verón corner. "We were very strong at set pieces because we practiced lots every day," Conigliaro said. "The corner-kick move was adopted from English soccer."

For the return, Estudiantes stayed in Lymm, where Brazil had been based during the World Cup two years earlier. As with the pictures of Rattin posing with guardsmen outside Buckingham Palace, there is a strange sense of the players as tourists as much as soccer players. Bilardo complained about the incessant rain, while Oscar Malbernat spoke of going to Liverpool, "not just to see the city of the Beatles but also because United played there."

George Best appeared on television, asking people to make Estudiantes feel at home, but two nights before the game a brick was thrown through the window of the room occupied by Ramón Aguirre Suárez. "In the morning," the defender said, "when the police and the journalists showed up, someone asked Zubeldía what was he planning to do. 'Well,' he answered, 'we are going to cover that hole so my boys won't catch a cold.' He never lost control." Such was the Machiavellian nature of that side, so bound up was their work with plot and counterplot, that it was even rumored that Bilardo had thrown the brick himself to help motivate his teammates; he denied it.

So well adjusted were Estudiantes that they took the lead after seven minutes, after which the tie resumed its acrimonious course. Best and José Hugo Medina were sent off for throwing punches at each other. The culmination of their battle was off-camera, but Medina seemed to come off worse and was pelted with coins as he made his slow way off the field and down the tunnel, feeling tentatively at his mouth to check for blood.

Willie Morgan stole in unmarked at the back post in the final minute to level the scores on the night, as Estudiantes' offside trap failed them for once, and, briefly, it seemed United might force a playoff. "In the last minute," said Bilardo, "I was running against someone, trying to prevent him from getting in the cross, but he did send the ball into the area, and we both fell. Suddenly I saw the ball in our goal, . . . but [goalkeeper Alberto] Poletti was celebrating in the center of the pitch. I hadn't noticed, but the referee had already blown his whistle."

"That was the high point," said Verón, but the reaction in Britain was one of disgust and fury. United midfielder Paddy Crerand called Estudiantes "the dirtiest team I've played against," while Brian Glanville in the *Sunday Times* was despairing. "Some of their tactics . . . ," he wrote, "draw us again to question how soccer, at the highest level, can survive as a sport. Tactical fouls as practiced tonight by Estudiantes, by Racing last year and by Argentina in 1966 at Wembley, simply make it impossible to practice the game." Amid the hyperbole—"the night they spat on sportsmanship," the *Daily Mirror* shrieked after the first leg—Glanville's was the most rational comment: the cynicism of the Argentinian game *was* becoming problematic.

Those doubts as to whether the ends really did justify the means reflected wider discontent: growing distaste for the cynicism of Estudiantes was mirrored by an increasing frustration at the bureaucratic authoritarianism of Onganía's reign, which brought neither stability nor prosperity. And then there was the youth movement, reflecting the events in Paris in 1968. As elsewhere, for many rebellion meant no more than having long hair or wearing miniskirts—although such mundane acts had been outlawed by Onganía as part of his Catholic-conservative program of recovering "Western Christian tradition"—but there was also a socialist, idealistic strand, inspired by Che Guevara, that tended to the revolutionary. The student movement was sufficient in number to be a significant force. Resistance to the regime became more visible, the most obvious example being what became known as the *Cordobazo*.

Early in 1969 students and workers' groups in Córdoba, which was going through a process of rapid urbanization, began a series of protests. By May, as

Estudiantes were winning the Libertadores, they'd become something more profound. Metalworkers, transport workers, and other trade unions called a strike. Leaving a meeting, they were attacked by government forces and fought back, prompting a pitched battle. At the same time, students across the country were protesting against the privatization of university dining rooms. In the northern city of Corrientes, a student, Juan José Cabral, was killed. The university was closed, leading to mass demonstrations.

On May 29 another strike and protest were called, prompting indiscriminate repression. After news broke that Máximo Mesa of the mechanics union had been killed, the police were attacked.

The uprising was quashed, but not without consequences. This was the first time civilians had shown they were prepared to use violence to challenge the state, and it both divided the military and led to an increasing radicalization of political groups. The struggle being played out in society was reflected in soccer: as much as anything else, the issue was one of generational change, as old hierarchies and conservative modes of behavior collapsed before the youth culture that, with its hedonism and vague egalitarianism, underlay the various risings in Europe in 1968.

As well as the growing national intolerance for cynicism, there were also simple soccer reasons for the backlash against Estudiantes. According to Verón, the delight the media had shown in the triumph of a "humble" team soon developed into resentment from the clubs and press from the capital, while a new, less cynical, more likable underdog rose up, as Chacarita Juniors, a team from San Martín, a poor suburb of Buenos Aires, beat River Plate 4–1 in the 1969 Metropolitano final. "Chacarita's victory validates the values that made Argentinian soccer great . . . ," wrote Juvenal in *El Gráfico*, clearly taking aim at Estudiantes. "Chacarita run, bite, sweat, give, sacrifice, but they also play soccer. Rather: they want to play, taking care of the ball throughout the park, and they also fight."

Poletti, meanwhile, insisted that Estudiantes' true crime had been to challenge the establishment, not just in the fleeting way of a fairy-tale underdog, but more seriously. "It's true that we had a reputation, but it's the kind of reputation you earn when you reach a position of power from humble beginnings," the goalkeeper said.

And then there was the shambles of World Cup qualification, which inflated the idea that something at the heart of the Argentinian game was badly wrong. Every World Cup in which they'd competed had been in some way a disappointment for Argentina, but at least they'd come home from 1966 with a burning sense of injustice and the feeling that they might have triumphed but for an Anglo-FIFA conspiracy. In Mexico in 1970, with fewer European referees, who knew?

The problem was, they had to get there. Longevity was never a trait of Argentina managers, but the late sixties was a time of particular turbulence. After the 1966 World Cup, Lorenzo had been replaced by Jim Lopes, who was replaced by Carmelo Faraone, who was replaced by Renato Cesarini. When he went, José María Minella came in for a brief caretaker stint. With World Cup qualifying looming, Ramos Ruiz, the *interventor*[1] of the AFA and a Racing fan, turned to Humberto Maschio, who was thirty-six and had just retired as a player.

With three wins and a draw from his first four games, everything seemed to be progressing well when Onganía forced Ruiz to resign. When he quit, the entire coaching staff was also ousted—"a big mistake," said Maschio—and only a couple of weeks before qualification began, Adolfo Pedernera took over. On the face of it, Argentina's task seemed simple. They had been drawn in a three-team group with Peru and Bolivia, with the winners to qualify. In retrospect, it can be seen that Peru, which topped the group, were just about to enter their second golden age, but at the time they were disregarded: they'd come fifth in the 1963 South American Championship and hadn't competed in 1967, forced to withdraw from qualifying because of the 1966 earthquake.

Eleven years after the embarrassment of Helsingborg—and the revolution it had provoked—came the counterrevolution, as an editorial in *El Gráfico* proclaimed "the school of Argentinian soccer" as the "great victim" of the "witch hunt" that followed the World Cup. "The desire to erase the memory of those six Czechoslovakian goals propelled us towards a more defensive game, towards the eternal fear of losing, making us forget the necessity and pleasure of scoring more goals than our opponents to win," it said. "The desire to overcome our lack of speed and physical power before the Europeans induced in us an indiscriminate imitation, a contempt for ability and intelligence."

Estudiantes didn't help themselves. Six weeks after Argentina had gone out of the World Cup, they went to Italy to defend their Intercontinental crown against AC Milan. They lost the first leg 3–0, and the return in la Bombonera became a battle. Estudiantes won 2–1, but the result was an irrelevance alongside the violence of the tie. Ramón Aguirre Suárez elbowed Néstor Combin, breaking his nose, and Poletti punched Gianni Rivera, an assault Eduardo Manera followed up by kicking him to the ground. Farcically, as a bloodied Combin, who had been born in Argentina but had moved to France while a teenager, was stretchered from the field, he was arrested on a charge of draft dodging. Combin even spent a brief time in police custody before mounting international pressure led to his release.

"Such shameful behavior has compromised and sullied Argentina's international reputation and provoked the revulsion of a nation," Onganía said. Suárez, Poletti, and Manera were sentenced to thirty days in jail for disgracing a public spectacle, while Poletti was given a lifetime ban from the game and Suárez suspended from international fixtures for five years. Zubeldía was vilified, although his apologists claim he merely sanctioned the pressing and the offside trap, not the gamesmanship. A more realistic defense may be that other Argentinian teams at the time were almost as happy to engage in skullduggery.

Estudiantes' final stand came in the Libertadores. As champions, Estudiantes again got a bye to the semifinal, where they beat River 1–0 at el Monumental and 3–1 at home to progress to the final against Peñarol. It was a grim, attritional affair, Néstor Togneri scoring the only goal with three minutes remaining in La Plata before a 0–0 draw in Montevideo sealed Estudiantes' third straight continental title. They lost to Feyenoord in the Intercontinental final without any repeat of the shame of the previous year, but the mood was against them. "The Estudiantes that we admired, applauded and defended, were a very different thing," another editorial in *El Gráfico* proclaimed. "When they won their first finals, their play was not *anti-fútbol*, but authentic soccer suffused with effort, vitality and sacrifice."

Zubeldía resigned and, after brief stints at San Lorenzo and Racing, moved to Colombia in 1976, where he managed Atlético Nacional. He won two league titles there before, in 1982, he collapsed with a heart attack while filling in a betting slip at Los Andes racetrack. He never recovered and died at the age of just fifty-four.

Whatever Estudiantes became, Zubeldía was a revolutionary, and, easy as it was for Argentinian soccer to blame only him or his club when it became disgusted by the excesses of the sixties, they were far from alone in adopting an approach that pushed pragmatism to its extremes. "If Argentina cannot, or will not, put their own house in order," warned Teófilo Salina, the Peruvian president of Conmebol, "the South American confederation will be compelled to recommend that the 1978 World Cup be transferred to a country of greater integrity."

In Argentina integrity was rapidly yielding to violence. As the sixties drew to a close, a section of the student movement, inflamed by the *Cordobazo*, began to espouse Peronism, if only because Perón, outlawed by the junta, had come to be seen as a force of radical liberalism. As a result, the younger part of Perón's support sought to reinvent what had been a broadly populist movement as something overtly left-wing. That was a process encouraged by Perón, who manipulated the Left to create an environment that might permit his return. From that grew a number of radical groups, most notably the Ejército Revolucionario del Pueblo—the People's Revolutionary Army (ERP), a band of urban guerrillas who eventually took to the jungles and hills of Tucumán in the North in an attempt to replicate the Cuban revolution of Fidel Castro and Che Guevara—and the Montoneros. Also inspired by Guevara, they were radical young leftist Peronists who carried out terrorist attacks, their ideology pitched awkwardly between pure Marxism and Peronism. On May 29, 1970, they kidnapped former president General Aramburu and gave him a mock trial for, among other supposed crimes, "the murder of twenty-seven Argentinians after an unsuccessful Peronist rebellion in 1956"—the deaths exposed by the journalist Rodolfo Walsh in his book *Operación masacre*. He was shot dead on June 1.

A few days later, Onganía was toppled by another army faction and replaced by the little-known General Roberto Levingston, who was serving as Argentina's representative on the Inter-American Defense Board in Washington, DC, and was perceived as a useful compromise candidate. So little known was he, in fact, that on his accession, a press release was sent out detailing his résumé. Levingston lasted only nine months, though, before being replaced by General Alejandro Lanusse, the head of the military who had been the driving force behind the coup against Onganía.

The Peronists continued agitating for the return of their leader in exile, in preparation for which the body of Evita was dug up from the grave where it had secretly been buried in Italy and flown to Madrid, where it took its place in a chamber above the bedroom where Perón slept with his third wife, Isabelita, a morbid detail that seems the perfect symbol of the instinctive Argentinian nostalgia for the myths of the past.

In September 1971 Lanusse promised that democratic elections would be held within two years; Perón's return had become inevitable. What followed was another cycle of violence. Banks were robbed, police and military officers were assassinated, foreign and local business executives were kidnapped. The left-wing radicals fought with right-wing groups, and the whole fabric of society seemed to unravel. When the Montoneros had kidnapped Aramburu, they had had only a dozen members; by 1973 they had well over a thousand. Novelist V. S. Naipaul reported seeing graffiti proclaiming *"Rosas vuelve"*—Rosas, the first dictator, is returning; a new terror was awaited.

PART FOUR

REBIRTH AND CONFLICT, 1973–1978

28

A TAINTED TRIUMPH

As a forest of blue and white flags waved in the stands at el Monumental, César Luis Menotti pulled his collar tighter around his throat. There was no outward sign of celebration: he had done a job, and done it superbly, but he must have also been aware that winning the 1978 World Cup had consequences. His success, Argentina's success, was necessarily also the success of the junta. On the field Argentina's leader, General Jorge Videla, grinning beneath his mustache, oiled hair gleaming in the floodlights, presented the World Cup trophy to Daniel Passarella, Argentina's captain. As Passarella raised it to a roar of celebratory patriotism, Videla turned to one side and raised both his thumbs in glee.

It's clear from his autobiography, *Football Without Tricks*, that Menotti was deeply uncomfortable about the propaganda coup the World Cup win provided the junta. At the time he claimed that "our victory is a tribute to the old and glorious Argentinian soccer," a phrase that appealed both to the conservatism of the military and to his own romanticism, but that wasn't enough to occlude the ethical issues.

Videla died in jail in May 2013, killed by internal hemorrhaging after slipping in the shower. He was less than a year into a fifty-year sentence for kidnapping: perhaps as many as 400 babies were taken from their mothers at detention centers during his reign and given to military families without children. That was only his most recent conviction. Videla had been found guilty in 1985 of multiple homicides, kidnapping, and torture and then, having been pardoned in 1990, was jailed again in 2010 for human rights abuses relating to the deaths of thirty-one civilians in military custody after the 1976 coup that installed him in power. In total, the junta was responsible for the deaths of between 15,000 and 30,000 of its own citizens. Whether the regime would have fallen sooner had Argentina not won the World Cup is difficult to say, but what is true is that the tournament was planned to provide a surge of nationalistic feeling on which the junta could capitalize and that it did so, ruthlessly, cynically, and successfully.

However joyous that scene of Videla handing the World Cup to Passarella may have seemed at the time, however thrilling and talented that Argentina team, it's impossible not to look at the presentation with hindsight and shudder. It might not be fair to Menotti or the players, but the tournament and the regime cannot be disentangled. Head out of el Monumental, turn right on Avenida del Libertador, walk for ten minutes, and you come to the Esma—la Escuela de Mecánica de la Armada, the Navy School of Mechanics. There, beyond the neat lawns, the whitewashed walls, and the four proud columns of the entrance, 5,000 prisoners were held and tortured between 1976 and 1983. Only 150 survived. It was the busiest and most notorious detention center of the Dirty War.

During the World Cup, with a dreadful symbolism that has been portrayed in numerous novels and films, prisoners could hear the celebratory roars of the crowd even as victims screamed down the corridor. Many detainees were allowed to listen to commentary of the final on the radio, supporting their country although they despised the regime that governed it. Anthropologist Eduardo Archetti relates the story of prisoners shouting "We won! We won!" in their cells and being joined in their celebrations by Captain Jorge Acosta, "el Tigre," one of the most notorious of the torturers. He then took some of the prisoners out in his car to witness the delight on the streets, so they could see that the people as a whole didn't care about the protests. One prisoner asked him to wind down the roof so she could see better. When he'd done so, she considered shouting that she was one of the disappeared. But she didn't, deciding she'd just be thought somebody celebrating crazily. As Carlos Fontanarrosa had put it after Racing's victory over Celtic a decade earlier, "in a troubled country, the greatest joys arise from sport."

But these were far darker troubles than those of 1967. As Bartolomé de Vedia wrote in *La Nación* in 2003, "In 1978 there was pain and death but also soccer and joy. Life always flows in this way, with light and shadow . . . and in this way, nations write their histories, with the soul full of jubilation and, at the same time, with the soul in tatters. . . . Let's play soccer without the shadow of death slipping into the stadiums through some crack. And let's mourn the lives lost without anything to distract us from our pain."

The contrast was desperately painful and desperately difficult, the divide he proposed, even if it was desirable, not universally possible. When the full extent of the Dirty War became known, how could those who had celebrated—essentially the whole country—not feel that they in some small, unconscious way had also been celebrating the regime? During the tournament alone, twenty-nine people were disappeared. Ricardo Villa later said that if he had known what was going on, he would not have played. Huracán defender Jorge Carrascosa, who had played twice in the World Cup in West Germany in 1974, did refuse to be selected, although he never explained why. Even before the (unproved) allegations of match fixing made in the *Sunday Times* in 1986, the World Cup win was tainted, an ambivalence with which the players have had to deal. "Critics aligned us to the dictatorship, and we did not have anything to do with it," said defender Rúben Pagnanini. "I believe that the journalists never gave our team the credit we deserved. And common people are very much influenced by what the press says."

On a soccer-playing level, their frustration is understandable: after all, what were they supposed to do? "We suffered from the fact that the military junta was involved," said goalkeeper Ubaldo Fillol. "To many people, the World Cup in 1978 means 30,000 disappeared. But none of us tortured or killed anyone. We just helped our country to have a bit of joy, and we defended the Argentinian colors with bravery. I cannot be ashamed of that."

The dilemma is perhaps insoluble: To what extent is a nation its government? What responsibility do the people have for that, and to what extent is a national sporting team the manifestation of the country? After all, not only would it be illogical to blame the players for playing to their maximum, but many who were opposed to the junta actively supported *la selección*.

At the center of the conflict stands Menotti, louche and long-haired, a former Communist who spoke of freedom and lived a notably liberal lifestyle yet an agent, however reluctant, of the junta. Too often it's assumed that a national soccer-playing ideology is congruent with the ideology of the state. Sometimes it is—Vittorio Pozzo's Italy side of the 1930s, for instance, clearly reflected the brusque militarism of Mussolini's government—but the relationship is rarely simple. The turn to *anti-fútbol* after 1958 can be seen as the rejection of idealism, an embrace of (in some cases, extreme) pragmatism against a backdrop of coups, economic chaos, and military involvement in politics. The rejection of cynicism, similarly, ran in parallel with the optimism of the youth movement and the belief that joyless technocracy had failed. By the time Menotti won the World Cup, though, his romantic invocation of the past—even in the compromised form it eventually took—was diametrically opposed to the murderous expediency of the junta.

29

THE GYPSY, THE CAR SALESMAN, AND THE OLD WAYS

Some would argue that the counterrevolution against *anti-fútbol* began at Racing under Pizzuti in the midsixties, but, attack-minded as they were, it's hard to square the violence and gamesmanship of their matches against Celtic with the idea that they reestablished a romantic ideal—not, of course, that the golden age had been free from cynicism. River Plate continued to play attractive soccer throughout the sixties, the ideals of la Máquina still firmly in place. But the real self-conscious return of *la nuestra* began in Rosario with the Newell's Old Boys of Miguel Antonio Juárez and César Luis Menotti.

"Gitano" (Gypsy) Juárez was born in El Tala, a village in the province of Salta in the Andean northwest of Argentina. Although his talent for soccer was obvious from an early age, his parents made him complete his education, and so he played for a number of the smaller northern teams before joining Belgrano de Córdoba and then, in 1956, Rosario Central. He spent eight years there, helping them to third in the league in his final season. Juárez was gifted enough to be called up to the national side, being an unused squad player at the 1957 Campeonato Sudamericano and scoring the winner in the Copa Roca against Brazil the following year. He helped Unión de Santa Fe to promotion in 1966 and finished his career at Central Córdoba de Rosario, where he was appointed coach in 1968. Although they failed to win promotion out of the third flight, Juárez impressed enough to be appointed by Platense, whom he led to qualification for the Nacional. Despite a 4–0 victory over River at el Monumental, though, they finished fourteenth, and Juárez left at the end of the 1969 season.

It was what followed that made Juárez a key figure in the evolution of Argentinian soccer. He had played with Menotti, in his day a tall, angular center-forward, at Central, and in 1970 he was appointed by

Newell's—something that former Newell's playmaker Mario Zanabria believes would be impossible today. Zanabria is a voluble and enthusiastic talker, forever leaping to his feet to act out key moments, and, unusually among soccer players, he has a precise recall for detail: who scored, where they scored, what it meant. As he said:

> There was no such thing as an assistant manager at the time, but because he loved soccer and he was retired, Menotti would attend training sessions, talk to us, sit on the ball, give us advice. He had a car dealership on Boulevard Oroño, but that didn't interest him at all. He was with us most of the time. A few months later, I had hepatitis and couldn't play the friendly tournament in Rosario, between Central, Newell's, River, and Boca. Juárez had a chronic lung disease because he smoked too much. And he got sick during the tournament, and the team was coached by Menotti. Newell's won it after defeating Central and River. He was caretaker, while Juárez wasn't fit to train us.

From then on, they were effectively joint managers.

Juárez and Menotti implemented an attacking approach, and Newell's finished fifth in the Metropolitano to qualify for the Nacional for the first time. That winter they went to Mexico to watch the World Cup together. Menotti had played briefly at Santos and knew Pelé, but he was still awe-struck by how Brazil performed in that tournament, their success hardening his resolve to play in what he saw as the traditional Argentinian style.

30

THE LITTLE PIGEON

The black-and-white footage is so grainy as to be almost indistinguishable. A circle of light moves permanently up the center of the screen, scrolling from bottom to top and then coming around again at the bottom. Look closely and you can just about make out a dark figure entering the picture from the left, approaching a shadow. For a moment there is a flicker of clarity, and you see a soccer player checking onto his right foot and passing the ball outside him, out to the right wing, beyond the frame. There, in a world that lives only in memory and imagination, Jorge González controls the ball and shuffles it onto his right foot. You see a defender in the left-back position hesitate momentarily, just backing away. A dark spot appears on the film and speeds across the ghostly pale of center frame. A blur appears from the left and then slowly separates, like the blades of a pair of scissors opening. The part that dips intercepts the spot, and for a fraction of a second the image clears again. There is a goal frame. There are a number of players all turned away from the camera toward the net. There is a goalkeeper, bent away from the camera, right arm down, the slump of his shoulders suggesting despondency. There is a ball bouncing into the net. And there, picking himself off the ground, arms stretching up in celebration even before his knees have left the turf, is Aldo Pedro Poy, who has just scored the most important goal in the history of Rosario.

Still photos make clearer what happened: Poy, wearing the blue-and-yellow-striped shirt of Central, getting in front of his marker, Ricardo De Rienzo of Newell's Old Boys, plunging forward, meeting the cross with a diving, downward header that bounces over the line, the winning goal in the semifinal of the 1971 Nacional. All diving headers are known in Argentina as *palomitas* (little pigeons), but this is La Palomita, a goal that has a quasi-mystical significance. In that sense, it seems appropriate that the video is so hard to discern: matters of faith perhaps shouldn't be seen with too much clarity.

In Rosario soccer there is before and after that goal. Every year on its anniversary, Poy reenacts it, jogging onto a ball tossed from his right, leaning forward, lifting his feet, heading the ball into the net, and then picking himself up to be hugged by fans. "Two months after scoring, I was approached by some people who asked me to re-create the goal," Poy said. "We did it outside a bar. It was funny, but I never thought that it would become something that important. But they called me again to celebrate the first anniversary, in December 1972. The reenactment usually involves a dinner with friends, memories, and laughter. It's a reunion, with that very special moment of the diving header. Ever since, we've been doing the same mad act."

The *palomita* marked the moment at which the absolute stranglehold of clubs from Capital Federal was broken. They have continued to dominate Argentinian soccer, but it was then, in December 1971, that the Nacional was first won by a club from the provinces. The slightly odd thing, looking back, is that the game it won wasn't the final but the semifinal, a Rosario derby played at el Monumental the day after San Lorenzo had progressed to the final by beating Independiente in a penalty shoot-out.

"Rosario is a city that loves soccer, and the city is split in two," said Zanabria, at the time a twenty-three-year-old attacking midfielder with Newell's.

Unlike Buenos Aires, which has Boca-River as a rivalry but many other clubs and derbies, Rosario is just about these two clubs. And the pre- and postmatch atmosphere is loaded in a completely different way from what I've experienced in other places. In Rosario, when you win the derby, you're allowed to go out. And by this I mean walk on the streets, leave your house. But if you lose, you have to stay inside. You can't go out. Because you go to the supermarket, the restaurant, the parking garage, and the cashier, the waiter or the parking guy will be either happy or sad because of what happened in the game. It's very difficult, it's impossible, to stay away from that. In Buenos Aires, there's space for neutrality, and that space lets you live. Rosario doesn't have that space. As a professional, you know that the derby of Rosario will influence your life. You're part of the derby day in, day out.

All Rosario derbies were special, but this was more special than any other. "It's important to put things in perspective," said Poy.

Until that afternoon, the Rosarian clubs had never been involved in a playoff, a direct match in which one would advance to the next stage and the other would be eliminated. Tragedy or glory, depending on the result, awaited. There was massive panic. People leaving the city or locking up their homes, pretending that they had left, just to avoid what would happen if their side lost and the mockery they'd suffer. But also there was an instinct that said that whoever won the game would also win the final and become the first Argentinian champions from outside Buenos Aires.[1] We were two great teams, playing one game, 175 miles from home.

"The first half ended 0–0," said Poy. "In the second half, there was a corner kick, and I tried to make the defenders feel nervous. Before the cross, I shouted to a photographer, 'Get your camera ready. My goal is coming.' The keeper intercepted the ball and moved quickly to try to set up a counterattack. But we recovered the ball, played a short pass, then opened it up to the right from where González crossed it. It was too far away from me to try to kick it. My only chance was to try the diving header."

Fortunately, Poy was good at those, thanks to a theory advanced by Labruna's predecessor as Central manager Carlos Griguol. "With Griguol as manager, we would practice this kind of technique," Poy said. "There is a particular type of cross when you usually try to use your feet, when it's easier and more profitable to use the head. Griguol encouraged us to do *palomitas*. It wasn't because they were spectacular, but because there's practically nothing a defender can do to prevent them."

Central held out for the win and went on to beat San Lorenzo 2–1 in the final, played at Newell's three days later. It's that semifinal, though, that has lived on. "They will remember this goal for the rest of their lives," Poy said in his immediate postmatch interview, and he was right; the veneration goes on and on. "When I say that sometimes I lose my potential for being surprised, I mean these kind of things that happen in Rosario," he said. "One celebration gave me the creeps. I knew people were waiting for me outside my house, but as soon as I opened the door, I found two thousand Poys cheering and waving their hands. I couldn't believe it, but they were all wearing custom-made masks of myself."

The masks, complete with downturned, slightly melancholic rubber mustaches, have become a key part of the celebrations because Poy, however much he is treated as a deity, is not omnipresent and cannot be with every group of Central fans every year on the anniversary. "In different parts of the world, on December 19, a group of people meets, one pulls on the Poy mask, and they do the reenactment," he said. On December 19, anybody can say, "*Hoy, soy Poy*"—"Today, I am Poy."

The masks aren't even the weirdest memorial. "One day, Ricardo De Rienzo, the player who was marking me for the goal, felt bad and was taken to hospital," Poy said. "He was suffering from appendicitis and went directly to the operating room. The surgeons instantly recognized him. And after performing the operation, they didn't throw away his appendix but saved it in a jar of alcohol. It was donated to the Ocal,[2] as the closest appendix to Aldo Pedro Poy on the day of his *palomita* against Newell's Old Boys, a distance calculated as eight inches."

Such is his popularity in Rosario that Poy has to keep the location of his reenactments secret for fear too many people will show up, forewarned by the scenes at his wedding in 1974. "There were fans two thousand feet deep waiting for me outside the church," he said. "If I hadn't come out of the main door, I think they would have set the church on fire. The priest told me that he was going to do everything in five minutes, because people were already jumping on top of the confessionals and stealing angels as souvenirs."

He insists, though, that the adulation doesn't get to him, that he does not feel like a soccer-playing version of Bill Murray in *Groundhog Day*, doomed to live out December 19, 1971, over and over again. "No, no, I'm not trapped in a time loop," he said.

It's a pleasure for me to remember that day, because we really were a fantastic team with a fantastic coach. The other day, a very serious man who was walking along with a seven-year-old girl saw me and stopped. "My daughter, do you know who this man is?" he asked. The girl looked terrified, afraid of saying that she didn't. The father continued. "This man is Aldo Pedro Poy, and he . . . " The girl's expression suddenly changed: "Oh yeah, the one who scored the *palomita*," she said. I couldn't believe it. But it happens. Every single day.

31

THE MIRACLE OF HURACÁN

Juárez and Menotti left Newell's after that disappointment, Juárez returning to Salta and leading Juventud Antoniana into the Nacional, while Menotti took up the manager's position at Huracán. As he preached his romantic doctrine, with his hawkish face, his intellectual air, and his chain-smoking, he seemed the embodiment of Argentinian bohemianism. For him, there was no point in soccer without beauty. "To those who say that all that matters is winning, I want to warn them that someone always wins," he said. "Therefore, in a thirty-team championship, there are twenty-nine who must ask themselves: what did I leave at this club, what did I bring to my players, what possibility of growth did I give to my soccer players? . . . I don't give in to tactical reasoning as the only way to win; rather, I believe that efficacy is not divorced from beauty."

Menotti proved it by leading Huracán to the Metropolitano title in 1973 with an approach that was startlingly attacking, so attractive that fans of other clubs went to the Estadio Tomás Adolfo Ducó to watch. "Menotti always insisted on the concept of small coalitions: [Carlos] Babington and me, Russo and Babington, Carrascosa and Russo," midfielder Omar Larrosa explained. That was a team full of fabled creators, liberated by a well-defined defensive plan based around the power and aggression of Basile, who had left Racing in 1970.

Babington moved to West Germany with Wattenscheid 09 in 1974, but only after giving serious consideration to a move to Stoke City so he could experience life in the land of his ancestors: he was nicknamed "el Inglés" and was portrayed in a remarkable *El Gráfico* cartoon in 1973 as a Victorian gentleman, complete with top hat, cape, and monocle. For Brindisi, broad-cheeked and seemingly permanently bleary-eyed, full recognition came only later, but he was a player whose delicacy of touch seemed out of keeping with his stocky frame.

René Houseman would emerge as one of the great bohemian heroes of Argentinian soccer. He was poor, growing up in the *villa* of Bajo Belgrano, learning the game in the streets, and working night shifts delivering meat before he was signed by los Intocables (the Untouchables), a neighborhood youth club. He signed for Defensores de Belgrano in 1971 and Huracán two years later. The club's directors were worried by tales of his heavy drinking and so moved him into a rented apartment to try to get him away from what they saw as the bad influences that surrounded him. He soon returned home. The drinking went on; he admits it became an addiction. So reliant was he that, he says, he played a game against River Plate drunk. "The night before was my son's birthday," he explained in an interview with *Efdeportes* magazine. "My teammates gave me like twenty cold showers and a lot of coffee, but it was no use. I couldn't start the game and went on during the second half with the score at 0–0. I got the ball, dribbled past three defenders, the goalkeeper, and kicked the ball in. My teammates tell me that I fell on the floor and started laughing. I then proceeded to fake an injury, got subbed, and went home to sleep. I don't remember any of that."

For all that incident may have been embellished, there is no doubting Houseman's talent, his pace, or the problems he had with alcohol. He ended up winning fifty-five caps for Argentina and was hailed as Argentina's best winger since Corbatta, who, of course, had his own battles with drink. Unlike Corbatta, Houseman sought help, spent three weeks at the Hospital Durand, and claims to have been dry since he was thirty-seven. Whatever happened later, however much alcohol may have affected him, he was always loved at Huracán for his part in the 1973 side.

"To watch them play was a delight," an editorial in *Clarín* asserted. "It filled Argentinian fields with soccer and after forty-five years gave the smile back to a neighborhood with the cadence of the tango." So beguiling were they that when they beat Rosario Central 5–0, the opposing fans applauded them. "The team was in tune with the popular taste of Argentinians," said Babington. "There were *gambetas*, one-touch moves, nutmegs, *sombreros* [a trick involving lifting the ball over the opponent's head], one-twos, overlaps."

Huracán started the 1973 season with a 6–1 win over Argentinos Juniors, then won 2–0 at Newell's, 5–2 at home to Atlanta, 3–1 at Colón, 5–0 against Racing, and 1–0 at Vélez, before finally dropping their first point in a 3–3 draw at home against Estudiantes. "After that start, especially the victories away, we realized that we were capable of challenging for the title," Larrosa said. "But Menotti always told us to think about the next game and not the championship, adjusting details to play better. That was the most significant objective, to keep playing well. I always thought about winning the championship, because I joined from Boca and that's the way Boca thinks. We were normally nervous before each game, but on the field we enjoyed ourselves, we enjoyed each pass, we had fun."

Only when they lost 4–1 at Boca in the seventeenth round of matches were there any real doubts. "We considered it an accident, which shouldn't change how we did things," said Larrosa. "We had to think of the next game, forget about that accident, and keep going. And that's what we did." The loss of six players—first Houseman, Brindisi, and Roque Avallay and, later, Babington, holding midfielder Russo, and left-back Carrascosa to join up with the national squad for World Cup preparations—meant that Huracán stuttered a little toward the end, but the tactical framework was strong enough to overcome the absences. Boca actually scored seven more than Huracán's sixty-two goals that season, but it was the style that was important; there had always been an indulgence in the golden age. Who cared if it was not the most efficient soccer? It was beautiful and it won. A late penalty from Larrosa sealed the Metropolitano title with a 2–1 win over Gimnasia La Plata with two fixtures remaining.

The following year offered further evidence of the soundness of Menotti's method. Newell's were by then managed by Juan Carlos Montes, the number 5 of the side that had lost in the semifinal two years earlier, but the team was based on the foundations Menotti had left. Playing open, fluid soccer, they topped one group in the Metropolitano and Central the other. They were joined in a final pool by the sides that had finished second in their groups, Huracán and Boca Juniors. Newell's won their opening two games, while Central beat Boca but lost to Huracán. That meant a draw for Newell's against Central in the final game would win them the title. Just before halftime, though, Gabriel Arias put Central ahead from the penalty spot, and midway through the second half Carlos Aimar added a second. A Central win would have meant a playoff seventy-two hours later. "Imagine what the team's morale would have been if we'd lost," said Zanabria. Within seconds of Aimar's goal, though, Armando Capurro pulled one back. "That gave us more energy," Zanabria went on. "And imagine what it meant to win the tournament in their stadium, with a late equalizer . . ."

The footage is not quite as obscure as for Poy's *palomita*, but it's difficult enough to make out, shot from a camera located low down somewhere between the goalpost and the corner flag. The ball drops into a dark huddle of players from which the willowy figure of Zanabria emerges. He shoots, his foot seeming to flick at the ball rather than crash through it, but the strike is pure, and from outside the box it whistles just under the bar. "I'd taken shots from that distance before," said Zanabria. "It wasn't the first time that I'd done that, but sometimes they ended in the stands and sometimes, well, it's not that you aim there, you aim there in your head, but sometimes the foot reacts differently. And it was a magnificent goal."

It was, and it came with just two minutes remaining, sparking crowd trouble that caused the game to be abandoned. The result stood, though, and Newell's had their first title.

32

THE RETURN OF PERÓN

As General Lanusse had promised, presidential elections were held in March 1973. Héctor Cámpora, a longtime ally of Perón who had been acting as his "personal delegate" since 1971, won the first round of voting without securing an absolute majority, but Radical leader Ricardo Balbín withdrew to allow Cámpora to become president without the need for a second round. Cámpora granted an amnesty to those convicted of political violence under the dictatorship and established diplomatic relations with Fidel Castro's Cuba. Strikes and labor disputes continued under his presidency, but the revolutionary Left had, at least temporarily, ended its struggle. The way at last was clear for Perón to go back to Argentina. Like Menotti, he sought to restore former glories, to return to a time before the turmoil of the late fifties and the adoption of pragmatism as an ideology; unlike Menotti, he failed disastrously.

Perón's return immediately brought bloodshed, confirming that the divisions between the Left and Right, even within his own support, were irreconcilable. Police estimated as many as 3.5 million people massed around Ezeiza to greet Perón as he landed from Madrid on June 20, a crowd made up of three main factions. There was the working class, those who remembered what he had done to increase wages and improve living conditions in the forties and fifties. There was the Tendencia Revolucionaria, a left-wing grouping of youth movements, and the Montoneros guerrillas, who had organized a huge march to hear Perón speak. And there was the Far Right, which believed in the top-down direction of the masses and was thus opposed to the Montoneros. From the podium from which Perón was to address the crowd, camouflaged snipers fired into the left-wingers. Twenty-five were killed and a further 365 injured.

The massacre was designed to force Cámpora to resign and effectively shattered any thought of an alliance between the two wings of Perón's support. Cámpora stood down on July 13, and on September 23, twelve days after the coup that toppled Salvador Allende in Chile, elections were held that returned Perón to power with 62 percent of the vote.

On May Day 1974, 100,000 gathered at the Plaza de Mayo, more than half of them organized by the Montoneros, who saw the rally as a final opportunity to make contact with Perón and urge him to end the campaign of violence against them. The organizers had permitted only two chants—"Perón, Perón" or "Argentina, Argentina"—but instead, when Perón appeared on the balcony of the Casa Rosada, the Montoneros asked, "What's happening, what's happening, what's happening, General? The popular government is full of gorillas [the term having been applied to anti-Peronists within the military since 1955]." Perón was furious and, yelling into his microphone, replied that the "stupid beardless fools who keep on shouting should shut up." He then claimed they were mercenaries in the pay of a foreign power. At that the Montoneros marched out of the square, leaving Perón haranguing a diminishing crowd.

Two months later Perón, by then seventy-seven, suffered a heart attack and died. As his body lay in state, it began to swell and visibly decay, slapdash embalming producing a potent image of the state of the nation. "He was the army man who had moved out of the code of his caste and shaken up the old colonial agricultural society of Argentina; he had identified the enemies of the poor; he had created the trade unions," V. S. Naipaul wrote at the time. "He had given a brutal face to the brutish land of the *estancias* and polo and brothels and very cheap servants. And his legend, as the unique revolutionary, survived the incompetence and plunder of his early rule; it survived his overthrow in 1955 and the seventeen years of exile that followed; it survived the mob killings that attended his triumphant return last year; and it survived the failure of his last months in office."

The myth perhaps survived because the man himself was so protean: the disaffected could always rally behind him because there was always something in what he had said or done that could be adapted to their cause. He became, in the end, just as much of an empty vessel as Martín Fierro, into which the beholder could pour his own prejudices and desires. Perón's return, Naipaul went on, became ultimately about personal rehabilitation as he reconciled with the army and the church. But in tackling any of the problems he had identified, he failed, although, as Naipaul said, "perhaps that task of reorganization was beyond the capacities of any leader, however creative. Argentina is a land of plunder, a new land, virtually peopled in this century. It remains a land to be plundered; and its politics can be nothing but the politics of plunder." So much for the utopianism of Argentina's emergence as a nation-state, those lofty ideals overwhelmed by those of the earliest settlers, of Mendoza seeking his land of silver and Garay hunting in vain for the City of the Caesars.

Naipaul's vision was bleak, but his pessimism was proved apposite by the horrors of the decade that followed.[1] Perón was succeeded by his third wife, Isabelita, whom he had met in 1956 in Panama City when he was in exile and she, thirty-five years his junior, was a dancer at the Happy Land Bar. As Perón took his gloomy seat by the stage each evening to watch Isabelita, twice widowed and exiled from the country he had revolutionized, they weren't the only future presidents of Argentina in the nightclub. The bar manager, Raúl Lastiri, having allied himself with Isabelita, became head of the Chamber of Deputies and then took over as president for four months in 1973 after Cámpora stood down.

Lastiri's father-in-law, José López Rega, had been a corporal in the Argentinian police who quit in 1960 to write books about the occult,[2] one of which he claimed had been coauthored by the archangel Gabriel. He went bankrupt, fled to Brazil, became an adept of *candomblé*, and then, making the most of Lastiri's links with Isabelita, visited Perón in exile in Madrid, being taken onto his staff. He became highly influential, on one occasion persuading Isabelita to return to Perón after a marital disagreement and on another sorting out a scandal in a bank run by the Argentinian unions by turning up with a suitcase full of cash. By the time Perón returned from exile, López Rega was in charge of the aging president's medical treatment. It was rumored that he and Isabelita would manipulate Perón by denying him *dulce de leche*[3] until he had agreed to sign documents they gave him. It was López Rega who put together the right-wing AAA death squads, while Colonel Osinde, who had directed the shooting of the Montoneros at Ezeiza, was an undersecretary at his ministry.

Perón's death finally freed the Montoneros of their subservience to the cult of his personality, which had persisted to a degree even after May Day 1974, and they turned on the government. Initially, the Montoneros had been able to claim a Robin Hood–ish charm: they chose their targets carefully, largely avoided civilian casualties, and handed out food to the poor, but as they became increasingly disillusioned, they were also radicalized. Their campaign of kidnappings brought financial resources that allowed them to broaden their ambitions. In September 1974, for instance, they seized brothers Jorge and Juan Born, executives in Argentina's largest industrial company, Bunge y Born, and ransomed them for what was at the time the highest fee ever received by kidnappers anywhere in the world: $60 million. By then they were in a state of open warfare with the government. Their allies, the People's Revolutionary Army, remained in the jungles of Tucumán, but their attempts to replicate the Cuban revolution were thwarted by the fact that Argentina's army was better equipped and trained than Fulgencio Batista's had been. As the ERP suffered a series of defeats, the Montoneros came to the forefront of the leftist struggle and increasingly became the focus of the army's counterinsurgency campaign.

Argentina, by then, was all but ungovernable, certainly by somebody as inexperienced and as influenced by quasi-mystical advisers as Isabelita Perón.

33

OF HEROES AND CHICKENS

I met Norberto "Beto" Alonso in a café next to el Monumental, which in retrospect probably wasn't wise. He is one of River Plate's most iconic players, a classic number 10, and, as a result, our interview was frequently interrupted by fans wanting to shake his hand or have a chat. Alonso was sixty when I met him, slim and sprightly, his wide eyes still flickering with the mix of intensity and insolence that used to glare out from beneath a dark mop. These days his hair is cropped and silver, so he looks like the insurance executive he became when his playing days were over.

Alonso, as Argentinian tradition dictates all great number 10s should, learned the game in the *potreros*. "I grew up in Los Polvorines [a poor suburb of Buenos Aires]. There were three houses, and the rest were *potreros*. We'd play for money, for things, for the sake of playing, but I learned a lot in that period."

He soon developed as a creator, his upright style, head always raised, making him appear taller than the five foot ten he actually is.

The number 10 is a magnet for masses, for those who come from the *potreros*—even though there are no numbers there, especially a left-footed number 10. My father used to say, "Look at how eye-catching and how much virtuosity left-footed players have," and he was right, partly because the right-footed were always a majority and partly because the left-footed are more elegant. They have a different attraction, are always capable of pulling something out of the hat. I wasn't left-footed, but *mi viejo* [my old man; that is, his father] made me left-footed. I would stand still on my right foot, wait for a ball he'd send, and hit a volley using my left foot.

When Renato Cesarini left River in 1944, he was replaced by former center-half José María Minella, who was thirty-five and had just brought his playing career to an end after two seasons in Uruguay with Peñarol and another in Chile with Green Cross. Minella had been schooled under Hirschl and Cesarini, and under his management their philosophy was confirmed as that of the club. From then on there was no debate: River's game was about an attacking style and forward fluidity. "I never liked improvising," Minella said. "River had a tactical plan, a style, and that style was good; that's why we won so many games and titles. So why would I change it?"

After the 1947 title win, there was a slight dip. River finished second in 1948 and 1949, and then, as the exodus to Colombia bit hard, they finished fourth in 1950 and third in 1951, although only a point off the top of the table. By 1952, though, River were back. Over the course of six years, they won the title five times. For one Argentina squad in 1958, thirteen River players were called up; even their reserves were internationals.

But in 1957 it all began to go wrong. First, Sívori was sold to Juventus, although the proceeds were used to extend the stands at el Monumental, then, on Christmas Day 1958, the decision was made that Labruna's contract would not be renewed. River began to be haunted by misfortune, which seemed to translate into a lack of self-belief. It began to be said that they were always missing five *centavos* in the peso—lacking that little extra that would carry them over the line. It would be eighteen painful years before they won another title.

That long drought haunted Alonso's time in the youth ranks at River. It wasn't even decline as such, just a failure to win: during the drought, River finished as runners-up eleven times.[1] La Máquina had been known as the Knights of Anguish for the way they squandered promising positions and never quite took full advantage of their ability, but this was far worse, a saga of almost incomprehensible misfortune and self-destruction. The week they'd squandered a 2–0 lead in a playoff for the 1966 Libertadores to lose 4–2 to Peñarol, Banfield fans threw a chicken onto the field in mockery. The image stuck, and River became "*las gallinas*" (the chickens).

Near misses became standard. In the eighteen years of their trophy drought, River won more points (788) and scored more goals (1,112) than anybody else and had the second-best defense (685 conceded). Boca, San Lorenzo, and Independiente all had worse records but won five titles each. River, though, remained true to the old ways, still trying to live up to the ideals of la Máquina even after the rest of the country had adapted following Helsingborg. As Alonso sees it, he was lucky. Although he made his first-team debut at seventeen in 1970, it wasn't until 1972 that he became a first-team regular, and so he suffered only three years of the drought. In that season he scored the goal that first elevated him to the River pantheon, pulling off the trick Pelé had narrowly failed to against Uruguay at the World Cup two years earlier, dummying so the ball ran one side of the Independiente goalkeeper Pepe Santoro as he went the other. Pelé had dragged his shot wide, but Alonso nudged the ball into an empty net. Footage of the goal does not appear to exist, even though there is film of other goals in the game: it's one of a group of "phantom goals" from the seventies whose disappearance prompted *El Gráfico* in 2013 to launch an investigation. It seems most were cut from the original reels to be used in other programs, most likely news bulletins.

Roberto Perfumo, by then thirty-two, arrived from Cruzeiro at the beginning of 1975, to form a fine partnership with captain Daniel Passarella. A natural leader whose role defied conventional description, Passarella was a central defender and a hard man, but he was only five foot eight and would ease forward from the back line into midfield and beyond. A consummate penalty taker, he was the highest-scoring defender of all time until Ronald Koeman took his record. Throughout an eighteen-year league career that began at Sarmiento and took in more than 250 games for River Plate, with whom he won six league titles, in spells either side of a stint in Italy, he maintained the same neat side parting, a look that seemed to reflect his spirit of discipline and order.

Ubaldo Fillol had arrived the year before, while midfielders J. J. López and Reinaldo "Mostaza" Merlo[2] were both twenty-four and coming into their prime. Perhaps the most significant addition, though, was the appointment of Ángel Labruna for his third stint as manager. He gave Alonso the number 10 shirt he'd so craved and furthered the sense of continuity, convincing players that the values of la Máquina still had a bearing. Alonso said:

> It was a process, a process that was never abandoned, and Labruna, as a symbol of the club, knew the River style. He brought in the players that were capable of giving the extra support that the players from the academy needed to form the great team.
>
> We played with responsibility, but the focus was always on having fun. This is a game, always has been, and my belief was that if we didn't have fun on the field, we couldn't make people in the stands enjoy it. And that was important for us, for the River style. We were never like Boca: the styles were completely different. The same victory at el Monumental and la Bombonera could be taken differently. Boca's soccer was about strength and tackling; ours was about playing and passing. Some victories applauded at la Bombonera would have been jeered at el Monumental.

After drawing their first game of the Metropolitano season 0–0 with Estudiantes, River won their next nine, taking a lead they never looked like surrendering until a stutter toward the end of the season. Alonso was suspended for six games for assaulting a linesman, and although River won their first two without him, they then lost three in a row before drawing against Temperley. "It looked like the story was repeating again," said Alonso, "but fortunately when I came back, I scored two goals against San Lorenzo. Boca lost to Huracán, and we were virtually champions."

They still needed a win against Argentinos, a game played at Vélez, in the penultimate round of games to seal the title, at which everything suddenly became far more complicated. The players' union, determined to negotiate a collective working agreement and to secure the annulment of a suspension imposed on Banfield's Juan Taverna for doping,[3] called a strike. The matches went ahead, but teams could use players only from their Under-18 sides, resulting in some curious results: Boca beat All Boys 7–0, Atlanta beat Gimnasia 6–0, and Rosario Central won 10–0 at Racing. River's youth team got the job done, though, leading 1–0 when crowd trouble forced the game to be abandoned with four minutes remaining. Union officials ensured that the striking first teamers couldn't even perform a lap of honor until they returned to work the following week.

The coincidence is striking. Argentina changed their approach after a humiliating defeat at the 1958 World Cup, ushering in the days of *anti-fútbol*, and River stopped winning. Then Argentina changed their approach again after a humiliating defeat at the 1974 World Cup, returning to a more traditional style, and River started winning, as though they had to wait for soccer to return to their way of doing things before they could again lift a title. Alonso remembered Labruna telling his players, "If we survive this plague, the day we win the tournament, other titles will come like we're producing sausages." And so they did. River won the Nacional later in 1975 and went on to win the Metropolitano in 1977 before doing the Metropolitano/Nacional double again in 1979.

It was that first title, though, that lives on in the mind, partly because it broke the drought, but also because it confirmed that the days of *anti-fútbol* were over. Alonso recalled the sense at the time of the game being in flux, of a rich variety of ways of playing:

> Once you lose your style, it's like giving up your soul. Our flag was the flag of *la nuestra*, the traditional Argentinian and River school. Argentinian style is about what the people like. And the people have always liked nutmegs, *sombreros*, luxuries, dribbling, through-balls. The discussion will always be there: whether we must copy Europe or we had to force Europe to copy us. And it comes and goes over the years. But you can play well with both styles; you only need to have

the players and respect them. If you leave out your best player because of a tactical style, then you've started on the wrong foot. You can play well in any style, but you only can play well in the Argentinian way with one style, *la nuestra*.

But even after winning the two domestic titles, the *gallinas* label couldn't easily be discarded. They reached the 1976 Libertadores final and came back from 2–0 to level in a playoff against a Nelinho-inspired Cruzeiro, only to lose to a last-minute Joãozinho free kick. The Libertadores, it seemed, would remain forever out of their reach.

34

THE AGE OF THE DEVILS

These days Francisco "Pancho" Sá is a teacher on the coaching course run by the AFA at el Monumental. He's tall and slim with wire-rimmed glasses and a fuzz of short white hair and is so quietly spoken that, as we sit opposite each other at school desks in one of the stadium classrooms, it's not always easy to hear him over the shouts and squeaks of the five-a-side game taking place in the hall outside. He was born in Las Lomitas in Formosa, a province in the far North of Argentina on the border with Paraguay, but was always an Independiente fan, gathering around the radio with his parents and brothers and sisters to listen to games.

In the 1960s he was playing in the youth ranks at Central Goya. He joined them on professional terms the following year and in 1968 moved to Huracán de Corrientes, a team from the capital of the province. Only when he was twenty-three did he finally achieve the breakthrough of a move to Buenos Aires, but in two seasons at River Plate he played only two matches. It was at twenty-five, having moved to Independiente, that his top-flight career really began, but by the time he retired in 1982 Sá had become the most successful player in the history of the Copa Libertadores.

The team Sá joined, managed by the former Racing great Pedro Della-cha, had won the Metropolitano the previous season. Miguel Ángel Santoro, who had been in goal for the first two Libertadores triumphs, was just coming into his prime at twenty-eight, while the side's creative play was based around the craggy elegance of José Omar "el Pato" (the Duck) Pastoriza.[1]

They retained the Metropolitano, after which Dellacha was replaced by his former roommate Humberto Maschio, who had been working at the club as a fitness coach. He was fortunate to inherit not only a title-winning side but on being refreshed by an influx of gifted young players, foremost among them Ricardo Bochini, who, despite being described by journalist Hugo Asch as "a midget, ungainly, imperturbable, without a powerful shot, or header, or charisma," would become the most popular player in the club's history. In fact, his lack of obvious athleticism or star quality enhanced his appeal: in his overt ordinariness, he embodied the imaginative genius of Argentinian soccer, the kid from the streets who made good not by any advantage of upbringing or physique but through his untutored technical ability.

"I gave Bochini his first appearance," said Maschio. "He played thirty minutes and was wonderful. If I put him on the bench, people whistled at me. People loved him because they knew him from the third team and the reserves. Every single number 9 was a top scorer with him."

Bochini doesn't like interviews, but, after much to-ing and fro-ing, he finally agreed to meet me on my final night in Buenos Aires. He told me to wait for him at a particular street corner in Palermo at 9:30, but by 9:50 he hadn't turned up. I called him, but there was no answer. I was on the verge of giving up when, just before 10:00, he rang and gave me an address a couple of blocks away. Two minutes later he was answering the door, and I was in the apartment of Independiente's greatest legend, the man Diego Maradona idolized.

Yet Bochini, although he lives in one of Buenos Aires's wealthier neighborhoods, has a disarmingly ordinary apartment for one so feted. The front door opened onto a sparsely decorated main room: at one end a small sofa and two chairs clustered around a television that was showing a Copa Sudamericana match, while at the other was a dining table on which lay some half-done schoolwork. Bochini, the top of his head entirely bald these days, sat awkwardly on the sofa, dwarfed by the large padded coat he kept on throughout the interview. In his right hand he cradled his car keys, as though at any time he might decide enough was enough and make a break for it. He spoke throughout in a dry monotone: he wasn't impatient, exactly, nor was he impolite, and he gave his answers significant thought, but his relief was clear when, after forty-five minutes or so, I decided there was no more blood to be wrung from the stone. He was, I think, just extremely shy, his discomfort hard to believe in somebody who had been so wonderfully instinctive as a player.

Bochini was born in Zárate, fifty-six miles north of Buenos Aires on the west bank of the Paraná River, in 1954. He showed early talent, playing for Belgrano in his hometown and, at fifteen, was taken by his father for trials with San Lorenzo and Boca Juniors. Neither offered much encouragement, so he tried again, this time with Independiente's academy. "Nito Veiga[2] was the coach in charge," he said. "He saw me in action, believed I had quality, and then promoted me to the Reserves, for a match I still remember, Independiente versus San Martín de Tucumán, played in Racing's stadium, because Independiente were fixing their field. So I can say that I played in the Independiente jersey for the first time at Racing's stadium."

Belgrano de Zárate loaned him to Independiente the following year to play for the reserve side in the seventh tier of Argentinian soccer. Bochini carried on living in Zárate, though, meaning that every Tuesday and Thursday he would have to make the long journey south for training, as well as joining the squad on Saturdays for matches.

Still, it was such a difficult journey that Bochini considered quitting. "I grew up in a humble family," he said. "We didn't have much money, and taking all those buses and trains, plus eating, cost a lot. And the club didn't pay me expenses, so one day I decided not to commute anymore, and I stayed in Zárate for about two months. But then they convinced me, told me that they were interested in me and that I had a future, and I started training again. The following year they bought me, so I moved to the club's lodge for kids from the interior. We lived there. The long trips were over."

As Libertadores champions, Independiente went straight into the semifinal group in 1973 and again found themselves needing to win their final game to progress. This time their opponents were San Lorenzo, and this time they went through with a single goal from Miguel Ángel Giachello. In the final they met Colo-Colo. A Sá own goal gave the Chileans a seventy-first-minute lead in the first leg in Avellaneda, but four minutes later left-winger Mario Mendoza leveled, and it finished 1–1.

The second leg was played in as fevered an atmosphere as Sá can remember. "Chile was going through a very tricky time politically," he said. "President Allende was very weak, and a few weeks later he was overthrown. The atmosphere was amazingly hostile, from the moment we stepped off the plane, to the hotel, the stadium, everything," Sá remembered. "They threw bottles at the bus and they made us travel miles around the city to get to the stadium, which was a way to make us feel more nervous. The power was cut off in the dressing room and the tunnel: it was very Libertadores indeed. Years later, I bumped into [Romualdo] Arppi Filho,[3] who refereed that final, and I asked him which was the most difficult game he'd ever been part of. And he told me precisely that Colo-Colo versus Independiente match." Hostile it may have been, but Independiente held out for a goalless draw.

That meant a playoff, staged in the Centenario in Montevideo. Mendoza gave Independiente the lead, but six minutes before halftime Carlos Caszely, the top scorer in the competition that season, leveled. The game went into extra time, and two minutes after the break Giachello lofted the ball over Colo-Colo keeper Adolfo Nef for the winner.

Maschio left after that success, to be replaced by Roberto Ferreira, who had been the right-back in the Independiente side that won the two Libertadores titles in the sixties. He would last only a year before making way for the return of Dellacha. The rapid turnover of coaches did nothing to shake Independiente's continental domination and made less difference to the style of play than the emergence of Bochini and the arrival from Quilmes of the player with whom his name would always be linked: Daniel Bertoni, a winger with a knack for cutting infield who was rapid, direct, and the perfect foil. "They were two key men who enriched all that toughness we already had as a team," said Sá. "Bochini was an extraordinary player, and Bertoni was a stunning forward. Few people acknowledge this, but he was quick, strong, could shoot with both feet, dribbled, and scored a lot of decisive goals. And Bochini was like Iniesta, a talented, intelligent kind of player."

Bochini became a master of that most revered phenomenon in Argentinian soccer, *la pausa*, the moment when a number 10, poised to deliver a pass, delays a fraction, waiting for the player he is looking to feed to reach the ideal position.[4] Bochini's explanation of the skill suggests an extraordinary soccer intelligence, a capacity to visualize and predict the behavior of others that recalls evolutionary biologist Stephen J. Gould's assertion that most top sportsmen have a capacity to make rapid calculations that would see them hailed as geniuses in almost any other field. Bochini said:

> The way I see it, there are two types of *pausa*, or two ways of doing *la pausa*: with the ball going slowly or with the ball traveling fast. Sometimes you have to go fast, carrying the ball with you, to wait another player to come into position. It happened for example in a game against Olimpia [in the Libertadores group stage in 1984]. [Alejandro] Barberón gave me the ball and started running, and I had to go fast with the ball, but I was also waiting for him. If I had stayed in my position, without moving, it wouldn't have been possible to assist him properly, so I had to run, with the ball, but knowing that I was waiting for him to come into the best position to give him the ball back. I did, he crossed it, and we scored.
>
> And another time, against Grêmio in Porto Alegre [in the first leg of the Libertadores final in 1984], I had the ball on my foot, but I had to wait, because they were sitting back very well and there was almost no space, so I had to hold the ball against a marker, knowing that I had to wait for [Jorge] Burruchaga, who had already started running, to break the lines. We were close to the box, so there wasn't much space, and it had to be a very sharp pass. I waited, and then I gave him the pass, and we scored.
>
> This is the typical explanation of *la pausa*, waiting for a teammate by holding the ball. The first one, the pause in speed, is a total revelation; nobody knows about it [he emitted a brief and slightly unnerving chuckle], and almost nobody has done it. If I had stayed in midfield, he would have been a hundred feet away, and even if he'd managed to get the ball, nobody would have been in the box to get on the end of

his cross and score, so I had to run fast, but waiting at the same time, because we were in midfield and therefore with plenty of space but plenty of ground to cover.

Bochini believes the capacity to understand movement in such a clinical way is innate. "None of this is something that you can teach," he said.

I believe it comes in the moment; it depends on the inspiration of your players. You have to know how to make *la pausa*, and another has to know that while the teammate is making *la pausa*, he's also watching who's going to make the proper movement in order to surprise the opposition. *La pausa* without a teammate who collaborates is just holding the ball until, perhaps, you get fouled and waste some time, if you need to waste time.

It's important to have players capable of fitting your purpose. If you don't have quick players, like Barberón or Burruchaga, who like to make vertical runs, then *la pausa* is useless. But technique can and must be trained. I had my share from the *potreros*, but during matches—I believe more in matches than training sessions—technique can improve because you face the real situations of the game, and you have to resolve them as quickly as possible, and therefore the more precision your foot has, the better it is for the team.

The relationship between Bochini and Bertoni was devastating, a partnership that required very little work. "With Bertoni we understood each other from the very first time we played together, and we didn't have to speak about it," Bochini said. "It was just natural; it really felt as though we had been playing together for our whole lives, based on our personal attributes: I was quick and skillful; he was powerful and good for one-twos, what we call *pared* [wall] in Argentina."

That had an impact on how the team played. "With the emergence of Bochini-Bertoni, the team shape changed a little, not that much, but it changed," said Sá. "We tried to keep the tactical scheme: a lot of work from the guys up front, in order to keep the balance and never be weak. And we always had a brain. First it was Pastoriza. The whole team looked to get the ball to Pastoriza. And then Bochini took over as the brain. He was the creative lad, the one who made the difference, and we were his support."

If there'd been any doubt as to Bochini's quality, it disappeared in that season's Intercontinental final. In 1972 Independiente had faced the great Ajax of Ştefan Kovács, drawing 1–1 in Avellaneda, before being thoroughly outplayed in Amsterdam, where a goal from Johan Neeskens and two from substitute Johnny Rep gave the Dutch side a 3–0 win. In 1973, though, Ajax declined to participate, and Europe was represented instead by the side they'd beaten in the final, Juventus, with the game being played over a single leg at the Olimpico in Rome.

"The natural reaction," Bochini admitted, "was to doubt if we were going to be able to deploy our game against one of Europe's strongest teams, but on the field we noticed pretty quickly that we were equals, that we could dribble at them, that we were as quick as they were, or quicker." Juve's Antonello Cuccureddu blasted a penalty over the bar early in the second half, but then, with ten minutes remaining, came the goal that first established Bochini—and Bochini-Bertoni—in Independiente legend. Bertoni surged from halfway and shoved a pass to Bochini with the outside of his right boot. Around thirty-five yards out and with a little space, Bochini received the ball on his right foot, turning as he did so and jinking to his left as Claudio Gentile closed him down. Suddenly, there was a channel, and he accelerated into it. Bertoni, having run beyond him, pulled away into the center as Sandro Salvadore went to block off Bochini. Bochini pushed the ball right, Bertoni, playing the *pared* perfectly, nudged it back into his path from the edge of the box, and just as the ball seemed to have lodged under Bochini's feet as Salvadore and Silvio Longobucco closed in, he scooped it over Dino Zoff. It was the only goal of the game, and Independiente had become the third Argentinian side to win the Intercontinental.

It was a goal that took on a mythical status when the tape of the Argentinian broadcast was lost. Fans began to refer to it as "*el gol invisible*" until, in 2009, the support group Independiente Místico had the bright idea of going to Italy and asking state broadcaster RAI for a copy. Even without that intrigue, it was the goal that established Independiente as a global power and Bochini as a bona fide star.

He was instrumental in the Libertadores final the following year as well, scoring the opener as Independiente won the second leg 2–0 to force another playoff. It turned on two penalties. First, eight minutes before halftime, Pablo Forlán[5] handled a Bochini corner to concede a penalty that was taken by his Uruguay teammate Ricardo Pavoni, a veteran of the 1965 Libertadores final. The left-back still sports an impressive mustache, but whereas these days it is slightly grizzled, suggesting experience and authority, back then it was pure black and drooped down to his jawline, giving him the look of a mournful balladeer. "I'm going to take it, because I was the one with that responsibility, and obviously as I'm walking up to the goal, well, it starts looking smaller," Pavoni said. "Because also, bear in mind that you're about to take the penalty and you've got the fans singing, '*Uruguayo, uruguayo* . . . ' but that '*Uruguayo, uruguayo* . . . ' also means . . . score it.

You're *not* going to miss it." He crashed the kick straight down the middle as goalkeeper Waldir Peres dived to his left. Then, in the second half, Carlos Gay saved a penalty from Zé Carlos, and Independiente had a third successive Libertadores title. "That victory opened up the possibility of a fourth consecutive Libertadores," said Sá. "That was something huge because no other team had won four in a row."

Their biggest obstacle had less to do with events on the field than with the fact that Bochini was forced to do his military service that year. "It wasn't that bad," he said.

> For the first two months I would attend [the army base] nearly all the times I had to be there, but then they would allow me to leave earlier, play the games, until I ended up just going there once every fifteen days. My supervising officer was a Racing fan, but we never had an argument or anything, and over time we became friends; we had dinner together. Just one time I remember that military service training was so hard, so hard, that I came home exhausted. That night I had to play for Independiente, and I couldn't move. I really felt my muscles were like logs.

They had to beat Cruzeiro by three in their final semifinal pool match to reach the final but did so, thanks in part to an Olympic goal from Bertoni. In the final Unión Española were beaten after a playoff, and Independiente won a record fourth successive title, the sixth in their history.

Independiente's continental success was part of a wider pattern. Between 1968 and 1980 there were no Libertadores finals that did not feature an Argentinian side. As dominant as Argentina were at club level, though, it took the national team a long time to recover from the shock of the failure to qualify for the 1970 World Cup. Omar Sívori replaced Juan José Pizzuti as national coach in 1972, and, determined to put right what had gone wrong in the qualifiers four years earlier, he and the AFA decided to implement the plan Maschio had proposed to cope with the altitude of the away game against Bolivia. They selected a second-string side, including Mario Kempes and Ricardo Bochini, and sent them to Tilcara in the northern province of Jujuy, eight thousand feet above sea level, for acclimatization and special training. They became known as *la selección fantasma* (the phantom national team), and those there felt as if they'd been forgotten. Kempes later complained about the quality of the hotel and explained how so little provision had been made for the players that they had to increase their schedule of friendlies from the proposed two to seven, just to get enough money to buy food from the local supermarket. Even then he estimated he lost "eighteen or twenty pounds." The plan worked, though: having beaten Bolivia 4–0 in Buenos Aires and drawn away to Paraguay, Argentina won 1–0 in La Paz, leaving them to complete qualification with a 3–1 defeat of the Paraguayans.

Qualifying was one thing; prospering at a World Cup finals was something else. For all the glib talk of how they'd been moral champions in 1966, the cold fact was that Argentina's best performance at a World Cup had been their first, in 1930, when they'd lost in the final to Uruguay. Given those complaints of eight years earlier, there was something mischievous in the appointment of a British referee for Argentina's return to the World Cup in 1974, against Poland in Stuttgart—and not just any referee, but Clive Thomas, a Welsh official whose idiosyncratic interpretation of the laws ensured he and controversy were never apart for long.

Thomas, though, had little to do with Argentina's 3–2 defeat. They got off to a dismal start, with goalkeeper Daniel Carnevali dropping a corner to allow Grzegorz Lato to put Poland ahead after seven minutes. An awful pass from Roberto Perfumo allowed Lato to set Andrzej Szarmach away to make it 2–0 before halftime, and the center-forward hit the post after another defensive slip early in the second period. Although Ramón Heredia pulled one back with an excellent finish, a terrible throw-out from Carnevali soon allowed Lato to make it 3–1. René Houseman did pull it back to 3–2, but Argentina's self-destructiveness had been too much.

They undermined themselves against Italy in their second game as well. Argentina took the lead after twenty minutes, as Houseman lashed in Carlos Babington's through-ball at the top of the bounce, but fifteen minutes later Perfumo's attempt to clear Romeo Benetti's header skewed the ball into his own net. Argentina, having had much the better of the game until then, lost confidence, and the match petered out into a draw. That meant that to reach the second phase, Argentina had to beat Haiti and hope Italy lost to Poland, with a swing in goal difference of at least three. They did their part, winning 4–1, then watched anxiously as Italy were denied a clear penalty when Pietro Anastasi was tripped by Antoni Szymanowski with the goal gaping and went on to lose 2–1, allowing Argentina to progress at their expense.

Not that there was any great joy to be gleaned from a second-phase group that featured the Netherlands, Brazil, and East Germany. The performances of Poland had hinted at just how far Argentina had fallen behind the best of Europe, but the Dutch hammered home the lesson. The Netherlands were brilliant in that tournament, but perhaps never more so than when outclassing Argentina. Where the Dutch were imaginative, graceful, and sleek, Argentina were lumbering, predictable, and sluggish. It finished 4–0, but the sense was that if the Dutch had really wanted to, they could have scored at least double that.

Facing the reigning world champions, Brazil, in their next game came almost as a relief for Argentina. Brazil were nowhere near the side they'd been in Mexico, but they scrapped their way to a 2–1 win, which eliminated Argentina. The following day Perón died, and as a result Argentina's final match, a 1–1 draw with East Germany, wasn't even shown on television back home. It was a campaign that, for all the talents of Houseman and Babington, had never really gotten going, but the tournament had a profound impact. "I believe that was a huge benefit for Argentinian soccer," said Sá. "At the time, we had a very good crop of players, with good technique, but I think our problem was the physical side. We just hoped to win because of technique, by keeping the ball, or controlling the game actions with the ball. And the other teams made us feel the fitness gap that existed: we suffered, especially when we faced Holland."

35

LORENZO AND THE
BOCA FULFILLMENT

After the fourth Libertadores success, Sá was one of a number of players granted free transfers to leave Independiente at the end of 1975. He intended initially to go to Colombia, but before he left he received a phone call from Juan Carlos Lorenzo, the manager of Boca. "Before you go," he said to Sá, "please talk to the president, Don Alberto J. Armando. He'll be waiting for you." Sá did so, and although they didn't reach an agreement, Armando had a photographer take a picture of them shaking hands. "Think about it," Armando said. "You have until this afternoon." He decided he had to accept the offer.

Sá was approaching thirty by then, his best days generally thought to be behind him, but in his first season Boca won the Metropolitano, finishing the championship group three points clear of Huracán, who many said were playing even better soccer than in 1973. "There was one major difference," said Larrosa. "Avallay was injured, and [Osvaldo] Ardiles came in to play as number 9, but he was Ardiles, so he was virtually a number 10 playing up front, and we even had more possession than in 1973, with Brindisi on the right and me on the left, with [Carlos] Leone as 5. And that diamond made us have 70 percent possession, but we lacked the power of 1973. But in terms of the style, it was brilliant, even more similar to Guardiola's Barcelona."

Boca then signed elegant playmaker Mario Zanabria from Newell's.

I had six months of the Nacional in 1976 to adjust. At Newell's I was used to getting the ball and having time to juggle with it, perhaps trying first to make an individual attempt, and if I couldn't succeed, I knew that my teammates were all coming to me, because we played a short-passing style, and we were all relatively close to each other. At Lorenzo's Boca, it wasn't like that. When the 10 did get the ball, the other players didn't come to him; on the contrary they'd run away from him, waiting for the pass. So I had to learn to play quicker, not to waste a second, because I had to learn how to survive without my teammates if I lost the ball. So I almost learned to play without thinking, because taking a second also meant that your teammates could end up in an offside position.

Boca qualified for the quarter-final of the Nacional and then beat Banfield and Huracán—a game in which Zanabria excelled coming off the bench—to set up a final against River, played at el Cilindro. "That's the superclásico I remember the most," said Sá. "There were hordes of people there. It was one of the best crowds I've ever seen, even if Independiente had an impressive atmosphere because we had very few seats and it was mainly terracing."

Rubén Súñe scored the only goal of the game, a controversial free kick. As Fillol stood by one post lining up his wall, Súñe looked at referee Arturo Iturralde, who held up his hands, a gesture that signaled he was happy for the midfielder to take the kick when he wanted. A still photo shows Iturralde with his hands above his head, a gaggle of River players on the edge of the box in the act of forming a wall and Súñe, foot having just struck the ball, body angled back, watching as it floated inside the post that Fillol wasn't guarding. Some footage of the early part of the game still exists and can be found easily enough on YouTube, raising a host of conspiracy theories as to what happened to the film. Some have claimed River fans in the military destroyed the tape, some that the cameraman was distracted by a brawl, some that the film was burned in a fire. Súñe himself, when asked by *El Gráfico* as part of their 2013 investigation into phantom goals, said he hadn't seen the goal but that he knew who had film of it; he then refused to reveal any more. The most likely explanation is probably that given for the missing Beto Alonso dummy goal: that the clip was cut out of the reel for use in another program.

"It was the first time that the Boca crowd really made me feel emotional," said Zanabria. "It was unbelievable, to see them there, packing the stands, singing all the time. Half an hour after the final whistle, they were all still there, singing and waving their arms. It created a hallucination; it appeared that the stadium was moving, that it was made out of rubber rather than cement." It might not have been entirely an illusion. La Bombonera is made up of a low stand and towers of executive boxes down one of the long sides, with the other three stands forming a shallow horseshoe. When the whole crowd sings and jumps together, the structure perceptibly sways.

For Lorenzo, tactics and an awareness of shape were vital. "We'd call him 'Ghost,'" said Zanabria.

"Oh, today we have Ghost,'" we'd say, because he'd deploy our first XI against nobody. Not cones, not players. Nobody. Eleven against none. We played against ghosts. He'd pick the ball up with his hand, and perform all the movements that the opposition would do. "And when we come here, you, Zanabria, will be here, and your marker, González, will be there and will run at you, so you need to cut inside, and you [signaling another player] will run free and get the ball, provoking a two versus one in this zone." That was Lorenzo. And most of the things he said happened. It was the most modern thing that existed.

What made Boca most unusual in the context of the time was their goalkeeper Hugo Gatti. "We had a unique thing," said Sá, "a *libero* behind the *libero*. That second sweeper was Hugo Gatti, 'el Loco,' who was always ready to leave the area and play with his feet, or smash the ball away, if necessary." Gatti and Fillol, Boca and River, came to represent the two different traditions of Argentinian goalkeeping: on the one hand, the conservative Fillol who hung back, preferring to stay on his line and react to events, and, on the other, the extrovert Gatti, who would proactively leave his box, looking to cut out attacks almost before they had begun. "Fillol followed Argentina's traditional school, but with greater abilities," said Hugo Tocalli, who played in goal for Quilmes before a highly successful career as a coach. "I didn't see Carrizo [generally regarded as Argentina's best goalkeeper before the seventies] in action, but I believe Fillol was Argentina's best goalkeeper ever, at least from the ones I saw. Gatti broke through with a completely different style. And for years there was a question regarding which school was better. So Argentinian! Like Bilardo and Menotti. But the intelligent people, like Fillol, knew that he had to incorporate attributes from Gatti in order to be better, like playing with the feet, because Fillol was about the hands only."

In that, surely, Tocalli is right: there is something characteristically Argentinian both in the willingness to theorize and in the division of the world into two camps—*fillolistas* and *gattistas*—as though no middle ground could possibly exist between them. As Enrico Udenio pointed out in his anthropological work *La hipocresía Argentina*, there are times when Argentina feels like a land without gray areas. "We have two completely different styles," explained Gatti. "Fillol is a goal-goalkeeper who has difficulties coming too far out. He's all reflexes, but I live the game. I play it. I go out far to stop the play. I'm sure some of the goals I let in, he wouldn't, and that many shots I save, he wouldn't. The controversy is pointless; we just each do our own thing,"

Winning Metropolitano and Nacional in the same season, and so matching River's feat of the previous year, was good, but far more important was the path it opened to the Libertadores, a competition that had taken on the nature of a quest for Boca. "The pressure was huge," said Sá, "because Boca, a giant club, had never won the Libertadores, while other clubs, like Independiente, Estudiantes, and Racing, had."

Conceding only twice in ten matches, Boca reached their first final since 1963, where they met the defending champions, Cruzeiro. The fact that the team they had beaten in the previous season's final was River Plate did not go unnoticed. It was then that Boca fans first composed the chant that became famous: "We will bring the Cup to Argentina, the Cup that the *gallinas* lost."

Understandably, the buildup to the final focused on Nelinho, the attacking right-back who had destroyed River the previous year. "He was an incredible player," said Zanabria. "He would take shots from virtually any position, including from corner kicks. So Lorenzo was obsessed about how to stop Nelinho and how to prevent his taking shots. We couldn't make fouls in the last quarter of the field."

Carlos Veglio's neat finish was enough to give Boca victory at home, but Belo Horizonte was a different matter. Zanabria recalled:

> We were doing quite well, even though they had a devil, Joãozinho, a lethal left-winger who played fifteen times better at home. In the Mineirão they really made you feel their presence, and the heat was terrible because it was still daylight.
>
> I received the ball, and the Brazilian who was marking me stuck out his leg, so I went past it but the ball went a bit far ahead, and suddenly there was another one coming, so I stretched my leg but couldn't get to the ball, and instead I brought him down. And after that I immediately thought, "Oh, shit, I'm close to the box. Lorenzo will kill me." But when I looked back, the goal seemed miles away, so I felt relieved. It was about twenty-five to thirty yards, true, in Nelinho's preferred zone, but still, it looked far enough.
>
> But suddenly it was as if the whole stadium was performing witch-craft. We were waiting in the wall, and the manager came on the field, waving his arms. He knelt down, then Nelinho came, saluted him; they hugged each other; the fans were crazy singing and celebrating, a hundred thousand fans waving their flags, and we were still in the wall, waiting, looking at what was happening in disbelief, and we were all saying, "He's doing a *macumba*,[1] this fat *hijo da puta*." The manager

was still on his knees, praying or something, Nelinho crying and hugging him. We had six men in the wall, imagining Nelinho's typical shot. And it went past me, inches away from me, and that meant that it was going to end far from the post, but after that the ball started swerving dramatically and ended up in Gatti's goal. *Hijo da puta!* The whole ceremony took four or five minutes.

Cruzeiro won 1–0, and so the game went to a playoff at the Centenario. According to Zanabria:

> Lorenzo was mad, jumping from one room to another, and the only topic of conversation in each room was Nelinho. Nelinho this, Nelinho that. There was a tremendous storm in Montevideo—we were lucky to land, actually. The game had to be played forty-eight hours after the Belo Horizonte game, so we traveled on the Monday and had to play on the Tuesday. But the rain was so thick, the airport was going to be shut down, and so they finally decided to postpone the game twenty-four hours. Lorenzo was mad at all of us: "I'm fed up with this," he'd say. "Any step I take, I hear about Nelinho. You're finalists of the Copa Libertadores. Think of all the things we've done to be here, and you're all talking about Nelinho. We are strong. We can beat them."

As they arrived at their final training session, a journalist told the squad that Nelinho was injured. The players wondered if this was a ploy of Lorenzo's to boost their confidence, but when he gave them two tactical plans, one for if Nelinho was playing and one for if he was absent, they accepted he had nothing to do with the rumor. Zanabria remembered:

> The Centenario was like a swamp, water everywhere. Lorenzo told us, "If Nelinho is there, then all the balls go to [Dario] Felman." And in the end Nelinho played. So I received the ball after kickoff and passed to Felman. And he faces Nelinho and goes past him. The plan was to take advantage of Felman's speed and dynamism to try to bring Nelinho down. One, two, three times. Felman was a lighting bolt. Against Nelinho, he'd get the ball, brake, accelerate, brake. We knew that we had to be close, but just for the sake of it because we weren't part of that game: it was going to be him against Nelinho—that was our tactical plan. Five minutes later Nelinho made a gesture to the bench and was substituted. Incredible. The plan had worked. Felman had finished him.

It finished goalless and went to a shoot-out. Boca hadn't practiced penalties, and Zanabria very rarely took them, although he was Boca's regular corner taker. He was the second Boca player to step forward. "I was lucky," he said, "because I slipped, the ball went slightly higher than I was aiming for, and that helped me beat the keeper, who managed to get a fingernail to it but couldn't save it. They missed the fifth kick, Palhinha. It might have been different with Nelinho on the field. But it might have been different if we hadn't had Lorenzo, too."

The reaction in Buenos Aires was euphoric. "The welcome in Argentina was amazing," Zanabria said. "There was still a terrible storm, but we were escorted by fans all the way to [the training base at] La Candela. It took us hours."

The success gave Boca, as they saw it, the chance of greater glory in the Intercontinental Cup, in which they should have faced the European champions, Liverpool. But Bob Paisley's side, as a number of European champions did in the seventies, mindful of the battles of the past, declined the invitation, and so the team they had beaten in the final, Borussia Mönchengladbach, took up the challenge.

Gladbach seemed to have the advantage when the first leg, at la Bombonera, finished 2–2, but in Germany Lorenzo pulled what probably ranks as his greatest masterstroke. "He dropped some of the historic names," said Sá, who was one of them. "I was actually close to being picked, but I was carrying an injury in the back of my knee. I didn't tell him anything, but he would ask about it every day; he was so canny."

Felman had put Boca ahead after two minutes, but it was two goals in the space of four minutes that won the game. Ernesto Mastrángelo, either dithering appallingly or showing remarkable composure, depending on your point of view, converted a left-wing cross after thirty-three minutes. Four minutes later Carlos Horacio Salinas clipped in a third, and Boca were Intercontinental champions.

36

THE FIRST STEPS TO GLORY

In its own way, the humiliation against the Netherlands in 1974 had as profound an impact on Argentina's style as the defeat to Czechoslovakia in 1958 had had. The difference was that this time, the effect was felt across South America: the Dutch had also put four past Uruguay and outplayed Brazil in beating them 2–0. The conclusion that was widely drawn was that South American soccer as a whole was outmoded, that Brazil's success in 1970 with an approach that eschewed the systematized play that had widely been adopted at the highest level in Europe might not have been possible had it not been for the way the heat and altitude of Mexico restricted the capacity of players to chase and play pressing soccer.

In Brazil and Uruguay, the reaction to defeat was to increase the physicality of their play. Argentina had already gone as far down that road as it realistically could, and so, while certain clubs—Lorenzo's Boca most notably—remained extremely physical, at national level the response was to return to the more artistic soccer of the past. In October 1974 former Racing and River defender Vladislao Cap was removed as coach and replaced by Menotti, the philosopher prince of the old romanticism. Aware of the debt he owed to Juárez, of the similarity of their thinking and the way they could work through problems together, Menotti promptly brought in his former assistant to work alongside him.

Just a week after his appointment, Argentina played Spain in a friendly, and they drew 1–1. "It was just another example of the lack of organization Argentina had in those days," Menotti said. "The national team was not a priority. Club officials decided what was best for their own interest, leaving Argentina to one side. A month before a World Cup, they would call up a bunch of players who were doing well and put together a tour. With that recipe Argentina had never won anything in their history. So I presented a plan, starting in 1975, to see if the AFA was willing to change, to start from scratch, to set up a serious calendar."

In a long interview with *El Gráfico* in 1974, Menotti laid out six key principles: talent and technical ability were to take precedence over physicality and power; there was to be a "dialectical articulation" between physical and mental speed—no running without thinking or thinking without running; the team would use a flexible system of zonal and man-to-man marking; going forward, Argentina would look to use two wingers and one center-forward as the best way of outflanking the 4-4-2 prevalent elsewhere; possession was to be regained as soon as possible after the ball was lost; and players were to be made aware of belonging to a soccer tradition with a canon of heroes.

Menotti later insisted he had no style of his own but was restoring the people's love for "the inner nature of the Argentinian soccer player: his creativity." At the same time, he was aware of the ideological impact his side could have—in soccer, and perhaps beyond. "If we could win the World Cup the way I would like us to," he said, "it would inspire others to reassess the way we play the game—our basic philosophy. Perhaps it would also stop us relying so much on violence and cynicism, which are the tools of fear." They were words that resonated in the political context of the time.

Intriguingly, given Menotti in part owed his appointment to the success of the Dutch, he was skeptical about the lionization of Total Football, insisting their principles were little different from those that underpinned the traditional Argentinian game. "People talk of speed and strength," he said in an interview with *World Soccer* in 1975, "but this is just silly. Soccer is a question of space on the field, of creation and the restriction of space. I do not believe in so-called 'Total Football.'"

He divided the country into six zones and selected a squad for each, pitting them against each other. "There were critics saying that we were using too many players for nothing, yet of the World Cup–winning squad, 90 percent came from those teams," said Menotti. "It was very important. We had hundreds of files, compiled by people who worked for me or by people who knew about soccer. Sometimes it's easier to ask the shoeshine boy from each town rather than a coach if you notice that he has a good eye for soccer." Whether he actually meant that is perhaps less relevant than the appeal he was making to the past: soccer, he was saying, wasn't a game for the technocrats; it was for anybody who understood it, however humble their origins.

There was a huge overhaul of personnel: of the thirteen players who played against Spain in Menotti's first game, only René Houseman made it into the World Cup squad four years later. The first sign Menotti was beginning to build something came in the prestigious Toulon Under-21 tournament in 1975, which Argentina won with a team including Daniel Passarella, Alberto Tarantini, Américo Gallego, and José Daniel Valencia. The Copa América (as the Campeonato Sudamericano was rebranded as it began again that July with a new home-and-away format after an eight-year hiatus) was a disappointment, as Argentina went out in the group, two demolitions of Venezuela irrelevant beside two defeats to Brazil. But the sense was of something beginning to stir, and Menotti had three years to get it right.

> The team is always formed and oiled off the field. Thinking otherwise is a mistake. You can never be a team on the field if you are not a team when the match is over. We were on tour in Europe [in March 1976], and it was nothing to do with a tour of professional and bourgeois players. We were soccer workers. Traveling from Kyiv to Moscow, after one and a half days without eating, we got a sausage and a loaf of bread. One slice for each player. From there we went to Warsaw, then traveled eight hours in a snowstorm in a bus to get to Hungary. And those were the best games, in which our players ran the most. There was this inevitable hunger of glory. You could sense it.

37

GLORY IN A TIME
OF TERROR

By the beginning of 1976 the cycle of violence and economic failure was beginning to spin out of control. Isabelita Perón had been left hopelessly exposed by the death of her husband, and by March monthly inflation had hit a record 56 percent. After Perón's death, there had been nothing to draw the radical groups to the center, and the result was an explosion of violence. As left-wing guerrillas clashed with paramilitary groups tacitly sanctioned by the state and the rightist wing of the Peronists, a bomb went off in Buenos Aires on average every three hours, and there was a political assassination every five hours.

Everywhere there was chaos. On February 5, Isabelita's forty-fifth birthday, she appointed her sixth economic minister since taking office in July 1974. In the week that followed, the daughter-in-law of former president General Lanusse was murdered by left-wing paramilitaries; Father Francisco Suárez, a member of the Third World Movement of Catholic priests, was killed with his brother in Tigre by a right-wing death squad; while the army announced the deaths of several dozen guerrillas in Tucumán. The bodies of the victims of the murder squads would be left in the streets on the outskirts of Buenos Aires as a warning to others, and in January and February alone there were thirty-two kidnappings in Córdoba. It became less a matter of if than when the military would take power again.

The final straw came on March 15 as a bomb exploded in the parking garage of a military headquarters in Buenos Aires, killing one person and injuring twenty-nine others. General Videla, at the time a senior commander of the army, narrowly escaped. On March 24, as River Plate beat Union Portuguesa 2–1 in the Copa Libertadores, the military seized power. Isabelita was taken in a helicopter from the roof of the Casa Rosada, in theory to go to her official residence, but the pilot landed at Ezeiza, where she was transferred to a plane to take her to Neuquén, in the southern Andes. She pointed out that she had no warm clothes to wear—a detail that hinted both at her priorities and perhaps at a lack of detailed planning by the coup leaders[1]—and so was allowed to write out a list of clothing for her captors to bring.

The same day hundreds of union officials were taken to ships moored in the River Plate and shot—murders that had been sanctioned by Isabelita the previous year. The junta went further and instituted the Proceso de Reorganización Nacional, which defined Argentina as a Christian country fighting communism. Over the seven years that followed, thirty thousand people were killed in the name of that cause. Congress and the judiciary were shut down, political parties were banned, and the press was forbidden "to inform, comment or make reference to subjects related to subversive incidents, the appearance of bodies and the death of subversive elements and/or of members of the armed and security forces in these incidents, unless they are reported by a responsible official source."

As so often elsewhere, the soccer terraces, where the weight of numbers offered a sense of anonymity, became a locus for limited dissent. There was, for instance, a widespread belief that Huracán were a pro-Montoneros club, although what that actually meant is hard to ascertain. Clubs are nebulous entities, their fan bases usually composed of a broad range of background and belief: Huracán's support was fairly evidently broadly leftist, but that's not to say all or even a majority of their fans supported the guerrillas, and certainly there was no official expression of political opinion. It is true, though, that before a game in May 1976 between Estudiantes and Huracán, Montoneros hung a banner in the away end. It was ripped down, and at half-time police moved into the stand, firing live rounds. A thirty-eight-year-old auctioneer, Gregorio Noya, who was at the game with his sixteen-year-old son, was killed. Police blamed "left-wing terrorists," and such was the familiarity of violent death and the servility of the media to the new regime that the incident passed almost without note.

FIFA had made the decision that Argentina should host the 1978 World Cup in July 1966; ten years later, it presented the junta with a huge problem. A tournament afflicted by bomb attacks and kidnappings was unthinkable; the World Cup had to be used to show that the coup had brought stability, that Argentina was safe. The prospect of global embarrassment might not have directly influenced the timing of the overthrow of Isabelita, but it didn't take long after the military had taken power for it to identify the World Cup as a priority and take control of the Ente Autárquico del Mundial (EAM), the local organizing committee. Decisive action was desperately needed: so far behind were Argentina's preparations that FIFA president Stanley Rous sounded out Montevideo and Porto Alegre about offering support and considered moving the tournament to Spain. But João Havelange, the Brazilian who succeeded Rous in 1974, insisted as early as 1972 that the only thing that would prevent Argentina from hosting the tournament was its economy, the poor performance of which he—typically—put down to "internal disturbances." There were significant doubts inside the country as well. "The 1978 World Cup," wrote Dante Panzeri, the editor of *El Gráfico*, in 1975, "should not take place for the same reasons that somebody who doesn't have enough cash to put gas into a Model T Ford shouldn't buy himself a Torino. If he does that, it's because he's stealing from somebody."

Around 10 percent of the national budget, more than $700 million (although the official total was only $521,494), was spent on remodeling the stadiums of River Plate, Vélez Sarsfield, and Rosario Central; building new grounds in Córdoba, Mar del Plata, and Mendoza; constructing a press center and facilities for color television transmission; and improving airports and roads. Most controversially, there was also the redevelopment of Buenos Aires, the most scandalous aspect of which was the construction of a vast concrete wall to hide the view of the *villas miserias*—the shanty towns—from the highway into the center of town from Ezeiza. Juan Alemann, the secretary of the treasury, described the World Cup as "the most visible and indefensible case of nonpriority spending in Argentina today." Organizers tried to justify the expenditure by saying it would be recouped by the arrival of an estimated fifty thousand tourists. Even that number wouldn't have come close; as it was, fewer than ten thousand turned up.

Finances were only part of it. The tournament logo, adopted in 1974, showed a pair of blue and white lines sweeping vertically upward before parting to embrace a soccer ball, deliberately evoking Perón's arms-aloft gesture. The EAM was well aware of the symbolism but concluded that a redesign—and the recall of merchandise and advertising it would have entailed—would only have drawn more attention to the former president.

General Omar Actis, who had played for River Plate's third team in the forties, was put in charge of the EAM, but in August 1976 he was killed by a car bomb. The attack was blamed on "subversive elements," but there is widespread suspicion, best articulated by Eugenio Menéndez in his book *Almirante Lacoste: ¿Quién mató al General Actis?*, that his assassination was planned by Admiral Carlos Alberto Lacoste, who replaced him as the head of the EAM and, it's alleged, subsequently embezzled millions from the World Cup funds.

A more robust media, perhaps, would have investigated that at the time, but the junta repressed dissent. Or at least forces unleashed by the coup did. On the first anniversary of the coup, journalist Rodolfo Walsh, who had exposed the Aramburu repression in 1957, sent an open letter to the junta asking about the dead, the imprisoned, and the missing. A day later he was murdered.

It would be misleading, though, to think of the junta as a single coherent entity; rather, there were a multitude of official and semiofficial bodies who carried out the atrocities of the Dirty War, run by the army, the navy, the air force, the National Gendarmerie, federal as well as city and provincial police, various ministries, and even YPF, the state oil company, each acting according to its own interest or trying to do, without direct authorization, what its leaders thought the junta might want. In such a climate, the forces of terror soon slipped out of control. While the program of abduction, torture, and murder might at first have been targeted at political opponents of the regime, it wasn't long before victims were selected so their property could be appropriated or to satisfy the perversions of their captors, made clear in Jana Bennett and John Simpson's book *The Disappeared*. In such a climate, the slightest sign of opposition, offering the slightest excuse to the intelligence services, could be fatal.

In that regard, the World Cup offered an opportunity: it was much easier to disappear an Argentinian than a foreigner. Accordingly, Amnesty International encouraged journalists to be vigilant for signs of oppression. Videla responded with the slogan *"Los Argentinos somos derechos y humanos"* (We Argentinians are honest and humane).

Many Argentinians simply couldn't believe their government could wage such a war on its own citizens, despite the efforts of those who had suffered to bring the Dirty War into the public domain. As early as April 1977, the mothers of some of those who had disappeared began to meet at the Plaza de Mayo to demand information and draw attention to the crimes of government agencies. Soon the march of the *madres* became a weekly event, as they made their poignant circuits of the Pirámide, holding aloft photographs of their missing children. Three of the original leaders—Azucena Villaflor, Esther Careaga, and María Eugenia Bianco—were subsequently themselves disappeared. The movement has become divided, but still, every Thursday, the *madres* gather in the Plaza de Mayo. During the World Cup, the *madres* became such a feature of international media coverage that West Germany goalkeeper Sepp Maier planned to join them before being warned off.

There was also the actual soccer for the junta to consider. The government needed a good performance from Argentina for reasons of morale, recognizing that success could create a sense of national euphoria and togetherness. The players, Videla said, were obliged "to show that they were the best of the nation and the best Argentina could present to the universe . . . and they were obliged to demonstrate the quality of the Argentinian man. This man who at the individual level or working in a team is able to carry out great enterprises when guided by common goals. . . . I seek from you the victory, to be the winners of the World Cup, winners because you will show courage in the games . . . and will be the right expression of the human quality of the Argentinians."

Menotti was clearly uncomfortable with the nationalist rhetoric that surrounded the team and sought to dispel the notion that his side was somehow representative of the government. "Playing we did not defend our borders, the motherland, the flag," he insisted in 1977. "With the national team nothing essentially patriotic dies or is saved." He saw himself playing less for the nation than for the great traditions of Argentinian soccer, through which the spirit of the people was tenuously expressed.

That didn't, though, make him any less determined to win. Menotti was meticulous in his planning and, in October 1976, persuaded the Argentinian federation to ban the sale of players to foreign clubs until after the World Cup. Of the twenty-two players on the squad for the finals, only Mario Kempes of Valencia was based abroad.

Not everybody was convinced by Menotti. Juan Carlos Lorenzo always lurked in the background, muttering that his reinterpretation of *la nuestra* had no hope of success against European opponents. There are even suggestions that Menotti would have been fired after the junta took power had the AFA had the money to pay up his contract.

It was precisely that thinking, though, the idea that the Europeans—inasmuch as Europeans could be bracketed together—could be taken on only at their own game, that Menotti was determined to challenge. The stylistic revolution of 1958 responded to defeat by a European side by moving toward a "European" model; the revolution of 1974 responded to defeat by a European side by moving away from it. "We had to get rid of the idea that in order to win, we had to play as the Europeans did," Menotti told *El Gráfico*.

> That was the wrong concept, thinking that we wouldn't be able to cope with them physically. . . .
>
> So I stuck to the idea of shaping the team I wanted to see: ball possession, rotation, and endless attacking movements, balanced with a very intelligent midfield commander, Américo Gallego, who for us was the Clodoaldo of Brazil in 1970. Defending without attacking is easy: you sit back and that's it. But we were not going to play a World Cup; we were going to win a World Cup. And to do so, we needed to think how to attack even when we were defending.

Pace became central to Menotti's conception and led him to omit the squat Bochini, even though Bertoni, Rubén Galván, and Larrosa were called up from the Independiente side that won the Nacional in 1977 and 1978. Larrosa found that emphasis on physical fitness the major difference between the Menotti he had previously played for and the one who led Argentina at the World Cup.

> He was the same when it came to thinking, philosophy, ball possession, but a completely new Menotti in terms of fitness, diets, and

training. Until then, it was common that before the games, we'd eat a *bife de chorizo*[2] with fries and salad, and we were used to that, even if some days you'd feel a bit full. Then Dr. [Rubén] Oliva came and told us that we needed pasta, and if possible without sauce, just olive oil or cream. And we'd say, "No, pasta makes you fat." But pasta— no stuffed pasta, of course—gave us more energy and the certainty that the food had already been processed by our bodies by kickoff, as opposed to the food we were eating before, which was probably still in our stomachs when we ran onto the field.

The tactical work changed, too. We worked a lot on pressing. Menotti would make us play soccer in reduced spaces, two against two, things like that, to improve our awareness. There were squares of fifty feet, and I'd play with the 5, against the 8 and 5 of the opposition. At Huracán, our mission when we lost possession was to retreat behind the line of the ball and wait to get it back. With Argentina, if we lost possession, we had to press for the ball, and to press for the ball, we needed to be close to each other, and that was the main concept of the team: *achique*—squeezing the space. Huracán retreated; Argentina pushed forward.

Ultimately, Menotti's decision to prefer Kempes in that attacking central midfield role was vindicated, but that Bochini failed even to make the squad caused some consternation. Beto Alonso, who effectively took his place, was clearly also a supremely gifted player—he ended up coming off the bench twice before his tournament was ended by injury—but there were rumors that the main reason he had been preferred was that he was the favorite player of Admiral Lacoste.

Larrosa's inclusion was also the source of some debate after an incident in the final of the previous season's Nacional. Independiente had drawn the home leg 1–1 against Talleres and took a first-half lead through Beto Outes's *palomita*. "It was such a difficult game," said Larrosa. A dubious penalty, given for a handball by Rubén Pagnanini, although the ball seemed to strike his chest rather than the arm, allowed Talleres to level on the hour, before, with sixteen minutes remaining, Ángel Bocanelli scored with his hand. Independiente protested so furiously that Larrosa, Galván, and Enzo Trossero were all sent off. "We probably called him everything but 'nice man,'" Larrosa said. Trailing, and down to eight men, the situation seemed hopeless. "They had two or three goal chances," Larrosa recalled, "and the one that had scored with his hand squandered two chances by being too selfish. And then Bochini got the ball, he played a one-two with Bertoni, shot, and it was a great goal, a *golazo*. I was watching from the tunnel with the other two sent-off players. And we couldn't believe it. After that, it was five minutes, plus stoppage time. And it was so clear that the ref was trying to bring us down that I wanted to invade and get the match suspended."

Larrosa restrained himself but was still given a twenty-match ban. "Some suggested that it'd be fair if I didn't play in the World Cup since I was still suspended from club soccer."

Looking to play down the militarism of his regime, Videla wore an ordinary suit rather than his uniform for the tournament's opening game, a goalless draw between West Germany and Poland. Before kickoff he gave a short speech in which he spoke of "a World Cup of Peace." *El Gráfico* wasn't alone among the local media in insisting that the staging of that first game exposed the "campaign of lies" that it alleged had been perpetrated against Argentina by internal opponents and outsiders with an agenda.

Argentina's entrance for their first fixture, against Hungary at el Monumental the following day, was dramatic, the teams walking out amid a blizzard of ripped-up paper, the cascades of ticker tape remaining one of the indelible images of the 1978 World Cup. Once the game had begun, it all seemed worryingly like 1974, as Hungary took the lead after nine minutes, Károly Csapó knocking in the rebound after Fillol had parried Sándor Zombori's shot. This time, though, there was a response. Five minutes later the authoritative Gallego was tripped by Péter Török just outside the box. Sándor Gujdár fumbled Kempes's low free kick, and River forward Leopoldo Luque forced in the loose ball. The extravagant celebrations suggested just how much of a relief the goal was. On the bench Menotti remained impassive, jutting his chin through the points of the upturned collar of his coat to take another drag on a cigarette. With nine minutes to go, it was still level. Then Gallego lofted a long pass forward to Luque, who chested it off for Beto Alonso. Twenty yards out he might have tried a shot, but as the ball bounced up, he nudged it forward into the path of Luque. Zoltán Kereki made a stretching tackle, but his goalkeeper had left his line and the ball bounced square for Daniel Bertoni to jab the ball into an untended net. It had been a game of repeated minor tangles, blocks, and obstructions—precisely the sort of tactical fouling Glanville had railed against twelve years earlier—and, in the final seconds, Hungary's frustration spilled over. First, András Törőcsik collected a second yellow card, thrusting an arm into Gallego's midriff as the Argentinian challenged him from behind, and then Tibor Nyilasi followed him after a dreadful high tackle on Tarantini.

France had lost their opening game to Italy, so, with Italy beating Hungary, they knew defeat against the hosts in their second match would eliminate them. Argentina won 2–1, thanks to a controversial penalty and a brilliant dipping twenty-five-yard strike from Luque.

With Italy and Argentina already through, their meeting in the third game mattered only insofar as it determined who would finish top of the group, but it did have profound consequences. Italy won 1–0, Roberto Bettega scoring a superb goal after receiving a pass from Giancarlo Antognoni and playing a sharp one-two with Paolo Rossi. Argentina were noticeably less prone to the cynicism of which they had at times been guilty in their first two games, kept in check by Israeli Abraham Klein, who was probably the best referee in the world at the time. He was in little doubt that the referees for Argentina's first two games, António Garrido of Portugal and Jean Dubach of Switzerland, had allowed themselves to be influenced by the crowd. "You can ask Platini what he thinks about that game," Klein told Rob Smyth in a 2012 interview in the *Guardian*. "You can ask Hungary for their opinion about that game."

Klein turned down two Argentina penalty appeals before halftime and was viciously abused as he left the field at the break. "The crowd was very upset," he said. "I had no problem with the players; they respect me. The crowd, you know, they pay, and when they pay they can tell you whatever they think about you and your mother." He later described the feeling as "very bad," but he gave the impression of absolute calm as he waited in the center circle for the players to head off down the tunnel. "There was nothing more impressive in this World Cup," wrote Brian Glanville in his history of the tournament, "than the way he stood between his linesmen at halftime in the Argentina-Italy game, scorning the banshee whistling of the incensed crowd."

Klein opted not to lead the players out for the second half but to follow Argentina, so any negative reaction toward him was lost in the adoration of the home side. "I felt stronger in the second half because I know all my decisions were correct," he said. "I feel very good with this. Even after the game, they told me, 'Don't go out. The crowd is waiting for you.' I told them, 'I'm not afraid.' I was never afraid in my career. I know that the crowd will do nothing after the game. I was not afraid to do what a referee must do in the game. There was no problem." Klein was praised across the world.

When Klein then had another excellent game in the second-phase game between Austria and West Germany, he was considered a certainty for the final. Pelé, Glanville, and Jack Taylor, who had taken charge of the 1974 final, all said so. But not the refereeing commission, which apparently on the casting vote of their Italian chairman, Artemio Franchi, and, it was rumored, after protests from Argentina, favored Franchi's compatriot Sergio Gonella, a decision Clive Thomas described as an "utter disgrace." "To tell you the truth, I was very disappointed," said Klein. "I think at that time I was fit to referee the final. But only one man can referee the final, and if I look back I am still happy with what I had in my life, in my refereeing life." The Dutch, perhaps, were less philosophical.

Before the final, though, there was the second-group stage to negotiate. Having finished second in the group, Argentina had to move from Buenos Aires and el Monumental to Rosario and el Arroyito, which might actually have been an advantage. Although the capacity was much smaller—forty thousand as opposed to seventy thousand—it was a compact stadium and generated a ferocious atmosphere. With Luque, whose brother had been killed in a car crash on the day of the Italy game, missing with an elbow injury sustained against France, Kempes was shuffled farther forward for the match against Poland, with the unpredictable talents of Houseman introduced behind the front three. Kempes, at last, showed why Menotti had been prepared to waive his guideline of selecting only Argentina-based players for him, breaking an eleven-game scoring drought as he darted to the near post to nod in Bertoni's cross after sixteen minutes.

Kempes also made a critical intervention seven minutes before halftime, diving to his right on the goal line to claw away a Lato header. In the modern era it would be as clear a red card, as you could imagine, but in those days a penalty sufficed. Kazimierz Deyna, in his one hundredth appearance for his country, struck his effort too close to Fillol, who saved low to his left. An Ardiles surge teed up Kempes to sidestep Henryk Maculewicz and seal the win eighteen minutes from time.

A brutal goalless draw against Brazil followed, the tone set in the opening ten minutes in which there were seventeen fouls. When Brazil then won 3–1 against Poland, it meant that Argentina had to beat Peru by at least three, while scoring at least four, in their last-group game to make the final. It's a match now tainted by suspicion, with Brazilians muttering darkly about conspiracy and pointing out that Peru's goalkeeper, Ramón Quiroga, had been born in Argentina.

Eight years later, on the day Argentina met England in the World Cup quarter-final in Mexico City, the *Sunday Times*, citing an anonymous civil servant, claimed that the Argentinian government shipped thirty-five thousand tons of grain—and possibly some arms—to Peru and that the Argentinian central bank released $50 million of frozen Peruvian assets. In 2012 a former Peruvian senator, Genaro Ledesma, gave evidence to a Buenos Aires judge that the game had been thrown as part of the Condor Plan, a grim agreement between a number of South America's dictatorships in the seventies to help each other deal with dissidents. Ledesma claimed that Peru's military leader Francisco Morales Bermúdez sent thirteen prisoners to Argentina to be tortured and that Videla accepted them only on the condition that Argentina got the result they required. "Videla needed to win the World Cup to cleanse Argentina's bad image around the world," said Ledesma, an opposition politician in Peru at the time who also says he was subjected to intimidation and torture. "So he only accepted the group if Peru allowed the Argentina national team to triumph."

Even more remarkable are the testimonies of several Peruvian players. "Were we pressured? Yes, we were pressured," midfielder José Velásquez told Channel 4. "What kind of pressure? Pressure from the government. From the government to the managers of the team, from the managers of the team to the coaches." Much was made of the fact that, having had an extremely good tournament, he was substituted after fifty-two minutes. "Something happened," he said. "Our team was changed. I was replaced in the tenth minute of the second half—when we were already losing by two goals. There was no reason to change me. I was always an important piece in our team. So what can one think?" That seems damning, except that Peru were actually 4–0 down when Velásquez went off; if removing him was part of a grand plot to secure an Argentinian victory, it happened too late to make any material difference.

There is, though, another odd detail. Shortly before kickoff, the Peruvian team was visited in their dressing room by Videla and Henry Kissinger, whose eight-year term as US secretary of state had ended in January the previous year. Kissinger was a lifelong soccer fan, and his pragmatic political outlook had led him to support Videla, so there is some logic in his being there, although his office claimed he had "no recollection" of having been in the Peru dressing room. Videla's visit, whether with Kissinger or not, left Peru's players disconcerted. "It seemed like they were there just to greet and welcome us," said captain Héctor Chumpitaz. "They also said that they hoped it would be a good game because there was a great deal of anticipation among the Argentinian public. He wished us luck, and that was it. We started looking at each other and wondering: shouldn't they have gone to the Argentina room, not our room? What's going on? I mean, they wished us luck? Why? It left us wondering . . ."

Proof of anything untoward, though, is hard to come by, and it's doubtful that anybody watching a video of the game without foreknowledge of the suspicions around it would see anything unusual. Larrosa is dismissive of suggestions the game was fixed, and, if it were, it's fair to say either that not all the Peruvians were in on it or that some of them were exceptionally good actors. Juan Muñante hit the post early on, while Quiroga made a string of improbable saves. "They had two chances in first ten minutes: one hit a post, and another shot from [Juan Carlos] Oblitas was almost a goal," said Larrosa. "Those are the details that are forgotten when they say, 'Oh, it was 6–0. What happened there?' And if you think about that shot that hit the post, give me the best player, give me Pelé or Maradona, make him dribble past a defender and hit a post on purpose, and he won't be able to do it."

Whatever the circumstantial evidence of a fix, from the match footage itself it looks as though Peru are guilty of nothing more than not fancying it very much once the goals started to fly in. During the game—it's said at the very moment the fourth goal was scored—a bomb exploded at the home of Juan Alemann, the minister of the interior who had publicly questioned the cost of the tournament. That and the surge in demands for wage concessions were indicative of a potential problem for the junta: if victory in the World Cup generated a surge of euphoria and nationalist feeling, to what extent would they be able to control it? It's estimated that after the final whistle in Rosario, 60 percent of the population of Buenos Aires took to the streets to celebrate.

Given it had been defeat to the Dutch that had prompted the change in style, it was perhaps appropriate that it was the Netherlands that Argentina met in the final. With expectation mounting, a stressed Kempes felt he needed to get away from the squad, so when the third-choice goalkeeper, Héctor Baley, suggested they should go fishing, he put aside the prejudice most Argentinian soccer players seemed to share and agreed. "I don't like fishing," Kempes said. "I've never liked it, but sometimes the pressure is too much. Menotti authorized us to go but asked us to be back for training at 10:00 a.m. Baley woke me in the middle of night, and we got our fishing gear ready—rods and everything. I don't know how he managed to get all that. You can't imagine how cold it was. In the morning we returned with four fish and handed them to the cook. The rest of the guys, watching us eat the fresh fish at lunch, really envied us."

There may be room for doubt over exactly what happened against Peru, but there is little defense for what happened before the final. There had been some clumsy propaganda in the days leading up to the game with *El Gráfico*, as well as attacking "the insidious and malicious journalists who for months pursued a campaign of lies about Argentina," taking a photograph of Ruud Krol writing a letter and fabricating its entire text to include farcical details about how harmonious life under the junta appeared.

Throughout the tournament, the magazine had shown startling disdain for the other nations. The Dutch, for instance, were explicitly linked with drugs, homosexuality, and excess and the Scots with alcohol. "The myth of beer as a form of athletic preparation is beginning to come apart," its match report sniffed after Scotland had lost to Peru in the group stage. The contrast to Menotti's austere training camps was obvious, but the comment also made clear just how different the 1978 incarnation of *la nuestra* was to the wine-sozzled glories of the golden age. *El Gráfico* weren't the only ones later to regret what they published amid the excitement of the tournament. In *La Razón* novelist Ernesto Sabato insisted that "the World Cup was a proof of maturity, nobleness, a popular mobilization marked by generosity and altruism."

The gamesmanship continued, as the bus carrying the Dutch team took a deliberately circuitous route from their hotel to the stadium, and fans were allowed to crowd around it, hammering on the windows, chanting, and generally being intimidating—an echo of what Celtic had experienced after the second leg of their Intercontinental final against Racing eleven years earlier. Argentina then delayed their arrival on the field before kickoff, leaving the Netherlands standing around, exposed to the full fury of the crowd, and when they finally did emerge, they protested about the cast on René van de Kerkhof's arm. Given he had been wearing it without controversy all tournament, their only purpose can only have been to try to unsettle their opponents. That Gonella allowed the game to be delayed while the cast was removed gave the first indication of just how weak his officiating would be.

Yet for all the chicanery, it was Argentina that appeared the more nervous. "The emotions as we stepped on the field were incredible," said Larrosa. "I think there were more than eighty thousand people in that stadium. We couldn't even see the aisles, the stairs, because the stadium was so full that people couldn't move." Menotti prowled the touchline, gasping on his cigarette. Although Passarella put a volley just over as he arrived late in the box to meet a right-wing cross, it was the Dutch who looked the more threatening. Rep put an early header from an Arie Haan free kick just wide, and then, as a defensive mix-up presented him with the ball fourteen yards out, he was denied only by a spectacular save from Fillol, who dived up and to his left to push a fierce effort over the bar. "I was in the goal that has the Rio de la Plata behind," the goalkeeper said.

> Américo Gallego and Daniel Passarella got in the way of each other, and the ball falls to Rep. He controls it and from very near the penalty spot takes a great shot that somehow I managed to save. I see that save these days, and I think it's incredible how I was able to stop that ball from going in. Falling 1–0 behind to a team like Holland would have been devastating for us. We'd played against Italy in that World Cup, and when they scored, we couldn't find a way back into the game. We ended up losing. So that save is still very special for me. It was the best save of my life.

The save seemed to inspire the home side. Passarella had a looping header turned over by Jan Jongbloed in the Dutch goal before, eight minutes before the break, Argentina took the lead with a goal of real quality. Ardiles began the move, weaving through two challenges before playing the ball in to Luque. He laid it off to Kempes, who used his strength to surge between two Dutch defenders and squeeze a finish past Jongbloed.

Even before halftime, though, the Netherlands should have leveled. Willy van de Kerkhof crossed from the left, René van de Kerkhof headed back across goal, and Rob Rensenbrink, six yards out, seemed certain to score, only for his shot to be blocked by the outstretched leg of Fillol as he scrambled across goal.

Argentina could have doubled their lead soon after the break, Bertoni bursting down the right and crossing for Luque, who was thwarted by Jongbloed's speed off his line, but the game soon settled into a pattern of Dutch control frustrated by resolute and at times cynical Argentinian defending. If Gonella had had any notion of booking players for deliberate handballs, the outcome might have been very different. With eight minutes to go, though, the Netherlands did finally equalize. René van de Kerkhof, released down the right, cleverly pulled his cross back toward the edge of the box from where the substitute Dirk Nanninga powered a header past Fillol. And the Dutch nearly won it in normal time. A free kick from deep seemed to have been overhit, but Rensenbrink, hunched and seemingly frail as ever, was able to run on and, at the farthest stretch of his right leg, get to the ball before Fillol. He jabbed the ball past the keeper, but it bounced back off the near post, and the Netherlands's chance was gone. Johan Cruyff, explaining his profound aestheticism, once said that he preferred to hear the noise of the ball striking the post to scoring a goal. Surely even he, watching back in Amsterdam, didn't think that then; the width of a post denied soccer—and perhaps Argentina—a profoundly different history. "The silence was like a cemetery after that," said Larrosa. "But that made us react. If that didn't go in, this was our World Cup. Menotti then said to us, 'Remain calm. Don't rush. We still have thirty minutes. I see you're fit. We have more physical reserves than them, and we will impose our rhythm.' And we did it."

As the tournament had gone on, the speed and directness of Kempes had become increasing features of Argentina's play and, in the end, proved decisive. In the final minute of the first half of extra time, Passarella drove a free kick forward from deep in the Argentina half. Bertoni controlled it, turned, and beat his man before slipping a pass just in front of the charging Kempes. His power took him through two Dutch challenges, and although Jongbloed saved his initial effort, the ball bounced back off Kempes and over the goalkeeper, and he ran on to stab in his sixth goal of the tournament, enough to win him the golden boot. Kempes was the architect of the third as well, another barreling run from deep leading to another ricochet, the ball falling for Bertoni to sweep in. With five minutes left, there was no way back for the Dutch, which lost their second successive final.

"The final against Holland was the greatest example of what I wanted from the team," said Menotti. But Brian Glanville, covering his sixth World Cup, deemed Argentina the worst winner he had seen, speaking of a tournament "disfigured by negative soccer, ill temper, dreadful refereeing, spiteful players and the wanton surrender of Peru."

To the Argentinians, though, none of that mattered, or at least not at the time. Yet in what was, ostensibly, a piece glorifying the victory the day after the final, *Clarín* happened upon the ambivalence at its core, writing that it "covers all the moments of darkness. Argentinian soccer is the best in the world. . . . [T]he achievement of Menotti is great. His style won. His convictions won. It is possible to be world champions with technical and attacking players. Argentinian soccer will always be remembered for this triumph."

The "moments of darkness" are undefined, but presumably referred most directly to the defeat to the Netherlands in 1974 and the failure to qualify for the World Cup four years before that. In hindsight, though, they take on a greater significance and seem to refer indirectly to the years of *anti-fútbol*. And with the full benefit of context, the term perhaps also takes on a political meaning and so acknowledges the point that Menotti made obliquely again and again in public and explicitly to his team before the final. "We are the people," he said in the dressing room before kickoff. "We come from the victimized classes, and we represent the only thing that is legitimate in this country—soccer. We are not playing for the expensive seats full of military officers. We represent freedom, not the dictatorship." In soccer, the old romantic, bohemian style of soccer, Menotti located the soul of *argentinidad*, just as Borocotó and Hipólito Yrigoyen had, in different ways, a half century earlier; in the victory of his team, playing a modified version of that style, one that had room for tactical fouling and cynical handballs, he saw a triumph for the Left. Videla insisted the "triumph was obtained with capacity, courage, and discipline"—omitting the technical ability Menotti insisted upon—while Menotti, as anthropologist Eduardo Archetti points out, tended to refer to a victory for the "people" rather than the "nation."

What should he have done, Menotti asked, "to coach teams that played badly, that based everything on tricks, that betrayed the feelings of the people? No, of course not." Instead, he argued, his soccer, being free and creative, offered a reminder of the free, creative Argentina that existed before the junta. That, though, is to overidealize it. Menotti took advantage of the political environment to prevent players from moving abroad; the selection of Alonso over Bochini was widely believed to have been politically motivated, and there was a sense throughout the tournament that if an advantage was to be had, Argentina would make sure they took it.

PART FIVE
A NEW HOPE,
1978–1990

38

THE NATIVITY

On October 30, 1960, thirty-two years after Borocotó had described the perfect *pibe*, the urchin with the mop of unkempt hair, the eyes that glittered with mischief, and the impudent smile that revealed teeth worn down by yesterday's bread, the ideal was made flesh in the Evita Perón hospital in Lanús, an industrial district to the south of Buenos Aires.[1]

Diego "Chitoro" Maradona and his wife, Dalma "Tota" Salvadora, were both from Esquina in Corrientes in the Northeast of Argentina, near the border with Paraguay. He was a boatman who lived in a riverside hut coated with clay and reeds and made his living by fishing and by taking cows to the islands of the Paraná Delta to graze, bringing them back when the tide came in. Tota moved to Buenos Aires, seeking a better life, and found employment as a servant. Two years later she persuaded Chitoro to join her, initially staying with some relatives in Villa Fiorito, a suburb to the south of Buenos Aires. Chitoro found work in a bonemeal factory on the Riachuelo, the inlet where Pedro de Mendoza had initially founded Buenos Aires and across which the Decamisados had swarmed in support of Perón in 1945. By then it had become a filthy and polluted canal that effectively marked the boundary between rich and poor in the city. Shortly after the Maradonas arrived in Villa Fiorito, their relatives moved, and Chitoro had to build his own house from loose bricks and sheets of metal.

The Maradonas had had three daughters when Tota fell pregnant again. There are dozens of stories about the birth of her fourth child, as though it had to be presaged by some acknowledgment on the part of the universe, but the most familiar has it that Tota was dancing when she felt a sudden pain. A few hours later, she gave birth to a son, who is reported to have been kicking even as he came into the world. "Congratulations," the doctor is supposed to have said. "You have a healthy boy, and he is pure ass." The Maradonas named their child after his father: el Diego.

Diego grew up in a shack with neither running water nor electricity. It was Villa Fiorito, Maradona always said, that taught him *viveza*, the sense of cunning or canniness that was prized as the virtue that allowed the impoverished to thrive. Those from the provinces, he insisted, were more honest, but *villeros* were tribal: they would gather their friends tightly around them, prioritizing loyalty above all else. He is, he proudly says, a *cabecita negra* (a little black head), descended from poor Italian and Guaraní stock, a laborer from the lowest reaches of society.

On his third birthday, Maradona was given a ball by his cousin Beto; that night he took it to bed with him. It became his constant companion. "There are many people who are scared to admit they come from a *villa*," he said, "but not me, because if I hadn't been born in a *villa*, I wouldn't have been Maradona. I had the freedom to play." But there can be no idealizing his childhood. There was no police station in Villa Fiorito for fear it would become a target for dissent; instead, police were bused in each day from outside. There were other, more mundane, dangers. While a toddler, Maradona fell one night into an open cesspit. "Diegito," shouted his uncle Cirilo as he helped him out, "keep your head above the shit." It's a story Maradona would tell often, his uncle's words becoming almost a mantra during the more difficult moments of his life.

As a child Maradona made money however he could, opening taxi doors, selling scrap, collecting the foil wrapping from cigarette packets. To survive was to live on your wits; it was a long way from the Peronist dream, but Chitoro and Tota kept pictures of Perón and Evita in the house. They seem to have realized early that Diego's future lay in soccer, supporting him at every stage of his development. An early photograph shows him, perhaps four or five years old, standing in front of a wire fence that is battered and twisted from how often he'd thumped a ball against it. On the way to school he would do keepie-ups with an orange, a crumpled newspaper, or a bundle of rags, not letting the ball touch the ground even as he went over a railway bridge.

In December 1968 Maradona was taken for a trial with the Cebollitas (the Little Onions), the youth side of Argentinos Juniors. The club had been founded in the central barrio of Villa Crespo in 1904 by a group of friends who held socialist or anarchist principles and initially took the name Martyrs of Chicago, after the eight anarchists hanged or imprisoned following the Haymarket Riots in Chicago in 1886.[2] The following year, as they began to grow, they changed their name to the more inclusive Argentinos Juniors. They were accepted into the association in 1909 and, after a series of moves, settled in the central barrio of La Paternal, just to the west of their original home, in 1921. By 1930 the club was at the forefront of the move to professionalism. Money was always tight, and they were relegated in 1936, returning to the top flight only two decades later. By then the quality of their youth development had begun to be recognized, and the club was appreciated for its entertaining, if not necessarily successful, soccer. It was then that they attracted the nickname *los Bichos Colorados* (the Red Bugs). Argentinos finished third in the championship in 1960—and had held out hopes of the title until a 5–1 defeat at River on the third-to-the-last weekend of the season—but they spent most seasons fighting relegation, knowing that if they did produce a good player or two, they would soon be sold to bigger clubs.

It didn't take long for Argentinos to realize that in Maradona they were dealing with a player very different from their usual intake. He was short and squat with an unusually large head—evoking memories of Sívori—and, said Francisco Cornejo, the coach, "he seemed to come from another planet." So gifted was Maradona that club officials initially assumed he must be older than he claimed to be but physically underdeveloped and insisted on seeing his identification card. Satisfied he was dealing with a prodigious eight-year-old, Cornejo took him to see Cacho Paladino, a doctor who worked with both Huracán and boxers, and he gave Maradona a course of pills and injections to build him up. From an early age, Maradona was familiarized with the idea that pharmaceutical assistance was normal and natural.

Almost immediately, he became a phenomenon. At halftime at Argentinos games, Maradona would perform tricks to entertain the crowd; at one game against Boca Juniors in July 1970, he was so impressive that the crowd chanted for him to stay on during the second half. He appeared on a Saturday entertainment show on television doing tricks, first with a soccer ball, then with an orange, and finally with a bottle. There is video of an early interview with him in which he was asked what his ambitions were. "To win the league and the World Cup," he replied.

On September 28, 1971, Maradona was mentioned by the national press for the first time, as *Clarín*'s reporter was captivated by the show he put on at halftime of a game between Argentinos and Independiente—although the tribute was rather spoiled by the fact that he referred to him as "Caradona." The ten-year-old, the report said, demonstrated a "rare ability to control and dribble with the ball," but what seems more significant is the way Maradona was immediately placed in the *pibe* tradition: "His shirt is too big for him and his fringe barely allows him to see properly. He looks as though he's escaped from a *potrero*. He can kill the ball and then just as easily flick it up with both his feet. He holds himself like a born soccer player. He doesn't seem to belong to today but he does; he has a very Argentinian love for the ball, and thanks to him our soccer will continue to nourish itself with great players."

That was a huge burden to place on one so young, yet nobody seemed in any doubt Maradona would succeed. What subsequently happened shapes perceptions, of course, and lends significance to episodes that in another life would be forgotten, but from an extraordinarily early age, there was a sense that Maradona was somehow marked for greatness, special. He was smuggled into overage teams and thrived, any issues with schooling smoothed over as his headmaster, enraptured having seen him play, gave him pass grades for exams he missed—an early lesson, perhaps, that the rules didn't necessarily apply to him. Talent, Maradona soon discovered, opened doors. His first trip was to a tournament in Uruguay, where he found himself staying in a shack without running water, while most of the team were billeted in pleasant homes. Soon, though, Maradona ceased to be the outsider. On a trip to Chile, his team stayed in a five-star hotel, and he insisted on room-service breakfast, reveling in the fact that he suddenly had power; he scored four that afternoon.

Maradona began to be indulged. He was a terrible loser. When los Cebollitas were beaten in the final of the national championship, he threw himself to the ground and wailed. Novelist Alicia Dujovne Ortiz made the incident part of Maradona's legend, describing how an anonymous man came up to him and told him to stop crying because he'd be the best in the world. In another game in 1972, he was sent off after flaring up at a referee. Maradona was hugely, perhaps uniquely, talented, but he was also temperamental, and it seems nobody in those early days had either the capacity or the inclination to tackle issues of his character.

When Maradona was fifteen, Argentinos gave him an apartment in Villa del Parque, which allowed his father to give up his job in the bonemeal factory. Soon after moving Tota found herself without sufficient cash in a local supermarket. A teenage girl behind her loaned her some money, and that evening Maradona was sent to repay the debt. The girl was Claudia Villafañe; she soon became Maradona's first serious girlfriend and, later, his wife.

By then Maradona had already met his first agent, Jorge Cyterszpiler. Cyterszpiler was two years older than Maradona, overweight, with a mass of curly hair. Having suffered from polio as a child, he walked with a limp and was resolutely unathletic. He loved soccer, though, and had become a mascot of Argentinos when his brother, Juan Eduardo, who was ten years his elder, began playing for the side. But when Juan Eduardo was twenty-two, he took a kick to the testicles, suffered a hemorrhage, and died. A shocked Jorge sank into depression, barely going out until he was told of Maradona and his genius. Intrigued, he rediscovered his love of the game. Cyterszpiler, who was from a comfortable middle-class background, began to invite Maradona to his home. The pair became friends, Cyterszpiler happy to pay for trips to the movies and pizzerias. He was always financially minded, working in the offices at Argentinos while still at school before studying economics at Buenos Aires University. Maradona trusted him and asked him to look after his business affairs.

On October 20, 1976, ten days before his sixteenth birthday, Maradona made his debut for the Argentinos first team against Talleres, coming off the bench to become the youngest player in the history of the Primera.[3] Argentinos were 1–0 down when he came on, and the scoreline didn't change, but Maradona did make his mark, nutmegging Talleres defender Juan Domingo Cabrera.

Four months later, having played only eleven professional matches, Maradona was called up to the national side by Menotti for a friendly against Hungary at la Bombonera. The crowd chanted his name, and he was brought off the bench in the second half with the score at 4–0. The experience, though, wasn't an entirely comfortable one. In his autobiography, published in 2000, Maradona said it was then that he began to feel the envy of others and that it so distressed and confused him that he would shut himself away and cry.

Tears were a regular feature of the young Maradona's life, in part, it's probably true, because others were jealous or had unreasonable expectations of his remarkable talents. At the same time, he was used to succeeding; he struggled to deal with failure or frustration. When he didn't win a prize at Argentina's Sportsman of the Year gala in 1977, for instance, he wept, and he locked himself in a room and sobbed when Menotti didn't select him for the final twenty-two-man squad for the 1978 World Cup, threatening to quit soccer and vowing never to forgive the coach for what he saw as a "betrayal."

Years later, having reconciled with Menotti, he was still insisting that was a mistake, even though, as well as Mario Kempes, Menotti had Beto Alonso and Ricardo Bochini who operated in a similar position. There were those who claimed that Menotti was concerned Maradona would eclipse him, but when a coach has won a World Cup, it's very difficult to suggest he erred by leaving out a brilliant but emotionally immature seventeen-year-old. Maradona was talked out of his threat to retire when Cyterszpiler and Chitoro took him out for pizza. In his next league game, fired up by *bronca*—a Buenos Aires slang term formed by reversing the syllables of *cabrón* (bastard) that Maradona uses frequently to denote the bitter energy fueled by anger or disappointment—he scored twice and set two up, as Argentinos beat Chacarita 5–0.

"Oh my God, what a player," said goalkeeper Hugo Tocalli, who played with him at Argentinos in 1977.

On top of his quality and the beauty of his soccer, after training sessions, he'd make me stay for half an hour or an hour, to practice shots, free kicks, using different techniques. I couldn't believe the things he did on the field. It was amazing. He took ten balls, he calculated where the wall would be, we imagined it, and then he'd announce where he was going to direct the ball, and even knowing that, you can't save it. And I got angry, and asked for another shot, and it happened again. But he needed to be challenged, because that made him better on the weekend.

The president of Argentinos Juniors at the time was Prospero Consoli, an official tailor to the Argentinian armed forces with the rank of corporal. He appointed as chairman of the club General Guillermo Suárez Mason, who was on the board of both YPF, the state oil company, and Austral, the state airline. It's indicative of how soccer was still seen as an essential component of political life that Mason would happily use his YPF helicopter for soccer business. He also shifted $250,000 from Austral to Argentinos Juniors to help keep Maradona at the club, making him pose in an Austral T-shirt and cap to justify the deal, an early sign of how Maradona's talent—and Cyterszpiler's clever exploitation of it—meant he was becoming too big for Argentinos. The use of what were effectively state funds to subsidize soccer was attacked by the popular daily *Crónica*, but it was a practice that was well established, going back to the cheap loans to fund stadiums in the late thirties and forties. Maradona dutifully made projunta statements about soccer players being soldiers fighting for their nation by other means.

Argentinos just about got their money's worth. They finished joint second in their group in the 1979 Metropolitano, but lost a playoff with Vélez Sarsfield for semifinal qualification, a game Maradona missed through suspension because of a red card he'd received in a friendly. "A referee took a dislike to me," he said. Nothing could ever be his fault, a theme that would recur throughout his life. It's hard not to wonder whether he might have had rather more of a sense of personal responsibility if he hadn't been indulged so readily for so long. But then messiahs—and Maradona was cast as one long before the Church of Maradona was founded on his thirty-eighth birthday in 1998[4]—perhaps don't have the same moral code as mortals.

39

THE UNLIKELIEST CHAMPIONS

A week after the World Cup final, the league season began again. Fifteen rounds of the forty[1] had been played when the Metropolitano broke for preparations for the tournament, with Boca leading River by a point. Quilmes were three points back, but nobody paid them much attention. After all, since winning the league in 1912 with a side made up of players left without a club after Alumni had disbanded, they'd been far more successful at hockey than soccer. Quilmes was the last of the old Anglo clubs still to have a presence near the top of the professional game.

Quilmes had had a difficult start to the 1978 season, and after taking six points from their opening seven games, their managerial pairing of Mauricio López and Rubén Caballero resigned. The previous year José Yudica had saved the club from relegation, so they turned back to him. Yudica had had a solid if unspectacular career as a player, first at Newell's, then at Boca, Vélez, and Estudiantes, where he played briefly under Zubeldía. "He was a very honest man," Yudica said. "I didn't agree with how he saw soccer, but he was ahead of his time, always studying. His sermons were useful at the time, but the real change in Argentinian soccer was thanks to Menotti." He then passed through a series of smaller clubs on his way to Colombia, where he won a title with Deportivo Cali.

When he returned to Quilmes, he was forty-two. "Yudica is from the Newell's Old Boys school, the father of all the Bielsas and Martinos, bringing sexy soccer and sacrifice together," said Tocalli, who joined Quilmes from Argentinos at the end of 1977. "I had the good fortune of playing with Maradona in 1977, and to be the manager of Messi when he was first called up to represent Argentina [at the youth level], but we at Quilmes had an extraordinary player that people hardly speak of: El Indio Gómez. He transformed three number nines into top scorers and made them earn transfers abroad. The problem was that his personal life was a disaster."

Omar Gómez was a broad-cheeked genius with a heavy fringe and an impishly lopsided grin. "We knew that López and Caballero were two workers in a particular kind of soccer, but they lacked joy," he said. "I've always trained professionally and always worked hard, but in a demanding sort of training there has to be joy. They failed in that regard. They were repressing joy, and that predisposes a player against them."

Yudica restored the sense of fun. "We knew he'd saved us from relegation the season before, and we knew what kind of person he was," said Gómez. "With him we became stronger, as the way we went through the matches shows." It may have been more enjoyable, but there was no slackening of the work ethic.

In 1978, the World Cup meant holidays for all clubs, but Yudica told us that if we worked while the other clubs were on holiday, we would come to the restart of the tournament with a great advantage. He wouldn't fine or say anything to those who didn't want to come to train, but that's what he underlined. He convinced us, meaning that nobody, not even one player, took a holiday. He was very persuasive, and it was the same when he spoke about the next game: we'll beat them if we do this, he'd say, and that's what we did, and that's how we won.

The decisive match came against Independiente, Quilmes's sixth to the last of the season, when they withstood intense pressure to win 1–0. "Everyone was convinced then that we were beginning to have the luck you needed to be champions," said Gómez. "It was a difficult game. Independiente had a terrific team, and beating the *grandes* wasn't easy at that time. When [Juan Carlos] Merlo came on and scored the goal, we realized what we had: a good squad. We were organized, hard to beat, we could beat anyone, and we had a bit of luck. From then on we were thinking more and more that we had a chance."

As Boca stuttered, Quilmes were left needing a win away to the Rosario Central of Carlos Griguol on the final day of the season to claim the title. "Before we went onto the field, Yudica said that we were just one step from touching the heavens with our hands," said Gómez. "That, going and touching the glory, was something soccer players had to feel deep inside. We weren't interested in collecting a prize or anything related to money; we were interested only in being champions."

The players seem almost to have been taken by surprise that they had gotten themselves into a position in which winning a championship was possible: no club as small as Quilmes had ever come close to success. There was a splendid naïveté about them: of everything Yudica instilled in the team, the most important was probably self-belief. "He made soccer players play better and convinced us that we were capable of winning," Tocalli said. "We didn't know about money, for instance. I think I earned three thousand dollars for winning the title. I didn't play all the games, but those who did probably didn't even get ten thousand dollars. Before the crucial game at Rosario Central, we didn't know about bonuses or anything."

Quilmes were nervous, and twice they fell behind, but on both occasions penalties from Luis Andreuchi pulled them level. And then, at fifty-two minutes, just five minutes after they'd gone 2–1 down, Jorge Gáspari got the goal that sealed the only professional title in their history. "It's impossible to say what you feel," said Gómez. "You have to live through it. Yes, you think of your father, your mother, your wife, your son, your friends, and the happiness they are guaranteed . . . but the feeling you have inside your body is impossible to explain. You don't know whom to hug, what to do, whether to jump or scream, whether you should throw yourself to the ground or swim."

There could be no building on the success: the title was not a platform for the future but a glorious one-off. Within a few weeks, Gómez had left. Quilmes were a team with a small budget and were effectively forced to accept any reasonable offer for their players, a paradigm that would become increasingly familiar to Argentinian clubs. When the North American Soccer League side Dallas Tornado made an offer for him, they had little option but to accept. In that, perhaps, lies the answer to Tocalli's question of why Gómez never gets the recognition he feels he deserves: he spent his prime years playing in the United States.

Still, Gómez will always be remembered for what he did with Quilmes. Their triumph was probably the most unexpected success of any side in Argentinian history, but it was part of a more general pattern. Part of the point of establishing the Nacional to run with the Metropolitano was to reduce the dominance of the *grandes*, and in that it was undoubtedly successful, even if the clubs that benefited weren't necessarily those from the provinces, as had been intended, but the two Rosario sides and smaller teams from Buenos Aires. "The big sides weren't that notorious anymore," said Zanabria, who, having scored the goal that won Newell's their first title before his move to Boca, had seen both sides of the equation. "Until then, the *grandes* put together their squads from the best players of the other clubs. It was very easy to snatch them. But in the seventies, the philosophy was to try to keep them as long as possible, and also clubs from abroad were interested in these names, so for the big clubs it wasn't as simple as before to get them."

As well as the economic factors, there were also tactical issues: although they came to be shunned, Estudiantes had offered another way of playing, a means by which smaller clubs could prevail. "That was the nice thing about Argentinian soccer then, because hard work started producing results," said Tocalli. "Before, the big clubs would buy the best players, and that was enough to win. But the managers who study soccer learned that there was another way of winning and also changed the mentality: River had Fillol, Passarella, Luque, an extraordinary team, but that didn't mean that we couldn't beat them at el Monumental. And we did. There had to be a way. And managers study those ways. Newell's, Talleres, Quilmes, Ferro . . . It was the sign of progress, a good thing."

Alexander Watson Hutton, the son of a Gorbals grocer who became the father of the game in Argentina. (Alexis Mariano Rodriguez)

Pancho Varallo, the great Boca Juniors forward who hit the bar in the 1930 World Cup final. (Getty Images)

Guillermo Stábile only played four games for Argentina but scored eight goals to finish as top scorer at the 1930 World Cup. (Getty Images)

Luis Monti, the hard man who lost his nerve in the 1930 World Cup final but won the tournament with Italy four years later. (El Gráfico)

Roberto Cerro, Boca's record goal-scorer until Martín Palermo bettered his tally. (El Gráfico)

Renato Cesarini, pictured here in his Chacarita Juniors days, although he would gain greater fame with Juventus and then as manager of River Plate. (El Gráfico)

Antonio Sastre, a great all-round midfielder who helped Independiente to two league titles. (El Gráfico)

Manuel Seoane (front row, fourth from left) with the national team during the 1927 Campeonato Sudamericano in Peru. (AFP/Getty Images)

The powerful Bernabé Ferreyra, River's world-record signing who changed the
style of Argentinian center-forwards. (El Gráfico)

The fabled front five of La Máquina. This page, clockwise from top left: Adolfo Pedernera (EFE/lafototeca.com), Ángel Labruna (EFE/lafototeca.com), Féliz Loustau (El Gráfico), and Juan Carlos Muñoz (El Gráfico). Facing Page: José Manuel Moreno. (El Gráfico)

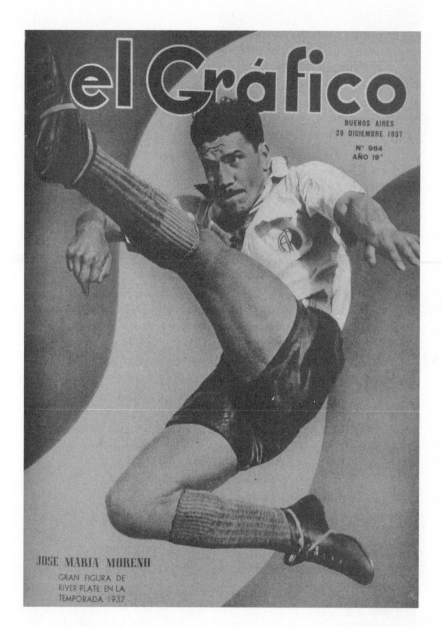

el Gráfico

BUENOS AIRES
29 DICIEMBRE 1937

N° 964
AÑO 19°

JOSE MARIA MORENO
GRAN FIGURA DE
RIVER PLATE EN LA
TEMPORADA 1937

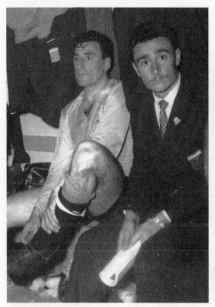

The River Plate *caudillo* "Pipo" Rossi unfastens his boots next to Norberto Boggio after Argentina's 3–1 win over Northern Ireland at the 1958 World Cup. (Getty/Haynes Archive/Popperfoto)

Amadeo Carrizo of River Plate, widely regarded as having been the best Argentinian goalkeeper before the seventies. (EFE/lafototeca.com)

Miguel Rugilo, the goalkeeping hero of Wembley. (El Gráfico)

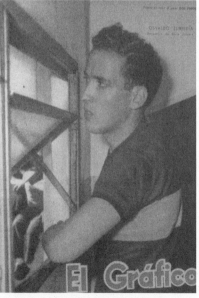

Osvaldo Zubeldía, later the high priest of *anti-fútbol*, seen here in his days as an inside-forward at Boca. (El Gráfico)

Argentina's 1957 Campeonato Sudamericano winning team, the last great national side of the golden age. Top row, left to right: Juan Giménez, Guillermo Stábile, Eduardo Domínguez, Pedro Dellacha, Nestor "Pipo" Rossi, Ángel "Pedro" Schandlein, Federico Vairo, Abajo. Front row, left to right: Omar Orestes Corbatta, Humberto Maschio, Antonio Angelillo, Omar Sívori, Osvaldo Cruz. (EFE/lafototeca.com)

As the goalkeeper Amedeo Carrizo looks on, the Racing center-half Pedro Dellacha heads clear against West Germany at the 1958 World Cup (Argentina forgot to bring a change kit so are wearing the yellow shirts of IFK Malmö). (Getty Images/Ullstein Bild)

The brilliant but doomed Racing winger Omar Orestes Corbatta. (El Gráfico)

A prolific goalscorer and a difficult man, the San Lorenzo and Boca striker José Sanfilippo. (EFE/lafototeca.com)

Silvio Marzolini, hearthrob, Boca Juniors attacking left-back and later their manager. (Popperfoto)

El Caudillo, the looming No. 5, Antonio Rattin. (EFE/lafototeca.com)

Carlos Bilardo celebrates beating Manchester United to win the Intercontinental Cup with Estudiantes. He would later take the principles of that side into management. (Getty Images/Popperfoto)

The tainted triumph: General Videla presents Daniel Passarella with the World Cup in El Monumental, 1978. (Getty Images/AFP)

Mario Kempes, top scorer at the 1978 World Cup, celebrates putting Argentina 1–0 up in the final against the Netherlands. (Getty Images)

The River Plate goalkeeper Ubaldo Fillol, one of Argentina's heroes at the 1978 World Cup. (EFE/lafototeca.com)

Diego Maradona's idol Ricardo Bochini, the great playmaker of Independiente. (EFE/lafototeca.com)

César Luis Menotti, who restored the attacking spirit to Argentina and led them to the World Cup. (Action Images/Sporting Pictures)

Raúl Gámez, later president of Vélez Sarsfield, punches an England fan during the 1986 World Cup quarter-final. (Getty Images/Billy Stickland)

Diego Maradona and Carlos Bilardo celebrate victory over Yugoslavia in the 1990 World Cup quarter-final. (Getty Images/Bob Thomas)

After dominating the tournament, Diego Maradona holds aloft the World Cup in 1986. (Getty Images)

Gabriel Batistuta runs away in jubilation after scoring against Japan at the 1998 World Cup. (Getty Images/Laurence Griffiths)

Juan Román Riquelme, the troubled throwback to the *enganches* of old. (AFP PHOTO/Toru YAMANAKA)

Carlos Bianchi, who led Vélez and
Boca to Libertadores success. (REUTERS/
Andrea Comas ACO/mk Reuters)

Marcelo Bielsa, the eccentric visionary
who has shaped the modern game.
(AFP PHOTO/Omar TORRES)

Lionel Messi surrounded by South Koreans at the 2010 World Cup.
(Action Images/Carl Recine Livepic)

40

THE PRIDE OF THE NATION

Having won the World Cup, Menotti's attention turned to the future, placing an emphasis on the 1979 Under-20 World Cup, staged in Tokyo, that no Argentina coach had previously given youth soccer. By then the AFA had a new president, Julio Grondona, who was appointed thanks to the lobbying of Admiral Lacoste. A thickset, lumbering man, Grondona had been born in Avellaneda in 1933, in a district so associated with the tango image of knife-juggling gangsters that it was said that around there, if you threw a potato in the air, it would come down peeled. He shared a room overlooking the cemetery with his ten siblings; in the *decade infame*, many of those whose graves he looked out on were still registered to vote.

He signed for River as a seventeen-year-old but had only ever played for their youth ranks and then played for Defensores de Belgrano in the lower leagues while working in his father's hardware store before, in 1956, buying a plot of land in Sarandí, a district of Avalleneda on the Riachuelo noted for its leatherworks, and becoming one of the cofounders of Arsenal. Grondona was initially a player and director of the new club, which combined the colors of Racing and Independiente, the two biggest clubs in Avellaneda, to wear pale-blue-and-red-striped shirts. He became president in 1957, but began working as a director at Independiente in 1962, eventually quitting Arsenal in 1976 to become president of Independiente. He might have become president earlier had he not been disbarred from elections in 1970 because of a year's ban imposed by the AFA for attacking a referee at Arsenal. Grondona, a hugely controversial figure, would go on to serve as a FIFA vice president in 1988, holding both that position and the AFA presidency until his death in 2014. In that time he was arguably the most influential off-field figure in Argentinian soccer.

With the Under-20 tournament beginning only two days after the end of the group stage of the Copa América, that inevitably meant compromise. Argentina needed to beat Brazil in their final-group game of the senior competition to go through to the last four. Maradona had scored on the senior side's previous group match, a 3–0 win over Bolivia, but he had been named as captain of the squad for Japan and so missed the decisive game, which Argentina could only draw 2–2.

If there was disappointment at Argentina's failure to make the continental semifinals for the second tournament in a row, it soon disappeared, as the Under-20s dazzled. It had been in a friendly against the New York Cosmos, featuring Carlos Alberto, Giorgio Chinaglia, and Franz Beckenbauer, played in Tucumán in November 1978, that it had first become apparent quite how good this Argentina Under-20 side could be. Maradona had just been brought onto the squad, but it was another addition, a five-foot-three forward from Chacarita, Osvaldo "Pichi" Escudero,[1] who made the biggest impact. Ernesto Duchini, who ran the national youth academy, had introduced him to the rest of the players only a week before the game, but in training "he made us all dance with his devilish dribbling," as defender Juan Simón put it. He was included on the team for the Cosmos game. "Those first thirty minutes were like an orchestra playing on the field," said Simón. "That was a milestone for that team. We were 2–0 up in twenty-five minutes." They ended up winning 2–1.

A weakened side finished second in the South American Under-20 championship, earning a place in the World Cup. Argentina beat Indonesia 5–0 in their opening game, but what really sparked them into life was Menotti's halftime team talk in the second game, when Argentina were drawing 0–0 with Yugoslavia. "'Why the hell did you come here?' he asked us," said Simón. "'If you're going to play like that, you should have stayed at home. You are here because you are ambassadors for an idea. That's what brought you here, and that's what you must show on the field, even if we lose 10–0.' The ball was our girlfriend, he'd tell us. You have to treat it as if it were your girlfriend."

Escudero scored the winner ten minutes into the second half, and Argentina went on to sweep aside Poland, Algeria, and Uruguay before beating the USSR 3–1 in the final; in six games they scored twenty goals. Ramón Díaz finished as the leading scorer, but it was Maradona who was the undoubted star of a tournament that was both promoted and vetted by the junta. Here, they said, was incontrovertible proof of the superiority of Argentinian youth, while at the same time they censored the television coverage, blacking out protesters and opposition banners in the crowd.

Shortly before the final, a delegation from the Organization of American States arrived in Buenos Aires to investigate allegations of human rights abuses. They based themselves in the Plaza de Mayo, encouraging anybody with evidence to come forward and speak to them. As the mood of celebration after the victory in Tokyo reached levels of hysteria, Radio Rivadavia commentator José María Muñoz urged his listeners to "show these men from the commission on human rights what is the real Argentina." Thousands flocked to the square, where Muñoz was paraded on their shoulders. The *madres*, who in many cases had lined up all day to give their evidence, were jostled and ultimately overwhelmed.

On his return to Argentina, Maradona was feted by the junta, who conscripted him, cut his hair, and then discharged him, urging him to carry on being a role model for the country's youth. Already, though, the sense was there of Maradona as a player who had outgrown his environment, a genius who was self-centered and suspicious of those around him. When he'd been taken off to be rested with the score 5–0 in the quarter-final, he'd wept and had begun to wonder if the rumors Menotti hadn't picked him for the 1978 World Cup for reasons of jealousy might have had some substance. He had dreamed, he wrote in his autobiography, of getting off the plane with the cup, and he was so concerned that Menotti might divert him to go and play with the senior side that he "wanted to die." In the end he was "saved" by the need for him to fulfill, in a very cursory way, his national service.

The following year Argentinos finished second in the Campeonato (the tournament that had been the Metropolitano), but Maradona couldn't stay at Argentinos forever. Barcelona made their first offer for him in 1979, prompting the AFA to make $400,000 available to Argentinos to increase Maradona's salary and keep him in Argentina. Early in 1981, though, after being insulted by fans as Argentinos lost a summer friendly to River Plate, Maradona decided to leave: he wouldn't stay where he was disrespected, he said, establishing a pattern that would be repeated at almost every club he played for by departing in acrimony. River Plate had first approached him when he was twelve, but he had always insisted his heart was set on Boca. Argentinos president General Suárez Mason was reportedly threatened by Admiral Lacoste, a River Plate fan who had retained an influence within the AFA after the World Cup by securing the appointment of Grondona as president, but there was never a serious offer from River for Maradona. Instead, having scored 116 goals in 166 games for Argentinos, he moved to Boca on loan for the 1981 season, his new club paying Argentinos $4 million and taking on $1.1 million of their debt.

The Boca Maradona joined had slipped a long way from their late-seventies peak. Having broken their continental duck in 1977, Boca promptly won the Libertadores again, beating Carlos Bilardo's Deportivo Cali in the final.

With their domestic form slipping, Boca lost to Olimpia of Paraguay in the Libertadores final the following year—denied in the second leg by the inspired goalkeeping of Ever Almeida and by their own ill-discipline, as they had three players sent off and the Paraguayans one. That year the government began to pressure Boca over the farcical situation of the Ciudad Deportiva. In 1965 the club had been granted forty hectares on a man-made island in the Rio de la Plata on which to construct a 140,000-capacity stadium and other sporting facilities. Fourteen years later, with construction having barely begun, the state repossessed the land, but allowed Boca to carry on the building work on the understanding that when the project was completed, rights would be returned to the club. Eventually, in 1982, the government granted Boca the land, even though there was no sign of construction ever being finished, but in 1979 there had been a genuine sense of economic threat. In 1980 results got only worse: Boca were seventh in the Campeonato and came in only fifth in their group in the Nacional. With their finances in trouble, they desperately needed the boost Maradona's signing brought.

Soon after joining Boca, Maradona went with Claudia and several other relatives to watch the final of a youth tournament at el Monumental. Already irritated that only he and Claudia were given seats in the directors' box, Maradona lost his temper when he was abused by River fans and got into a fistfight, for which he was thrown out. In itself it was a minor incident, but it summed up two emerging themes that would become central to his career: that he was always a target for others and that he was quick to anger. He was a star who was loved by most in Argentina, but that adoration and its antithesis made it almost impossible for him to remain there.

In the context of Argentina's creaking economy, the deal that took Maradona to Boca would have far wider ramifications. Despite the government's austerity measures, inflation began to climb again, while output collapsed, unemployment rose, and the standard of living slipped. Opposition, in the form of secret trade unions, remnants of the old political parties, and social movements like the *madres*, began to reemerge. Soccer, again, became a barometer of the state of the nation, both reflecting the financial chaos and offering a locus for dissent.

In 1981 River, despite also being given free land, had slipped $30 million into debt. The bonds Boca had issued in the seventies had less than junk status. Racing were massively in the red, sliding ever further into trouble as they struggled to meet interest payments. But nobody was in such a desperate state as San Lorenzo. In 1979 Osvaldo Cacciatore, a brigadier in the air force who was the de facto mayor of Buenos Aires and had undertaken a program of radical urban redevelopment, building nine highways and clearing slums, decided that there were too many soccer stadiums in the city and that the land could be better used. It's said he looked at the grounds of San Lorenzo, Vélez, and Huracán and decided that as the Gasómetro was showing signs of age (it had been opened in 1916), largely constructed of wood, and in a neighborhood that made ready access difficult, it was the one that had to go. Heavily in debt, San Lorenzo had little way of resisting pressure from the government and sold, drawing 0–0 with Boca in a tearful final game on December 2, 1979. The government subsequently sold the land at a huge profit to the Carrefour supermarket group. San Lorenzo were reduced to a nomadic existence, wandering glumly from one small crumbling stadium to the next before eventually settling into the Nuevo Gasómetro in the rundown barrio of Bajo Flores in 1993. So straitened were their circumstances in the early eighties that there were collections just to buy towels and soap for the players.

As the general economic situation worsened, for the first time in years serious opposition to the government began to be heard in stadiums. There were Peronist chants from the fifties at Chacarita, for instance, while at Huracán Montoneros flags would be unfurled and then rapidly hidden again. Videla, following the principle of five-year terms, stood down in March 1981 and was replaced by General Roberto Viola, although this appointment was opposed by hard-line nationalists within the military. Viola began talks with the opposition—who were at the time still technically illegal—about a return to civilian rule, his hand partly forced by the catastrophic state of the economy. Conservative forces rallied behind General Leopoldo Galtieri, and in December 1981 he led a coup that deposed Viola, becoming president after an eleven-day interim government headed by Lacoste.

Maradona's $4 million fee was enormous anyway, but it was made even more enormous by the fact it was paid not in pesos but in dollars. In June 1981, four months after the initial agreement had been signed, the peso was devalued by 30 percent as part of desperate anti-inflationary measures. Boca, already in debt, were crippled. According to Maradona, he should have been given ownership of some apartments as part of the deal, but the deeds were never produced: they "might as well have been made of cardboard," he said.

While Boca and Argentina struggled, Maradona Productions, which Cyterszpiler had set up in Liechtenstein to manage his client's assets, was thriving. A series of sponsorship deals had been struck to help keep Maradona in Argentina: he promoted Puma and Coca-Cola and advertised toothbrushes, soaps, exercise bikes, and a doll, although he refused to put his name to cigarettes or wine because he regarded them as pollutants.

By 1981 Maradona's salary was $65,000 a month before bonuses, but he also brought in $1.5 million a year from "other sources." He paid $1 million to buy a huge house for himself and his family in Villa Devoto, an upscale neighborhood in the northwest of the city. It was then that the backlash that he had feared since making his first international appearance really began. In December 1979 Maradona had given an interview in which he'd complained of constantly being at the center of attention and of how the public endlessly demanded things from him. People, he said, had asked him for sunglasses, for houses, and to be the godfather to their children. The media reported a string of partners, some real, some imagined, while the ever-loyal Claudia stayed at home. In one of his final games for Argentinos, Maradona pushed a fifteen-year-old who had bumped into him while asking for an autograph. He was given a two-month suspended jail sentence, although—as allowances were made again for his talent—that was subsequently scrubbed from the record.

There were regular accusations that money had gone to his head, and while many stories were exaggerated, Maradona and his family clearly did find it difficult to adjust to his new status. Shortly after the move to Villa Devoto, Tota collapsed on the pavement outside the house, overcome by nerves, seemingly because her relationship with her new neighbors was so fraught. And the constant games, the demand for Maradona always to be his Maradona-ish best, even in exhibitions, took a toll. In February 1981 a friendly was arranged between Argentinos and Boca to mark Maradona's transfer, with him playing forty-five minutes for each side. Seventeen minutes into the first half (for Argentinos), he was forced off with a muscle strain in his left leg. A painkilling injection allowed him to hobble through the second half for Boca, but the reaction was so bad that, he said, he was unable to sleep for three nights. To Maradona's fury, a newly suspicious public suggested he hadn't been fully committed to the half he'd played for the club he was leaving.

He was certainly committed to the club he was joining. From childhood Maradona had been desperate to play for Boca, and that he signed for them when they were struggling and had gone four years without a trophy merely added to his determination: this was his chance to be their savior.

It was an attitude that met with a mixed response. Silvio Marzolini, the great left-back who was by then Boca's coach, warned him that he had to remember he was part of the side and travel with the team to games rather than with his family, words Maradona seems to have regarded as a grave insult: "He made a mistake speaking to me like that." Still, it was never a bad idea to fire the *bronca* in Maradona, and he responded by scoring three and setting up another for his experienced strike partner, Miguel Ángel Brindisi, who had joined the club from Huracán for the start of the 1981 season and became more of a central forward than the right-sided attacking midfielder he had been. "The Boca manager knows that if he loses the tournament, bye-bye, he's out," said Marzolini. "When Boca brought Maradona and Brindisi, we knew that both of them had to play, because it was key to success. To me, in terms of how I treated him, Maradona was an ordinary player, like everybody else. I didn't make distinctions because it wouldn't have been right. He knew that he was the best, I knew he was the best, but our relationship was rather cold because I wasn't offering him any privileges. He was a great person and gave everything."

Boca had won seven and drawn two of their first nine games of the Metropolitano season when they faced River, which had lost only one of their opening nine games, at the Bombonera. Maradona scored a hat trick, including one goal with a run from inside his own half, as Boca won 3–0. As Maradona celebrated his *gambeta*, Marzolini came to the touchline, arms spread to embrace him, whatever differences they had had seemingly forgotten. "Maradona Is Gardel," screamed a headline. A few hours after the game, Marzolini suffered a heart attack. "The stress of being Boca manager is not easy to take," he said. "The first stint I'd smoke sixty cigarettes a day, and my cholesterol was at a record high. They had to perform a bypass after that."

Boca lost the following week, but they still seemed in command of the title race. At the beginning of May, they traveled to their closest challengers, Ferro Carril Oeste, and drew 0–0 in a ferocious game. Maradona said that in that match he got the worst kicking of his career to that point and seemed a little baffled as to why, given the quality on the Ferro side. One celebrated photograph showed Maradona "six feet in the air," as he put it, after a foul by Carlos Arregui.

"When the first half of the season was over, Brindisi had more goals than Maradona," Marzolini recalled. "So Diego said to me, 'Silvio, it's either him as forward or me as forward, but one has to go forward and one has to play behind.' And I told him, 'No, Diego, don't worry, because we are playing well, and they don't know who to mark because there are no fixed positions.' In the end, Maradona scored more goals than Brindisi, but he was also a born leader." Boca remained dominant until July when, as nerves got to them, they drew four matches in a row. The *barra brava* were incandescent as the title seemed to be slipping away and invaded the *concentración* at la Candela.[2]

Maradona was waiting for left-winger Hugo Perotti to get off the phone when he saw him being knocked to the ground. Led by José "el Abuelo" Barrita, around two thousand fans, some of them armed, took over the table-tennis room. They threatened Tano Pernía, Jorge Ribolzi, and Pancho Sá, saying their intervention was a warning as to how angry the fans were. "We were left unattended, on purpose, with no board members or security or anything," said Marzolini. "They wanted to grab [midfielder Jorge]

Benítez, because he was struggling with his crosses, but he wasn't there. They were accusing us of not wanting to win, because we hadn't won against Vélez. It was terrible."

One told Maradona he was exempted from the criticism. He replied that if they didn't leave, he wouldn't play the next day, at which the *barra*, if Maradona is to be believed, fed his paranoia by telling him that there were some of his teammates who wouldn't pass to him or run for him. Marzolini, Maradona said, hid himself away, leaving him to face down Barrita, telling him that the team couldn't play under such circumstances.

Eventually, the *barra* were persuaded to leave. "We were losing the tournament, we had to do something, so we cut the friendlies and focused on the league," said Marzolini. More immediately, he restored the adventurous Hugo Gatti to the starting lineup for the following day's game against Estudiantes. The official line was that the goalkeeper had been injured, but the truth was rather more complicated. "I did military service with Gatti, and he was also on the national team when I was there," said Marzolini. "I dropped him from the team because he was thinking that we wouldn't win the league. Carlos Rodríguez replaced him and had some good performances. When Gatti returned, he got the ball on the halfway line and then assisted a teammate and set up the [only] goal [for Perotti]. But Gatti had a difficult character. He had to wait for a few games."

The following week Boca went to Colón and were 2–0 up when, with twelve minutes remaining, the home side stormed off in protest at the refereeing. They then faced Ferro, all but wrapping up the title, as Gatti made a series of fine saves and Maradona laid in Perotti to give Boca a 1–0 win. Boca needed a draw at Rosario Central on the penultimate weekend of the season to seal the championship. But Maradona hit the bar with a penalty, and they lost 1–0. A week later, though, they got the point they needed, Maradona converting a penalty, as they drew 1–1 with Racing in a game that featured five red cards, four of them—two for each side—coming in the opening quarter hour.

For Maradona at Boca, that was as good as it got. Three weeks after the title had been secured, Boca admitted they were unable to pay the next installment of his transfer fee. Argentinos Juniors sued them, and, at the same time, Boca's assets were frozen by the central bank after a series of checks bounced—one of them to Maradona Productions. Amid the uncertainty, São Paolo offered to buy him for $7 million.

At the time, Maradona was away on a three-week tour with Boca, resentfully playing a further series of friendlies. He returned to find himself being blamed for the club's situation, with some claiming that it was his demands that had gotten Boca into the mess. There was some truth to that, but it was hardly Maradona's fault. Not surprisingly, the criticism hurt. He was, after all, still only twenty, and had played more than two hundred league games despite a persistent thigh injury that required regular pain-killing injections. The problem, really, was the other way around: Boca—Argentinian soccer, even—was so financially dependent on Maradona that he had to play, and that had become debilitating. On October 19, in an interview with *Clarín*, Maradona begged for a break, saying he wanted "to be able to go on enjoying the game and not feel it like a weight that tortures me." It was a plea that would be repeated in various forms throughout his career and seemed to encapsulate something rather sad in what soccer had become for him—had become, perhaps, for Argentina. It was still a game he loved, but it produced extraordinary and intolerable pressures.

In February 1982, Galtieri visited the Argentina squad at their pre–World Cup training camp, embracing Maradona for the cameras. Menotti had by then spoken out against the junta, while Maradona retained an understandable reluctance to be drawn out on political issues. Asked about the government a month earlier, he had replied, "I don't know. . . . All I want is for my country to be the best in the world." In terms of soccer, that was all the junta wanted as well. Galtieri had seen the impact of success four years earlier and was desperate for a repeat in Spain, particularly as, after certain restrictions on free speech had been lifted, protests calling for a return to democracy had become an increasingly common occurrence. At the end of March, thousands demonstrated against the government in the Plaza de Mayo, the first concerted protest against the regime. Galtieri sent in riot police, who cleared the gathering using sabers, truncheons, tear gas, and live ammunition.

The performances of the national team offered only limited hope for a repeat of 1978. Maradona was poor in a 1–1 friendly draw against West Germany, a performance only partly explained by a series of heavy challenges on him. The junta decided radical action was required: even better than a World Cup for generating a sense of national unity, Galtieri decided, was a war. He considered conflict with Chile over the disputed border in the far South, but decided instead to invade the Falklands, assuming the British would grudgingly accept occupation of what were, to most people in Britain, a group of little-known rocks in a far-off ocean. It proved a terrible miscalculation. Argentinian troops landed on April 2, and three days later Britain sent a task force of 127 ships to reclaim the islands, while the United States, whom Galtieri had assumed would stay out of it, supported the British action.

For Ardiles and Ricardo Villa—both of whom had joined Tottenham Hotspur after the 1978 World Cup and been instrumental in winning the FA Cup in 1981, Villa scoring one of the tournament's most famous goals in the final replay against Manchester City—the invasion presented particular difficulties. The day after Argentina occupied the Falklands, Tottenham faced Leicester City in the FA Cup semifinal. "The fuss in the press was big," Ardiles recalled. "Very big. It was an important match, but the number of journalists in our hotel trebled."

Spurs won 2–0, and the following Monday Ardiles returned to Argentina to join up with the national team. Villa remained in London. "My teammates were terrific," he told *El Gráfico*. "Rather than saying it was 'hard,' I'd say it was an 'uncomfortable' situation. Generally, the English are used to these sort of conflicts. Throughout their history they've taken control of lands that aren't theirs, so they're more experienced than us with this kind of issue. The news was there and reported, but nobody thought it would go as far as it did."

Ardiles left to play in the World Cup and then was loaned to Paris Saint-Germain (PSG), but Villa stayed at Spurs—although he was left off the side for the 1982 FA Cup final. "Had it just been soccer, he undoubtedly had to be on the field for that match," said Ardiles. "But as the conflict was reaching its peak and due to various types of pressure, he didn't play—which I consider was a very sad thing. Because in a country like England, politics defeated soccer: you may see that in other parts of the world, but in England it was more unusual." Generally, though, both players remember the protectiveness of Spurs and their fans and the general lack of hostility.

It wasn't easy either for the player who had been remorselessly promoted as the embodiment of Argentina. The day after that FA Cup semifinal and the day before Britain launched the task force, Argentina drew 1–1 with the USSR in another friendly. Again Maradona looked unfit and played poorly. Criticized on all sides, he fled to Esquina, hiding himself away before finally giving an interview to *El Gráfico*. He said:

> What the people have to understand is that Maradona is not a machine for making them happy. He is not a machine that gives kisses and smiles. I'm a normal guy, common and down-to-earth, who happens sometimes to make people happy, sure, and that makes Maradona happy too. But the fact is that people think differently if Maradona doesn't do things right sometimes or has one or ten bad games. And why can't they forgive Maradona? It sometimes takes just one game in which Maradona doesn't play well or doesn't score a goal, and all hell breaks loose.

Maradona kept playing for Boca in the Nacional, but he wasn't happy, despite scoring eleven goals in twelve games. When director Pablo Abbatángelo accused the players of not giving their all after a defeat to Instituto,

Maradona went on *60 Minutes* and said that only "somebody stupid" could have said such a thing. Boca reached the quarter-final, where they met Vélez. With the score at 0–0 in the home leg, Maradona, frustrated at the tight marking of Abel Moralejo, lashed out and was sent off. Boca battled on to win 2–1, but a 3–1 defeat in Liniers, with Maradona suspended, saw them eliminated and ended his first stint at the club.

Not only could Maradona make more money outside Argentina, but the pressure of staying at home had become intolerable. A deal was—at last—done with Barcelona, which paid a total of $7.3 million, $5.1 million to Argentinos and $2.2 million to Boca. Maradona himself received a salary of $70,000 a month.

In Buenos Aires, the mood during the Falklands conflict was surreally detached. Television interspersed news of the war with reruns of games from 1978, while crowds at matches and in the Plaza de Mayo joined in the chant "He who doesn't jump is an Englishman." The link between soccer and war was made explicit by leaflets funded and distributed by the intelligence services, depicting a cartoon Maradona accepting the surrender of a British lion. The World Cup and the Falklands War both allowed Argentinians to lose themselves in a blind patriotism that ignored the reality of a faltering economy and a government that had no mandate and increasingly little sense of control.

On April 10, as US secretary of state Alexander Haig made his way to the Casa Rosada to present a peace proposal, he found his route lined by Argentinians. More than three hundred thousand had packed the Plaza de Mayo, the biggest demonstration since the days of Perón. They burned British and US flags while presenting a carpet of blue and white. To the junta this was vindication; to outsiders this was the symptom of a political malaise that went back at least as far as Perón, a sign of, as Jimmy Burns put it, "the suppression of individuality and a negation of history and their replacement by an extreme nationalism verging on xenophobia. In political terms it signified the victory of totalitarianism over democracy." After all, why would anybody wish to assert their individuality when to stand out was to be a threat, and to be a threat was to risk being disappeared?

As in 1978, it became almost impossible even for those who opposed the regime not to support their country. Novelist Ernesto Sábato, who had railed against Perón and been prepared to criticize the junta from the start, typified the conflicted emotions many Argentinians felt, giving an interview to Spanish radio in which he could barely be heard between his sobs. "In Argentina," he said, "it is not a military dictatorship that is fighting. It is the whole people, her women, her children, her old people, regardless of their political persuasion. Opponents to the regime like myself are fighting for our dignity, fighting to extract the last vestiges of colonialism. Don't be mistaken, Europe; it is not a dictatorship that is fighting for the Malvinas;[3] it is the whole nation."

As more than three hundred lives were lost when the Argentinian Navy cruiser *Belgrano* was sunk by a British nuclear submarine,[4] the disaster competed for coverage with Maradona completing his move from Boca to Barcelona. Before departing for Spain, the World Cup squad paraded with a banner proclaiming "Las Malvinas son Argentinas." Amid the grandstanding there was the odd spark of self-awareness, most notably a piece in *La Nación* ten days before the tournament under the headline "Knowing How to Lose." Given the general atmosphere, it precisely skewered the lunacy of allowing soccer and war to become entwined: "The progressive disintegration of Argentinian optimism," it wrote, "is causing a real national neurosis observable in certain social phenomena, such as compulsive attention to the 1978 World Cup, at which the triumph against the best teams of other countries restored to the public the lost certitude that they could be the best in the world. Such glory, achieved in a gladiator circus . . . gave an ersatz consolation for wounds to the national soul, lacking more significant triumphs in other meaningful areas of international competition."

Even Menotti, difficult as it must have been to square his leftism with one of the most brazenly nationalistic acts of the junta, was able to justify an act of opportunistic saber rattling as part of Argentina's ongoing fight for self-determination, placing the 1982 World Cup alongside the military campaign. "Each man has a part in the struggle," he said. "In these moments there is national unity against British colonialism and imperialism. We feel immense pain for our brothers in the battle fleet, but we have been assigned a sports mission, and we will try to fulfill it with dignity."

For the most part, the media at home continued cheerily to propagandize the war in quasi–soccer playing language, even as it became clear to any neutral that Argentina's ill-equipped and undertrained conscripts had no hope of victory. When the Argentina World Cup squad reached Spain, they found newspapers in their own language and with no reason to be biased telling a very different story. The sense of shock was profound. "We were convinced we were winning the war, and like any patriot my allegiance was to the national flag," said Maradona. "It was a huge blow to everyone on the team."

As the holders, Argentina played in the opening game of the World Cup, against Belgium at Camp Nou. Maradona admitted that the expectant mood in Buenos Aires meant they had arrived in Spain believing success was so necessary as to be all but inevitable. Nine of their starting eleven had played in 1978, but there was little of the fluency or drive they had shown on home soil, and they fell behind after sixty-three minutes. Franky Vercauteren found Erwin Vandenbergh behind the defense with a sweeping pass from the left, and although he took forever to get the ball under control, Fillol hesitated, and the defense had given up any thought of trying to get back, allowing him to jab a shot into the net. Maradona, who was struggling with a hamstring injury, hit the bar with a free kick ten minutes later, but Argentina became the first defending champions to lose their opening game since Italy in 1950. "In soccer," Maradona said, "spirit is contagious: if the team is in good form, then even the biggest donkey on the team can pick up on it. And like boredom, mediocrity is also contagious."

The following morning, *Clarín* split its front page between two headlines: "Bombardment of the British Troops" and "Failed Debut at the World Cup." Later that day, the British accepted the Argentinian surrender in Port Stanley, the news announced, as though to confirm that war's weird interconnection with soccer, during the BBC's coverage of Brazil's 2–1 win over the USSR.[5]

For the junta, that was the beginning of the end, but at the World Cup Argentina staggered on amid a sense that they lacked discipline. Menotti was frequently photographed leaving his room with his arm around a German model. His appetite for women was hardly a secret, but in the context of a struggling World Cup campaign, it became an issue. Alberto Tarantini's wife argued with the fullback on the beach, threatening to go to bed with another man, a row gleefully reported in the Spanish press. Other Spanish journalists were openly skeptical of Maradona, while Pelé, in a column in *Clarín*, wrote, "My main doubt is whether he has sufficient greatness as a person to justify being honored by a worldwide audience." Three years earlier, Maradona had flown to Rio to meet Pelé; he regarded the criticism as a betrayal.

Ramón Díaz was dropped and Kempes pushed deeper to give Maradona greater freedom for the game against Hungary, which had beaten El Salvador 10–1 in their opening game. Maradona scored twice in a 4–1 win, leaving Argentina needing only to beat El Salvador to make it through. They did so, although it was far from a convincing win, Passarella converting a debatable penalty and Bertoni getting the other in a 2–0 victory.

The punishment for failing to top the group was severe, Argentina finding themselves in a second-phase group with Italy and Brazil. In the first of those games, in the Sarrià in Barcelona, Maradona was kept quiet by the attentions of Claudio Gentile—footage from a camera that tracked the defender all game showed a master class in spoiling and fouling on the blind side of the referee—while Ardiles was left with a ripped shirt by Italy's rugged interpretation of defending. Italy scored with two counterattacks, and then Maradona and Passarella both hit the bar before Passarella smacked in a late free kick. But when Gallego was sent off for a late tackle on Tardelli, the game was lost.

That left Argentina needing to beat Brazil by a wide margin in their second game to have even a chance of reaching the semifinal. That never seemed likely once Zico had given Brazil a twelfth-minute lead, and when Serginho headed a second and Júnior added a slick third in the second half, all hope was gone. Maradona, frustrated after not being awarded what looked a clear penalty earlier in the half, lost his head, and when Batista clattered Juan Barbas with three minutes remaining, he responded by thrusting his studs into the Brazilian's midriff and was sent off. Maradona later said that he'd meant to kick Falcão, who had been tormenting Argentina with his passing from deep, but in the heat of the moment had gotten the wrong man. Ramón Díaz did pull one back, but a 3–1 defeat with their best player red-carded was an ignominious departure for the world champions, nine of whom were never capped again.

After the defeat in the Falklands, the navy and air force abandoned the junta, leaving the army to govern alone. Galtieri was replaced by General Reynaldo Bignone, who promised a return to civilian government the following year. With inflation reaching an annual rate of 200 percent—it would later rise as high as 900 percent—the economy contracting by 10 percent per year, and foreign debt at $39 billion, the situation was desperate, and Argentina was forced to turn to the International Monetary Fund (IMF) for help.

Elections were held in October 1983, with the two main parties the Peronists, led by Ítalo Lúder, who had served as acting president for a month in 1975 when Isabelita Perón had fallen ill; and the Radicals, led by Raúl Alfonsín, a lawyer who had been jailed toward the end of Perón's first presidency, helped fight for the rights of the disappeared, and vocally opposed the invasion of the Falklands.[6] The Peronists continued to promote the cult of *el Líder* nine years after his death, broadcasting his greatest speeches over loudspeakers across the country and producing chocolates decorated with the face of Evita. The days when Argentinian politics could readily be divided into Peronists and anti-Peronists, though, were over, and Alfonsín swept to power.

41

THE RETURN OF
ANTI-FÚTBOL

Menotti left the national job after the World Cup, but, as so often in Argentina, there was no simple transfer of power, no suggestion of continuity. Argentina's triumph in 1978 had not led to a complete reversion to the values of *la nuestra*. Once *anti-fútbol* had been introduced, it could never be entirely extirpated. What had happened in Helsingborg in 1958 ensured that the two schools—*menottisme* and *bilardisme*, as they had come to be known by the eighties—would always coexist, fighting for precedence. Perhaps understandably, it was the smaller clubs who reveled in *anti-fútbol*: that was how they could challenge, how they could compete. As Tocalli said of Quilmes's success, it was an era when hard work brought results.

The backlash against Menotti and his philosophy was such that the AFA turned to somebody whose ideas could hardly have been more different: Carlos Bilardo. He had retired from playing in 1970 and succeeded Zubeldía as manager of Estudiantes the following year. While coaching he also helped run his father's furniture business and practiced as a gynecologist, retiring from medicine only in 1976, when he moved to Deportivo Cali in Colombia. He then had spells with San Lorenzo, the Colombia national team, and Estudiantes, which he had led to the Metropolitano title in 1982.

At first, Bilardo spoke warmly of Argentina's performances in winning the 1978 tournament, and he met Menotti at the Arena Hotel in Seville in March 1983. Menotti told him that Estudiantes had set back the development of Argentinian soccer by ten years, but they still parted on good terms. But when Bilardo then ignored his predecessor's advice and left Alberto Tarantini and Hugo Gatti out of the squad for his first game, a friendly against Chile, Menotti reacted by writing a highly critical piece in *Clarín*. The détente over, they became implacable enemies. Bilardo's case wasn't helped by another Copa América failure, as Argentina again went out in the group phase, drawing 0–0 away to Brazil in a final match they needed to win.

The terms of the debate were soon set. Menotti spoke romantically of *la nuestra* revisited—so insistently that it feels at times as though he was trying retrospectively to justify what had happened in 1978. Bilardo just cared about winning. "I like being first," he said.

As the nation cast off the authoritarian pragmatism of the junta, idealistically embracing democracy, the national soccer team turned in the other direction, from the (professed) romanticism of Menotti to somebody for whom the ends pretty much always justified the means. Bilardo's appointment would be the beginning of eight years of struggle, in every sense. In no decade has the Argentina national team ever had a worse win-loss ratio than between 1981 and 1990—yet in that time they reached two World Cup finals, winning one. "Later, when you see the results, everything seems easy, when in fact it was so hard," said Bilardo. "The front of my house was attacked twice. I had to tell my wife to put up a 'Sold' notice before some key games, just in case."

While Estudiantes' success continued the school Osvaldo Zubeldía had founded in the sixties, albeit in a diluted way, there was also a less aggressive, less cynical side to the *anti-fútbol* of the eighties, as Carlos Griguol, the man who had led Rosario Central to the Metropolitano title in 1973, showed with Ferro Carril Oeste. Spiritually at least, he was Spinetto's heir.

Ferro were the epitome of the neighborhood club. They had been founded in 1904 by a hundred workers from the Buenos Aires Western Railway, the company's management providing funds to develop a clubhouse and field. Ferro joined the second division in 1907 and five years later were promoted into the top flight. Their history thereafter was largely one of mediocrity, not that anybody minded too much. The club is based in the leafy district of Caballito, its ground located almost at the exact geographical center of Buenos Aires, and its fans are among the more relaxed in the capital. Ferro has strong basketball, hockey, and volleyball sides, but it also has tennis courts open to members and a restaurant where locals commonly pop in for Sunday lunch.

Ferro's rise in the eighties was the result of two factors: the decline of the *grandes* amid the financial chaos of the end of the junta and the abilities of an exceptional coach. After leaving Rosario, Griguol had managed América in Mexico before returning to Argentina with Kimberley. He led them for only a few games, though, before, in 1979, Ferro's president, Santiago Leyden, asked him to take over from Carmelo Faraone, who had taken the club to promotion to the top flight the previous year. He found a club that had little sense it could challenge for titles. "When I first started at Ferro, after the games everybody would ask about the results of the teams who were relegation candidates," Griguol told *El Gráfico*. "It took a year to change that attitude."

Griguol continued slapping players across the face to motivate them, as he had at Central, and promoted players from the youth side, looking always for those who worked for him and bought into his methods, rather than stars. He tended to wear a beret or cap to hide his baldness, and his thin, slightly crooked smile combined with a vaguely disapproving air often gave him the appearance in photographs of somebody who had just heard a slightly racy joke, but he was tough, innovative, and driven by the conviction that the smaller sides could win trophies. By 1981 Ferro's hard-running, well-organized, possession-based style was beginning to have a major impact. They finished second behind Boca in the Metropolitano and then lost to River in the final of the Nacional. The following year, though, they delivered on their promise.

As the junta's grip on power loosened, violence at matches increased and attendance dropped, decreasing the advantage of the traditional giants. Exacerbating the problem was Menotti's demand that he should have months to work with his World Cup squad before the 1982 tournament in Spain, depriving the *grandes* of their best players and further lessening public interest in attending their matches. That in turn increased the pressure on clubs that were already struggling financially. Not only did Boca sell Maradona, but River had to return Mario Kempes to Valencia when they were unable to keep up with their payment plan and then had to sell Daniel Passarella to Fiorentina.

The effect was profound, the process of decentralization begun fifteen years earlier taken to extremes: in 1982 none of the *grandes* reached the quarter-finals of the Nacional. Ferro won 1–0 over two legs against Independiente Rivadavia of Mendoza—whose stadium had that year been renamed el Estadio Malvinas Argentinas—and progressed to the semifinals. There they met Talleres of Córdoba, winning the first leg 4–0 before letting their concentration slip and drawing the second 4–4.

It would be unfair, though, to suggest that Ferro got their chance only because others were weak. Theirs was consistently a very fine side through the early eighties. By 1982 the core that would sustain the club for much of the decade was in place. Carlos Barisio was a calm, authoritative goalkeeper who in 1981 went a record 1,075 minutes without conceding, protected by two top-class center-backs in Juan Domingo Rocchia, an imposing *caudillo*, and Héctor Cúper, who had come through the youth setup and was a thoughtful passer of a ball—and would later become a coach who took Valencia to successive Champions League finals. The reliable Roberto Carlos Mario Gómez played at right-back with Oscar Garré, later a World Cup winner, an attacking left-back.

The three-man midfield was industrious and intelligent: Carlos Arregui on the right and Gerónimo Saccardi in the middle were also products of Ferro's academy, although Saccardi, a gritty and composed player who could drop in to become a third center-back, was a veteran, having played for Spinetto's 1974 title challengers. On the left, there was the Paraguayan Adolfino Cañete, who added craft and guile to a side that was otherwise largely unimaginative. The front three featured the rapid dribbler Claudio Crocco on the right, with Miguel Ángel Juárez a goal-scoring left-sided forward. In the center, either Julio César Jimenez or Alberto "Beto" Márcico would drop back as a sort of proto false 9, linking with the midfield and creating space for the wide men. "The group was very strong, respectful, and had a great deal of heart," Griguol said. "For us it was normal to run and keep playing for ninety minutes. For other teams it was a sacrifice to play against Ferro. To that you have to add that if the other teams focused on one wide area, running up and down the wing, we would look to the middle. If you reinforced the flanks, I would play through the center, and vice versa."

Ferro sealed the Nacional with victory over Quilmes in the two-legged final. They were, *El Gráfico* said, "a well-oiled machine that reached the summit with simplicity as its emblem. . . . A resounding demonstration of how conviction and total unity can take a group to the very top."

Griguol was a pioneer of zonal marking in Argentina, working with Ferro's basketball coach León Najnudel to develop the best structures for pressing, videoing one another's games, and analyzing them afterward. "They came up with the zonal marking where grabbing and chesting other players was vital," Marzolini said, although his tone suggested he wasn't impressed. Griguol's Ferro side pressed hard all over the field, with players often having to interchange positions as a result. Their fitness was supreme, usually attributed to their conditioning coach Luis María Bonini, who went on to work with Marcelo Bielsa.

Ferro, with their focus on industry, were widely regarded as being *anti-fútbol*, but once they'd regained the ball, they liked to pass in tight triangles, which was usually seen as a *menottista* trait, which perhaps gives some indication of how reductive the *bilardisme-menottisme* dichotomy can be. The 1983 season was a disappointment, as Ferro lost to Estudiantes in the last sixteen of the Nacional, finished third in the Campeonato, and came in at the bottom of an extremely tight Libertadores group, repeatedly throwing away leads in the final minutes of games, as though the criticism of their conservative approach goaded them into taking unnecessary risks.

In 1984, though, they were back. Ferro had passed unbeaten through the group stage of the Nacional and ground their way through the knockouts. They beat Huracán on penalties after a 1–1 aggregate draw in the last sixteen and won 2–1 on aggregate against both Independiente in the quarter-final and Talleres in the semi. Against River in the final, though, they cut loose. Cañete put them in front with a near-post header, Hugo Mario Noremberg ran clear to add a second, and a penalty from Márcico, in what he described as the best game of his career, completed a 3–0 victory. A superb Cañete header that flew into the top corner from the edge of the area made it 4–0 early in the second leg, but the game was never finished, as River fans set fire to a stand. The match and the title were awarded to Ferro.

Still, Argentinian soccer was unsure what to make of Ferro. "Are Ferro a boring team?" asked Natalio Gorin in *El Gráfico* in 1984, publishing a diagram of them passing the ball along the back four and back to the keeper. Gorin picked carefully through the stereotypes of *anti-fútbol*, and there is a strange sense that it needed explaining that the term does not come as a package, that a team can be cautious and hardworking without lapsing into the violence and unpleasantness of the Estudiantes of the late sixties. "It is not a team that aims to hurt opponents," Gorin wrote. "They play hard but fair."

It's true Ferro were masters at killing the game once they'd taken the lead, practicing what would later be termed "sterile domination" by retaining possession, but ultimately, Gorin concluded, "since soccer has been soccer, only teams who play well win."

42

MARADONA IN EUROPE

B arcelona hadn't signed Maradona purely for his soccer-playing ability. The club's president, Josep Lluís Nuñez, believed that, amid the opportunities that had sprung up since the death of Franco, Barcelona could become a worldwide brand. Maradona, who already had global popularity, was the centerpiece of that strategy—which meant even more draining friendlies. Maradona himself was hugely ambitious.

He began with a series of impressive performances—notably in a 4–2 away win over Crvena Zvezda that prompted the crowd in Belgrade to applaud him off—but right from the start there was friction. Maradona employed as his personal doctor Rubén Oliva, who had been the Argentina national team doctor but was by then working in Milan, and as his trainer Fernando Signorini, a locally based Argentinian, much to the frustration of Barcelona's medical staff. There was disquiet too about how he moved his family and a large number of friends—the so-called Maradona clan—into the house the club had provided for him. There were stories of drug taking and parties, and there was a brawl at a nightclub; the whole atmosphere was one of ill-discipline and licentiousness. Ten years later, Maradona finally admitted that it had been at Barcelona that he first began taking cocaine. "When you go into it," he subsequently explained, "in fact you're wanting to say, 'No,' and end up hearing yourself say, 'Yes.' Because you believe you're going to control it, you're going to be okay . . . and then it gets more complicated." At the time, he was fronting an antidrug campaign.

On the field, Maradona, by his own admission, struggled with the "fury" of the Spanish game. Other players were far fitter than him, while he couldn't adjust to the insistence of the coach, Udo Lattek, on training by running while carrying medicine balls, with—he said—heavier weights for bigger games. In his first six months at Barcelona, Maradona scored just six goals. That December he fell ill with hepatitis. He found his first Christmas away from home difficult. "Loneliness scares the shit out of me," he told *Marca*. His relationship with Nuñez never recovered after the president had criticized him for taking the team to a Parisian bar following a friendly victory over PSG, yet the club in some ways went out of its way to accommodate him. When Barcelona decided Lattek had to be replaced, they brought in Menotti, influenced seemingly by the desire to keep their superstar happy. Menotti's first act was to shift training from the mornings to three in the afternoon, which was far more in keeping with both his and Maradona's lifestyles.

It had been a poor season. Barcelona had finished fourth in the league, fifteen points behind the champions, Athletic of Bilbao; they'd lost to Aston Villa in the Super Cup, and they'd gone out of the Cup Winners' Cup to the unfancied Austria Vienna. Only the Copa del Rey offered salvation. Barça reached the final, but the buildup to that game brought further controversy. Maradona and Bernd Schuster were both invited to play in a testimonial for the West Germany great Paul Breitner, who was retiring. That game, though, came four days before the Copa del Rey final. Although Breitner sent a private plane to collect Maradona, Nuñez banned him from traveling to Munich. Maradona planned to go anyway, only for the club to refuse to let him have his passport, which it was looking after with those of the rest of the squad. Maradona saw that as an unconscionable restriction on his freedom and not merely said so in forceful terms but also smashed some trophies in the trophy room; the following day, a group of fans attacked him as he drove away from practice. Barça nonetheless beat Real Madrid in the final, Maradona laying on the opener for Víctor in a 2–1 win.

Still Maradona wasn't happy. He criticized Spanish referees for not offering skillful players sufficient protection and suggested that poor television direction allowed cynical players to commit fouls off camera. His critics, of whom there were many, said he dived and exaggerated contact. At the same time, Menotti and Athletic coach Javier Clemente had a public falling-out. When Barça met Athletic in the fourth game of the season, the atmosphere was rancorous.

On the morning of the game, Maradona went to a local hospital to visit a boy who'd been hit by a car. As he left, the boy said to him, "Diego, please be careful because they're going after you now." Characteristically superstitious, Maradona had a sense of foreboding. The match seemed to be going well, with Barça racing into a 3–0 lead. There was, though, an unpleasant undercurrent. Schuster had gone in hard on Athletic's Andoni Goikoetxea in revenge for an injury he had suffered after a challenge from the center-back the previous season, prompting the crowd to chant his name. Seeing Goikoetxea becoming worked up, Maradona warned him to calm down, but a couple of minutes later Goikoetxea lunged in on him, breaking his left ankle.[1]

Early indications suggested Maradona would be out for the rest of the season, but, working with Oliva, he recovered within three months. He was typically eye-catching on his return, scoring twice in a 3–2 win over Sevilla. Three games later, Barça met Athletic again. Maradona scored twice in a 2–1 victory: the *bronca* had struck again. It wasn't enough, though, to inspire Barça to the title, and they finished third. That March Barça faced Manchester United in the quarter-final of the Cup Winners' Cup. Maradona needed painkilling injections in his back to allow him to take the field, but after playing poorly he was forced off with twenty minutes remaining. The crowd booed him, and he sat in the dressing room and wept. A change of scene hadn't lessened the demands of the public.

His relationship with Nuñez went from bad to worse, as Maradona refused to freeze out a journalist, José Maria García, who had been critical of the president. Nuñez in turn hinted to the press that Maradona's hepatitis was the result of his lifestyle. That made the fans only more skeptical, and Maradona decided he had to leave, a request in which Cyterszpiler was happy to assist. Quite apart from anything else, Maradona needed cash.

By the end of his time at Barcelona, First Champion Productions, as Maradona Productions had been renamed, was losing money. The injuries and a failure to win trophies had rendered Maradona less marketable—one McDonald's advertisement had had to be shot entirely above the waist so as not to show his plaster cast—while a $1 million investment in a film of Maradona's life came to nothing.[2] Then there was the fact that Maradona's lifestyle was expensive: he bought cars on a whim and was funding not just himself but his whole clan. There was further friction when a check to Oliva bounced and Nuñez refused to cover it. Cyterszpiler began agitating for a move, deliberately provoking Nuñez. The final straw, though, came in the Copa del Rey final, as Barcelona again faced Athletic.

Clemente and Maradona sparred in the press in the buildup to the game, and a tense atmosphere was made worse when Athletic fans booed during a minute's silence for two Barcelona fans killed in an accident on their way to the match. Athletic won a tetchy game 1–0, and at the final whistle Maradona lost all control. He claimed he'd been provoked by a V sign from Athletic defender José Núñez, with whom he'd clashed during the game, going forehead to forehead, but even if that were the case, there was no excuse for his brutal and cowardly assault on the unused Athletic substitute Miguel Ángel Sola. He was on his knees celebrating, and as Maradona passed him, he booted him in the face, knocking him out. That prompted a full-on brawl, players high-kicking each other, as substitutes, riot police, journalists, and fans poured onto the field. Maradona was one of six players, three from each side, who were subsequently given three-month bans. "I ended up lashing out at everybody," Maradona said in his autobiography, "because they were beating us and teasing us, until one of the Bilbao players gave me the two fingers, and then the shit really hit the fan. We beat the shit out of each other in the middle of the field. . . . Thank goodness [defender] Migueli and the guys came out to defend me, because otherwise they would have killed me."

Menotti resigned, Terry Venables was appointed, and Maradona was sold for $13 million to Napoli, making him the only player twice to be transferred for world-record fees. The pressure would be no less in Naples, though; if anything, in fact, it was greater. Arriving in Italy in July 1984, Maradona used a decoy in Capri and took a series of back routes from the airport to avoid the crowds before descending on the San Paolo by helicopter, a messiah from the heavens, whose coming was enthusiastically welcomed by tens of thousands of fans. Barcelona had demanded a deposit of $600,000 on the fee; it's said that thousands of Neapolitans each made small deposits at a local building society to raise the money. That perhaps gave an indication of just how desperate Napoli fans were to have Maradona at the club—or perhaps it merely showed the extent to which the club and the city were in the grip of the Camorra.

Cyterszpiler soon found that the rules of commerce were different in Naples. On the streets there was a brisk trade in Maradona products, from cassettes to cigarettes. Cyterszpiler tried to assert control, insisting that all Maradona products had to be officially licensed, but the Camorra warned him off: these were traders working under their protection (having paid the associated costs). Eventually, a deal was reached: First Champion Productions continued to handle promotion and advertising, but local merchandising was controlled by the Camorra.

Maradona and his clan fitted far more easily into life in Naples than they had in Barcelona. Still, things didn't exactly run smoothly. Maradona's form was decent without being spectacular, and by Christmas in his first season Napoli had just nine points from thirteen games and lay third from the bottom of the table. There were also difficulties in Maradona's relationship with Claudia, and in January 1985 he had a much-publicized affair with Heather Parisi, a Californian television presenter.

The second half of the season, though, went rather better, and Napoli ended up missing out on UEFA (Union of European Football Associations) Cup qualification by just two points, with Maradona finishing as the third-highest scorer in Serie A. He told the club hierarchy that they needed three or four new signings, stipulating that they should buy defender Alessandro Renica from Sampdoria. The club complied and also brought in goalkeeper Claudio Garella from Verona and, vitally, forward Bruno Giordano from Lazio. Rino Marchesi was replaced as coach by Ottavio Bianchi, who had been at Como. Maradona took an instant dislike, deeming him "too German."

As the 1985–1986 season began, Maradona's relationship with Cyterszpiler broke up: First Champion Productions was in trouble, and Maradona seems to have come to the conclusion that his childhood friend had been exploiting him, although the truth was rather that the influence of the Camorra meant there was less money coming in. He replaced him with Guillermo Coppola, an Argentinian businessman who represented more than two hundred other players.

On the field the season went well, Napoli continuing their development by finishing third. Off it, though, there were constant rumors and reports about Maradona's social life, of partying and drug abuse. In January 1986 two emissaries of the Giuliano clan approached Maradona at training and told him that the family wanted to get to know him better. It wasn't an invitation Maradona could realistically have refused, and so he attended a party hosted by Carmine Giuliano. A number of photographs were taken, which would later come back to haunt him, but given how many Giuliano events Maradona would subsequently attend, it would be wrong to portray him as an innocent exploited. He knew with whom he was associating, and he benefited from it, his connection with the Giulianos meaning no journalist was ever seriously going to criticize him, for either on- or off-field activities.

In December 1985 Maradona began a relationship with Cristiana Sinagra. He cleaned up while he was with her, cutting out the cocaine and reducing his alcohol intake, but in April 1986 she fell pregnant, and Maradona broke off the relationship. Shortly before the World Cup in Mexico, Maradona's brother-in-law, whose sister had introduced the couple, discovered that Sinagra planned to make the affair public. It seemed the worst-possible buildup.

43

OPTIMISM AND THE
LIBERTADORES

D emocracy may have returned to Argentina and with it a sense of positivity, but the economy remained desperately weak. By the time Alfonsín
took office, inflation had reached 400 percent. Nonetheless, he was initially
popular, as he sought to provide food for the poorest citizens and rescinded
the blanket pardon Bignone had issued in April 1983 for those guilty of
human rights abuses under the dictatorship. He also prosecuted left-wing
groups that had engaged in violence, leading to a jail sentence for Montoneros leader Mario Firmenich.

Alfonsín's election encouraged artists and scientists who had fled the
country under the junta to return, particularly after he appointed playwright Carlos Gorostiza as secretary of culture and computer scientist
Manuel Sadosky as secretary of science and technology. Gorostiza abol-
ished the National Film Rating Entity, effectively a board of censors, and
the result was that film and theater production doubled during his time
in office. There were also official attempts to come to terms with the Dirty
War, as Alfonsín established the National Commission on the Disappearance of Persons, headed by novelist Ernesto Sábato. It documented 8,960
disappearances, which, although some way short of other estimates, at least
represented an official acknowledgment of the crimes of the state. At the
same time, though, he had to play the political game and offered an olive
branch to the Peronists by pardoning Isabel Perón for persecution of dissidents under her presidency and the alleged embezzlement of public funds.

The return of democracy and the cultural boom brought a sense of
buoyancy to Argentina, and the return of success in the Libertadores can
only have reinforced the sense of a nation beginning to renew and reassert itself. After Boca's defeat to Olimpia in the 1979 final, five years passed
before another Argentinian side reached that stage. If only vaguely, sub-
consciously, to a nation that derived so much of its self-esteem from soccer,
those years of failure must have added to the sense of stagnation.

It was Independiente, perhaps not surprisingly given their reputation as the king of cups, who made the breakthrough. José Pastoriza, the great midfielder of the late sixties and early seventies, took over as coach and led the club to the 1983 Metropolitano. Only the balding playmaker Bochini remained from the team that had won the club's sixth Libertadores in 1975, but Jorge Burruchaga, who would go on to have a key role to play in the 1986 World Cup, had emerged as an energetic attacking presence. That close-season Alejandro Barberón returned to the club from the Colombian side Millonarios. He was a forward who cut in from the left and shared an understanding with Bochini almost as profound as that Daniel Bertoni had once enjoyed. After a shaky start in the Libertadores, their impressive home form helped them through to the final against Grêmio.

The first leg, in Porto Alegre, was perhaps the last great flowering of Bochini's talent, as he laid in the bustling Burruchaga for the only goal—the incident he described as being characteristic of *la pausa*, waiting for the teammate to make the run from deep before delivering the pass at the perfect moment.

At la Doble Visera, a 0–0 draw ended Argentina's six-year drought in the competition and gave Independiente their seventh Libertadores title, making them the most successful side in the competition's history. A third Intercontinental title followed with victory over Liverpool in Tokyo, nineteen-year-old forward José Alberto Percudani running on to Claudio Marangoni's ball over the top to score the only goal of the game after seven minutes. To an extent, though, Independiente's reputation for success meant that welcome as their triumph had been, it didn't necessarily signify an Argentinian revival. Far more significant in that regard was what happened the following year, underlining the returning strength of the Argentinian game, even as faith in Alfonsín's capacity to reform Argentina began to wane.

The issues of the economy and tackling the crimes of the junta dominated Alfonsín's presidency. Although gross domestic product grew by 2 percent in 1984, Argentina was still left with a federal budget shortfall of $10 billion, 13 percent of GDP. It responded by printing money, which only worsened the inflationary crisis, reaching 30 percent per month by June 1985. Prices were frozen and a new currency, the austral, valued at one thousandth of a peso, introduced. There were cutbacks in public spending across the board, but particularly to the military, whose funding was slashed to half its 1983 level. In the short term, the policy worked, inflation dropping to 2 percent per month in the final half of 1985, while the fiscal deficit was reduced by two-thirds.

But there were consequences. The unions were angered by the fall in real wages caused by the failure to bring inflation under control; the

Catholic Church objected to liberal measures such as the legalization of divorce, at one point ordering clergy to deny communion to congressmen who had voted in favor of the bill; and, most troublingly, there was discontent among the military. In October 1985 General Suárez Mason, the former president of Argentinos, fled to Miami after a warrant was issued for his arrest following a number of acts of sabotage at military bases. There had been friction already over the military's refusal to court-martial officers over offenses committed during the Dirty War, leading Alfonsín to sponsor the Trial of the Juntas, the first hearings for which were held at the Supreme Court in April 1985. That December Videla and former navy chief Emilio Massera were given life sentences. Three others were handed prison terms of seventeen years, while four defendants, including Galtieri, were acquitted, although he was subsequently court-martialed for malfeasance during the Falklands War and sentenced to twelve years in jail.

Aside from the Cebollitas, Argentinos Juniors' impact on Argentinian soccer had been minimal, but the coming of Maradona changed everything. His presence was enough to lift Argentinos to second in the Campeonato in 1980, and his loss the following season was felt keenly. As Boca won the Campeonato, Argentinos slumped. On the final day of the season, they went to San Lorenzo second-bottom of the table, trailing them by a point; they needed to win to stay up. With San Lorenzo homeless, the game was played at Ferro, where a record crowd packed in. Argentinos's Uruguayan goalkeeper Mario Alles saved a penalty from Eduardo Delgado after seventeen minutes, and then, just before halftime, Carlos Horacio Salinas, one of the players transferred to Argentinos as part of the Maradona deal, converted a penalty. In the face of intense pressure, Argentinos hung on and survived, while San Lorenzo became the first of the *grandes* ever to be relegated.

For San Lorenzo, that was another step in the degradation that had begun with the sale of the Gasómetro, but just because it was predictable didn't mean the blow was any less profound. "I mourned as much as I did the day my father died," said novelist and San Lorenzo fan Osvaldo Soriano,[1] who was living in exile in Europe at the time. "I remained alone and as helpless as a woman in the darkness." A decade earlier, other teams had begun to win titles; now the *grandes* weren't even guaranteed their place among the elite anymore. San Lorenzo won promotion at the first attempt and were only a point off winning the Campeonato in 1983. The shock, though, was a warning: the thought of a Primera without the *grandes* wouldn't do: they brought tradition and, perhaps more important, fans and thus money. From 1983 relegation was determined by the *promedio*, an average of points won per game over the previous two seasons (that saved River, which had finished second from the bottom, but only at the expense of Racing). From 1984 relegation was decided over a three-year term, the theory being that the *grandes* would never be that bad for that long. It proved not to be quite that simple.

The sale of Maradona to Barcelona at the end of the 1984 season brought Argentinos $5.8 million, but the initial reaction of the board, perhaps recognizing Argentinos's natural level, was to spend it on infrastructure rather than directly on the team. The result was another year of struggle, with Argentinos staying up by a point—their final point of the season having come in a 0–0 draw against Nueva Chicago that was abandoned at halftime. Only then were funds released, with Ángel Labruna appointed as coach and four major signings, including goalkeeper Ubaldo Fillol and midfielder J. J. López from River. There was an immediate improvement, but that September Labruna was admitted to the hospital for surgery on his gallbladder. He was being visited by his son, Omar, and Fillol when he suffered a heart attack and died, at the age of sixty-four.

To replace him Argentinos turned to Roberto Saporiti, the former Estudiantes and Talleres coach. Under him Argentinos played bright, lively soccer and scored at a rate of almost two goals per game. All season they and Ferro, the Nacional champions, traded blows at the top of the table, and going into the final weekend they were level on points. Ferro could only draw at Estudiantes, while Jorge Olguín's first-half penalty was enough to give Argentinos a 1–0 win over Temperley—in a game played at Ferro—and with it their first-ever title.

That was just the beginning. Saporiti was replaced as coach by José Yudica, who had led Quilmes to the title in 1978 and then taken San Lorenzo to promotion back to the top flight. At Quilmes circumstance had made Yudica relatively cautious, but at Argentinos he found a team suited to the more expansive approach he naturally favored.

In 1985 the Nacional took on an even more baffling format than usual, a low even in the tangled history of the structure of Argentinian championships that was thankfully abandoned immediately. Argentinos beat Vélez on penalties to reach the final and then beat them again in the final. The next step was the Libertadores.

"Argentinos are one of the great teams in Argentina at the moment," Yudica said in an interview with *El Gráfico*, "and it's partly because we have the perfect player in each position." The real question, though, in a country beginning to reassert itself internationally, was whether being one of the best sides in Argentina meant they were competitive at the continental level.

Argentinos needed to beat the defending champions, Independiente, in their final game in the semifinal group to reach the final. They led 2–1, but with two minutes remaining Independiente were awarded a penalty. If Marangoni had scored, Independiente would have gone through, but Enrique Vidallé, the charismatic goalkeeper, plunged low to his left to keep it out, and it was Argentinos that progressed. In the final they beat the Colombian side América de Cali on penalties in a playoff after Vidallé saved from Ántony de Ávila.

For Yudica, what was important wasn't just that Argentinos had won, but how they'd won. "We always play the ball," he said, "no matter the result. And we do it for the respect of the profession, for the spectacle and the people that believe in our style. I wouldn't spend much time speaking about the opposition, underlining each player's ability or weakness."

Penalties were the undoing of Argentinos in the Intercontinental final later that year, when they drew 2–2, with Juventus having twice taken the lead, and within a few weeks Yudica was gone, having fallen out with Batista and Claudio Borghi.

That was the end of Argentinos as a serious force, but the point was nonetheless made: Argentinian soccer was preeminent again in South America, and not only that, but its smaller clubs could compete not merely with the *grandes* in their own country but also with the best of the rest of the continent and the world. The rise of the smaller clubs was in part down to a general improvement in Argentinian soccer and wasn't—or not entirely—the result of the decline of the *grandes*.

44

HIS FINEST HOUR

A rgentina's preparations for the 1986 World Cup were terrible and not just because Maradona was facing exposure over his affair. Bilardo had known from the moment he took the national job that if Argentina were to do anything, he needed the support of Maradona, so in January 1983 he went to visit him in Lloret de Mar on the Costa Brava, where Maradona was recuperating from hepatitis. He borrowed a tracksuit jacket from him, and the two went running along the beach. They discussed the national side, and Bilardo offered him the captaincy, although Maradona didn't actually play for Argentina between the 1982 World Cup and a pair of friendlies against Paraguay and Chile in 1985. Through 1984, as speculation understandably intensified around Maradona's position, Bilardo kept repeating that he was the only player guaranteed to be a starter in Mexico. "We received criticism for our way of playing, for the players I called up. . . . [S]ome even criticized me for picking Maradona as captain," Bilardo said.

A tour of Europe in September 1984 was key to the development of the side. It was in those games that Bilardo unveiled his tactical master plan: a highly unusual 3-5-2 formation. He always claimed he had invented it, reasoning that if nobody was using wingers anymore, there was no need to play orthodox fullbacks. Although the truth is rather that 3-5-2 was a system with many fathers and that Ćiro Blažević at Dinamo Zagreb and Sepp Piontek with Denmark came to similar conclusions at around the same time, that doesn't diminish Bilardo's tactical imagination or his courage in being prepared to challenge the orthodoxy. "That was the cornerstone of the process, when we played against Switzerland, Belgium, and Germany, and deployed a new tactical system: three defenders, five midfielders, and two forwards," said Bilardo. "It was very difficult to set up, but I was convinced it was the best shape for us. But everyone, from fans to journalists to players, kept asking me, 'But who's the right winger? But who's the left-back?' It was very difficult to explain that fixed positions were no longer useful. So I said, 'Right now, I prefer to be understood by 30 players rather than by 30 million Argentinians.'" Argentina beat Switzerland and Belgium 2–0 and West

Germany 3–1, at which Bilardo, not wanting to alert the rest of the world to what he was doing, hid the formation.

For the 1978 World Cup, Menotti had been able to select a squad that was, Kempes aside, entirely based in Argentina. Six of the twenty-two Bilardo ended up picking for the 1986 World Cup were based in Europe, while José Luis Brown was in Colombia and Héctor Zelada in Mexico; the modern exodus that had begun with Ardiles and Villa joining Tottenham was well under way. By 1990 only eight of the squad were based in Argentina. "It was very hard to work," Bilardo said. "That's why I once said, 'To practice, Burruchaga has to take free kicks in Nantes and [Oscar] Ruggeri head them home in Madrid.'"[1]

Argentina began the qualifying campaign for the World Cup superbly, with home and away wins over Venezuela and Colombia. Defeat away to Peru, though, meant they then had to manage at least a draw against the Peruvians at el Monumental to qualify automatically and avoid a four-team playoff for Conmebol's final slot. They managed it, but only just, Daniel Passarella squeezing in a shot after a half-cleared corner had been returned to the box to make it 2–2 with nine minutes remaining. "The qualifiers were very tough," said Bilardo, "but we knew it's always more difficult to qualify than to play in the World Cup. Still, the press wanted me out. Nobody had confidence in us. The day we left, the airport was almost empty. When we arrived home, five hundred thousand people were there celebrating."

It wasn't just the fans who looked at Argentina's chances without great optimism. When they beat Israel 7–2 in their final friendly before the tournament, it was their first win in seven games, and there was disquiet in the camp almost as soon as they arrived. Maradona and three teammates turned up fifteen minutes late for a team meeting, prompting Passarella to lecture the captain, seemingly under the assumption that the four had been delayed while taking drugs. Maradona admitted to the squad that he did at times use cocaine, but insisted that he wasn't during the World Cup. He then went on the offensive, accusing Passarella of having run up a two-thousand-peso phone bill at the hotel that the squad had to split between them and of having an affair with a married woman. The elegant center-forward Jorge Valdano, having previously supported Passarella, turned on him, and the former captain soon left the squad, claiming he was ill.

As Maradona put it in his autobiography, fans watched their opening game against South Korea "with their eyes half-closed," fearing the sort of humiliation that was eventually inflicted upon them by Cameroon four years later. "They didn't even know who was playing," he went on. "Passarella had left; Brown, [José Luis] Cuciuffo and [Héctor] Enrique had come into the squad. We trusted, we trusted, but we had not yet had a single positive result to build on. . . . All Bilardo's meticulous plans, all his tactics, his obsession with positions, suddenly it all fell into place."

What is remarkable to modern eyes is the punishment Maradona took, whether because opponents deliberately targeted him or because he was so quick and so adept at changing direction that what would ordinarily have appeared reasonable challenges were made to look thuggish. It took just six minutes of Argentina's first game, against South Korea at the Olimpico in Mexico City, for Kim Pyung-seok to catch him with a dreadful thigh-high challenge, and he would be fouled a further ten times during the game. Maradona's free kick came back to him off the wall, but he headed the ball into the box for Valdano, who had time to measure a finish into the far corner. For a team short on confidence, it was the perfect start.

Kim pulled Maradona down again twelve minutes later, and again Maradona took the free kick, floating a cross to the back post for Ruggeri to bury a header. Maradona created the third as well, darting to the byline after Nery Pumpido's long clearance had been knocked down for him and squaring for Valdano to roll in. Park Chang-sun belted in a consolation, but Argentina, after Bulgaria and Italy had drawn their opening game, to their surprise and relief, had control of the group.

There was little onus on Argentina to attack Italy, and Bilardo accordingly deployed Ruggeri to man-mark center-forward Alessandro Altobelli. Italy nonetheless took an early lead, Altobelli converting a penalty after Oscar Garré had handled. Maradona was also man-marked, by Salvatore Bagni, but it was Gaetano Scirea who was picking him up when, after thirty-three minutes, Valdano received the ball from Ricardo Giusti with his back to goal and chipped it around the corner for Maradona to run onto. Maradona let the ball bounce and got far enough away from the Italy captain to guide a shot back across goal and inside the post. Bruno Conti hit a post in a drab second half, but as the game became increasingly fractious, few on either side were unhappy with the point.

It meant that a draw from their final game, against Bulgaria, was likely to be enough to guarantee Argentina first place in the group, while the Bulgarians knew they would probably make it through as a best-placed third team with a narrow defeat. From the moment José Luís Cuciuffo broke down the right and crossed for Valdano to head Argentina into a third-minute lead, no other result seemed likely. With eleven minutes remaining, Maradona pushed the ball one side of Andrey Zhelyazkov, ran around the other, and crossed for Burruchaga to confirm the win.

Despite winning the group, all was not well. Bilardo was just as much a disciplinarian as Zubeldía had been, imposing a strict curfew, which was broken on one occasion by the reserve goalkeeper, Luis Islas of Estudiantes.

Bilardo gathered the squad together the following morning and raged at his players, saying he knew one of them had been out late and that whoever it was would be sent home. He called on the guilty player to own up. Islas sat in silence as his teammates glanced anxiously about. Bilardo's fury increased. He said whoever was responsible was a coward and that he was destroying Argentina's World Cup and again asked the player to confess. Islas still said nothing. By that stage, Bilardo was almost spitting with anger. For a third time, he demanded the guilty party to admit it, at which Maradona raised his hand. "Boss," he said, "it was me."

"Okay," said Bilardo, clapping his hands and heading for the door. "Training at the usual time this afternoon."

Argentina's opponents in the last sixteen were a familiar rival, Uruguay. Having been fined and warned by FIFA for their conduct in the group stage—when José Batista had picked up the fastest red card in World Cup history, sent off after fifty-five seconds of the 0–0 draw against Scotland—Uruguay perhaps felt restricted in how they could deal with Maradona, who hit the bar with a free kick, had a goal ruled out, and created a number of chances for Valdano and Pasculli. Only one chance was taken, though, and Maradona was only tangentially involved. It was his turn and pass from deep in midfield that released Batista, he forced the ball wide for Burruchaga, and when his attempted pass to Valdano was intercepted, the ball ricocheted kindly for Pasculli to sweep in.

It was not a goal that would keep the striker on the side. "You can't play against the English with a pure center-forward," Bilardo explained. "They'd devour him, and the extra man in midfield will give Maradona more room." Argentinos striker Pasculli was dropped for Héctor Enrique, a dependable attacking midfielder from River Plate, and at last Bilardo unleashed the 3-5-2 that would win Argentina the tournament. José Luis Brown was an uncomplicated *libero*, with Ruggeri and Cuciuffo as the two markers in front of him; Batista operated in front of them as a ball-playing ball winner, with Julio Olarticoechea—preferred to the more defensively minded Garré—and Ricardo Giusti wide. Burruchaga provided the link between midfield and attack, with Maradona operating as a second striker behind Valdano with a license essentially to drift wherever he wanted.

And there was, of course, an additional edge to the game, just four years after the end of the Falklands War. At the time, players on both sides seemed frustrated by constant references to the conflict. "Look," snapped Maradona then, "the Argentina team doesn't carry rifles, nor arms, nor ammunition. We came here only to play soccer. How can I talk about the war when only last month thirty thousand Tottenham fans cheered me in Ossie Ardiles's testimonial?"

Maradona's first goal, after fifty-one minutes, became notorious, an example of *viveza* at its worst, as he punched Steve Hodge's sliced clearance past a flat-footed Shilton. As he ran to the corner flag, Maradona gave an anxious glance over his shoulder, as though unable quite to believe that the goal would be given. "I was waiting for my teammates to embrace me, and no one came . . . ," he said. "I told them, 'Come and hug me, or the referee isn't going to allow it.'" Asked about the incident after the game, Maradona said it had been scored "a little with the head of Maradona and a little with the hand of God."

There has been much pontificating about the incident, but criticism of Tunisian referee Ali bin Nasser, much of it based on the spurious logic that officials from countries outside the soccer-playing mainstream should not be given major games, should be tempered by the fact that it took almost two minutes for English commentator Barry Davies to realize England's players were appealing for handball rather than offside; it was by no means as obvious at the time as still photographs and familiarity have made it appear. Besides which, English attempts to claim the moral high ground are rather undermined by the brutal treatment meted out to Maradona. As Scott Murray pointed out in the *Guardian* in 2014, Terry Fenwick arguably committed four red-card offenses in the game yet got away with only a booking.

Maradona's second goal, scored four minutes later, was breathtaking, instantly surpassing in the popular consciousness Corbatta's goal against Chile in 1957 as the greatest scored for the Argentina national team. He received the ball from Enrique about ten yards inside his own half—"With a pass that good, he couldn't really miss," the midfielder joked—and turned away from Peter Beardsley and Peter Reid. Reid gave chase but couldn't close the gap on Maradona as he darted inside Terry Butcher. Maradona slipped by Fenwick, and although Butcher got back to make a desperate challenge he couldn't prevent him sidestepping Shilton and sliding the ball into the net.

Victor Hugo Morales, commentating on Argentinian television, exulted, "What a goal! Diegooooooo! Maradona! I'm so sorry, it brings tears to your eyes. Maradona, in an unforgettable run, in a move for all time. . . . You barrel-chested cosmic phenomenon. . . . From what planet did you come to leave so many Englishmen in your wake, to turn the country into a clenched fist screaming for Argentina? Argentina 2, England 0, Diego Armando Maradona, thank you God, for soccer, Maradona, for these tears and this Argentina 2, England 0." Or, as Davies put it on the BBC, "And you have to say *that*'s magnificent." Gary Lineker pulled one back, but it was not enough.

Like England, Belgium, which had beaten Spain on penalties in their quarter-final, eschewed wingers and packed the midfield. They too could only hold out until just after halftime. Burruchaga drifted in from the right and slipped a pass into the path of Maradona as he darted into the box. Goalkeeper Jean-Marie Pfaff came off his line, and Maradona calmly stabbed the ball over him with the outside of his left foot. Twelve minutes later he added a second of dazzling brilliance. Picking the ball up forty yards from goal, he had a phalanx of three defenders in front of him and another, Eric Gerets, ten yards behind them. He skipped through the first three and surged left of Gerets, before hooking his finish back across Pfaff. His momentum almost caused him to fall over, but, arm windmilling, his balance extraordinary, he stayed up to wheel away and take the congratulations of his teammates.

With five minutes remaining, Ricardo Bochini, by then thirty-two, came on for Burruchaga to make his only appearance in the finals of a World Cup. Maradona had insisted Bilardo select the player who had been his idol, who had been left out of the previous two tournaments by Menotti, seemingly because of his lack of pace. As Bochini shuffled onto the field, Maradona jogged over to him. "Maestro," he said, "we've been waiting for you." Bochini claims he can't remember what was said, but it's believed he wasn't overly impressed by the gesture, feeling patronized by the whole episode.

West Germany, Argentina's opponents in the final, had also switched to three central defenders as the tournament progressed. Their wingbacks Hans-Peter Briegel and Andreas Brehme were rather more defensive than Argentina's, but essentially they matched them shape for shape, with Lothar Matthäus used to man-mark Maradona. For a long time, the pair effectively canceled one another out.

Argentina's opener, though, had nothing to do with tactics and everything to do with an uncharacteristic error from Toni Schumacher, who had probably been the best goalkeeper in the tournament until then. He came for Burruchaga's right-wing free kick—awarded for a foul by Matthäus on Maradona—midway through the first half and missed by a distance, allowing Jose Luís Brown to head in his only international goal. Eight minutes into the second half, Argentina added a second, Maradona feeding Héctor Enrique, who slid in Valdano. With Schumacher tentative—having been ordered by his teammates, he said in his autobiography, to stay back—Valdano casually rolled the ball past him.

At that stage the game seemed done, but the replacement of the ineffective Felix Magath with Dieter Hoeneß and the release of Matthäus from his marking duties gave them renewed thrust. Bilardo had been tormented in the buildup to the game by West Germany's strength from set plays. So anxious about them was he that, at four on the morning of the final, he burst into Ruggeri's room, pounced on him, and, with the defender disoriented and half-asleep, asked whom he was marking at corners. "Rummenigge," came the reassuringly instant reply, but with Brown nursing a fractured shoulder, Argentina's marking structure at set pieces collapsed. With sixteen minutes remaining, Rudi Völler flicked on Brehme's corner, and Karl-Heinz Rummenigge stretched to turn the ball in from just inside the six-yard box. Eight minutes later, Brehme took another corner from the same flank, Thomas Berthold headed back toward the near post, and Völler nodded in from close range.

The momentum seemed to be with the Germans, but three minutes later, as the ball dropped near the halfway line, Maradona volleyed a perfectly weighted pass for Burruchaga to chase. With Schumacher again slightly slow off his line, the midfielder got away with a heavy touch and poked the ball into the bottom corner. Argentina had won the World Cup for the second time, and Maradona had fulfilled the ambition he had revealed on television more than a decade earlier. As players and coaching staff celebrated on the field afterward, Bilardo broke down in tears and spoke of the debt he owed to Osvaldo Zubeldía.

Even in victory, Bilardo wasn't entirely satisfied. "After beating Germany, I was very angry and couldn't celebrate," he said. "Somebody asked me, 'Carlos, but what's going on?' And I answered, 'They scored two goals from set pieces. With the number of times we had practiced and emphasized their moves, they still scored two goals from corners!'"

He was also frustrated by the claim that the success was due to the excellence of one man. "During the World Cup, Maradona was brilliant, but so were other players," Bilardo said. "It wasn't just Diego, even if he was fundamental: we knew how to surround him and make him feel comfortable. For example, the movement of Valdano[2] in the final, starting almost as left-back and ending as a right-winger to score, that's when you say: these players know everything."

Argentina returned in triumph, and, as was expected, Alfonsín allowed the team to celebrate on a balcony at the Casa Rosada in front of a packed Plaza de Mayo. It was characteristic of his style of politics, though, that he didn't join them; he sought neither cheap publicity nor to promote himself through reflected glory.

45

BURYING THE CHICKEN

The *gallinas* tag hung heavy on River Plate, even though they'd won the Metropolitano and Nacional in 1979, the Campeonato in 1980, and the Nacional in 1981. That side of Ubaldo Fillol, Daniel Passarella, J. J. López, Renato Merlo, Beto Alonso, and Leopoldo Luque was clearly a superb one, probably the best River team since the days of la Maquinita, but the Libertadores remained beyond them, despite the fact their squad was so stuffed with talent that they effectively used one midfield for domestic games and one for continental competition.

With the team in chaos—they went through seven managers in the two and a half years after Di Stéfano's departure for Real Madrid in 1982—they didn't qualify for the 1983 tournament. That year was the nadir: the players went on strike for forty-seven days over unpaid wages, meaning youth teamers played instead, and River finished second from the bottom of the Metropolitano and avoided relegation only because of the introduction of the *promedio*, which determined who went down on an average of points per game over the previous three seasons.

The first signs that River were beginning to grow again came under the Uruguayan Luis Cubilla in 1984 as they lost to Ferro in the final of the Nacional and finished fourth in the Campeonato, despite a 5–1 defeat away to Unión that led to Cubilla's being sacked. He was replaced by Héctor "el Bambino" Veira. In 1964, at eighteen, Veira had been the top scorer in the Primera with San Lorenzo, and four years later he'd helped them to the Metropolitano title, but there was a sense his playing career had never quite delivered on its early promise. When River named him manager, his coaching career was still in its infancy, comprising stints with San Lorenzo and Vélez and two impressive seasons in the second flight with Banfield. He was already attracting a reputation for his sense of humor and idiosyncratic pronouncements.

"If we have order, discipline, and humility, with this squad we can make history," he wrote on a board in the dressing room. His first step toward that was working out the best way to use the sublimely talented Uruguayan Enzo Francescoli, at the time only twenty-three, converting him from a number

8 into a center-forward. "If he doesn't succeed," Veira told club president Hugo Santilli, "I'm going to quit managing teams." He wasn't a typical 9, though: Veira defined Francescoli as a 9 and a half, midway between a 9 and a 10. Héctor Enrique, meanwhile, who had been playing as right-winger, became the number 8, a sort of 10 on the right. It was a move that appealed to Veira's audience: since the days of la Máquina, River was a club that had believed in accommodating as many playmakers as possible.

They lost only three times all season and made a habit of racking up big scores: 5–1 against Newell's, 4–1 against Vélez, 5–1 against Estudiantes, 5–4 against Argentinos, and 4–0 against Racing de Córdoba. On March 9, 1986, a 3–0 win over Vélez saw them crowned champions with five rounds of the season still remaining. The great celebration came with a 2–0 win over Boca—both goals from Alonso—in a game made instantly recognizable in video clips by the use of an orange ball because of the amount of ticker tape on the field.

The league title was important to restore a sense of calm, but the dream was the Libertadores and putting to an end the stigma of not having won it—a need made all the more pressing, of course, by Boca's victories. Impressive early performances meant a draw at home against Argentinos in their final game in the semifinal group would have them through to the final, but River lost 2–0 in what their rivals were quick to highlight as a classic *gallinas* choke. Argentinos then beat Barcelona of Ecuador to force a playoff, although River's superior goal difference meant they needed only a draw to progress. "We played with our balls in our throats," said Alonso, but they held out for a 0–0 draw to reach their third Libertadores final, where their opponents were América de Cali, which had lost in the final the previous year.[1]

Midway through the first half in Cali, River's Uruguayan forward Antonio Alzamendi found space on the right, checked back inside, and slipped on the rain-sodden field as he attempted to cross. His delivery was surely lower than intended, but Juan Gilberto Funes, "el Búfalo,"[2] showed a deftness that defied his nickname, turned, and finished smartly. Three minutes later a cleverly worked free kick led to Alzamendi knocking down a left-wing cross for Alonso, who fired in an awkwardly bouncing ball from the edge of the box. Paraguayan midfielder Roberto Cabañas pulled one back early in the second half, but River held on for a 2–1 victory.

Seven minutes after halftime at el Monumental, River defender Alejandro Montenegro was sent off along with Ricardo Gareca, who had left River for América the previous year, but after sixty-six minutes Enrique played a quick, low ball forward to Funes, who held the ball up, turned superbly, and hit a low shot inside the left-hand post of América's Argentinian goalkeeper Julio César Falcioni. It was the only goal of the game, and River, at last, had won the Libertadores. "I was raised on people's arms and carried like that all the way around the lap of honor," Alonso said. "To be a River fan, as well as a soccer player, made that even more special—particularly for somebody who was practically born there. Everything I do for River comes from my heart."

It was in Tokyo a little under two months later, though, that, as Gallego put it, "the chicken was finally buried," as River won against Steaua Bucharest, the European champions. "Finals are like *superclásicos*: you play not to lose, to keep the nil in your goal, because if you can score, you know that 1–0 will be enough to make you a champion," said Alonso.

> That was a team that could go to war and know that we'd win. We were like the home side in every stadium, in terms of how we set out and how we managed to seize games and control the action. We forced others to retreat and see what they can do against us. It was the last great Argentinian side I've seen. And it wasn't 100 percent River DNA. There were just three of us born in River, for a start. But the ones who were brought in adapted quickly and efficiently. And we all wanted achievements; we were humble and hungry.

Alzamendi's twenty-ninth-minute goal secured a 1–0 win in a tight, tense game.

Already the process of dissolution had begun. Francescoli had gone even before the Libertadores, sold to Racing Paris. Alonso retired in 1987 and Gallego in 1988. Roque Alfaro left in 1987 and Pumpido, Nélson Gutiérrez, Ruggeri, Alzamendi, and Funes in 1988.

Also in 1987 Veira was replaced as coach by Carlos Griguol. That October Veira, by then working for San Lorenzo, was accused of sexual assault by a thirteen-year-old boy, who said he'd been invited into Veira's apartment after asking for an autograph. Veira, who continues to protest his innocence, was convicted of attempted rape and the corruption of a minor in April 1988 and sentenced to four years in prison. After an appeal, the conviction was amended in August 1991 to rape and the sentence lengthened to six years. The following September the Supreme Court recategorized the offense again as attempted rape and set the sentence at three years. As Veira had already served more than a third of his sentence, he was paroled, prompting unproved allegations that President Carlos Menem, whose party had a majority on the Supreme Court at the time, may have influenced the decision.

46

THE NEAPOLITAN GLORY

After the World Cup, Maradona went on a "honeymoon" with Claudia, who—seemingly in response to the public revelation of his affair with Cristiana Sinagra—had had a nose job and dyed her hair blonde. The message was clear: they were back together and presenting a united front. That September Sinagra gave birth to Maradona's child, although it would be years before he accepted that the boy was his. Public sympathy was on her side, yet for all the complications Maradona carried his form of the World Cup into the new season.

The unique achievement of Maradona, when he is compared with the other contenders to be considered the greatest player of all time, is to have led, almost single-handedly, a moderately sized club to a major championship in an era in which money had started to be not merely an advantage but a decisive factor. That's not necessarily to say he was better than Pelé or Di Stéfano or Cruyff or Messi or Puskás, but it is to say he was different. Not for him the knitting together of exceptional talents, taking the very good and inspiring them through his own genius to be great; Maradona perhaps needed to be the central figure, needed to have a side around him that relied on him. It wasn't just about his technical ability, about his *gambetas*, his free kicks, and his goals, but about him as an inspiration and an organizer. Of the other greats, perhaps only Cruyff—although in a different way—could match his on-field tactical brain.

Just as it would be wrong to portray Argentina's World Cup winners of 1986 as Maradona plus the rest, it would be wrong to suggest Napoli were Maradona and ten stooges. There were others of a high level on the squad: after the World Cup, they brought in Andrea Carnevale to create a formidable front three. They had Ciro Ferrara at center-back and Fernando De Napoli and Salvatore Bagni in midfield. They were far from no-hopers, but, still, it was clear that without Maradona they wouldn't have been mounting a serious challenge for the title. He gave them their spark, their creativity, and their drive; he made them believe extraordinary things were possible, just as he had with Argentina.

With Maradona exceptional, in 1986–1987 Napoli won the *scudetto* for the first time in their history, sealing the title on the penultimate weekend of the season with a 1–1 draw against Fiorentina. That night the Giulianos organized a mass celebration, distributing food and champagne to fans and arranging a party that journalists were instructed not to report on. According to Bruno Passarella, *El Gráfico*'s man in Rome at the time, it was held in Nola, a village outside Napoli, in a secret and well-protected mansion. Nobody at the party said who owned it; nobody had to ask.

Perhaps there was nothing sinister about the Camorra's interest in Napoli. Perhaps this was simply local businessmen rejoicing in a local triumph. But the following season, the influences around Napoli came in for far more scrutiny. They'd signed Brazilian striker Careca that summer, creating the Ma-Gi-Ca front three of Maradona, Giordano, and Careca, and started the season superbly. When they beat Inter 1–0 on April 10, Napoli were four points clear at the top of the table, but they failed to win any of their last five matches of the season and were overhauled by Arrigo Sacchi's Milan, which had beaten them 3–2 at the San Paolo on the third-to-the-last weekend. Nothing was ever proved, but there were allegations that the Camorra, fearing huge losses for the bookmakers they ran if Napoli were champions again, had instructed them to throw the title. Maradona dismissed the claims as "people . . . talking crap." He blamed referees, problems he was having with his lower back, and also his teammates, who, after a defeat to Fiorentina, had called for Bianchi to be fired. Maradona, who had never been particularly impressed by the coach, said that Bianchi had "started experimenting" and was largely to blame for the downturn in form, but he felt the protest by the players was ill-conceived because it turned the coach into a martyr.

Sure enough, the crowd chanted the coach's name, and, at the end of the season, Bianchi was given a new contract. He reacted by firing six players. Maradona told Conrado Ferlaino, the club chairman, that he couldn't tolerate playing under Bianchi anymore and that he would have to choose between them. Ferlaino simply pointed out that the previous December Maradona had signed a contract until 1993 worth $5 million a year. There was a further loss of public sympathy.

As the injury problems began to worsen, Maradona began to train less. It was almost certainly a sensible precaution, but it did little to mollify fans who had begun to suspect their hero was looking for a way out of the club. Napoli finished second in the table, but they were eleven points behind Inter and had never seriously threatened to win the title. They did win the UEFA Cup, beating Stuttgart over two legs in the final—Maradona winning a mystifying penalty when he rather than a defender had handled—but when Maradona limped out of a game against Pisa with a thigh injury in June

1989, fans jeered at the directors' box, where Claudia was sitting with their daughter Dalma and his agent, Guillermo Coppola. Maradona was furious and railed against the abuse.

Many blamed his erratic form on his nightlife, which was notorious despite the code that kept newspapers from publishing stories about it. Yet Maradona himself believed that he was the subject of a conspiracy, the pressure he had felt in those early days in Argentina developing into paranoia. He used the show he presented on Italian television to attack journalists who had criticized him, on one occasion forcing a newspaper into the mouth of a reporter. The season over, he returned to Esquina, vowing he wouldn't return to Italy.

Yet while the cries of conspiracy were largely absurd—and became a regular feature of Maradona's tirades against the world—it is true that something strange was going on. His sister's apartment and his car had been damaged, while there'd been a break-in at his apartment in which nothing was taken but items were moved around. Warnings from the Camorra? Maradona thought so. Once he'd raised the possibility of staying in Argentina, the response in Naples was rapid. He was seen to have broken the bond: fans and journalists had indulged his excesses, but they would do so only if he kept his head down and played good soccer. Photographs of Maradona in the company of the Giuliano family were published in *Il Mattino* with the caption "It's ridiculous to think that anybody would want to challenge the Camorra by threatening its idol." There are multiple possible interpretations, but the one favored by Jimmy Burns is that the Camorra were pulling Maradona back into line.

Reluctantly, bound by contracts written and, perhaps, less tangible, Maradona agreed to return to Naples. Before that, though, he married Claudia in an extravagant ceremony at a Buenos Aires cathedral. It was another public relations disaster: the opulence of the reception, at which it was alleged cocaine and prostitutes were provided for guests, was set against the backdrop of a public transportation strike. The timing was unfortunate, but Maradona was left looking like somebody who had abandoned his roots and wasn't too bothered. Yet still he was feted: presidential candidate Carlos Menem, for whose election campaign Cyterszpiler would act as manager, went out of his way to court him.

When Maradona arrived back in Naples, he was palpably unfit. So bad did things get that an hour before a UEFA Cup tie against Wettingen in November 1989, he was suspended by Napoli manager Alberto Bigon, who had replaced Bianchi in the summer of 1989. Once again he insisted he was the victim of a conspiracy. A month later Maradona claimed the World Cup draw was fixed. "Either he is stupid or bad," said FIFA general secretary

Sepp Blatter. Yet Napoli went top of the Serie A table on the second weekend of the season, and they held that lead until February, when Milan edged by them.

With a World Cup approaching, Maradona was focused, and his fitness improved. In the spring he came into a patch of golden form. A 4–2 win at Bologna as Milan went down at Verona took them top again in their penultimate game, and they clinched their second title with a 1–0 victory at home to Lazio. Somehow, amid all the chaos and the scandals, Maradona had done it again. It's a measure of his achievement that Napoli, after those two *scudetti* in three years, have never come close to winning one since.

47

MORAL CHAMPIONS AGAIN

There were many who urged Bilardo to resign after the 1986 World Cup, unable to see how he could take the team further. With a typical mix of stubbornness and self-belief, he refused. "I felt we had not seen the full potential of 3-5-2," he said. It pretty quickly seemed that he was wrong. As soon as the World Cup was over, Argentina's form returned to the indifference they had shown in the buildup. They hosted the Copa América in 1987—as it reverted to being held in a single nation—desperate for a first success in the tournament since 1959, but with Maradona struggling with tendinitis, they never played like potential champions and lost in the semifinal to Uruguay.

Argentina did beat West Germany in a friendly that December, but otherwise their only victory before the next Copa América was against Saudi Arabia. Some form, at least, returned at the Copa América in Brazil in 1989, despite Maradona's struggles with a thigh injury, but this was a far more defensive Argentina than the one that had won the World Cup three years earlier. It's probably just as well that, as champions, they didn't have to qualify for the 1990 World Cup.

A collapse in global commodity prices in 1986 derailed Alfonsín's economic plan. As inflation began to rise again, there was a fall in wages in real terms of around 20 percent, which prompted a series of strikes, while capital flight continued, as did the exodus of soccer players seeking the greater rewards of Europe. The picture was worryingly familiar: a worsening economic picture weakened the president's hand against the military, and on Alfonsín's initiative, in December 1986, Congress passed the Full-Stop Law, limiting civil trials against the roughly six hundred officers implicated in the Dirty War to those who had been indicted within sixty days of the law being passed. Nevertheless, on Easter weekend 1987, a section of the army mutinied. Alfonsín personally negotiated the rebels' surrender, but that June Congress passed the Law of Due Obedience, which granted immunity to officers under the rank of colonel involved in the Dirty War on the grounds that they had been operating under orders from superiors who had already been convicted. That effectively halted all remaining trials relating to human rights abuses under the junta. While appeasing the military may have been a political necessity, it also cost Alfonsín a lot of public support. He was a humble and decent man, and his habit of clasping his hands together to form a circle with his arms seemed indicative of his desire to embrace all Argentinians, but the circumstances in which he found himself were as good as impossible.

The economy continued to deteriorate. A severe drought early in 1987 led to a decline in exports, all but wiping out the trade surplus. The austral lost about half its value between June and October, prompting a leap in inflation from around 5 percent per month to 20 percent and, as earnings were eroded, provoking two general strikes and a series of smaller stoppages. The Wall Street crash of 1987 stemmed foreign investment, which in turn meant an increase in taxation; taking inflation into account, that left household incomes lower than they'd been in 1983. There was another mutiny—again swiftly quelled—in January 1988, but Alfonsín was also losing public support, which led him to bring elections scheduled for October 1989 forward to May. As 1988 went on, Argentina slipped back into recession, and inflation continued to rise. Another wage freeze prompted a general strike, which then brought clashes on the Plaza de Mayo between demonstrators and police.

Not only were wages falling in real terms, but the feeling began to grow that Alfonsín wasn't serious about tackling white-collar crime. In 1988 executives from Banco Atlas were convicted of fraud against the Central Bank totaling $110 million, but they were given a suspended sentence for returning half of the missing funds. The prosecution should have been a sign of Alfonsín's determination to stamp out corruption, but the verdict called his commitment into question, as did the revelation that what was effectively a parallel system of custom duties had been in place for certain businesses.

Alfonsín did secure the extradition from the United States of General Suárez Mason, the former president of Argentinos, and General López Rega, the occult writer who'd put together the AAA death squads, to face trial in Buenos Aires,[1] but that only antagonized the military, which was furious anyway about further spending cuts, leading to a third mutiny in December 1988. The following month a leftist organization attacked the regiment of la Tablada, leading to thirty-nine deaths and prompting fears that the cycle was beginning again, particularly when the military was accused of having tortured suspected perpetrators.

With the austral collapsing (it was eventually replaced in 1991 by the peso at a rate of 1:10,000) and inflation raging, Alfonsín's hopes of reelection all but disappeared. His Peronist opponent, Carlos Menem, the flamboyant son of Syrian immigrants, won in nineteen of twenty-two provinces. Although the election had been brought forward, Alfonsín had intended to stay on as president until December 1989 as originally scheduled, but further economic chaos that took per capita GDP to its lowest level since 1964, combined with rioting and looting in Rosario and other cities, led him to hand over power in July, the first time since Yrigoyen had taken office in 1916 that an Argentinian incumbent had peacefully surrendered power to a member of the opposition.

With the economy in crisis and the government contemplating radical reform, there was a perceived need from those in power for Argentina to have a good World Cup. The feeling may not have been as intense as it had been under the junta, but Menem, a showman and an opportunist, demonstrated none of the restraint Alfonsín had in terms of linking his fortunes and the country's to those of the national side. He even took part in a training session at el Monumental.[2]

By then Menem had grown his hair and a pair of bushy sideburns while affecting a poncho, consciously evoking the image of Facundo Quiroga, the most celebrated of the *caudillos* who had fought against European liberalism in the nineteenth century. Like Perón, he sought to awaken romantic notions of Argentina's past to harness a popular nationalism. He referred to the British as "pirates of the world" and vowed to continue the fight for the Falklands, promised to improve the lot of the poor and the working class and made great play of his love of soccer and fast cars. People flocked to support him, tens of thousands turning out at rallies. At the same time, he developed secret contacts with key figures in the financial sector.

Menem portrayed himself as the heir to Perón, but once in power he began ruling in a quasi-presidential manner and soon embarked on a program of almost Thatcherite economic reforms. He dismantled the welfare state and overrode many of the labor laws established under Perón. State industries were privatized—often corruptly—and the proceeds used to hold off Argentina's international creditors. In 1991 the peso was pegged to the dollar, which provided a short-term solution to the perennial problem of inflation, although it did nothing to check soaring unemployment.

To enact his policy of radical change, Menem had to curry favor with the old guard. Accordingly, in 1990 he pardoned Videla, Massera, and Galtieri and others convicted in the Trial of the Juntas. Alfonsín called it "the saddest day in Argentinian history." There were other reasons for popular opinion to turn against Menem, even before it became apparent just what his economic program entailed. His family life was a staple of gossip columns: he was accused of various affairs and of mistreating his wife, Zulema, while she was noted for her tantrums and their two children were infamous for their extravagance. In a typically brazen act of populism, Menem sought the support of the one Argentinian figure whose popularity could be guaranteed: Maradona. Shortly before the World Cup, at a press conference in the San Siro in Milan, Menem appointed Maradona as ambassador for sport, granting him a diplomatic passport.

Eventually, in December 1990, Menem too faced an uprising. He forcefully repressed it, cut military funding further, and appointed as the army's general chief of staff moderate Lieutenant General Martín Balza, who had opposed every military coup during his senior career and been a vocal critic of the Falklands War. Even more remarkably, given his rhetoric in the election campaign, Menem made a conscious effort to improve relations with Britain. When conscription was ended in 1994, the army's grip over civilian life was at last released.

For Argentina, those final four matches in the 1989 Copa América were the beginning of a ten-game streak without a victory that would be ended—as a similarly bleak run had been four years earlier—only by victory over Israel in their final friendly before the World Cup. This time, though, there would be no gentle start to the tournament itself. African teams had been improving steadily since Tunisia had become the first side from the continent to win a game at the World Cup by beating Mexico in 1978, but few expected much of Cameroon, which had endured a miserable Cup of Nations a few months previously and whose players seemed bewildered by their Russian coach, Valery Nepomnyashchy. Their players had threatened to strike over unpaid bonuses, while the squad had been destabilized by the ongoing spat between their two great goalkeepers, Thomas Nkono and Joseph-Antoine Bell.

Maradona knew he was likely to be on the receiving end of some robust tackling and so wore shin pads not only on his shins but also on his calves. He was in poor condition anyway, needing to have a carbon-fiber implant inserted into his boot to prevent further damage to a toe swollen by an ingrowing nail. The fans at the San Siro, mindful of how he had just led Napoli to the title over AC Milan, hated him, cheering every brusque challenge on him. "I cured Italy of racism that night," Maradona said sardonically. "The whole stadium was roaring for Cameroon."

It was goalless at halftime, but, just after the hour, the game seemed to have taken a decisive lurch Argentina's way, as André Kana-Biyik was sent off by French referee Michel Vautrot for a foul on Caniggia. Although the foul—a deliberate trip about fifteen yards inside the Cameroon half—was cynical, it seemed an extraordinarily harsh decision given how far out Caniggia was and the fact that there were at least two covering defenders, one of them no more than five yards in front of him when the foul was committed. Six minutes later, though, it was Cameroon that took the lead.

As the clock ticked down, there came the incident for which the game has become most famous. Caniggia broke and was knocked off balance by Emmanuel Kundé, looked certain to fall after evading a lunge from Bertin Ebwellé, and was finally sent to the ground by a terrible foul from Benjamin Massing, who kicked the forward so hard his boot came spinning off. The big center-back had already been booked and was shown a second yellow, but the challenge was bad enough that it could have been a red in its own right. Yet even with nine men, Cameroon held on to inflict what Bilardo described as "the worst moment of my sporting career."

Maradona was devastated. "We were all dead, dead of shame," he said. The players passed the bus journey to the airport in silence. When they got there, they found their flight delayed by two hours. Maradona used the time to speak to Claudia and drag himself out of his despair. On the plane, Bilardo set the players a target, refocusing them on what was still possible in the tournament. "Either we reach the final," he told his players, "or let's hope the plane carrying us back to Argentina falls out of the sky."

Otherwise, Maradona was magnanimous in defeat. "I don't think they had any intentions of beating us up to win the game," he said, although he must have had plenty of bruises that would have suggested otherwise. At the same time, though, he railed against FIFA and the refereeing of Vautrot, blaming them for their failure to impose "Fair Play." In this, at least, he was consistent: it was up to the officials to apply the rules, and up to players to get away with as much as they could.

In the days that followed, both Menem and Alfonsín telephoned Bilardo to offer advice. The coach made four changes for the game against the USSR, which were soon followed by a fifth, as the luckless goalkeeper Nery Pumpido broke his leg after ten minutes and had to be replaced by Sergio Goycochea. What saved Bilardo ultimately was another hand-of-God moment, Maradona's third in four years, to go with his goal against England and a handball that had won a penalty for Napoli in the 1989 UEFA Cup final. Goycochea had just come on when he was beaten by an Oleh Kuznetsov flick, only for Maradona to hook the ball off the line with an unseen arm. Reprieved, Argentina took the lead after twenty-seven minutes, as Pedro Troglio headed in a Julio Olarticoechea cross and confirmed the win twelve minutes from time, Kuznetsov playing a strange backpass that laid in Burruchaga. Argentina secured qualification as a best third-place team with a 1–1 draw against Romania.

It was hardly inspiring, but Bilardo had developed a habit of getting his side to do just enough, peaking just when they needed to, getting results in key games almost despite themselves. "Without the individual brilliance of 1986," said the defender Juan Simón, "our tactics became a measure we took to survive." In the last sixteen, they faced Brazil in a game that remains shrouded in controversy.

What definitely happened is that Argentina were pummeled. Dunga headed against the post. Goycochea, having pushed a cross against the woodwork, recovered to divert Alemão's long-range drive against the angle of post and bar. Careca headed over, and Müller lashed a clear chance far too high. But Argentina clung on. Maradona, struggling with his inflamed toe, was fouled repeatedly. And then, with nine minutes remaining, he collected the ball in the center circle. He started dribbling left, toward the touchline, then cut back sharply to make for goal. Alemão vainly stuck out a leg. He held off Dunga, but there were still four Brazilians between Maradona and the goal—and Caniggia. There shouldn't have been a problem, but Brazil collectively panicked. All four defenders converged on him, at which Maradona hooked a pass through for Caniggia. As Ricardo Rocha and Ricardo Gomes ran into each other, the forward steadied himself, side-stepped Taffarel, and clipped a shot high into the empty net. "The Cameroon game put us on the ground," said Simón, "but the Brazil game lifted us up again and made us feel that we couldn't lose. We were revitalized."

What might have happened is that Argentina incapacitated Brazil with drugged water, one of those legends that it's impossible to prove but that several people involved in the game clearly believe to be true. At a break in play, Argentina physio Miguel di Lorenzo threw a water bottle to Branco, Brazil's left-back, who later claimed that he'd felt dizzy after drinking from it. Brazil striker Bebeto insisted many years later that he'd been at a dinner at which Di Lorenzo had admitted everything. "He said that he left the bottles already prepared," Bebeto claimed, "and by the way he said it he probably didn't do it just with us." Asked directly about the allegation in 2005, Bilardo said teasingly, "I'm not saying it didn't happen." This was *viveza*; cunning, real or imagined, was to be celebrated, not denied.

Argentina went on to meet Yugoslavia in the quarter-final. Again they were under pressure, again they rode their luck to survive until, with a half hour played, Refik Šabanadžović collected a second booking for the familiar offense of fouling Maradona. Yugoslavia held their own, even if Ruggeri hit the bar and Burruchaga had a goal controversially ruled out for a handball. The game went to penalties, and although Maradona and Troglio missed, so too did Dragan Stojković, Dragoljub Brnović, and Faruk Hadžibegić, and Argentina, improbably, were through to the semifinal.

There they faced Italy in Naples. As Antonio Matarrese, the president of the Italian soccer federation, recognizing the sympathy Neapolitans were likely to have for their hero and the resentment they felt at the way they were regarded by the rest of Italy, called for unity, Maradona was quick to try to make capital. "For 364 days of the year," he told the fans who supported him every Sunday, "you are considered to be foreigners by your own country; today you must do what they want by supporting the Italian team. By contrast, I am a Neapolitan for 365 days of the year." Two years earlier, perhaps, before Maradona's relations with the club and its support had become strained, his words might have carried more weight. Quite how committed local fans were to Italy remains open to debate, but it certainly wasn't a case, as some had feared it would be, of the San Paolo making Argentina seem like the home team. "Maradona," read one banner, "Naples loves you, but Italy is our country."

Argentina were duly physical from the kickoff and fell behind after seventeen minutes, as an offside Totò Schillaci followed in the rebound after Goycochea had blocked Gianluca Vialli's shot. Italy seemed in control to all but their most superstitious fans: the goal hadn't just come after seventeen minutes, but this was the seventeenth international staged in Napoli—and seventeen is the Italian unlucky number.[3] Slowly, anxiety crept over the hosts. Following decades of tradition, they sat back and obeyed the stereotype, looking to defend their lead. As they did so, Argentina began to grow in confidence. Simón recalled:

Bilardo had said to us, "Italy have two wide midfielders: [Luigi] De Agostini on the right and Donadoni on the left. So we'll put [Gabriel] Calderón and Olaticoechea to stop them. But when they lose the ball, they never go back to defend quickly, so when we recover the ball, we'll always have a two-to-one advantage on each side, plus two gaps to take advantage of each wing. It's the easiest game we'll have in this World Cup." And the truth is that it was like that. When you're on the field and you realize that he's seen the game in advance, then you say, "Chapeau!" Even their goal was totally by chance, an accident, and it was offside, too. We even had more ball possession than them.

Midway through the second half, Argentina equalized, Caniggia glancing Olaticoechea's cross past Walter Zenga, who had blundered hopelessly off his line, the first goal Italy had conceded in the finals. The game went to extra time, but even after Giusti had been sent off for flattening Roberto Baggio with eleven minutes remaining, Italy couldn't find a winner.

The penalties had a strange sense of inevitability about them. The first six penalties were scored, but then Roberto Donadoni, Italy's number 17, stepped up. He hit his shot to his right, at roughly waist height, and just inside the post; it wasn't a bad penalty, but Goycochea read it and, diving full-length to his left, pawed the ball away. Maradona sent Zenga to his left and rolled the ball the other side, meaning Aldo Serena had to score. He didn't, his hard, low shot being kept out by the body of Goycochea.

Somehow, Argentina had scrapped their way to the final, although suspension robbed them of four players, including Caniggia, who had picked up a wholly avoidable yellow card in the semifinal for handling the ball as a cross flew over his head. Still, there was a sense that how they'd gotten there mattered less than the fact that they had. "I've never seen anything like it before in my life," Bilardo said. "I've never seen anything unify the nation like that. Not politics or music or anything. Everyone was watching and hoping for the team. And when we came home, they were happy for us. We were proud to have reached the final."

Italians were rather less happy, leading Maradona to spy yet another conspiracy. Two days after the semifinal, Maradona's brother Raúl—known as "Lalo"—was arrested for speeding in Maradona's Ferrari. He didn't have his identification papers on him, so police accompanied him back to Argentina's *concentración* near Rome. According to Maradona, they arrived "with the wrong attitude," and a brawl broke out, with Gabriel Espósito, Maradona's brother-in-law, to the fore. The following morning, the Argentinian flag at the *concentración* was torn down, leaving just a rag fluttering on the pole.

The hostility Maradona had felt from the crowd in the opening game against Cameroon was nothing compared to the final. Bilardo was so concerned by the antipathy of the crowd that he considered cutting the anthem short to reduce the amount of time he and his players would have to hear it being whistled. In the end, with a certain irony given how stridently Maradona had protested about a supposed global conspiracy against Argentina and the three handballs he'd gotten away with at key junctures over the previous four years, Argentina were undone by a combination of the referee—Edgardo Codesal, who had been born and raised in Uruguay before taking Mexican citizenship—and their own lack of discipline.

Monzón's sixty-fifth-minute foul on Jürgen Klinsmann was a bad one, but there was little reason for the West Germany forward to react by pivoting up on his shoulder. The red card Codesal produced with an arched back, straight arm, and theatrical flourish, the first sending-off in a World Cup final, seemed excessive. Equally when he awarded a penalty after eighty-five minutes for a supposed foul by Néstor Lorenzo on Rudi Völler, the defender appeared to have taken the ball before his hip followed through into the German. At that Argentina lost any semblance of composure. Troglio could have been sent off for barging the referee in his protests, and it was little surprise when, two minutes after Andreas Brehme had converted the penalty,

Gustavo Dezotti was sent off for grabbing Jürgen Kohler around the neck. As Argentinian players surrounded Codesal, he was barged at least twice more and could easily have shown further red cards, but he contented himself with booking Maradona.

Argentina went home with a familiar sense of outrage, railing against Italy, FIFA, and the world in general. Menem greeted the players as returning heroes and insisted they were an example to follow. Artlessly, he hitched their progress to his program of socioeconomic reform. "We had 11 titans on the field," he said. "Today we need 33 million titans to draw Argentina out of this situation."

The opportunism was so blatant as to be almost patronizing, but it did highlight both the ongoing power of soccer in Argentina and the almost universal sense among Argentinians that they were, once again, moral champions. Perhaps they had been unfortunate in the final, but, having snarled and spoiled their way to that point, few outside Argentina had much sympathy. A cynical team that had played on the edge of the laws was consumed ultimately by its own negativity.

PART SIX
DEBT AND DISILLUSIONMENT, 1990–2002

48

THE THIRD WAY

S anta Fe is a flat, nondescript town in northeastern Argentina that grew up as a center for the transportation of grain, vegetable oil, and meat. On its dusty street corners, stray dogs sleep, moving only when the summer heat forces them to seek shelter. The Conquistador Hotel is an unremarkable concrete block on an unremarkable street that stands out only because of the figure of a portly man in armor that projects from the wall, above a mesh of telephone wires, the word *HOTEL* picked out uncertainly in neon lights down his back. It's as ordinary as city-center business hotels come, yet it was there, in 1992, that one of the main prophets of soccer's new tactical age wrestled with his doubts and, having conquered them, set upon a course that would forge a third way between the extremes of *menottisme* and *bilardisme*.

History may not judge Marcelo Bielsa as a great coach: three Argentinian titles and an Olympic gold, after all, are not a spectacular return over the course of a career. As a theorist, though, he stands among a very select few. His quirks—the neck cord on his glasses, the circumlocutory syntax, the way he would insist on taking thirteen steps to cross his technical area while at Athletic of Bilbao, or the occasion when he drew on his sneakers to explain a way of kicking the ball and wandered around with the chalk marks for days afterward—have perhaps made him a caricature and obscured just how significant a figure he is, but it's probably fair to say that, since the back-four spread from Brazil in the late fifties and early sixties, no South American has had such an influence on how the world played as Bielsa did in the first decade of the twenty-first century.

From childhood, Bielsa was intense, driven, and intellectual. There seems always also to have been an idealistic streak in him, something that made him awkward as a teenager—and, for many, infuriating as an adult. He became known as "el Loco" and even in wanting to be a soccer player, he was marking out his difference. His family members were all lawyers or politicians or both: his brother, Rafael, served as minister of foreign relations under Néstor Kirchner's presidency, while his sister, María Eugenia, is an architect who has served as vice governor of the province of Santa Fe. So keen was Marcelo to be a soccer player that he left home at fifteen to move into club accommodation at Newell's Old Boys. Typically, he was kicked out two days later because he refused to leave his two-stroke Puma motorcycle outside.

Bielsa may have rebelled against his upbringing, but it conditioned him. It's said Bielsa's grandfather had more than thirty thousand books at home, and Bielsa developed a similar respect for knowledge and learning, subscribing at one point to more than forty international sports magazines and collecting thousands of recordings of matches.

It's characteristic of Bielsa that he doesn't regard his obsession as unusual; rather, he always seems slightly taken aback that others don't also spend their days poring over DVDs of old soccer. Once, when asked how he planned to spend Christmas and New Year's, Bielsa said deadpan that he intended to do two hours of physical exercise each day and spend fourteen hours watching videos. He has, apparently, developed the ability to watch two games simultaneously.

Bielsa was born in Rosario in July 1955, the son of Rafael, a lawyer who supported Rosario Central, and Lidia, a schoolteacher. Largely to annoy his father, it seems, he decided to support Newell's, as did his brother. He played soccer almost as soon as he could walk but from an early age also began to learn about it, having his mother buy him copies of *El Gráfico* and then index them. As such, his mother began the process of taxonomizing soccer that he would later take to extremes. "The influence of my mother was fundamental in my life," he said. "For her, no effort was sufficient."

Bielsa is somebody who divides soccer, but apologists and critics both agree that he is relentless, a workaholic who expects others to work as hard as he does. "At first he seems tough, and he may even annoy you with his persistence and don't-take-no-for-an-answer resilience, but in the end he is a genius," said center-forward Fernando Llorente, who played under him at Athletic. "He convinces you to keep working and running, and it can be seen in his teams' games and practices. He knows more than anyone in the world; he is elite. Once you get used to him, you love him."

Effort and discipline, though, couldn't make Bielsa a soccer player. He was a defender who was good on the ball, but he lacked pace and managed just four games for Newell's before leaving at twenty-one. Eventually, the club released him, after which Bielsa drifted around the lower leagues and studied agronomy and physical education before, at twenty-five, moving to Buenos Aires to coach the city university's soccer team. His approach was characteristically thorough (he watched three thousand players before selecting a squad of twenty) and unusual (he carried a thesaurus with him at training and addressed players using the formal pronoun *usted*). He treated his players like professionals, insisting they trained properly. There was, a number of those who played for him said, a new "seriousness" about training, while his belief in the importance of verticality, of getting the ball forward quickly, was evident even then.

Bielsa spent two years with the university before returning to Rosario to work in the youth setup at Newell's. Deciding there were probably players from the interior who were being missed by the big clubs, he divided a map of Argentina into seventy sections and visited each one in the hunt for new talent, driving more than five thousand miles in his Fiat 147 because he was afraid of flying.

By 1990 Bielsa was established enough to replace José Yudica as coach. Yudica had joined the club in 1987, leading them to the Campeonato the following season. He was also, perhaps, a necessary step in the transition to a *bielsista* approach, more pragmatic than his successor, gentler, more modest in both demeanor and ambition. Even with Yudica's grounding, the first dose of Bielsa was bracing. "When Marcelo took over, there was a radical change," said former midfielder Juan Manuel Llop.

Training was altered beyond recognition. "It was nothing that would shock us now," said Llop, "but at that time it was very surprising. All the training sessions were short but very intense. The ball was nearly always present, but tactics were always present. We started training at different times, three or four players doing specific, zonal exercises: for example number 5, number 4, and number 8 together; or number 5, number 3, and number 11. The young players were used to training like that. But we, of course, weren't."

With most games taking place on Sunday, players had Monday off and then would work with the fitness coach on Tuesday and Wednesday mornings, while Bielsa locked himself away and watched videos of the opposition. On Wednesday afternoon, the tactical work would begin. "The youngsters had to read the papers and bring some detailed dossiers on the next team we were going to face," Llop said. "It was a way to make them feel committed and to make them understand soccer better." Bielsa would then take them through videos, never full games, but isolated moments and sequences to highlight key points.

On Thursday there'd be a practice match in the afternoon, "a short game," Llop said, "but played with the intensity of a Primera match. It was amazing. We'd never seen anything like that. The other team played like our next opponents. And our mission was to beat them, to win the game. We couldn't afford to lose on a Thursday."

Friday was for specific game preparation: Bielsa would lead his side through 120 different attacking situations and 120 different defensive situations. "It was about movement, coordinated movement," said Llop. "The ball has to come here, you must curtain there, you have to run here, in case they play the offside trap, two would come out of the play, and one will have to take action to counter it. It was very, very detailed."

It worked. Or at least, it worked at times. That 1990–1991 season, for the first time, the championship was split in two halves, *apertura* and *clausura*, with the winners of each playing off for the title. Newell's began the *apertura* hesitantly, beating Platense 1–0 but then drawing away at Argentinos Juniors and losing at home to Huracán. When they went to Santa Fe to face Unión in the fourth game of the season, there were major doubts about Bielsa. "There were rumors," said Llop. "We hadn't started well. I don't know if he would have been fired after the fourth game or later, but after a bad start, if we'd kept on that path, it would have happened. Marcelo was seen as a weird guy, there was scrutiny over his methods, so everybody was eager to see if he was right or wrong. If we'd lost in the fourth round, perhaps Bielsa wouldn't have made it. Who knows?" They didn't lose, though: they won 3–1. "We took off and never stopped," Llop said. Newell's lost only once more in the *apertura*, as they finished two points clear of River Plate. Santa Fe would soon have a far greater part to play in Bielsa's development.

Winning the *apertura* effectively meant Newell's had nothing to play for in the second half of the season (which was why, in subsequent years, the *apertura* and *clausura* were both declared championships in their own right—there were two titles contested each season with no playoff). Newell's, demotivated, finished eighth in the *clausura*, which was claimed by Boca Juniors. "It wasn't normal," Llop said. "It wasn't that we didn't care, or that we were saving our energies for Boca. Actually, when we faced Boca we were a little wary because we knew we weren't playing well. I'd say we were more alert, and that ended up being a positive for us, because we weren't feeling overconfident. That was our chance, at la Bombonera, to win it and be part of Argentinian soccer history. And that made us be brighter and sharper than during the rest of the tournament."

Newell's won the first leg in Rosario 1–0, but that still left an almighty task in la Boca. Absurdly, the Copa América began between the two legs, which meant both sides lost players—Fernando Gamboa and Dario Franco from Newell's and Diego Latorre, Blas Giunta, and Gabriel Batistuta from Boca.

Boca dominated, Cristian Domizzi and Juan Simón were sent off, and Gerardo Reinoso scored with nine minutes remaining to give the home team a 1–0 win. Newell's, though, won the penalty shoot-out 3–1. "It was the best game of my life," said Llop. "We played in the mud. It was very mystical."

Newell's were victorious, but their form had deserted them, and in the *apertura* of 1991–1992 they got even worse. In the whole of 1991, Newell's won only nine games. Fatigue was a major issue. "It's a method that provokes a certain level of tiredness," Llop said. "Not just physical tiredness, but also mental and emotional tiredness because the competition level is so high that it's difficult to keep up with it after a period of time. Not all human beings are the same, or think the same, or react in the same way.

And the style of Bielsa, his training sessions, demand continuity, and it's difficult. We were a squad that seemed perfect for him, but after he left, we ended up in a relegation battle, in 1993 and 1994. And that's because there comes a time that the human being relaxes. It's not that you abandon everything, but you let something go, because you feel worn out."

By the start of the *clausura*, the pressure was beginning to build. Newell's at least began with a 2–0 home win over Quilmes, but then they were hammered 6–0 by San Lorenzo in their first game in the group stage of the Libertadores.

And so they went on to Santa Fe, where the charge to the title had begun the previous season. At the Conquistador, Bielsa's doubts overwhelmed him. His was a method that required faith, and in the aftermath of the 6–0, he began to question himself. "I shut myself in my room," he said, "turned off the light, closed the curtains, and realized the true meaning of an expression we sometimes use lightly: 'I want to die.' I burst into tears. I could not understand what was happening around me. I suffered as a professional, and I suffered as a fan."

He phoned his wife, Laura, "and presented an argument that for many would be irrefutable." Their daughter, he said, had been seriously ill. For three months they hadn't known whether she would live or die. That, he knew, was real emotional turmoil. "Does it make any sense that I want the earth to swallow me over the result of a soccer match?" he asked. He knew it didn't, but it made no difference. "The reasoning was brilliant," he said, "but, nonetheless, my suffering from what had happened demanded immediate vindication." This was his crisis: what had happened against San Lorenzo wasn't just a defeat; Bielsa wasn't just questioning his capacity as a coach. His choice of words was telling: it wasn't merely a solution he was looking for; it was vindication for the entire philosophy by which he played his soccer and lived his life. Bielsa called his players together. "If we have to rethink the project," he said, "we will do it together. We will seek a new way of doing things if we don't feel able to achieve what we set out to do at the start of preseason."

Bielsa was set on his new path. It wasn't, he decided, that what he'd done before had gone too far; rather, it hadn't gone far enough. "Still under the emotional shock," he said, "there was born a new manner of understanding the tactics of the team. For quite some time I had had some ideas about individuality and its contribution to the joint effort, which I hadn't put into practice because they involved too many rotations in the field. We came through our failings to refresh the structure, and a seemingly unfortunate situation allowed us to relaunch the general idea, through a series of changes of position." The phrasing is characteristic of Bielsa: put simply, he wanted his team to absorb the patterns of the opponent and, using a rotating system of man-marking, press them accordingly—if an opposing center-back liked to initiate moves with a pass to the right-back, Bielsea's side would attack the center-back and the line of a pass to the right-back.

Llop remembers it as a stressful time. "Marcelo was trying to find the proper tactics, and there were days of talking and talking." Newell's drew 0–0 in Santa Fe, but it was the start. The following week they beat Rosario Central 1–0 in a game that had to be stopped with two minutes remaining because of crowd trouble. They went to Racing and won 1–0, then beat Gimnasia y Esgrima by the same score. "The main difference was fitness," said Simón. "Newell's were like a tractor that would shatter all opposition. That team would suffocate you; that was the Bielsa touch, adding mad pressing to Newell's existing soccer style. After facing them, you'd go back to the dressing room feeling that you were going to pass out, that they had made you run as never before." The revolution gathered pace. Saldaña's wife was killed in a car crash that year, but he played on, finding strength in Bielsa and the team unit.

Results picked up in the Libertadores as well. Newell's went unbeaten through the group stage and gained a cathartic 1–0 away win over San Lorenzo. The better Bielsa did, the more his methods were examined and the more the question was asked: What was this new style? Was he *bilardista* or *menottista*? "Bielsa was not aligned to Bilardo or to Menotti," Llop insisted. "He was an attacking tactician. A tactician is often seen as a negative, defensive style of manager, but tactics are not just defending and blocking the opponents' main virtues. Bielsa proved that. He was a mix between the two, a fusion of the two schools."

That was certainly how the coach saw it. "I spent sixteen years of my life listening to them: eight to Menotti, who is a coach who prioritizes inspiration, and eight to Bilardo, who is a coach who prioritizes functionality," he said after becoming national coach in 1998. "And I tried to take the best from each."

Menotti and Bilardo responded exactly as every stereotype about their personalities suggested they should. "Bielsa is a young man with concerns," said Menotti. "He has ideas, and he knows how to develop them. But we do not agree on the starting point: he thinks soccer is predictable, and I do not." Bilardo, meanwhile, claimed Bielsa was simply repeating what he had done. "I share his thinking because it seems to me that we did that in 1986," he said. "They have many videos to study opponents, as I did back then."

There are those who would argue the drills—those 120 repetitions on a Friday—were *bilardista* (not that Menotti was as bohemian as some of his devotees would claim), but Bielsa's ideas on the need to attack whenever possible were far more toward the *menottista* end of the spectrum.

When it came to actually defining his philosophy, Bielsa said it could be broken down into four terms. The first three are *permanent focus*, *mobility*, and *rotation*. The fourth term is rather harder to translate and is a classic Bielsa term. In music, *repenitización* is used for the discipline of playing a piece without having practiced it first: it's not extemporization as such in that it involves sight-reading, but the use of the term in soccer clearly has some sense of improvisation, while also carrying a sense of urgency. It's a term that sums up the counterintuitive idealism of the *bielsista* philosophy, demanding that players repeatedly do things for the first time, a paradox that perhaps suggests the glorious futility of what he is trying to achieve. "The possible is already done," Bielsa said during his time at Newell's. "We are doing the impossible." When Llop speaks of playing mystical games and of having to have faith, that is what he means: there is always a sense with Bielsa that he is as interested in reaching for the absolute as he is in winning matches—and it is that, of course, that gives him his cultish appeal.

Like so many South Americans of his generation, Bielsa had been heavily influenced by the Dutch side of the early seventies, but a more direct influence was the Uruguayan Óscar Washington Tabárez, a coach whose pragmatism seems oddly incongruent with his own idealism. "Soccer," Bielsa said, "rests on four fundamentals, as outlined by Óscar Tabárez: (1) defense; (2) attack; (3) how you move from defense to attack; (4) how you move from attack to defense. The issue is trying to make those passages as smooth as possible."

Newell's lost only once in the 1991–1992 *clausura* in the league and took the title by two points from Vélez. In the Libertadores, they beat Defensor Sporting in the last sixteen to set up a quarter-final against San Lorenzo. The pain of the 6–0 was still fresh, but this time they beat them 4–0 in Rosario to take the tie 5–1. That meant a semifinal against the Colombian side América de Cali. The first leg finished 1–1, but five minutes into the second Mauricio Pochettino got on the end of a free kick to head Newell's in front. It had been a ferocious game played before a crowd so hostile that even getting into the stadium had been an ordeal. Newell's clung on, but América leveled with a last-minute penalty, and the game went to a shootout. Twice Cali missed kicks that would have won it, but when Norberto Scoponi saved from Orlando Maturana, Newell's were through, 11–10. Before they could begin to think about the final, they had to get off the field, as fans reacted furiously. Eduardo Berizzo was left with a badly gashed head after being struck by a battery thrown from the stands.

The final, against the São Paulo of Rai and Cafu, also went to penalties, but this time Newell's lost. Bielsa, seemingly exhausted by the emotional strain of coaching the team he supported to play in the style for which he was an evangelist, resigned. "We tried to convince him to say," said Llop, "but the process was worn out. He wanted to quit before then, and I went with midfielder Gerardo Martino to his home and convinced him to stay a little longer, but after a month or two, he resigned. He probably understood that his era had ended, that he wouldn't be able to keep up the results. I wanted him to stay. I knew he was positive for Newell's. When he left, we ended playing to avoid relegation. It was terrible."

49

TABÁREZ AND THE
BOCA REVIVAL

Maradona had been a glorious distraction who had brought Boca Juniors the Campeonato in 1982, but he was only covering over the cracks. After his sale to Barcelona, Boca fell into a slump from which it took them a decade to emerge. Results deteriorated, and the financial situation was desperate. By the end of 1984, the players were threatening strike action over unpaid wages, and in 1985 there was a serious possibility that Boca might be declared bankrupt. They were saved by the newly elected president, Antonio Alegre, and his deputy Carlos Heller, who invested their own money and sold off the Ciudad Deportiva to settle 183 outstanding claims from creditors.

There was a second-place finish under José "el Pato" Pastoriza and Carlos Aimar in 1988–1989, eight points behind Independiente, and there was a Supercopa Libertadores in 1989 and a Recopa Sudamericana[1] in 1990, but it was the arrival of Óscar Washington Tabárez in 1991 that sent a jolt of energy through the club. Tabárez had been no more than a moderate defender and had worked as a teacher—the source of the nickname "Maestro"—when he began coaching Bella Vista in Uruguay. He soon gained a reputation as a tough and principled coach, an image reinforced by his rigorously parted hair and his preference for sensible tie-and-jacket combinations that gave him the air of a precinct chief in a 1970s US police drama. He is Uruguayan, but slotted readily into a typically left-of-center Argentinian intellectual tradition, as made clear by his admiration for Che Guevara. He even named his daughter Tania, after the revolutionary's last known lover. On the wall of his house in Montevideo hangs a plaque bearing the motto "One must toughen oneself without ever losing tenderness," a line attributed to Guevara that encapsulates Tabárez's soccer-playing philosophy: he prioritizes defensive rigor while still encouraging his teams to play with a certain swagger.

Yet violence marked the beginning of Tabárez's reign at Boca. After scraping through their group in the Libertadores, Boca beat Corinthians and Flamengo to set up a semifinal against Colo-Colo. Boca won the first leg at la Bombonera 1–0, thanks to a goal from Alfredo Graciani, but the circumstances of the game enraged the Chileans. On the way to la Bombonera, they claimed, their bus had mysteriously gotten lost, driving into a rough neighborhood, where they were pelted with stones and other missiles. In the dressing room, there was only hot water, and for a while it seemed Colo-Colo might refuse to play. In the end they did take the field, but Colo-Colo director Jorge Vergara warned of a dire revenge back in Chile.

Mirko Jozić, Colo-Colo's Croatian coach,[2] took his squad into the basement of the Sheraton hotel before traveling to the stadium. He could see they were nervous, so he turned off the light and made his players sit in darkness until laughter began to fill what had been an anxious silence. "Colo-Colo are great," he said, "but we can make this an even greater story." It was by some way the biggest match in the club's history, arguably the biggest game in the history of any Chilean club, given their lack of success in continental tournaments to that point.

There were sixty-four thousand fans rammed into Santiago's Estadio Monumental, but the bigger problem were the one thousand accredited journalists and photographers. With no space for them in the stands, hundreds were lined up along the running track by one touchline, creating a sense of anarchy from the start. At halftime it was goalless, but nineteen minutes into the second half, Marcelo Barticciotto darted down the right, made space for a cross, and found Rubén Martínez, whose calm side-foot volley gave the Chileans the lead. A few dozen fans leaped over the advertising billboards in their glee. Two minutes later Gabriel Mendoza cut through that same space on the right and crossed deep for Patricio Yáñez, stretching beyond the back post, to turn the ball over the line. This time the celebrations were even more fervent, hundreds of fans and photographers spilling onto the field.

Carlos "el Mono" (the Monkey) Navarro Montoya, Boca's goalkeeper, complained to Brazilian referee Renato Marsiglia about the flashes from the photographers' cameras, suggesting they were being deliberately set off to blind him. When, after seventy-four minutes, Boca pulled one back with a neat header from Diego Latorre, the mood behind his goal became so hostile that Navarro approached the official again. "I'm going to get the shit kicked out of me here," he said. With eight minutes remaining, Martínez exchanged passes with Yáñez on the left of the box, ran on, and dinked the ball over Navarro Montoya to make it 3–1.

Fans and photographers poured onto the field. The brawl became wild, Boca players lashing out at cameramen as well as Colo-Colo players and staff. An Agence France-Presse photographer, Rodrigo Arangua, was left temporarily blinded. Tabárez, in a rare loss of cool, chased another, Miguel Ángel Allendes, who swung his camera into Tabárez's face, leaving the coach with two gashes on his right cheek. There is an extraordinary photograph of Tabárez, immaculately dressed in a check jacket and white V-neck sweater, dark tie fractionally askew, jaw tight with rage, blood running down his face, restraining Batistuta by grabbing his nipple though his shirt as the forward glares at somebody off camera, mouth open as though midtirade.

For seventeen minutes the battle raged. "It was a war, a street fight, and we were afraid," said Arangua, who was helped to the hospital by two colleagues. The violence was ended only when a police dog called Ron bit Navarro Montoya, leaving him with a bloody wound in his thigh.

Marsiglia made the token gesture of sending off Yáñez and Boca midfielder Blas Giunta before restarting the game. Colo-Colo held out through a desultory last few minutes and went on to the final, where they beat Olimpia of Paraguay 3–0 on aggregate. Ron became a national hero, hailed as "the dog who bit a monkey," but died a year later from a heart attack. Boca, their behavior seen as both shameful and heroic—a characteristic Argentinian blend—paid Arangua 98 million pesos in compensation and probably came out of the game stronger than they'd gone in, a ferocious team spirit forged in adversity. Batistuta, in particular, seemed elevated by the experience.

It helped as well that Tabárez was a coach of great authority with a clear vision of how he wanted the side to play. In the face of his certainty, much of the confusion and doubt that had undermined Boca melted away.

While Tabárez sorted out the defense, he was fortunate that his attack was energized by the sudden upturn in the form of Batistuta. At twenty-one, he was seen as a useful forward but little more. After the fight in Santiago, though, he was transformed. "When he first arrived, Tabárez asked for a number 9, even though Batistuta was in the squad," said Simón. "He missed a lot of chances, and he was being played as right-winger, but then he switched back to number 9 and he exploded. Soccer can be a matter of luck."

Boca improved dramatically in the early nineties, narrowly missing out on both *apertura* and *clausura* in 1991–1992, which only intensified the pain of the drought. If Boca had own their penultimate game of the 1992–1993 *apertura*, at home to Deportivo Español, they'd have taken the title. They lost, 3–2. "La Bombonera," said Simón, who'd ruptured knee ligaments and was reduced to watching anxiously from the stands, "was a pressure cooker."

Boca needed a point from their final game, at home against San Martín de Tucumán, for the title. At halftime, they trailed 1–0, but two minutes into the second half, Claudio Benetti scored the goal that clinched the league. "I don't know what the dressing room must have been like at halftime," said Simón. "But Tabárez never lost his cool: after the game, you could see him in the midst of total madness and all the celebrations, walking with his jacket on, crossing the field toward the tunnel. And he waited for us in the dressing room. He was always the same, very calm, in defeat and in victory."

Tabárez returned to Peñarol after a disappointing sixth-place finish in the 1992–1993 *clausura*, but the drought had been broken, and Boca, precarious as their financial position remained, were a team that won things once again.

50

THE FATAL URINE OF
FOXBOROUGH

B ilardo finally left the Argentina job after the 1990 World Cup and was
replaced by Alfio "Coco" Basile, a former Racing defender whose fifteen-
year managerial career had already taken him through thirteen jobs. Always
stocky of frame, he'd filled out after his playing career had ended, while
retaining the same greased-back demi-mullet with which he'd ended his
playing days; a tangle of chest hair sprouting from the collar of a shirt he
always wore with at least two buttons open and a voice of startling huskiness
completed an idiosyncratic image. The start of his reign was unremarkable,
seven friendlies yielding two wins and five draws, but at the 1991 Copa
América in Chile, with Gabriel Batistuta and Claudio Caniggia, a pair of
long-haired, explosive, intelligent forwards in tandem, they hit a spectacular
patch of form. Argentina, without Maradona, won all four games in their
five-team group, racking up eleven goals as they did so.

That took them through to a four-team final group, in the first match
of which they faced Brazil, with memories of their controversial victory in
Turin the previous year still fresh. Both sides had two men sent off, but
Argentina clung on for a 3–2 win. They then drew against the hosts, Chile,
meaning they faced Colombia in their final match, needing a win to take
the title from Brazil. They went ahead with a Diego Simeone header after
eleven minutes. Eight minutes later Leonardo Rodríguez played an angled
chip over the Colombian back four for Batistuta to lash in a second, and
although Ántony de Ávila pulled one back in the second half, the Copa
América was Argentina's for the first time since 1959.

F or Maradona, the World Cup had offered only brief respite from the tor-
rent of bad news. By the autumn of 1990 his fitness had again become
a major issue, and when he withdrew from Napoli's Serie A game against
Fiorentina on November 22, journalist Franco Esposito wrote in *Gazzetta
dello Sport* of his being afflicted by a "dark evil" and "an obscure mysterious

illness." It didn't take much background knowledge to work out what he was hinting at. A crackdown on the Camorra meant there was little inclination to protect Maradona, and with Napoli wearying of their errant star, they did nothing to repudiate the rumors. Police launched an investigation into Maradona for alleged possession and distribution of cocaine, news of which brought a string of kiss-and-tells. At the same time, Piero Pugliese, a security guard for the club who worked as a chauffeur for Maradona and, it turned out, had been a hired gun for the Camorra, told police that the player had been involved in transporting two kilos of cocaine. Maradona was never charged, never mind convicted, but few were sympathetic as he raged about the "vendetta" he said was being enacted against him.

It got worse. On March 17, 1991, after a game against Bari, Maradona was selected for a random drug test, itself a telling detail; previously it had been possible to protect him. On other occasions, he'd used a plastic penis that could be filled with somebody else's urine, positioning it in his tracksuit pants before visiting the testers, squirting the "clean" sample into the specimen jar.[1] On this occasion, though, there was no escape, and Maradona tested positive for cocaine. "There's no doubt in my mind," he said, "that it was Italy's vendetta because Argentina knocked them out of the World Cup." He admits now that he was a regular user, but insists that he would test himself and that he knew he was clean. The logic of his *viveza* demands unpacking: he admits he broke the rules, but still had to find somebody else to blame. He was guilty, yet he was still the victim. The issue becomes not whether he was guilty but the fact that he was caught; he is outraged not because he was wronged, but because his ingenuity in avoiding the testers was thwarted.

Having been banned for fifteen months, Maradona returned to Buenos Aires on April 1. On April 26, he was arrested in Caballito for possession of cocaine. That August police raided his chauffeur's apartment in El Soldadito and found Maradona passed out after a day of heavy drinking and cocaine abuse. Menem refused to protect him, and at last Maradona accepted he needed help.

He began a radical detox program, eating only fruit and vegetables and drinking only water, while working out regularly in a gym and going jogging in Plaza Holanda. He saw a psychotherapist who, along with his family, highlighted what they saw as bad influences they felt Maradona should cut from his life. Among them was Coppola, his manager. The family got in touch with Cyterszpiler, Menotti, and Bilardo and encouraged them to offer Maradona support. A former Argentinos Juniors player, Adrian Domenech, meanwhile, volunteered to eat and train with him. Batista was a regular presence at the Maradona home. Jorge Valdano, buying heartily into the conspiracy theories, claimed that Maradona's arrest was part of a plot to divert public attention from the failings of the Argentinian government. Maradona had regular therapy sessions, in which the image that kept recurring was that of his childhood fall into the cesspit, as though his whole life had been a constant struggle to keep his head out of the shit.

Maradona still had popular support: a poll in *Clarín* showed that 71 percent of Argentinians believed him innocent; others were just as ready to accept claims of conspiracy. In a world of profound disillusionment, it was as though Argentina couldn't bear to give up their faith in the incarnation of Borocotó's *pibe* ideal.

Menem's amnesty for those involved with the junta—a process that had begun under Alfonsín—had provoked fury, especially among the young. While some accepted that a soldier couldn't be blamed for following orders, and some saw immunity from prosecution as a necessary sop to preserve democracy in the face of increasing military resentment, many regarded it as another example of the old establishment getting away with it. The term *careta*—literally "mask"—began to be used of mainstream politics: it was fake or hypocritical. Menem's lurch into neoliberalism had made him seem duplicitous and thus characteristic of that facet of the political class. Soccer and rock music were seen as being free of that taint, their very distance from orthodox politics making them political. Maradona came to be regarded as the representative of that spirit of resistance and had, in a typically ad hoc and unstructured way, begun to embrace a political role. "I am the voice of those who don't have a voice," he said, "the voice of the many people who feel I represent them." Journalist Carlos Ares even described him as "the Perón of the nineties . . . a postmodern leader," perhaps the greatest unifying force in Argentina.

Maradona, by admitting his drug use, was not merely acknowledging he was one of them, but also free of *careta*, the issue given an extra twist by the widespread legend that the government permitted drug trafficking and took a slice of the proceeds. Eventually, the fury of the fans fell upon an embodiment—as they saw it—of *careta*: Constancio Vigil, a friend and golf partner of Menem and a director of *El Gráfico*. He had attacked Maradona in print, but was later found to have fraudulently imported luxury cars with permits made out to the physically handicapped.

Popular support, though, couldn't save him, nor, Maradona believed, could psychotherapy. What he needed was soccer. When Judge Amelia Berraz de Vidal, who first questioned him three hours after his arrest, asked him what drugs he'd dealt in, Maradona replied, "The only thing that I've dealt in my life is soccer." After three months, he quit counseling and began playing again, first for a local amateur club and then in a charity game.

Bilardo had become coach of Sevilla in 1992 and wanted Maradona to join him when his ban had been served. The city had just held the Expo to celebrate the five hundredth anniversary of Christopher Columbus's departure across the Atlantic and had invested in a new airport and better road and rail links, aimed at making it more culturally and commercially integrated with the rest of Spain and Europe. Signing Maradona was seen as another part of that self-promotion. Maradona, though, still had a year remaining on his contract at Napoli, which rejected a $3.75 million bid. With his drug arrest and paternity issues still to resolve with the Italian courts and convinced there was a vendetta against him, Maradona refused to return. Sepp Blatter, the general secretary of FIFA, offered to arbitrate and negotiated a $6.75 million fee. Within four days of the transfer being confirmed, Sevilla had brought in an additional $3.3 million in ticket sales. Maradona was still a major draw.

He was also still overweight. Maradona played twenty-six games for Sevilla, and although there were flickers of the old magic against Real Madrid and Sporting Gijon, his second spell in Spain was a disappointment. It was also marked by regular controversies; there was no sense of his being cowed by the drug ban. He was arrested for driving a Porsche at 125 mph and was involved in a brawl outside a nightclub to which he'd been denied entry for wearing sneakers. The final straw came with a magazine exposé of the whole team going to a brothel, an escapade for which Maradona, rightly or wrongly, was widely blamed. In Sevilla's following game, against Burgos in June 1993, Bilardo substituted him. Maradona, who claimed in his autobiography that he'd had three painkilling injections in his knee ten minutes earlier, regarded that as a betrayal and, as he left the field, clearly called his coach an "*hijo de puta.*" In the dressing room they almost came to blows. Although the pair subsequently made up, Maradona never played for Sevilla again, quitting after being told to knuckle down.

For five years the Argentinian economy soared, and soccer was a clear beneficiary. This, though, was different from the boom under Perón, which had been stimulated by an interventionist and protectionist state that recognized the benefits of developing infrastructure. Menem's boom took place in a rapidly globalizing environment that left Argentina at the mercy of liberalized world markets. Menem had a box at el Monumental and would pose for photographs wearing the national team shirt, but that was as far as state involvement in soccer went: there were no subsidies, no equivalents of Perón's *padrinos*, and no way to restrict the sale of players overseas, even if that had been desired.

In the short term, none of that seemed to matter. The peso rose in value. Inflation was brought under control. Consumption increased, and a lot of what was consumed was soccer. Cable television became hugely popular—disproportionately so when compared with equivalent and wealthier nations—a phenomenon that was almost entirely driven by soccer: in 1997 the ten most watched programs on Argentinian television were all soccer matches. Broadcast revenue and sponsorship deals were huge.

The split into *apertura* and *clausura* meant twice the drama and even more grist to the media mill. It gave smaller sides, which could never have hoped to sustain a title challenge over thirty-eight games, the hope of putting together a run over nineteen. In some ways it was a tremendous success, but the short championships ultimately led to an even shorter-term outlook than usual.

Still, the international successes kept coming. In 1992 Argentina beat Côte d'Ivoire and Saudi Arabia to lift the King Fahd Cup, the forerunner to the Confederations Cup. By February 1993 Argentina had gone unbeaten in twenty-three games. It was then that Basile decided to recall Maradona. He took over the captaincy from Ruggeri, but Argentina were disappointing in a 1–1 draw with Brazil. The team, critics said, had become "Diego dependent," the first hint that the luster of Maradona's reputation—previously inviolable on the field, if not off it—was beginning to fade. A week later he retained his place for a game against Denmark to decide the Artemio Franchi Trophy, a competition between the winners of the Copa América and the European Championship that was played only twice.[2] Bilardo, his club coach, had warned Maradona not to play more than ninety minutes, but when the game went into extra time, he stayed on, further undermining his position at Sevilla. Caniggia had canceled out an early own goal by Néstor Craviotto, and after extra time produced no further goals Argentina won on penalties, another trophy in the brief golden period of the early nineties.

Then came the 1993 Copa América in Ecuador, the first to include twelve teams, with Mexico and the United States invited to join the ten Conmebol members. Maradona this time wasn't included, and Argentina weren't particularly impressive in the group stages, two draws and a 1–0 win over Bolivia seeing them through in second place, which meant a quarter-final meeting with Brazil in Guayaquil.

Brazil had much the better of the first half, and Cafu had hit the post before Müller, drifting in from the left, put them in front. Argentina improved a little after the break but were still far from dominant when Leonardo Rodríguez headed an equalizer. Brazil had further chances, but, with Simeone outstanding, Argentina hung on for penalties. Simeone had come through at Vélez, where his tenacious approach developed in an environment that valued commitment as much as ability. As a youth player he was nicknamed "Cholo" by Victorio Spinetto, after former Boca midfielder Carmelo "Cholo" Simeone (the roommate who had failed to stop Omar Corbatta's drinking on that 1963 tour of Europe and no relation), whose style of play he supposedly replicated.[3]

The first ten penalties were all scored before Marco Antônio Boiadeiro, in what would be his final game for Brazil, stabbed a tentative kick that Goycochea saved diving to his left. That left Jorge Borelli to slam in the winning kick and take Argentina through to a semifinal against Colombia. Again they drew, this time 0–0, and again the first ten penalties were all scored. Again Goycochea saved the sixth kick, from Víctor Aristizábal, and again Borelli held his nerve and side-footed his penalty just inside the right-hand post.

In the final Argentina faced Mexico. Batistuta put Argentina ahead after sixty-three minutes with a typical Batistuta goal, running onto a ball over the top, showing great strength to hold off Ramón Ramírez, and cracking in an early right-foot finish. Four minutes later Mexico leveled, Goycochea felling Luis Roberto Alves and Benjamín Galindo rolling in the penalty. But seven minutes after that, Batistuta struck again, seizing on Simeone's quick throw-in, turning by Claudio Suárez, and curling a left-foot finish just inside the post to complete a 2–1 triumph and win a fourteenth South American title.

As the national team thrived, though, the national icon struggled. Having left Sevilla and with no soccer to sustain him, Maradona began using cocaine again. Early one morning, his daughter, Djalma, walked in on him snorting a line in the bathroom. That was too much. Maradona broke down and talked for hours, before realizing he had no idea what he was saying. He went back to Esquina to be with his parents.

In October 1993 Maradona was ready for a return to soccer. He had almost rejoined Argentinos Juniors, only for members of their *barra* to visit him at his home and demand $50,000 they said they'd been promised as their cut of the deal. Maradona had been aware of the increasing power of the *barra* but had never previously come up against it himself. He refused, at which the Argentinos fans graffitied a wall by his house before being chased away by fans of Defensores de Belgrano, the local club. Instead, Maradona joined Newell's Old Boys, which offered participation in the Copa Libertadores.

When Maradona arrived in Rosario, he was greeted as the best player in the world. "The best," he supposedly replied, "has already played here: Carlovich." Perhaps Maradona was showing unusual political acuity and playing to his audience, but Carlovich hovers always in the background when the greatest Argentinian players are discussed. There is Messi; there were

Maradona, Di Stéfano, Pedernera, Moreno, Sastre, Seoane; and there was also Tomás Felipe Carlovich, "el Trinche" (the Fork), more myth than man, a player whose only negative was that hardly anybody saw him play. He helped Central Córdoba, Rosario's third club, to promotion out of the third flight in 1973 and 1982, but it seems no video footage of him exists. He played only two games in the first division. Photographs show a tall, slight man, but, height aside, he was the classic player of the *potreros*, shaggy-haired and resistant to authority. José Pékerman described him as the greatest central midfielder he'd ever seen.

Carlovich, who was born in 1948, was one of seven sons of a Yugoslav immigrant. He played in the streets as a child and regrets that those spaces are being lost, that so many young players grow up on the artificial perfection of Astroturf. "Before," he said, "there were a lot of fields, but now there are no more fields. I tell you why I like to play on the streets—a player who goes onto the field and looks up into the stands where there are sixty thousand, one hundred thousand, people, how is he going to enjoy the game? He can't play, ever. Those people in the stands, their demands, their insults."

He was elegant if slow and joined Rosario Central when he was fifteen. At twenty he played twice for them in the top division. He was called up to the squad for an away game in Buenos Aires and arrived in plenty of time for the team bus. He took the back seat and waited ten or fifteen minutes for other players to arrive and then, bored, got off and went to play for the amateur Rio Negro club in his home neighborhood. He never returned to Rosario Central. "He was a phenomenon of a player," said Carlos Griguol, "but he does not like sacrifice, so he didn't succeed playing with me at Central and preferred to go hunting or fishing.[4] He had unique technical abilities."

Carlovich eventually joined Central Córdoba, for whom he played a total of 236 games in four separate spells. If he found a home anywhere, it was there. His legend spread, particularly after he responded to a shout from the crowd to perform a trick by nutmegging an opponent first forward, then backward. The double nutmeg became his signature move. "The directors paid me a special bonus for a nutmeg and a double bonus for a double nutmeg," he said. In one game for Independiente Rivadavia in Mendoza, he got himself sent off just before halftime: it was the only way he could catch the bus back to Rosario in time for Mother's Day.

His defining match came in April 1974. As part of their preparation for the World Cup, Vladislao Cap's national side faced a Rosario Select XI in a friendly to raise funds for the Sports Journalists Circle. The Rosario side included five players from Newell's, five from Central, and Carlovich. They'd never trained together or even discussed playing together until they arrived at the stadium two hours before kickoff. Carlovich promptly nutmegged Pancho Sá and then, as he turned, nutmegged him a second time. The stadium erupted. What had been a friendly became something rather more serious. On LT8, radio commentator Héctor Vidana spoke of "the dance of the Rosarinos." By halftime Argentina were 3–0 down. Cap asked for Carlovich to be taken off. He stayed on, but the second half took a more conventional course, and the game finished 3–1 to Rosario.

Carlovich retired in 1983 and then again in 1986, but even after that, he would stroll through games in his barrio, hitting the same raking passes. He worked for a time as a bricklayer before being stricken by osteoporosis that afflicted his hips. A benefit evening featuring two exhibition matches was arranged to help pay for treatment. The crowds again sung his name, and then a journalist asked if there was anything he would change about his career, anything he would do differently. "No," he said, voice wavering. "No, sir, don't ask me that." He bit his lower lip. "No, not that." Then the tears fell from his eyes. This is the curse of the player who embraces the ethos of the *potreros*: freedom comes at a cost.

Maradona was a very different figure from Carlovich, but he too had paid for a lack of what others would have seen as basic professionalism. The eating, the drinking, and the drugs had left him in no shape for the increasingly high-octane soccer of the nineties. There was something absurd in the thought that he, at thirty-three, with his inflated waistline, could slot happily into a team brought up on *bielsista* pressing. Some of the weight came off, but although Maradona would start games ferociously, he was rarely able to finish them. He played just seven matches, and the initial excitement soon dissipated.

Argentina had carried their form from the Copa América into World Cup qualifying, beating Peru and Paraguay away. Even after a 2–1 defeat to an improving Colombia in Bogotá, nobody was too concerned. Peru were beaten at home to leave Argentina still in charge of the group, but when they were held by Paraguay and Colombia thumped Peru 4–0, there was suddenly pressure. They had to beat Colombia at home in their final game to take the top spot and automatic qualification, or they would face a playoff against the winner of a playoff between the second-place team from the Concacaf region and the best Oceanian team—Australia. What happened at el Monumental that night, September 5, 1993, was a humiliation as great as any Argentina had suffered since Helsingborg, greater even than that the Dutch inflicted in 1974.

The game remained level until four minutes before halftime, when the Colombia captain, Carlos Valderrama, "el Pibe," a player whose style represented everything Argentinians thought great about their own game, made a forward burst and shoved the ball outside for Freddy Rincón, who hurtled past left-back Ricardo Altamirano and rounded Goycochea to score. Down 1–0 at halftime, there was still hope. It vanished five minutes into the second half. Rincón sent a long diagonal ball from the right in behind Jorge Borelli, Faustino Asprilla ran on, turned back inside the center-back, and hooked a finish through the legs of Goycochea. At that Argentina effectively gave up. Seventy-four minutes in, Leonel Álvarez crossed from the left, and when the ball looped over Asprilla, Rincón mishit a volley that bounced past a wrong-footed Goycochea. A minute later Borelli was dispossessed by Asprilla, who ran on and beat Goycochea with a superb chip. Any semblance of defensive discipline having gone from Argentina, Asprilla then laid in Adolfo Valencia to touch home a fifth. The crowd chanted for Colombia and then for Maradona, who was watching in horror from the VIP box. "*Vergüenza!*" roared *El Gráfico*: Disgrace!

That night, as the celebrations took on a violent edge, eighty people died in Bogotá. In Cali the mayor had had the foresight to close all the bars and kept the death toll to three. "I never want to think about that match again," said Basile. "It was a crime against nature, a day when I wanted to dig a hole in the ground and bury myself in it."

Such was the impact of the defeat that, two days later, the current affairs show *Tiempo Nuevo* was devoted to the game. It was mesmerizing television. Goycochea, dressed in a green suit,[5] sat glumly, two fingers to his lip, looking shamefaced as José Sanfilippo ripped into him, his hand leaving his mouth occasionally to form—seemingly unconsciously—a clenched fist. So furious was Carlos Bilardo, who was watching at home, that he drove to the studio and demanded to be put on air. Wearing a white leisure shirt patterned with red and blue diamonds—surely not something he had ever intended to be seen on television—he defended the players who had been part of his World Cup squad three years earlier.

Basile kept his job, but before the playoff against Australia in November 1993, he recalled Maradona. Argentina weren't particularly good, but Maradona was inspired. He set up a goal for Abel Balbo by beating two men, being tackled, bouncing up, winning the ball back, and whipping in a perfect near-post cross. Australia leveled through Aurelio Vidmar, but 1–1 gave Argentina the advantage heading back to Buenos Aires. They did win in el Monumental to secure their progress to the United States, but it was hardly an impressive performance, the only goal coming as a Batistuta cross flicked off Alex Tobin and looped over goalkeeper Robert Zabica.

Maradona's return to the national team was far from simple. His early enthusiasm at playing for Newell's soon evaporated, largely because of a change of president. Indio Solari was replaced by Jorge Castelli, after which

Maradona found his "freedoms" restricted. On February 1, 1994, he quit the club. Later that month, journalists seeking to find out what he was planning gathered outside his country house in Moreno, where he was relaxing with his father, his uncle Cirilo, and a number of friends. Maradona asked them to leave. They said they would if he gave them a brief statement, which he refused to do. One of his friends sprayed the journalists with a garden hose. Another pretended to masturbate. Maradona then took an air rifle, leaned on the roof of a car, and shot at the journalists, injuring four. They sued. Two accepted a payment as settlement, but the other two pressed on.

As the case headed for court, Menem urged the judge to show leniency. Julio Grondona, the president of the AFA, said nothing, which seemed revealing of his relationship with Maradona. Again, the public mood was broadly sympathetic to the old messiah. Heroes were heroes, each flaw seemingly heightening the appeal; of course the *pibe* got up to mischief—how could he not? If, as sociologist Sergio Levinsky argued, the veneration of the *pibe* was at some level rooted in a desire for him not to grow up, but to remain childlike, then how could he be expected to take responsibility? As the case progressed Maradona announced he was willing to captain the national side at the World Cup. The public reaction was one of euphoria, although there was little to justify their faith. Maradona hadn't played well since the previous World Cup, he was unfit, he was fighting legal action in two countries, and he was struggling with drug addiction. This was an investment in an empty dream no different from the lionization of Evita after her death or the embracing of gaucho culture in the 1920s or even Mendoza's primal lust for the mythical silver mines when he'd first set off across the Atlantic. Whatever Basile felt privately about bringing Maradona into the squad, he had no choice: he had announced he wanted to be captain in the United States, and so he had to be captain.

The dream of a glorious farewell for Maradona was established, despite his behavior, despite his clear lack of conditioning. In March 1994 when he was substituted at halftime in Argentina's first defeat to Brazil in five years, Maradona looked overweight and out of sorts. "Maradona is totally out of shape," Basile acknowledged, "and our objective is to prepare him slowly for the World Cup."

Three months later he looked sleek again, perhaps not as quick as he had been, but certainly sharp enough to direct a team that, the defeat to Colombia notwithstanding, went into the 1994 World Cup with high expectations; after all, they had won the previous two Copas América. And Argentina began well, with a comfortable 4–0 win over Greece. Batistuta took advantage of some chaotic Greek defending to squeeze in the opener in the second minute. He went on to complete a hat trick with a superb finish from outside the box and a penalty. It was the third goal, though, scored by Maradona, that would prove the most memorable. In itself, in his catalog of brilliance, it barely registered—a couple of one-twos and a touch to the left to create space before an accurate shot from the edge of the box into the top corner—but his celebration, racing to a television camera and roaring, which at the time seemed to speak of his passion and his delight to be back playing for his national team, soon began to attract more sinister interpretations.

It would turn out to be Maradona's last goal for Argentina, but he had one more game to play, against Nigeria in Foxborough. Nigeria took the lead, Rashidi Yekini laying in Samson Siasia to sidestep neatly before beating the onrushing Luis Islas from just outside the box. Argentina leveled midway through the half, Maradona backheeling a free kick to Batistuta, whose low shot was saved by Peter Rufai, only for Caniggia to follow in. Six minutes later the striker, who had returned just a month earlier from a year-long ban for taking cocaine, had a second, calmly curling a finish just inside the post after running onto a quick free kick from Maradona.

And that was the end—for Maradona and for Argentina's hopes. After the game he was chosen for a random drug test, which he seems to have given blithely enough. Footage shows him being led off the field by a nurse, happily waving to the crowd. The test, though, proved positive for a cocktail of five substances aimed at suppressing the appetite and increasing endurance. Maradona was withdrawn from the tournament and subsequently given a fifteen-month ban from soccer. "I killed myself training, and now they do this to me!" Maradona complained at a press conference, as though his effort somehow outweighed the fact he had broken the rules. He then broke down in tears.

Man-on-the-street interviews on radio revealed an extraordinary level of general distress. Television showed Argentinians sobbing on the streets. Some compared the mood to the day of the surrender in the Falklands in 1982 or Perón's funeral in 1974—the link between the events strengthened by the fact that the confirmation that the B sample was positive fell on the twentieth anniversary of Perón's death. They were two figures in whom many Argentinians continued to believe, excusing their faults long after their powers had waned.

To most, Maradona remained a god—and that wasn't just the case in Argentina. So strong did Maradona's international appeal remain that in Bangladesh, twenty thousand took to the streets of the capital, chanting, "Dhaka will burn unless Maradona is allowed to play." The sense in Argentina seems to have been one of sadness rather than anger, with television channels broadcasting maudlin montages of his best goals set to music, as though he had died rather than failed a drug test. There was little sense of shame or disgrace. As ever, Maradona cried conspiracy, insisting this was part of a dastardly plot by outgoing FIFA president João Havelange, a Brazilian, to ensure Brazil won the tournament. "They've really cut my leg off . . . ," he said. "This is a real dirty business. I'd like to believe in Havelange and Blatter, but after this, well . . . I don't want to say anything."

The truth was far less complex: he'd been taking drugs—recreational if not necessarily performance enhancing—for years and had finally been caught. There were no plastic penises in Foxborough. After leaving Sevilla for Newell's, Maradona's weight had dropped from 200 pounds to 160, something he put down to hard work with Daniel Cerrini, a bodybuilder who had become part of his inner circle, and a Chinese nutritionist called Liu Guo Cheng. Maradona probably wasn't absolutely clear what he was taking, and it may even have been the case, as he claimed, that the US version of a particular supplement had contained ephedrine, while the one available in Argentina didn't, but the regulations are clear: the responsibility was his, and his guilt was undeniable. "The only truth," Maradona said, "is that my personal trainer made a mistake, and I took the brunt of the fallout."

That certainly wasn't the only version of events, but perhaps the deepest truth was that outlined by Bernardo Neustadt, the journalist who had presided over the Sanfilippo-Goycochea affair after the Colombia defeat and whose willingness to criticize Maradona made him an outsider. "Ours," he said, "is a country in which it's the speculators who win, a country that violated its own constitution every time it felt like it. . . . Argentina paid with Maradona for a way of life, for not heeding the law." Maradona himself stayed in the United States after being banned from playing in the tournament and picked up a reported $1.3 million as an analyst for Channel 13.

A 2–0 defeat to Bulgaria in their final group game meant Argentina qualified only as one of the four-best third-place teams and had to travel from Massachusetts to Pasadena in California to face a Romania team whose fluent passing soccer had beguiled in the group stage. It was one of the great World Cup matches, which was of little consolation to Argentina, as they lost 3–2. Argentina were out and, with Maradona in disgrace, facing a future without their genius.

51

THE RISE OF VÉLEZ AND THE RIVER REVIVAL

Raúl Gámez seemed to stare at the mess of muffin crumbs on the leather sofa, but he either didn't see them or didn't care. He sat down, straightening his camel coat behind his knees with a wave of his left hand, on which he wore a large signet ring. He is tall and, even in his early seventies, exudes a sense of power. His face is heavily lined, each cheek carved with a deep vertical canyon. He is a man who has known violence, the cracks around his eyes evidence of a life lived hard.

In 1986, as a leading *barra* at Vélez, he went to the World Cup with Argentina. There is a photograph of him from the day of the quarter-final against England that shows him in the lower tiers at the Azteca, bare-chested, his T-shirt in his hand, fist drawn back to throw a punch at a chubby blond man wearing a white vest on which is written "Viva England." Another blond man in the foreground, also shirtless, seems already to have felt the force of a Gámez punch, his eyes half-closed, mouth scrunched. Gámez reformed, though, and in 1992, with Vélez in financial trouble, he was appointed vice president. He was later twice elected to the presidency of the club.

There was something incongruous about his suggesting meeting in the Starbucks on Avenida Corrientes, but then there is something incongruous about him, a hooligan who became not only a director but a highly successful one. While he may have left violence behind, it continues to stalk him. Four days after our interview, Gámez was kidnapped by an armed gang. They forced him and a friend to sit on the back seat of his car as they drove to a house, where they intended to keep him prisoner until a ransom was paid—a not uncommon practice in Buenos Aires. There are softer targets than Gámez, though. As they drove past a police speed trap, he managed to open the car door and throw himself out. The police gave chase and rescued his friend, while Gámez received medical attention on a badly gashed head. He appeared on the television news that night, his part almost invisible beneath a thick bandage, face and hands badly scratched. The attack, he said, had had nothing to do with soccer.

When Gámez became vice president in 1991, he was also made president of the soccer section of the club. He was starting, he said, "from scratch."

He was determined to do things properly. "I'd tell the Racing president I was going to be knocking on a player's door. I wanted to be respectful. Not like Boca, which would announce in the press every time they wanted goalkeeper José Luis Chilavert, so I had to pay him an extra ten thousand dollars to keep him happy."

Vélez finished second in the *clausura* in 1991–1992 and sixth in the *apertura* in 1992–1993. "We could see there was good material," Gámez said, "but it was too much for Coach Eduardo Manera and he decided to step aside. His assistant, Roberto Mariani, took over as caretaker. And he won four games and drew two. Brilliant. The players wanted him, but every time players ask me for a manager, I have doubts. Why are the players asking for him? Are they becoming friends? Doesn't he work enough?"

A number of coaches, Bielsa among them, turned Gámez down. Then "a pharmacist, a Vélez fan and friend of most of us at the club," suggested Carlos Bianchi. Bianchi had been a legend of the club as a player, a wiry forward who scored a club-record 206 goals in 324 games. He'd helped his father with his sales job at a newspaper—there's a certain irony in the fact that Spinetto and Bianchi, the two greatest heroes of Vélez, a club that self-identifies as outsiders scrapping against the *grandes*, should both have been from middle-class backgrounds—before making his debut in July 1967 at the age of eighteen. The following year Bianchi scored nine times as a dogged Vélez, under the management of Manuel Giúdice, took the title.

That was Bianchi's only trophy with Vélez, but he was the top scorer in the Nacional in 1970 and the Metropolitano in 1971. In 1973 he moved to France, where he remained just as prolific. In seven seasons there, he was top scorer five times, three times with Reims and twice with Paris Saint-Germain. He'd coached Reims and Nice, but when Gámez got in touch in December 1992, he hadn't worked in more than two years.

The only goal Vélez conceded in the first six rounds of the championship was in a 1–1 draw against Boca Juniors, and that game was subsequently awarded to them as a 1–0 win following crowd trouble. "As a team, Vélez were still not defined in soccer terms," Gámez said. "There are clubs famous for playing nice soccer, other clubs that are known for strength and defensive style. . . . Vélez was neither one nor the other. No style. The Vélez style started with Bianchi."

Ricardo Gareca left for Independiente, while Oscar Ruggeri, having been named South American player of the year in 1991, was sold to Ancona, which "went bankrupt before they could pay us," Gámez said. "That's how Vélez started. And two years later we were beating Milan to win the Intercontinental Cup." In nineteen games in the 1992–1993 *clausura*, Vélez scored just twenty-three goals, but, more important, they conceded only seven times. It might have been Bianchi who defined the modern team's style, but Spinetto, the scourge of *la nuestra*, would have approved.

The title earned Vélez their place in the 1994 Libertadores, scrapping their way to a final against São Paulo, which were seeking a hat trick of titles. With Chilavert brilliant, the tie went to penalties. The Paraguayan saved from Palhinha and then scored his own penalty, as Vélez claimed the first international title in their history.

Three months later Vélez went to Tokyo for the Intercontinental final to take on Fabio Capello's AC Milan, the team of Franco Baresi, Paolo Maldini, Marcel Desailly, Zvonimir Boban, and Dejan Savićević. A fiftieth-minute Trotta penalty put Vélez ahead, and, seven minutes later, Assad seized on an underhit backpass from Alessandro Costacurta, rounded Sebastiano Rossi, and curved his finish in from an awkward angle. Eighteen months after winning their second Argentinian title, their first in twenty-five years, Vélez had won the world crown—something that perhaps mattered more in South America than in Europe—and they had done it with a starting eleven that included seven players who had been developed at the club.

For a time, Vélez seemed the model of how to run a club. They kept their spending in check—a rare quality in the early years of the Menem boom—and they kept winning, lifting both *apertura* and *clausura* titles in 1995–1996. "We were humble," Gámez said. "We kept agents out of the club, which is a very difficult thing for boards. It's very simple to be an honest man, but to prove it in a soccer club, that's way too complicated. Especially now."

By then Bianchi's achievements had caught the attention of wealthier clubs, and his departure was inevitable. He accepted an offer from Roma, moving there for the start of the 1996–1997 Serie A season, before the 1995–1996 *clausura* had finished. Bianchi's assistant Osvaldo Piazza oversaw the final games of the 1996 *clausura* success (although Bianchi, bizarrely, returned for one game at the denouement), and the foundations that had been left underpinned the *clausura* success of 1998 when Bielsa finally took the job.

Bianchi's gift was less any great tactical insight than the way he used his force of personality to inspire his players. Although he insisted the coach should never "be a star," he also suggested coaches should "cultivate *el liderazgo*," which for him clearly meant not just "leadership" but a projection of that leadership into something approaching a cult of personality. When

Bianchi laid out his ten "unwritten rules" for being a successful coach for the magazine *Management Deportivo*, he didn't discuss on-field strategy at all. His theory was all about motivating players and ensuring the overall structure of the club was coherent: "Surround yourself with intelligence," he said.

The only time he came close to outlining how his teams actually played was to express his belief that soccer should be kept as simple as possible. "Orders are orders, and they have to be clear, but you have to give them with tact," he said. A director praised his capacity to give plain and simple instructions, "to put the toilet in the bathroom and the oven in the kitchen." He was a leader whose greatest gift was leadership.

B ut this was not an age in which one style dominated. As Vélez espoused a philosophy of effort and solidity, River remained true to the ideals of the past. When Daniel Passarella returned to River Plate in 1988, he was thirty-five. He'd spent eight years at the club before leaving in 1982 for Fiorentina, by which time he was regarded as perhaps the greatest central defender in Argentinian history. Reinaldo "Mostaza" Merlo's resignation as coach following the club's presidential elections in December 1989 left Passarella as a natural choice to take over, despite his lack of coaching experience. He would lay the foundations for a decade of domination. "I took to it with a calmness that surprised even me," he said.

A point behind Independiente at the halfway stage in 1989–1990, River grew in strength as the season went on and ended up winning the league by seven points. In *El Gráfico*, Juvenal described them as being "as precise as surgeons, cold, accurate, clinical, no-nonsense." They were a team that pressed hard in midfield, thanks largely to their two "Pac-Men," Leonardo Astrada and Gustavo Zapata, who gobbled up possession.

Passarella went on to win the *apertura* in 1991–1992 and 1993–1994, and River won it again in 1994–1995 under Carlos Babington. In part their success was put down to their comparative wealth, well deployed, and in part to two forwards who had come through their youth system. Ariel Ortega was quick and inventive and a fine dribbler, a modern version of the number 10, while Hernán Crespo was powerful and explosive and a born finisher. In 1994 Enzo Francescoli, "el Príncipe," was brought back to the club after seven years in Europe with RC Paris, Marseille, Cagliari, and Torino. He was thirty-three and slower than he had been, but still had a wonderfully quick soccer brain.

After a third title in three years, 1995 was a disappointment. River finished tenth in the 1994–1995 *clausura*, lost on penalties to Atlético Nacional of Colombia in the semifinal of the Libertadores, and then came in seventh in the 1995–1996 *apertura*. Babington was replaced by former River forward Ramón Díaz, a bold choice given that he had only just retired from playing with Yokohama Marinos and had no coaching experience.

River started the 1995–1996 *clausura* poorly, ensuring the Libertadores would be their focus. Victory over Universidad de Chile in a brutal semifinal saw them to the final for the first time in a decade. Their opponents, as they had been in 1986, were América de Cali, which were looking to avoid a fourth defeat in four finals. Ántony de Ávila scored the only goal of the first leg, brilliantly chipping Germán Burgos from a narrow angle, but back in el Monumental, it was all about Hernán Crespo. First, charging across a carpet of ripped-up paper, he turned in Ariel Ortega's cross, and then, after Ortega's persistence had forced a goalkeeping error, he headed Francescoli's cross into an empty net. River, at last, had a second Libertadores and so pulled level with Boca.

Crespo left for Parma after the final, but River signed the explosive Chilean striker Salas to replace him, and for the eighteen months that followed they were unstoppable, their style becoming increasingly about the team and less about moments of individual brilliance. When they beat Gimnasia y Esgrima de Jujuy 3–0 at the end of October 1996, it meant they had scored twenty-five goals in nine games that season—and that after drawing their opener, against Gimnasia y Esgrima de La Plata, 0–0. In *Clarín* Juvenal made the case for them as la Máquina of the nineties. "This River defined the big picture, the strategy, aligning themselves with the historic values," he wrote. "This goes beyond the tactical details, set pieces, or marking: they decided that they want to search for the goal in the opposition area, and they want to do it by playing: not pushing, not grabbing, not running, not crashing into others . . . but playing."

River won that *apertura* and then both *clausura* and *apertura* in 1997. By the time Salas joined Lazio in 1998, Colombian striker Juan Pablo Ángel had already been bought to replace him, and River won another *apertura-clausura* double in 1999–2000. When Díaz left the club in early 2000, he had won four league titles. A fifth followed as he returned for the 2001–2002 season.

52

THE FAILURE OF
NEOLIBERALISM

With open markets and an overvalued currency, the result was inevitable: in the 1990s imports became cheaper, and Argentinian manufacturing and the smaller industries suffered crippling blows. As the decade went on, unemployment became an increasing problem. The general shift in power toward business was reflected in soccer. In 1995, for instance, Boca's *socios* elected Mauricio Macri as the club's president. He was a civil engineer who also happened to be the eldest son of the family that owned Argentina's largest construction firm. The Macris had been great beneficiaries of Menem's economic policy, particularly the privatizations, and Mauricio understood business on a global scale. He sought to make Boca an international brand, self-consciously prioritizing the Libertadores and the Intercontinental Cup; in that he was successful, as attested by the number of tour groups from all around the world taking in la Bombonera, whether for matches or on stadium tours.

In December 1994 the devaluation of the Mexican peso prompted what became known as the Tequila Effect, rippling through Latin America and thrusting the Argentinian economy into recession. Once it bit, it bit dreadfully hard, exposing the sense of economic well-being for the chimera it had been, a typical short-term fix that not merely did nothing to tackle fundamental structural problems but ended up exacerbating them. As the downturn began, the unions rallied and in 1996 declared a general strike. Austerity measures hit the interior particularly hard, and by 1997 there were protests across the country, with demonstrations blocking roads and rioting in parts of Patagonia and the Northwest. In January 1997 journalist José Luis Cabezas was murdered; he had been investigating Menem's program of privatization. Corruption and violence were nowhere near as prevalent as they had been in the 1970s, but they hadn't disappeared.

The economy deteriorated further, and the aftershocks of the Asian financial crisis of 1997–1998 had a profound effect, as global interest rates rose and

Argentina struggled to pay off a mounting debt. Menem's neoliberalism had dealt with inflation by further impoverishing those at the bottom end of the economic scale and by limiting the aspirations of the middle class as wages fell in real terms and workers' rights were curtailed. His economic policy essentially killed the immigrant dream of self-advancement that had sustained Argentina for a century. According to sociologist Javier Auyero, recognition of that led to a belief that Argentina is cursed and, in the *villas*, a profound sense of resignation. Whereas before the slums had been seen as a necessary stepping-stone from the countryside to a better life in the city, from the nineties they began to be regarded as a place from which there was no escape.

Aside from the cycle of boom to bust, the other defining feature of soccer under Menem was increasing instances of off-field violence and the growing power of the *barra bravas*. At their most benign they create a vibrant atmosphere, occupying the space behind the goal, organizing banners and streamers, and leading chants—although it's probably a little naive to believe that's all they ever did. "They first started in the days before games were on television," said Diego Murzi, the vice president of Salvemos al Fútbol (Let's Save Soccer), a group set up to try to combat violence in the Argentinian game. "In the 1950s and '60s, there was always a suspicion that away teams would be victimized by corrupt referees, that games would be fixed, so groups of fans formed to try to redress the balance, to fight for the club's interests. These were the original *barras bravas*." Boca's *barra* was the first to gain real prominence, thanks to the encouragement of their coach Juan Carlos Lorenzo. "He invented the *barra brava*," said Silvio Marzolini. "He set it up—they were on the plane with us. But they were fans with drums and stuff like that, not thugs like today."

By the late nineties, though, most *barras* were connected to organized crime, dealing in drugs, smuggling and engaging in extortion, and controlling parking and merchandise sales around the ground. In Argentinian soccer there had always been fans ready to fight on behalf of their team, but the changing role of the *barras* represented something rather more sinister, something that suggested a toxicity at the heart of Argentinian society.

In 1986 Argentinian soccer saw 46 officially recognized instances of violence, 81 injuries, and 451 arrests. By 1990 there were 258 instances, 413 injuries, and 2,255 arrests. The contrast to the Perón era was striking. Whereas it had then, as historian David Goldblatt put it, "served to integrate urban *barrios* and the wider nation, soccer in the 1990s deepened local, neighborhood and tribal affiliations to clubs." That both reflected and exacerbated growing divisions within society as a whole, so the homogenous, broadly working-class crowd of the forties and fifties became fragmented "by class, consumption patterns and belief systems."

For Raúl Gámez, the problems with the *barra* began at the 1978 World Cup. "They [the *barra*] started earning money to make some minor repairs in the stadiums, then they [the authorities] gave them money to help on match days, and also paid them to sing," he explained. "The stadium atmosphere was like a theater . . . and that changed. I was part of a *barra*, the *barra* of *aguante. Aguantar* meant to travel away with all your flags and defend them. And defend your fans in away matches. That was it. No business. Players didn't give us so much as a pair of socks! And they didn't like us, because we demanded sacrifice and commitment."

There probably is no simple explanation for the escalation in violence in the late eighties. In part, there were wider societal issues at play—the transfer of the political violence of the seventies into other spheres, a less repressive state apparatus, and a growing disillusionment with the reform process—but soccer's leadership was also to blame. "Grondona and Bilardo, who is very stupid with this kind of thing, took them to the World Cup in 1986," Gámez said. He himself, of course, had been in Mexico in 1986, but he is adamant he paid his own way—that, along with fighting only with fists and not weapons, seems central to his code of honor. The problem, as he sees it, came as those within soccer began to try to use the *barra* to force their own agenda. Just as Yrigoyen had discovered when he used military insurrections for political ends in the late twenties, it turned out that once muscle becomes aware of its own power, it becomes extremely difficult to control.

"Managers gave them clothes," Gámez said.

Board members used them to force managers to quit rather than be fired. Soccer players became the victims of other players who gave the *barra* clothes or money; there was a rupture between the players who supported the *barra* and those who didn't. That produced what you see today: everything is a business and they fight against each other because of money. Now they are gangs. It's more profitable for a thug who's just left prison to join a *barra brava* than to join a band of robbers. Money is as good, and the risks are considerably less. Police are involved. Board members are involved. They earn money from public parking spaces around the ground, and nobody does anything to prevent this.

In 1991, as soccer-related deaths became commonplace, the government established a commission to investigate the issue. It reported back and proposed that closed-circuit television cameras be installed at stadiums and that there should be regular inspections to monitor safety, security, and hygiene. The money for the initiatives was supposed to come from Prode, the national soccer pools, as well as the clubs themselves—but it never did, and the proposals came to nothing. The clubs at the same time were told to take more responsibility for ticketing—a fairly obvious coded warning that they should stop letting *barras* in for free, which was also ignored. After all, many club directors used the *barras* as political muscle; the relationship may have been unhealthy, but it was mutually beneficial.

The following year there were 502 incidents of violence, 660 injuries, 6,036 arrests, and 12 deaths, which suggested just how inadequate the response had been. In 1993 incidents were down, but arrests went up to 10,703. Fans continued to fight among themselves, but also began to target team buses and press conferences. There was a sense of anarchy, with the clubs rendered powerless by a lack of money, competence, and will. In 1993, for instance, after Racing had taken the lead in an away game against Vélez, their directors taunted the home fans. One responded by throwing a chair through the window of the directors' box, at which a director pulled a gun and began firing. By that stage, the sound of gunfire within grounds wasn't especially unusual. As the nineties went on, there were countless anti-violence campaigns, all of which faltered on the same basic problems: the clubs and police were often complicit with the *barras*, and, even when they weren't, the police were as likely to provoke violence as to quell it.

In 1994, after a *superclásico*, Boca fans riding in a flatbed truck shot and killed two River fans. Three years later José Barritta, "el Abuelo" (the Grandfather), as he was nicknamed, the leader of Boca's biggest *barra,* la Doce, was charged with the murders. Although he was acquitted of those charges, he was convicted of extortion and racketeering and jailed. Perhaps more significantly, the investigation into him revealed that la Doce had $3 million in their bank account and who knew what assets elsewhere.

Finally, on May 13, 1998, two games from the end of the *clausura*, Buenos Aires judge Victor Perrotta ordered a judicial suspension of soccer, demanding that, before the league could start again, cameras should at last be installed in all grounds, that fireworks and flags be banned, and that lists of known hooligans be compiled and those on them banned from stadiums. The clubs refused to pay for the cameras, agreed to the ban on fireworks and flags but insisted it was the police's job to enforce it, and, remarkably, handed over the lists—with such alacrity that it confirmed what everybody had always suspected: they knew exactly who the *barras* were and were in league with them.

After a two-week break, soccer began again. With many of those who had been banned turning to lawyers to claim that their exclusion was unconstitutional—they had, after all, been convicted of nothing—things went on pretty much as they had. The following year, after another spate of violence, a further suspension was imposed, this one lasting three months.

53

THE DWINDLING
OF A GENIUS

As he served his 1991 playing ban, Maradona took over as manager of Deportivo Mandiyú, a fourth-tier side based in Corrientes in the far North of Argentina, working with his former Argentinos Juniors teammate Carlos Fren. The season ended in relegation, with Maradona this time blaming a conspiracy of referees, one of whom he called "a thief and a liar" and "a gutless coward without balls." The following year the pair had a stint in charge of Racing that was notable less for anything that happened on the field than for Maradona's occasional absences on drink and drug binges. Again Maradona blamed referees. "They had it in for me," he insisted. "It was personal."

Coppola returned as his manager, and, the ban served, he negotiated for Maradona to resume his career at Boca, which were coached once again by Silvio Marzolini, the deal funded by the television channel America 2 in return for exclusive broadcast rights to matches. He played a total of thirty games, scoring seven goals, and toyed with a glorious finale. With five games of the 1995–1996 *apertura* remaining, Boca were five points clear of Vélez Sarsfield at the top of the table. "I knew what had happened to him in his life, and again he showed me that he gained the respect of his teammates, because he didn't have any privileges," Marzolini said. "We went many games without conceding goals—we won games 1–0 comfortably—but the thing is that with the new three-points-for-a-win rule, a draw was like a defeat."

That fifth-to-the-last game, Boca were denied what seemed a clear penalty and drew 0–0 with Rosario Central. "That was crucial," said Marzolini. They drew 0–0 against River and then on "a terrible afternoon," as Marzolini put it, lost 6–4 to Racing. "That was the day Mauricio Macri was elected president, but the defeat had nothing to do with it—the elections were before the game. Maradona ended up playing as a five, throwing passes forward to see if we could get goals back, but we'd score one, and they'd score another. In the dressing room, Maradona was crying on the floor: I've never forgotten that image. The title was ours, and it had just slipped from our hands." They lost to an eighty-eighth-minute goal at Estudiantes and then drew with Deportivo Español. Bianchi's Vélez won their last five games and, with them, the title.

Bilardo took over as coach before the 1996 *clausura*, as Boca sought to tap once again into the magic of 1986. The reformed Bilardo-Maradona partnership began with a 4–0 win against Gimnasia y Esgrima de Jujuy, and, with Caniggia in sensational form, the season opened promisingly. Maradona, though, missed a penalty and suffered another muscle pull in a 1–0 defeat away to Newell's. Without him, Boca's form dipped, most notably in a 6–0 home defeat to Gimnasia y Esgrima La Plata. Maradona took time to return, partly because of the injury and partly because his relationship with Bilardo had suffered another downturn, seemingly because of the coach's reluctance to select former Vélez midfielder José Basualdo.

When he did come back, there was another missed penalty, this time in a 2–0 win over Belgrano, but Boca were harboring thoughts of a title push again. Then they went to Vélez. Caniggia put Boca ahead, but Vélez hit back to win 5–1, goalkeeper José Luis Chilavert scoring twice, with a penalty and a free kick. For Maradona, this was intolerable. "Vélez," he insisted, "were awarded a goal, a free kick, and a penalty, and none of them were valid. None of them!" He was sent off for dissent. On his return Maradona missed another penalty, against Central, and then another one, against River. When he missed a fifth in a row, against Racing, all hope of the title was gone. Maradona wept and said witches had placed a curse on him. The following week he played what he thought might be his last game for Boca, against Estudiantes.

It turned out to be his last game for a traumatic eleven months. He had a panic attack after getting trapped in an elevator in a hotel in Alicante, screaming and smashing tables and chairs long after the fire department had released him. He went to a rehab clinic in Switzerland to try to kick the cocaine, and then Coppola was arrested on a charge of drug trafficking, although the case against him collapsed amid claims the cocaine found at his apartment had been planted by police. Maradona drifted, playing exhibition games, before finally deciding to knuckle down for one last season, hiring the disgraced Canadian sprinter Ben Johnson as a coach. The *apertura* began against, of all teams, Argentinos Juniors. Maradona was, perhaps not surprisingly, selected for the postmatch drug test. He played against Newell's and managed forty-five minutes in a 2–1 win over River. Then it was announced that the sample he had given after the Argentinos game had tested positive for cocaine. Protesting his innocence again, he announced his retirement from soccer on his thirty-seventh birthday.

54

THE LURE OF THE PAST

By the mid-1990s, disillusionment with Menem was widespread and fostered both a sense that Argentina was doomed and a nostalgia for an age when Argentina had been a more optimistic nation with aspirations to play a major role on a global stage. By the midsixties, that myth was unraveling. Development in local infrastructure had slowed and in some cases regressed, Brazil had emerged as a major industrial power, the shock of the series of coups had undermined confidence in the apparatus of government, and exposure to global markets had laid bare inefficiencies in the Argentinian economy.

"Very little is left of what Argentina was as a nation," cultural theorist Beatriz Sarlo wrote, before reaching a conclusion redolent of that made by Borocotó, the editor of *El Gráfico*, seventy years earlier. "In the explosion of identities that some call postmodernism," she went on, "soccer is an adhesive: it is easy, universal, and televised." In the declining days of Menem's second term, it was one of the few things that bound it together.

Pablo Alabarces, in arguing that there was a difference in degree in soccer's roles as nation unifier in the nineties when compared to the twenties, placed the responsibility for the sense of dissolution squarely on Menem, noting that the withdrawal of the state had left many without access to education, health care, water, electricity, gas, and housing, let alone welfare provision such as unemployment benefits. There were disaffection and anger, which led many to violence and crime: there could hardly have been a better symbol of social decay than the announcement in September 1998 that the prisons in Buenos Aires were full, and as a result thirty-seven hundred convicts would be held in abandoned factories.

After the 1994 World Cup, Alfio Basile was replaced as national coach by Daniel Passarella, who had led River to three league titles in the early nineties. No friend of Maradona, he was determined to stamp out the laxity of approach that he believed had contributed to the forward's issues with drugs. He banned long hair, earrings, and homosexuality, which brought him into conflict with a number of players. Batistuta was exiled from the national side for ten months before a cursory trim permitted his return, but both Caniggia and elegant midfielder Fernando Redondo ended up refusing to play for Argentina as long as Passarella remained coach.

The defense of the Copa América in 1995 was undone first by a sloppy 3–0 defeat to the United States in their final-group game and then by a dreadful refereeing decision. Argentina were already through after winning their first two games, but the decision to rest a number of key players upset their rhythm, and the defeat to the United States meant that instead of topping the group and facing Mexico in the quarter-final, Argentina came in second and faced Brazil. They took a ninth-minute lead, Ariel Ortega and Juan José Borrelli combining to set up Abel Balbo to finish with a crisp, low shot. Edmundo soon equalized, but just before the half hour Taffarel let a fierce Batistuta drive slip through his grasp, and the Argentinian lead was restored. River Plate midfielder Leonardo Astrada was sent off for a second bookable offense shortly before halftime, and the dynamic of the game was transformed. Still, though, Argentina held on until, with nine minutes left, Túlio pulled down a Jorginho cross with an extended left hand. The offense was so obvious that everybody stopped as Túlio lifted the ball over Hernán Cristante's halfhearted dive, yet Peruvian referee Alberto Tejada allowed the goal to stand.

César Sampaio was later sent off, it finished 2–2, and Brazil won on penalties, but the focus in Argentina was on only one thing. "Brazil, with the hand of God," raged *La Prensa*. As journalist Pablo Vignone noted in *Página/12* a decade later, to speak of karma and retribution for Maradona's handballs against England and the USSR was to miss the point; outrages like this were a direct result of the culture of *viveza*. "When it comes to reproaching sins," he wrote, "it must be admitted that both the hand of Túlio in the Copa América in 1995 and that of Diego in the Mexico World Cup . . . were the product of an instant craftiness, steeped in the *potrero*, outside the law in regulatory terms, although characteristic of a folklore linked intimately with the spirit of soccer."

Argentina's hopes in the 1997 Copa América were undermined by the reluctance of European clubs to release players. A last-minute Marcelo Gallardo penalty secured a draw against Paraguay in the third-group game that took them through second in the group, but Argentina were eliminated in the quarter-final by Peru. Still, with a full squad, Argentina romped through South American qualifying for the 1998 World Cup, finishing top of the nine-team Conmebol group (Brazil, as defending champions, didn't have to go through qualifying) and earning Passarella the accolade of South American coach of the year for 1997. The expectation on the side going into the World Cup wasn't without justification.

The draw was gentle. Argentina started against a compact, organized, but largely unthreatening Japan and beat them 1–0 thanks to a deft finish from Batistuta, who lifted the ball over Japan goalkeeper Yoshikatsu Kawaguchi after a ricochet fell kindly for him at the edge of the box. Argentina cut loose against Jamaica, Ortega scoring two and Batistuta three in a 5–0 win. A much-changed team then beat Croatia 1–0 to secure the top spot in the group and a last-sixteen meeting with England.

The sides had met at Wembley in an ill-tempered friendly in 1991, when Argentina came from 2–0 down to draw 2–2, but the buildup, inevitably, was dominated by the previous competitive meeting, the World Cup quarterfinal in 1986. The game was one of the most thrilling in World Cup history, an epic of seemingly endless twists and subplots. Six minutes in, Simeone ran on to a Batistuta flick and tumbled over a clumsy challenge from David Seaman. Gary Neville, arms raised, charged toward referee Kim Milton Nielsen, insisting Simeone had dived, but while there was something theatrical about his fall, Seaman's thigh had clipped the Argentinian's ankle. Batistuta's penalty was not a great one, firmly struck but at a comfortable height for Seaman, who got his right hand to the ball but could only push it down against the inside of the post, from where it rebounded into the net.

The lead didn't last long. Ten minutes in, Michael Owen ran onto a Paul Scholes flick and charged into the box. Roberto Ayala stepped into his path, Owen threw himself down after minimal contact, and England had a penalty that Shearer thumped into the top corner.

There might have been a question as to the extent to which Owen had manufactured the fall, but what he did six minutes later was truly remarkable. Sol Campbell made a half challenge on López, and Paul Ince picked up the loose ball no more than five yards outside the England box. He laid a pass forward to David Beckham, who chipped a pass toward Owen in the center circle. His first touch, dragging the ball down from behind him with the outside of his right foot, took him by José Chamot, and he had the pace and strength to hold off the defender. By the time he reached Ayala just outside the box, Owen was at full tilt, and a touch to the right was enough to go by him, opening the angle for a delicious clipped finish past Carlos Roa.[1] It was, perhaps, the greatest individual goal scored by an Englishman at the World Cup, and, to those who see patterns echoing back through the generations, there was something appropriate about it: just as Maradona in 1986 had downed England first with *viveza* and then with brilliance, so had Owen inflicted two differing blows on Argentina.

Argentina leveled in first-half injury time. López, carrying on a theme of the game, went down cheaply under pressure from Campbell to win a free kick just outside the box, and, with England expecting a shot, Juan

Sebastián Verón rolled the ball down the side of the wall to Javier Zanetti, who slashed a finish past Seaman.

The second half was two minutes old when the game took its decisive shift. Simeone barged over Beckham just inside the Argentina half, a foul for which he was booked. As he walked away, having tousled—or pulled?—Beckham's hair, the midfielder flicked out his foot, catching him behind the knee. Simeone staggered, making sure Nielsen saw the incident: he did and showed a red card for an act of petulant silliness. As retaliation goes, it was relatively mild, but it was also undeniable. Even in England, sympathy for Beckham was limited: "Ten Heroic Lions, One Stupid Boy," as the *Mirror*'s headline had it the following day.

What followed was a performance of supreme doggedness and effort from England, as they held Argentina at bay and created sufficient chances to prevent the pressure on their goal from ever becoming intolerable, prompting *La Nación* to speak approvingly of "the great swipes made by the wounded lion of England."

And so it went to penalties, already becoming a bête noire in the English consciousness. Seaman saved Crespo's penalty, Argentina's second, but immediately Roa denied Paul Ince, and when David Batty's effort, England's fifth, was beaten away by the goalkeeper, Argentina were through to a quarter-final against the Netherlands. If anything, it was an even better game than the match against England had been.

Wim Jonk had already struck a post when the Dutch took a twelfth-minute lead, Dennis Bergkamp subtly heading Ronald de Boer's forward pass into the path of Patrick Kluivert, who nudged his finish over Roa. Within five minutes, Argentina had leveled, Verón's sumptuous pass slitting the Dutch defense for López, who delayed his shot before rolling the ball between the legs of Edwin van der Sar. They were two wonderful goals, but what followed meant barely anybody would remember them. With fourteen minutes remaining, Arthur Numan, already booked for a late challenge on Ortega, lunged in on Simeone and was sent off.

Argentina's advantage lasted only ten minutes. Then Ortega, having isolated Jaap Stam on the right side of the box, dived over his dangling leg—one of those instances in which, if he'd just kept running rather than leaping, flicking his heels up, and arching his back, he'd probably have gotten the penalty. Referee Arturo Brizio Carter of Mexico gestured for Ortega to get up, at which Edwin van der Sar ran over to remonstrate. Ortega sprang to his feet, thrusting the top of his head into Van der Sar's jaw. The red card was inevitable.

Two minutes later Frank De Boer launched a long forward pass from the back of midfield into the path of Dennis Bergkamp as he advanced into the box. His first touch, made several feet off the ground, plucked the ball out of the air, his second turned back inside Ayala, and his third dispatched a finish past Roa. It was a stunning goal born of extraordinary technical ability and a clinical, minimalist mind-set, and it put Argentina out. It also, perhaps, confirmed two strands of thought about the state of the nation: on the one hand, Argentina had self-destructed, needlessly surrendering a man advantage; on the other, it was cursed, undone by one of the greatest goals in the history of the World Cup.

Passarella resigned, at which national youth coach José Pékerman was asked to take over. He declined, instead taking on a role as general manager and recommending the appointment of Marcelo Bielsa, while Tocalli took on the Under-20 side.

55

BOCA'S AGE OF GLORY

Boca had been in financial crisis when Mauricio Macri was elected president in 1995. A qualified civil engineer, Macri had been president of Sevel, which held the license to produce Fiats and Peugeots in Argentina. In 1991 he was kidnapped by rogue officers of the Argentinian federal police and held for twelve days before his family reportedly paid a ransom. It was during that time, Macri has later said, that he decided to enter politics; his time as president of Boca can be seen as a way of honing his electoral skills and building a power base within Buenos Aires. There is an immediate contradiction in the colocation of the center-right Macri and Boca's broadly working-class fans, but the plan worked; in 2015 Macri was elected to succeed Cristina Kirchner as president of the republic.

For the first time, Boca had a clear business plan, and that helped them out of debt. The club introduced such innovations as telephone service centers, a decentralized ticket sales system, and a separate section in the stadium where companies could rent boxes; there was, for the first time, an effort to maximize revenue from members.

Whatever the off-field developments, Macri's revolution meant nothing without on-field success. Macri recognized early that the only way for Argentinian clubs to survive was to accept their position as breeding grounds for the far richer clubs of Europe. Under him Boca prioritized their academy, sweeping up promising teenagers from around the country, and signed players from other Argentinian clubs who had a resale value. Buenos Aires had boomed as a city that exported Argentinian goods to the Old World; Macri reinvoked that past, positioning Boca as the key conduit for players seeking a move to Europe. He was hugely successful, his twelve years as president yielding more than $120 million in player sales and bringing sixteen trophies.

Understandably, the policy took time to take effect. By the time Carlos Bianchi was appointed as coach in July 1998, it was six years since the *apertura* triumph under Óscar Tabárez.

Bianchi's critics would say that, as at Vélez, he inherited a squad that was almost fully formed, and while it is true that the players he led to greatness were already at the club when he arrived, he got more out of them than either Bilardo or Veira had managed, in part perhaps because he no longer had to deal with the distraction of Maradona. Bianchi left out Caniggia, who ended up breaking his contract; sold Diego Latorre, who had described Boca's dressing room as "a cabaret"; and off-loaded Néstor Fabbri, Norberto Solano, and Sergio Castillo to create the tight, committed squad he believed was essential. Not that everybody got along: forwards Martín Palermo and Guillermo Barros Schelotto had a notoriously difficult relationship, something Bianchi dealt with head-on. "He put us together in the same room and told us that he knew that we didn't like each other," Barros Schelotto said, "but that we were going to change that because we would play the nineteen games of the tournament in the first XI."

Boca didn't lose any of those nineteen games, winning thirteen and drawing six to take the title by nine points. They were finally beaten by Independiente in the third-to-the-last game of the *clausura* season, having stretched their unbeaten record to forty matches. River also lost that weekend, though, which was enough to give Boca the title.

Bianchi's was a hard, cautious team—they conceded less than a goal a game in both *apertura* and *clausura* that season—but they had in Juan Román Riquelme a glorious, creative presence. He was twenty, a thoughtful, almost ponderous visionary. He had a mournful demeanor, seeming always slightly put upon, as perhaps befitted a player out of time. He lacked pace, having none of the acceleration from a standing start that had characterized Maradona and would later characterize Lionel Messi, and he seemed to revel in his slowness. He was a master of *la pausa*, the greatest exponent of that moment of stillness since Ricardo Bochini. Even more tantalizingly, it may be that he was that last master of the art. Increasingly since the fifties—since Helsingborg, for Argentinians—soccer has become a frenetic, urgent game; even Menotti demanded speed. In part, that's because soccer players are fitter now than they've ever been, thanks to improvements in diet and sports science. But it's also, Valdano argues, because of the way soccer has come to be consumed. "Soccer is no longer mysterious," he said. "We no longer experience it according to our own imagination because the cameras are everywhere. Pictures on a screen can't compete with the pictures you can form in your head. And it's impacting the way the game is played."

"The *enganche*," columnist Hugo Asch wrote in a column in *Perfil* in 2007, is "an artist, almost by definition a difficult, misunderstood soul. It would, after all, hardly seem right if our geniuses were level-headed. . . . Our man is a romantic hero, a poet, a misunderstood genius with the destiny of a myth. . . . Riquelme, the last specimen of the breed, shares with Bochini the melancholy and the certainty that he works only under shelter, with a court in his thrall and an environment that protects him from the evils of this world." Boca was that environment; he should, perhaps, never have left.

Palermo, five years his senior, was a bustling target man, all chest and elbows, a player who specialized in goals that would be described as having been bundled over the line. Aesthetics meant little to him; to him, being a center-forward was just about getting the ball in the net as often as you could, however you could.

He broke Boca's goal-scoring records with 236 goals, 193 of them in the league. By the end the records were tumbling so regularly that fans hung a banner from one of the executive boxes at the Bombonera, listing the numbers from 180 to 221 (221 being the all-time, all-competition record of Roberto Cherro). Every time he scored, they hauled it in and crossed off another one. By the end, they needed another banner. Yet Palermo remains best known—at least to an international audience—for having missed three penalties in the same game, as Argentina lost 3–0 to Colombia at the 1999 Copa América, or perhaps for celebrating one of his rare goals for Villarreal by jumping on a wall, only for it to collapse, breaking his leg and sidelining him for six months.

Boca lost only twice in the 1999 *apertura*, which left them third, and the focus then shifted to the Libertadores. Boca finished top of their group and, in the last sixteen, achieved a typical 0–0 draw away to Nacional of Quito. Back at la Bombonera, Riquelme, with almost no back lift, shaped an opener around a defender and inside the post, a stunning goal that set Boca on their way to a 5–1 lead by halftime. As Nacional pulled two back in the second half, the suspicion was that they'd already begun to think about the quarter-final, for there they faced River, which were on the way to their own *apertura-clausura* double. It was the most eagerly awaited *superclásico* in decades.

In the first leg, at el Monumental, River took an early lead, Javier Saviola getting to a cross in front of goalkeeper Óscar Córdoba and diverting it back for Juan Pablo Ángel to score. Riquelme leveled with a sumptuous free kick before Saviola scored a superb winner, surging forward and whipping his shot into the far corner from twenty-two yards.

Palermo had been out for six months with yet another knee injury, but he vowed to play in the second leg. River coach Américo Gallego was so dismissive of his chances of recovering in time that he said that if Palermo played, he would select Francescoli, by then thirty-nine and retired for three years. Bianchi put Palermo on the bench. It was his other *grande*, though, who got things going early in the second half, Riquelme beating two men on the left before carving a low, diagonal ball to the back post, where Marcelo Delgado turned it in.

And then it was Palermo's turn. Although clearly unfit and still favoring his good leg, he was introduced with fifteen minutes remaining. Sebastián Battaglia was tripped in the box, and Riquelme converted the penalty. But there was more. Riquelme, toying with a tiring River on the left, rolled the ball inside for Battaglia, bursting forward. He cut the ball back a little behind Palermo on the penalty spot. The striker's first touch was heavy but seemed to wrong-foot poor Víctor Zapata, giving him an eternity to turn. His second touch teed up the shot; his third jabbed it into the bottom corner for what has become known as *el gol de las muletas* (the goal on crutches). When Palermo reached 180 goals, a series of 180 pairs of boots were produced, each autographed and inscribed with the details of one of his goals. They were then auctioned off for charity. The pair that fetched the highest price was number 73, the goal that gave Boca a 3–0 win over River on the night and made it 4–2 on aggregate, *el gol de las muletas*.

It took a late Walter Samuel header in the second leg to get Boca past América of Mexico City in the semifinal, even though they'd won the first 4–1. Two draws in the final against Luiz Felipe Scolari's Palmeiras meant penalties. Ivan Córdoba saved from Faustino Asprilla and Roque Júnior, leaving Guillermo Barros Schelotto, whose twin brother, Gustavo, had also played in the first leg, to convert the decisive penalty and give Boca the title for the first time in twenty-two years.

As it turned out, that wasn't even the summit of what Boca achieved under Bianchi. Five months after the success in Brazil, Boca went to Tokyo for the 2000 Intercontinental Cup final against a Real Madrid side at the beginning of their *galácticos* era.

Bianchi knew his side couldn't compete in an open game, so he set out to stop Real Madrid, precisely the sort of challenge he relished. He sat his back four deep, with the three midfielders in front of them, essentially as runners to block the gaps. Riquelme was then the sole creator, often drifting left, with Marcelo Delgado cutting in from the right: a lopsided 4-3-1-2 with a huge gap between the back seven and the front three. It was a system set up to hold an opponent at arm's length and wait for mistakes.

Boca didn't have to wait very long. Two minutes in, Madrid right-back Geremi took a throw-in straight to midfielder Mauricio Serna. He nudged the ball on to Basualdo, who slipped a quick pass into the path of Delgado as he, peeling off Fernando Hierro, attacked the space behind Geremi. Delgado made for the line and, as Palermo rumbled between Aitor Karanka and Roberto Carlos, waited and waited before rolling the ball square for the center-forward to tap in.

It was a barely credible start, and it soon got even more unbelievable. Three minutes later Madrid won a throw-in on their left. Roberto Carlos lofted the ball forward to Raúl, who attempted to chest it down to Guti. Battaglia stole in and shoved the ball forward to Riquelme. His job was to link front and back of the side, to be coordinator of counterattacks. His first touch was typically perfect, allowing him to turn and open his body. Palermo had already set off, clanking between Hierro and Geremi. Riquelme lifted the ball forward, an effortless, perfect sixty-yard pass loaded with backspin so that when it landed in front of Palermo it checked, meaning he didn't have to break stride or take a touch but could simply run on and, as it bounced a second time, thrash it under Iker Casillas. Palermo ran off, tried to celebrate with a slide, and collapsed awkwardly on his belly.

Goaded by the two early goals, Madrid tore into Boca, Roberto Carlos hit the bar, and then, as Hugo Ibarra headed a Luis Figo cross aimlessly up into the air, the Brazilian fullback smacked a volley past Córdoba. Still only eleven minutes had been played. As the onslaught continued, Boca could easily have buckled, but a Riquelme free kick twenty minutes in steadied the nerves, forcing Casillas into a fine save and offering a reminder that Boca could still trouble the European champions. That was the story of the rest of the game, furious Real Madrid attacking, with Riquelme, elegantly and calmly leading the resistance, holding possession, delivering just enough jabs to prevent a full-on assault, just enough menace that the siege never became overwhelming. For Bianchi, it was a second world title in six years. "It's hard to compare the two," he said. "Both are special for different reasons. But this victory is not only for Boca, but for Argentina. We were able to prove that Argentinian soccer is the best in the world."

Nobody, perhaps, really believed that, but over the three years that followed Boca proved they were the best in South America. Three weeks after the Libertadores success, Boca wrapped up the *apertura*, as River took only a point from their final two games of the season. In the Libertadores they beat Palmeiras on penalties in the semifinal and then Cruz Azul in the same way in the final.

Boca cruised through the group stage of the Libertadores in 2001, winning five of six matches. Junior of Colombia were beaten 4–3 on aggregate in the last sixteen, and Vasco da Gama dismissed 4–0 in the quarter-final to set up a repeat of the previous year's final against Palmeiras in the semi. Again Boca were at home first. Palmeiras twice took the lead, but twice Boca leveled, so that it again finished 2–2, with both sides finishing with ten men after Fernando and Antonio Barijho were sent off. A series of defensive errors allowed Walter Gaitán to give Boca a second-minute lead in São Paulo, and Riquelme doubled that quarter of an hour later, finishing off a hypnotic run with a shot squirted into the bottom corner. Fábio Júnior pulled one back, at which the game took a violent turn. Two Palmeiras fans ran onto the field, and after one had failed to lay out the linesman with a punch, the second followed up with a flying kick. Alexandre was then red-carded for a horrendous lunge on Cristian Traverso, who was lucky he was fractionally off the ground when contact was made, so he was sent spinning into the air rather than breaking a bone. Boca's Aníbal Matellán was also sent off, before a corner deflected in off Jorge Bermúdez. The second leg, too, finished 2–2, and, as they had the previous year, Boca prevailed on penalties. A pair of 1–0 away wins in the final against Cruz Azul of Mexico meant more penalties. Boca again triumphed. It was a very Boca way of winning.

The next task was to defend the Intercontinental title, but against Bayern Munich there was no repeat of the previous year's triumph. They had Delgado sent off and were beaten 1–0 by Sammy Kuffour's 109th-minute goal. Bianchi resigned, saying it was best for the club, although it was widely believed that he was frustrated with the number of players who had been sold. He was replaced by Óscar Tabárez, but results dipped. Boca finished third in both the *apertura* and the *clausura* in 2001–2002, while their bid for a third successive Libertadores was ended in the quarter-final by the eventual champions, the Paraguayan side Olimpia.

56

THE CRASH

Menem's popularity had disappeared long before the 1999 general election, but the constitution anyway prevented him from standing for a third successive term. His unpopularity also undermined the chances of Eduardo Duhalde, the Justicialist candidate, with the result that the Radical mayor of Buenos Aires, Fernando de la Rúa, was elected president. Through the nineties public debt had continued to rise, partly because government spending remained high and partly because corruption, money laundering, and tax evasion reduced the revenues available to pay off the deficit. The IMF continued to extend credit, but the problems kept mounting. A crisis in the Brazilian economy followed the one in Mexico and further reduced Argentina's exports, while a revaluation of the dollar led to the devaluation of the peso against the euro.

Inevitably, the economic issues affected soccer. In March 2000, Racing were declared bankrupt—an astonishing emblem of the nation's collapse: their title success in 1913 had signaled the end of British control and the start of an Argentinian sensibility; their downfall seemed to symbolize the end of it. Fans, in a typical show of defiance, flocked to the stadium and went through the full ritual of songs and flares, but that couldn't alter the basic fact that the money had run out. Eventually, in January 2001, a company called Blanquiceleste became the first corporate owner of an Argentinian club, running it as a concession for ten years while paying off the debt. Fans decided the ill fortune must be put down to the curse imposed by Independiente in 1967 and so arranged an exorcism. One hundred thousand turned up to witness it, but Racing's results didn't improve until coach Reinaldo "Mostaza" Merlo, the former River midfielder with the mustard-colored hair, ordered that the concrete moat around the field be ripped out. The skeleton of the seventh cat buried by Independiente fans in 1967 was discovered. Later that year Racing won the league, their first major title since the Intercontinental success thirty-four years earlier. Nobody, though, thought that signified any kind of national renaissance.

In March 2001, Argentina went through three ministers of finance. In July 2001 civil service salaries and government pensions were cut by 13 percent, sparking a nationwide general strike that was soon followed by a players' strike, as they claimed $50 million in unpaid wages. The AFA provided a short-term loan to get things moving again, but the wider problems went on. In August the highest-paid government employees received their payments in IOUs.

The Radicals suffered badly in the midterm elections in October 2001, leaving them without a majority in Congress, but the most worrying development perhaps was the 20 percent of those who voted who spoiled their ballot papers or left them blank as "anger votes."[1] By the end of November, with unemployment at 20 percent and inflation soaring toward 40 percent, fears of devaluation led to a run on the banks, as those with savings in pesos sought to convert them into dollars and get them out of Argentina. The government responded on December 2 with a series of measures known as the *corralito*, effectively freezing bank accounts for twelve months, limiting withdrawals to $250 a week.

The *corralito* sparked fury, and thousands took to the streets in the major cities to protest. Initially, they simply banged pots and pans together as a gesture of disgust, but soon there were attacks on property, particularly that belonging to banks or major European and US companies. On December 5 the IMF, citing a failure to reduce the budget deficit to an agreed target, refused to release a $1.3 billion tranche of a loan and demanded cuts amounting to 10 percent of the federal budget. With the situation worsening, De la Rúa declared a state of emergency. Soccer stopped. Racing sealed the *apertura* title with a 1–1 draw away at Vélez on December 27, but it wasn't until the following February that the season was finally completed.

Clashes between demonstrators and police became increasingly common until, on December 20 and 21, thousands gathered in the Plaza de Mayo and ended up fighting running battles with police, who deployed tear gas, water cannons, and rubber bullets. Eventually, live rounds were fired, resulting in five fatalities. In total, thirty-nine people were killed in the protests across Argentina. De la Rúa was left isolated and impotent, his government collapsing around him and violence raging outside as he sat in the Casa Rosada watching cartoons on television. He fled in a helicopter and was left with little option but to resign, although he insisted he had never authorized the level of force used by police.

De la Rúa was succeeded by Adolfo Rodríguez Saá, the Peronist governor of the province of San Luis. On December 23 Argentina defaulted on a debt of $132 billion. The Rodríguez Saá administration reacted by proposing a third currency, the argentino, that would exist only in cash form and would be nonconvertible, allowing a fiscal flexibility impossible with convertible pesos. Critics of the scheme, though, suggested it was devaluation by another name, and when it became apparent Rodríguez Saá didn't have the political support to push the scheme through, he resigned, to be replaced by Eduardo Duhalde, who had run as a Peronist candidate in the 1999 presidential elections.

In January 2002 Duhalde accepted the inevitable and unpegged the peso, forcing those who held bank accounts in dollars to convert to pesos at an official rate. By the end of the year the peso had fallen from parity with the dollar to trading at four to the dollar, which, because of the Argentinian reliance on imports, forced up prices. Another wave of protests and riots swept the country in April, and the banking system was suspended once again. By the end of the year, though, the situation had stabilized sufficiently for Duhalde to call elections for April 2003.

What cultural critic Beatriz Sarlo had observed about the national soccer team being one of the few remaining institutions that bound Argentina together in 1998 was even more true four years later; by then it was pretty much the only entity capable of engendering a sense of pride in the nation. Argentina were unbeaten in almost two years under Marcelo Bielsa, even though he had gone eight months without being paid. A number of players—Ayala, Verón, Caniggia, Batistuta, and Almeyda—went into the World Cup in Japan not fully fit, while Riquleme, his thoughtful style incongruous with Bielsa's incessant verticality, was left out altogether, but there was widespread hope in Argentina that the crisis would be a motivating and unifying force that could carry the national team to glory. Bielsa, after all, having won the league at Vélez before taking the national job, was excitingly radical and as near to a guarantee of success as there could be in Argentinian soccer.

They began well enough, controlling an uninspiring game against Nigeria and winning 1–0 thanks to a back-post header from Batistuta. As the nation celebrated, the government quietly revealed it intended to convert all remaining savings into government bonds of dubious value. Further riots followed.

The national mood was only worsened when England proved rather more valiant—and fortunate—than they had in the previous two World Cup meetings between the sides. Michael Owen had already hit the post when, a minutes before halftime, he collapsed over Mauricio Pochettino's attempt at a tackle, a penalty born of a defender's carelessness and a forward's instincts. David Beckham, desperate for personal redemption after his red card against the same opponents four years earlier, hit his penalty hard and low and just to the right of center. Pablo Cavallero, having jerked about on his line, was wrong-footed, and the ball zipped past his tamely outstretched left leg.

As England struggled to maintain their intensity, Pochettino should have equalized, his free header from six yards hitting David Seaman and bouncing wide, but, as against Nigeria, Argentina found that the ball just wouldn't go in. A 1–0 defeat meant they faced Sweden, which had beaten Nigeria 2–1, needing to win to go through, assuming England avoided defeat against the Super Eagles.

That final match followed a familiar pattern. Argentina had chance after chance, but it was Sweden that took the lead, Anders Svensson crashing in a thirty-yard free kick just before the hour. Andreas Andersson then had an effort brilliantly tipped onto the crossbar by Cavallero, before, with two minutes remaining, Ortega dived to win a penalty. He missed, but Hernán Crespo followed in the rebound. But a draw wasn't enough. At the end of the group stage, Argentina had had more shots and won more corners than any other side at the World Cup, but as England and Nigeria played out a tedious 0–0, they were eliminated.

What was striking was the lack of outrage. "We are sad," said Fernando Niembro of cable TV channel TyC, "but this doesn't change our lives. People in Argentina have the same problems as yesterday and continue to worry about getting a job and avoiding being mugged on street corners." The paradox is striking: in the 1920s, *El Gráfico* had sought to define *argentinidad* through soccer, yet, eighty years later, even the Argentinian soccer-playing identity was a fractured one, the ties of barrio and club far stronger than those of the nation, in which faith was rapidly dwindling.

In soccer nobody had any money. Racing, despite the Blanquiceleste takeover, were still $60 million in debt. San Lorenzo's debts weren't far short of that, while Boca, River, and Independiente all owed around $40 million—and that was with television and advertising revenues having been paid in advance. All five had been caught in the same trap: loans taken out in dollars had effectively been trebled by the devaluation. Belgrano Córdoba put their entire squad up for sale. At Boca Macri arranged a premium-rate phone line, urging fans to pay $2 each to keep Riquelme at the club. He was sold to Barcelona anyway.

Duhalde, recognizing soccer's role as an opiate, reduced the tax on ticket sales and released the clubs from the obligation of paying for policing outside the grounds, but such assistance went only so far. Many clubs abandoned their reserve sides, while the AFA stopped paying and supplying fourth officials. What made the financial misery all the more shocking is that since the restrictions had been lifted after the 1978 World Cup, almost fifty-five hundred players had been sold abroad for a total of $570 million, the vast majority of them in the previous five years. The clubs were running out of assets to sell, and disillusionment was growing.

The end of the *apertura* in 2002 saw an increase in violence. In October Banfield went 5–0 up at home to River Plate ten minutes into the second half, at which River fans invaded the field to end the humiliation. The following week River lost 2–1 at home to Boca. The regulation was already in force that away fans leave first, and only when they've fully dispersed are the home fans let out; la Doce, though, refused to move, staying on the terrace, celebrating in teeming rain. Frustrated, some River fans tried to leave the stadium, pushing past police and hurdling barriers. The police responded with rubber bullets, baton charges, and tear gas, some of it fired not only onto the open terrace—which under the circumstances would have been dangerous enough—but into the enclosed concourses, stairwells, and corridors. There was panic, the bathrooms packed with people, many of whom had been innocently caught up in the trouble, washing out their eyes and vomiting, while the *barras* fought with police in the streets, some even invading the postmatch press conference and attacking River coach Manuel Pellegrini. In the dressing room, River's club doctor removed a rubber bullet from a fan's eye. Some 750 miles to the west, in Mendoza, River fans rioted in sympathy.

On the final day of that season, Independiente went to San Lorenzo needing a win to clinch the title. When they went 3–0 up, San Lorenzo fans cut through the fencing in an attempt to prevent any postmatch celebrations on the field and were kept back only by the use of water cannons. Violence had become endemic.

PART SEVEN

OVER THE WATER,
2002–2015

57

THE SECOND COMING

S alvador Ricardo Aparicio was frustrated. Only thirteen of his fourteen players from the 1986 age group had turned up at the stadium in the Rosario suburb of Grandoli, which meant he was one short for the game of seven versus seven he usually oversaw. There was one other boy there, messing about in the dust, kicking a ball against the front of the dilapidated stand, but he had been born in 1987. He was small, even for a four-year-old. His two older brothers were regulars at practice, and his grandmother was sitting on one of the hard wooden benches in the stand. She had already asked Aparicio to let the youngest boy play.

The exact details of what happened next are disputed. Aparicio says that in desperation he asked the four-year-old to play, and when his mother or aunt—he can't remember which—objected, he promised to stop the game if it got too rough. The family, meanwhile, maintains that the grandmother demanded the boy should play and Aparicio agreed only reluctantly, saying he had to play on the wing so they could take him off quickly if he started to cry. Either way, the four-year-old started the game. The first time the ball came to him, he ignored it. Aparicio wasn't particularly surprised. The second time it came to him, this time on his left foot, he nudged it in front of him, started running, and beat three opponents with a startlingly instinctive *gambeta*. Aparicio had never seen anything like Lionel Messi.

M essi had been born on June 24, 1987, at the Garibaldi hospital in Rosario. Later that day fifteen bombs went off across Argentina, including one in Rosario and one in Villa Constitución, the small town about thirty miles outside the city where Messi's father worked. The precise reasons for the bombing remain unclear, but it seems they were a protest at Alfonsín's Law of Due Obedience, which had come into effect the previous day.

Messi's parents, Jorge and Celia, had married in 1978, eight days before the World Cup final. In a nation in which all history can feel like a magic-realist novel, the symbolism seemed significant, that Messi's coming was somehow preordained. Rosario lies on the Paraná River, about three hundred miles downstream of Esquina, the home of Diego Maradona's parents. The day of his birth was the fifty-second anniversary of the death of tango singer Carlos Gardel. And on his first birthday his aunts and uncles presented him with the red-and-black shirt of Newell's Old Boys, the club for whom Maradona would later unsuccessfully play: what Maradona couldn't finish, it turned out, Messi wouldn't even begin.

The presentation of the shirt to the infant was a symbolic act, one that foreshadows "The Adoration of the Cage Fighters," the first in Grayson Perry's remarkable 2012 sequence of six tapestries "The Vanity of Small Differences." In Perry's work, the baby, Tim Rakewell, is given a Sunderland shirt, an emblem of his tribe that comes to represent not only a sense of belonging but also of entrapment. Had Messi stayed at Newell's into his midteens, had the *barras bravas* that came to have an unhealthy influence on the club's finances taken more of an interest, the entrapment may have become more than merely figurative. Alabarces deals gloomily with this notion of soccer as an easy bestower of identity, making the point that as the population has become consumers, both material and symbolic, rather than citizens, the role of soccer has changed.

That Newell's shirt is emblematic of Messi's identity. For all the accusations that have dogged him throughout his career that he doesn't care about the Argentina national team, he has always remained firmly Rosarian: his girlfriend and the mother of his child, Antonella Roccuzzo, is from Rosario; his favorite actor is Argentinian Ricardo Darín, the star of *El secreto de sus ojos* and *Nueve reinas*; and, despite moving to Spain when he was thirteen, his accent has remained strongly Argentinian.

His favorite food, meanwhile, is *milanesa*, the typically Argentinian breaded beef fillet his mother served with tomato sauce and cheese. There is something oddly unsophisticated in general about Messi's diet, even if it did improve after Pep Guardiola became coach at Barcelona. He had to be warned in his early days at the club that he was drinking too much Coke, while a list released in September 2014 showed that his preferred post-match meal was a cheese pizza and Sprite. Even before taking into account that typical Argentinian pizza tends to be short on tomatoes and heavy on cheese,[1] that sounds, as Irish journalist Ken Early pointed out, like something you'd order off a children's menu: this perhaps is a manifestation of the necessary infantilism of the *pibe* that Levinsky discussed, the idea that the kid from the *potrero* cannot be allowed to grow up if the full impishness of his talents is to be maintained.

Tellingly, when *Corriere della Sera* interviewed Messi about his family's Italian background, he knew nothing about Recanati, which had been the home of his grandparents before they emigrated, or about the poet Giacomo

Leopardim who was born there, or the nearby Virgin of Loreto: his life was just Rosario until, at thirteen, he went to Barcelona. That broke the bonds with home, but exile hasn't been without its difficulties, particularly in terms of how people back home have reacted to him (there is additional nuance, of course, in that for so many, particularly in Argentina, soccer is a way of breaking free of an ailing economy and escaping the rundown neighborhoods like Grandoli).

Despite the shirt, it took time for Messi to gravitate to soccer. He was given a ball for his fourth birthday, but still preferred collecting picture cards and playing marbles, at both of which he was highly competitive. Then one day he went out to join his father and brothers playing in the street. "We were stunned when we saw what he could do," said Jorge. "He had never played before." It wasn't long after that he started playing for Grandoli, regularly scoring four and five goals per game, even though he was so small that the ball came up almost to his knee.

Jorge Messi had played for the lower sections of Newell's before his national service. He gave up the sport to work in steel production, becoming a manager at his plant. Messi, his brothers, and his cousins would play for hours in the streets while visiting his grandmother. The games would often end in tears; Lionel hated losing.

Messi stayed at Grandoli until the age of six, scoring dozens of goals. The time was probably coming anyway for him to move on to somewhere more professional, but the issue was forced one day when Jorge arrived to watch Lionel and Matías without the two-peso admission fee and was denied entrance. Messi never played for the club again.

He was taken on by Newell's Old Boys on March 21, 1994, three months shy of his seventh birthday, despite being only four feet in height. Three months earlier, Maradona had played his final game for the club. At the time, Newell's had an exceptional reputation for youth development, thanks largely to the work done by Jorge Griffa through the eighties. Messi's early coaches were struck by how natural a player he was, how he needed a little guidance rather than a full-on education. They and his schoolteachers remember a quiet, reserved child, but one who was nonetheless a leader. Even Cintia Arellano, his best friend in childhood, described him as "solitary"; later, with the Argentina national team, his reserve antagonized more senior players. Perhaps that's simply how he was, but it's tempting now to wonder whether genius placed him at a distance, whether he knew that he could do things nobody else could and realized that made him different from everybody else, perhaps even that it gave him a certain responsibility to his talent.

His ability gave him a natural authority, even if he spoke only rarely. Quique Domínguez, one of those first coaches at Newell's, left Messi to lead the warm-ups, knowing that the other players would follow him. And there remained also that hatred of losing; sometimes it manifested in frustration and tears, but more often it just led him to win games almost single-handedly. There was one game in Pujato, for instance, when Newell's found themselves 2–0 down after a quarter of an hour. Messi focused, got "the face," as his teammate Gerardo Grighini put it, and scored a hat trick to turn the game. His tricks meant defenders often looked to foul means to stop him, but, according to Adrián Coria, who coached him in the tenth team, the highest level he reached at Newell's, being kicked simply spurred Messi on.

Messi was still small. At ten he was just four-foot-two, far smaller than his contemporaries and far smaller than his siblings at a comparable age, so he was referred to Dr. Diego Schwarzstein, who discovered that his body wasn't producing a particular growth hormone. It could be treated with daily injections, but they cost fifteen hundred dollars a month. They worked: at eleven, Messi was four-foot-four; by twelve he was four-foot-ten. At first, Jorge was able to pay, helped by social security and the company he worked for, but he sought help from the club (the details are a little puzzling; Schwarzstein insists the treatment should have been available from the state). Newell's made various promises, but, according to Jorge, only three hundred pesos were ever paid, so he began to seek alternatives.

Although Messi was a fan of Newell's, he also had great admiration for River Plate, largely because his idol, inasmuch as he had one, was Pablo Aimar, their subtly gifted *enganche*, who moved to Valencia in 2001. In 2000 Messi went to River for a trial. It followed a familiar pattern. Coaches looked at his diminutive frame and doubted he could cope. He was left on the bench for the preliminary practice game before finally being brought on with a couple of minutes to go, whereupon he nutmegged his marker twice. He was asked back for another game, played from the start, and scored at least ten goals. River wanted to sign him, but the problem was that they had accommodation only for boys over the age of thirteen. It's debatable anyway whether Jorge really wanted his son to join River or was simply looking to pressure Newell's into honoring their promises to pay for the medical treatment. If that was his plan, he failed: there were more promises but no more money. And so he began to consider an even more radical plan.

In February 2000, a video was made of Messi as he performed 113 keepie-ups with an orange and then 140 with a tennis ball. There was a table-tennis ball lying around as well, so he gave that a go and managed 29. A couple of months later, a tape of that, along with more conventional footage, was passed on by Horacio Gaggioli, a Rosarino who owned significant amounts of property in Barcelona, to Josep María Minguella, an agent who, thanks to his friendship with former Barça player and coach Carles Rexach, was influential at the club. He told Barcelona that if they agreed to pay for Messi's growth hormone treatment and find Jorge a job, they could sign him. So, on September 17, 2000, at the age of thirteen, Messi got on a plane for the first time and flew to Spain.

A few days earlier, the Rosario newspaper *La Capital* had run a profile of Messi under the headline "A Very Special Little Leper." In it, as well as revealing uncertainly that he liked chicken and that his favorite book was the Bible, he spoke of wanting to play for the first team and then becoming a phys-ed teacher. He also said the saddest moment of his life had been the death of his grandmother, the first person who had really believed in his talent, when he was ten.

In Barcelona Messi was nervous and barely spoke, initially preferring— in an echo of Carlovich—to change in the corridor rather than go into a dressing room with the likes of Cesc Fàbregas and Gerard Piqué. Coaches, worried by his small stature, warned other players not to "break him." And then he got the ball. Piqué responded to calls to go easy on Messi by asking, "How can we? We can't get close enough to him to be careful." Within a week Rexach, who had been in Australia, asked to see Messi play against boys two years older. He walked once around the field, his first sight of Messi. He knew immediately he wanted to sign him.

Other directors, though, were less sure. Barça were in crisis, enduring the difficult final season of Louis van Gaal's first spell as manager. They were suspicious of Argentinians, having seen Juan Román Riquelme and Javier Saviola fail to adapt, and they were extremely doubtful about the wisdom (and cost) of transplanting such a young player and his family from Rosario to Catalonia, particularly when he was still undergoing hormone treatment for which they would have to pay. They remembered the Maradona clan and the chaos they had caused. After ten weeks they were still quibbling, while Jorge Messi and Minguella were becoming increasingly impatient.

Minguella played tennis with Rexach. Afterward they had a beer. Minguella put pressure on Rexach, who wrote the outline of a contract on a napkin and signed it. Minguella had it notarized the following day, and the napkin has since been venerated, although it's doubtful it would have been legally binding. Nonetheless, it was a gesture of intent, and, finally, a contract was agreed. As soon as it was, Jorge and a friend walked fifty miles to give thanks at the Shrine of the Virgin of Saint Nicolas in the North of Buenos Aires Province, with Messi joining them for the final half mile, which he covered barefoot. On March 15, 2001, he flew back to Spain to begin his new life.

58

THE ASCENT FROM
THE ABYSS

Argentina's constitution barred candidates from standing for a third term as president, but that was not the sort of detail to restrict the ambitions of Carlos Menem, who believed an ad hoc interpretation would allow him to do so. His main opposition came from Néstor Kirchner, a little-known lawyer from Río Gallegos in the South of Patagonia.

Kirchner had supported the return of Perón from exile and had been at Ezeiza in 1973 when the massacre had taken place. He became a doctor of law in 1976, the year when he met Cristina Fernández, whom he married six months later. After the restoration of democracy in 1983, Kirchner took public office and was briefly president of the Río Gallegos social welfare fund. By 1986 Kirchner was popular enough to run as the Justicialist candidate to be mayor of Río Gallegos. In 1991 he was elected governor of the state of Santa Cruz, by which time Cristina was also a member of the provincial legislature. Kirchner had little national profile, something he used to his advantage, skillfully presenting himself as an outsider and winning the presidency when Menem accepted the inevitable before a second round of voting.

Kirchner's priorities in office were twofold. There was, of course, the economy, but he also made radical changes to the judiciary and the military, seeking to remove conservative forces and to oust anybody who had been involved in atrocities during the Dirty War.

Kirchner also set up yet another commission into soccer, headed by Javier Castrilli, a former referee known as "el Sheriff," who had become renowned in the nineties for his probity and strictness. The fighting between rival *barras*, though, continued. In 2004 Talleres players admitted they were still paying protection money to their own fans, while at that year's Paralympics the Argentina team brawled with Brazil. At every level, it seemed, the game was run through with violence.

I n December 2002 Carlos Bianchi returned to Boca. He inherited a side that had just finished second in the *apertura*, and they went on to be runners-up in the *clausura* as well. The sale of Riquelme may have taken some of the artfulness from the side, but there were great pace and directness. And there was Carlos Tévez, a player who, for all his technical skill and goal-scoring ability, often seemed to win games by will alone. Having grown up in Fuerte Apache, a *villa* of notorious lawlessness, he was an authentic child of the *potreros*, something that contributed to his huge popularity. By the middle of 2003, Boca were at their peak, hammering Santos 5–1 on aggregate to claim their fifth Libertadores and their third in four years, while Bianchi surpassed Osvaldo Zubeldía as the most successful coach in the competition's history with his fourth triumph.

Boca also won the 2003–2004 *apertura*, beating second-place San Lorenzo 1–0 on the final day to secure the title. The focus by then, though, was firmly on the Libertadores. In 2004 they topped their first-round group, as did River, which won the *clausura*. Tévez scored in both legs as Boca beat Sporting Cristal in the second round, while River edged by Santos Laguna on penalties. Boca needed penalties in the quarter-final to see off São Caetano, while River swept by Deportivo Cali. And so the stage was set for an apocalyptic semifinal.

Boca's Rolando Schiavi stooped to head the only goal in the first leg at la Bombonera after twenty-eight minutes, after which Marcelo Gallardo and Raúl Cascini were sent off. Boca goalkeeper Roberto Abbondanzieri was extremely fortunate to escape a red card after grabbing Gallardo by the neck, and Guillermo Barros Schelotto also escaped punishment after punching one of River's team doctors.

Boca had Fabián Vargas sent off for a second yellow card just after halftime in the return, and, at fifty minutes, Lucho González leveled the tie with a drive from twenty-five yards. Rubens Sambueza was then sent off for River, a decision that provoked such anger on the River bench that their coach, former midfielder Leo Astrada; his assistant; and the team doctor were all dismissed. When Ricardo Rojas limped off with all three substitutes having already been used, River were left to battle on with nine men. That looked to have been decisive when Tévez smashed in a cutback from the left with six minutes remaining to give Boca a 2–1 lead. Tévez pulled off his shirt in celebration and then flapped his arms by his sides like a chicken— *las gallinas*, he was clearly saying, had lost their bottle again. He was sent off for the gesture, and in the final minute a Fernando Cavenaghi free kick from wide on the left was flicked on for Cristian Nasuti, arriving at the back post, to steer in a low volley. And so it went to penalties. Abbondanzieri saved from Maxi López, leaving journeyman midfielder Javier Villarreal to score the decisive kick and take Boca through to the final. "It was like a game in a film," Villarreal said. "I don't think you'll have another game like that for years. I've never celebrated after a game like that."

All that stood between Boca and a fourth Libertadores in five years was Once Caldas, a team from Manizales in the heart of Colombia's coffee country whose league success in 2003 had been only the second in their history. They held out for a goalless draw in the first leg, although both sides struck the bar. The second leg at the Palogrande finished 1–1, and Once won on penalties.[1] Bianchi left soon after the final, and hasn't won another trophy since. He'd more than done his part, though. As the economy collapsed around the turn of the millennium, his Boca were just about the only Argentinian institution that functioned in a global environment.

S oon there was another. Argentina had refused to travel to Colombia for the 2001 Copa América because of security concerns after death threats were made against a number of their players, but they arrived at the 2004 tournament in Peru with a fine squad and determined to put right what had gone wrong at the World Cup in Japan. With Javier Saviola, a diminutive and explosive forward nicknamed "the Rabbit," linking well with Tévez, they played some fine soccer, but lost on penalties to Brazil in the final. There was some sense of redemption a month later at the Olympics. Argentina were brilliant and took gold, as Tévez got the only goal in the final against Paraguay. In six games Argentina had scored seventeen goals without reply, an emphatic assertion of their superiority. True, it was only the Olympics, but the evidence of recovery was everywhere.

For Bielsa, that was it. Saying he no longer had the "energy" required for the job, he resigned at the end of 2004 and didn't take another job until Chile approached him in 2007. He returned to club soccer in 2011, first with Athletic of Bilbao and then with Marseille, apparently doomed always to follow the same paradigm, spreading first bewilderment, then enlightenment, and finally exhaustion.

59

THE GROWTH OF
THE LEGEND

For Messi, the early months in Barcelona were hard, quite aside from the difficulties of settling in. As a foreigner, Messi couldn't play for the A team (Under-17s), and, besides, that year's side was already settled. Newell's, meanwhile, furious at having lost such a prized asset, were less than helpful, as Barcelona sought to register Messi with the Spanish federation. Then, playing for the B team (Under-16s) against Tortosa in the April, a tackle left him with a broken leg. He returned in June, but almost immediately fell down some stairs and damaged ankle ligaments, putting him out for a further three weeks.

He stopped the hormone treatment at fourteen, but at fifteen he was still only five-foot-four and weighed just 120 pounds. He struggled to finish games and, by his own admission, lacked speed and resistance. Not for nothing did his teammates call him "Enano" (Dwarf). Finally, in March 2002, Messi was registered, which meant he could play in the youth championship. Barcelona won it, the first flowering of what became known as "the Machine of 87." There was a tacit agreement that Barcelona's A side played in the same league as Espanyol's B side and vice versa, so the A sides could effectively share the trophies between them. The Machine of 87 won as a B side, the first time that had happened.

By 2002–2003, as the senior side, in Louis van Gaal's second spell as manager, struggled to sixth, their worst finish in fifteen years, the fifteen-year-olds, with Messi, Gerard Piqué, Cesc Fàbregas, and Víctor Vázquez, were superb. Messi scored thirty-six goals in thirty games, the only ever-present as they won their league. Barcelona's youth coach, Alex García, said practices were of such high standard and so ferocious that matches felt almost relaxing by comparison.

In the crucial game in the title run-in, in April 2003, against Espanyol, Messi suffered a fractured cheekbone. Eight days later they faced the same opposition in the cup final. Messi was desperate to play, so he borrowed a mask Carles Puyol had worn to protect a similar injury earlier in the season. It was too big for him, restricting his vision, and midway through the first half he wrenched it off as he dribbled toward the Espanyol box. He threw it to the bench and kept playing, scoring soon after. By halftime it was 3–0, and, the game won, García substituted him. The match became known as "the game of the mask," and it confirmed both Messi's toughness and his prodigious will to win.

The trophies kept coming, while Messi continued his rapid development as a player. García would encourage him to learn other roles, playing him all over the field; Messi, though, always gravitated to a position just behind the strikers. He remained reserved, although he became good friends with his compatriot Pablo Zabaleta, who was at Espanyol. His teammates remember tears after games if he'd played badly, evidence, as they saw it, less of a sense of entitlement than of his competitive spirit. It wasn't confined to soccer; nobody ever beat Messi on PlayStation either.

Messi's style, García said, was a fusion of the individualism of Argentinian street soccer and the more team-oriented game that had been Barcelona's philosophy since the days of Rinus Michels and Johan Cruyff. The negotiation between the two was a happy one: when Barcelona were at their peak under Pep Guardiola, Messi gave them an unpredictable edge. Spain's version of *tiki-taka* was highly structured, based on protecting possession and grinding sides down with the constant attrition of passing excellence; Barcelona did all that but also had in Messi a player who could suddenly take two opponents out of the game with a *gambeta*; they had an element of individuality that made them less mechanistic and rather better to watch.

By November 2003, Messi had been called up to the first team. Admittedly, it was only for a friendly to inaugurate Porto's new stadium, and he probably wouldn't have been selected had a number of players not been away on international duty, but when he came on after seventy-five minutes, Messi was just sixteen years and 145 days old and so the third-youngest ever debutant for the club after Paulino Alcántara in 1912 and Haruna Babangida in 1998.[1] After that, he trained one day a week with the first-team squad.

The next step was to gain international recognition. In June 2004 Claudio Vivas, Marcelo Bielsa's assistant with the national team, sent a tape of Messi to Hugo Tocalli, who was working as José Pekerman's assistant with the Under-20 side. With Spain trying to encourage Messi to commit to them, two friendlies were arranged, against Paraguay and Uruguay, to give Argentina's national coaches a chance to take a look at him. As soon as they did, his future with the side was safe.

That October Messi made his first-team debut for Barcelona, coming off the bench to replace Deco in the derby against Espanyol. At seventeen years and four months, he was the youngest player ever to represent Barcelona in a competitive game—a record he subsequently lost to Bojan Krkić. He made six other league appearances that season and played against Shakhtar Donetsk in the Champions League. On May 1 Messi came on for Samuel Eto'o with Barça 1–0 up against Albacete. Ronaldinho slipped a pass through for him, and Messi scored, only to be denied by an incorrect offside call. Almost immediately, they repeated the move, and this time the goal stood. Barça won 2–0, and the title was all but secured. Ronaldinho jogged over to Messi and picked him up, carrying him on his shoulders. The two were extremely close: after his first training session with the Argentinian, Ronaldinho called a journalist friend and said that he'd just played with somebody who would be better than he was. He began to join in the games of foot tennis in the dressing room. Previously, Ronaldinho had always vied with the Brazilian fullback Sylvinho to be the squad champion; Messi was better than either.

A month later Messi signed his first long-term contract with Barcelona and then headed off for the Netherlands to join the Argentina squad at the Under-20 World Cup. Even with all Argentina's success in the competition, that side—with Messi, Sergio Agüero, Pablo Zabaleta, Fernando Gago, Ezequiel Garay, and Lucas Biglia—and its performances in that tournament are feted. Pékerman and Tocalli had succeeded Bielsa with the senior national side after the Olympic success, leaving Pancho Ferraro in charge. Apparently still distrusting the player's slight physique, he left Messi on the bench for the opening game against the United States, and Argentina were beaten 1–0. Messi started the second-group game, against Egypt, and scored the opener, Zabaleta adding a second in a 2–0 win. That meant Argentina had to beat Germany to be sure of qualifying for the last sixteen—although a draw would have been enough to carry them through as one of the best third-place teams. A characteristic Messi dribble set up the only goal of the game for Neri Cardoso.

Messi scored again as Argentina came from behind to beat Colombia 2–1 in the second round to set up a quarter-final against the European champions, Spain, whose side included Fàbregas, Juanfran, José Enrique, and David Silva. It was 1–1 with nineteen minutes remaining when Messi teed up Gustavo Oberman to make it 2–1 before, two minutes later, flicking the ball over a defender and running on to add a third. This was Messi's tournament, a point he confirmed by scoring the opener in the semifinal against Brazil—Zabaleta got the winner in a 2–1 win—and then converting two penalties, the first of which he had won himself after a *gambeta*, in a 2–1 victory over Nigeria in the final. Maradona telephoned Messi to congratulate him. "Do you know what it means to get a call from Diego?" Messi asked. "It's really, really unforgettable."

"What I like most about Messi," said Maradona, "is that as well as his play, he is a leader. Against Spain, he put on a soccer concert that left me very impressed."

Two months later, Messi made his full international debut in a friendly away to Hungary. It could hardly have gone worse. He was brought on by José Pékerman after sixty-four minutes to replace Lisandro López with Argentina 2–1 up. The second time he got the ball, he made a typical forward dart. Defender Vilmos Vanczák grabbed his shirt. Messi tried to push him off, but Vanczák held on. Messi swung his arm hard and struck the defender in the chest. It was, fairly clearly, an attempt to free himself, the contact a sharp push rather than a punch, but Vanczák went down clutching his face, and referee Markus Merk, a dentist from Kaiserslautern, showed a red card. Messi's debut had lasted forty-four seconds. As Vanczák was booked for the tug, Messi wandered around as though in a daze. By the time he finally reached the touchline, he was in tears. His international career, arguably, has never quite escaped the ill omen of its beginnings.

From a club point of view, things soon picked up. In September 2005 Messi gained Spanish citizenship in addition to Argentinian, which removed some of the opposition to his playing in the league. In October he made his first league start in a 3–0 win over Osasuna. By the end of the year he was doing almost as much advertising as Maradona had, endorsing, among other products, burgers, soft drinks, oil, yogurt, potato chips, shoes, and a credit card, while Nike and Adidas competed to sign him up. That he was a star in the making was no longer in doubt, something confirmed by his performances in the Champions League. Messi had had a key part in Barcelona's second-round victory over Chelsea, suffering the body check from Asier del Horno that led to the fullback being sent off, but he missed the final victory over Arsenal through injury. There would be further frustration before the summer was out.

60

THE LIST IN THE SOCK

A rgentina went to the 2006 World Cup a settled and talented side. They'd finished second to Brazil in Conmebol qualifying on goal difference, and had a squad packed with neat, technical attacking players that, vitally in terms of how they were viewed by the Argentinian public, played in the prescribed Argentinian way, with Javier Mascherano a classic number 5 in front of the back four, Maxi Rodríguez and Esteban Cambiasso or Lucho González as shuttlers—*carrileros*—alongside him, and Juan Román Riquelme restored as the *enganche* behind Hernán Crespo and Javier Saviola. The only real concern was an appallingly difficult group, with the Netherlands; a promising Côte d'Ivoire side that had been a little unfortunate to lose on penalties to the hosts, Egypt, in the final of the African Cup of Nations four months earlier; and Serbia and Montenegro, which had conceded only one goal in qualifying and, thanks to a quirk of the FIFA rankings, had been demoted from the European pot to join the Concacaf and AFC teams in the draw.

Concerns began to dissipate as Argentina started off with a comfortable 2–1 over the Ivorians in Hamburg. By the time the finals began, Serbia and Montenegro were perhaps not quite the side they had seemed when the draw was made and they'd lost their opening game 1–0 against the Netherlands, but, still, nobody quite expected what Argentina did to them.

They were ahead inside six minutes, Saviola slipping a ball inside for Rodríguez to score. It was the second goal, though, that will live in the memory as perhaps the greatest team goal in the history of the World Cup, a move of twenty-six passes culminating in Crespo's backheel for Cambiasso to fire in from the edge of the box. Rodríguez knocked in his second just before halftime after Saviola's shot had been saved, and he was then on the receiving end of a two-footed lunge that saw Mateja Kežman sent off twenty minutes into the second half. What followed was of significance largely in retrospect. Lionel Messi came off the bench with quarter of an hour to go and, three minutes later, scuttled into the box to provide a low cross for Crespo to score. Another second-half substitute, Carlos Tévez, dribbled through to add a fifth before, with two minutes remaining, Tévez laid in Messi to score the sixth, his first World Cup goal; it seemed implausible then that it wouldn't be until eight years later (to the day) that he scored his second.

A goalless draw against the Netherlands saw Argentina top the group on goal difference, setting up a second-round tie against Mexico. Within six minutes they were behind for the first time in the tournament, the aerial weakness that had emerged against Côte d'Ivoire exposed, as Pável Pardo's right-wing free kick was flicked on for Rafael Márquez, arriving unmarked at the far post, to guide in with a jab of his right boot. It took only four minutes to equalize, though, Crespo turning in Riquelme's corner with a waist-high flick. As Crespo and Saviola both spurned one-on-ones, it remained level until eight minutes into extra time, when Maxi Rodríguez took down a cross-field ball on his chest just outside the box and thrashed a dipping volley into the top corner for a brilliant winner.

The quarter-final was against Germany in Berlin. Argentina took the lead from a familiar source, Riquelme's corner being met by a powerful downward heard from Ayala. Everything seemed to be going perfectly, but with eighteen minutes remaining Pékerman took off Riquelme and replaced him with Cambiasso. For many, it was the moment at which the coach lost his nerve and with it the World Cup. Tocalli, though, insists it was the injuries that undid them. A minute before Riquelme was withdrawn, goalkeeper Roberto Abbondanzieri was forced off, with Leo Franco taking his place. Seven minutes later Pékerman also had to replace the injured Crespo. With Messi, Aimar, and Saviola on the bench, Pékerman turned to Julio Cruz, a tall and awkward striker. "We knew Riquelme so well, we'd had him since he was fourteen, when he was a number 5," said Tocalli.

We knew that if he lost three consecutive passes, it was because either he was tired or had another problem. . . . We had Cambiasso on the bench, a good ball winner but also very technical when it came to passing the ball. So winning 1–0, we said, Cambiasso for Riquelme, we keep playing soccer but with more ball winning. The same with Cruz. Why Cruz and not Messi? Because we felt that Germany were lethal in the air, and we had to balance that. We thought that the only way for them to score was with headers from set pieces. And they ended up scoring with a header but with a 40-yard ball: nobody could have predicted that.

A minute after Cruz came on, Tim Borowski flicked on Michael Ballack's cross, and Miroslav Klose headed in at the back post. The match went to penalties, and Argentina crumbled, seemingly spooked by the way German goalkeeper Jens Lehmann, before each of their kicks, took a sheet of hotel notepaper from his sock and consulted it. It subsequently turned out that, of the seven Argentinian names on Lehmann's list, only two actually took penalties, although both put their kicks precisely where Andreas Köpke, the Germany goalkeeping coach, had told Lehmann they would. The rest was simply suggestion; Lehmann seemingly knew where they would place their penalties, and that illusion was enough to spread panic. Ayala and Cambiasso both missed, and Germany scored four in a row to reach the semifinal.

It had been a spectacle of magnificent drama, but it ended in ignominy, with a mass brawl in the center of the field in which Leandro Cufré was shown a red card after kicking Per Mertesacker. "The first provocation came from Argentina," insisted Germany midfielder Michael Ballack. "They were shouting at our players as they were going to the penalty spot. They shouted something in Spanish, and we didn't understand what they were saying. But they were definitely trying to influence our strikers. After Tim Borowski scored [to make it 4–2], he put his finger to his lips to tell them to shut up. They were a bit mad at that. After that I didn't see much, but I saw one or two lying on the ground." What is clear from the video is that Rodríguez caught Bastian Schweinsteiger with a punch to the back of the head, while there was a scuffle between Torsten Frings and Fabricio Coloccini and another involving Germany's general manager, Oliver Bierhoff, and Juan Pablo Sorín.

Suddenly, there were rumors of splits within the Argentina camp, and, amid a familiar storm of backbiting and recrimination, Pékerman wearily resigned. That he had correctly identified the German threat—that weakness in the air undoing them again—was little consolation.

61

THE ECSTASY OF GOLD

Messi may have been peripheral for Argentina in Germany, but back at Barcelona he became an increasingly central figure. If any doubt had remained as to his greatness, it disappeared in 2006–2007. Messi scored a hat trick against Real Madrid in a 3–3 draw at the Camp Nou and then, against Getafe in the Copa del Rey semifinal, scored a goal that would have guaranteed comparison with Maradona even if he had not been Argentinian. Receiving a pass from Xavi on the halfway line on the right flank, he skipped past one challenge; dodged inside another with a nutmeg; accelerated thirty yards; ducked between two more tackles as a third player, having chased him, tried vainly to claw at his shirt; rounded the goalkeeper; and then, from a tight angle, lifted the ball over a defender sliding back on the line. If he had tried to replicate Maradona's second goal against England, Messi couldn't have produced a more perfect imitation. Bilardo and Maradona both pointed out the context was different and that there had been that thirty-yard section in which Messi hadn't faced a challenge; they may have had a point, but it was the mimetic quality of Messi's goal that made it so remarkable. And, in guarding the primacy of the original so jealously, Maradona and Bilardo seemed to invoke one of the great early myths of the Argentinian game, that of the player who dribbles through a number of challenges to score and then, as he returns to his own half for the kickoff, erases his footprints from the dust so nobody can repeat his virtuosity. Messi dedicated the goal to Maradona, who had just been admitted to a psychiatric clinic.

Having re-created one of Maradona's goals against England, six weeks later Messi reproduced the other, scoring with his hand in a 2–2 draw with Espanyol. "It's Diego!" screamed the Argentinian commentary. "Tell me it isn't! To me it's Diego. It's the same guy. . . . He's reincarnated."

But for all that the *gambeta* provided confirmation of Messi's genius, it was a disappointing season for him and for Barcelona. The brilliant *gambeta* had been part of a 5–2 win, the margin leading to Messi's being rested for the second leg. Without him Barça, unthinkably, lost 4–0. The concession of late goals against Espanyol and Real Betis proved costly in the race for the title, in which Barça were edged out on goal difference.

After Pékerman's resignation, Argentina turned again to Alfio "Coco" Basile, who had just led Boca to an *apertura* and a *clausura* in the space of two years. His hair was gray by then, but he still wore it long, slicked back from his forehead so it clustered on his collar. After Pékerman's academic approach, in terms of image at least, this was a return to something earthier. Yet Basile changed little in terms of the team's style. The shape remained a classic Argentinian 4-3-1-2, with Javier Mascherano as the 5, Cambiasso and Verón a nicely balanced pair of flanking midfielders, and Riquelme as the *enganche* to a front two of Messi and Crespo. For seventeen days at the 2007 Copa América in Venezuela, they were stunningly good, reaching heights far greater than those achieved by either of Basile's Copa América sides of the early nineties.

A ninth-minute Eddie Johnson penalty gave the United States the lead against Argentina in their opening group game in Maracaibo, but within two minutes Argentina were level, Crespo taking advantage after Kasey Keller had failed to deal with a floated Riquelme free kick. They went ahead on the hour: Riquelme found Messi on the edge of the D, and his precise angled pass laid in Crespo to drill a first-time finish across a wrong-footed Keller. On the bench Basile, wearing an extraordinary purple-striped shirt open to midchest, beat two fists in the air in celebration: this was exactly the sort of goal the side he'd selected should have been scoring. Aimar, on as a substitute, headed a third before Tévez, another substitute, got behind a tiring US defense to make it four.

Argentina fell behind in their second game as well, Edixon Perea scuffing in a shot from the edge of the box after a right-wing free kick was cut back to him to put Colombia ahead. A foul on Messi allowed Crespo to level from the spot after twenty minutes, but the striker strained a thigh muscle in scoring and had to be replaced by Diego Milito. Two Riquelme goals—a header from a Zanetti cross and a superb free kick—made it 3–1 by halftime. Jaime Alberto Castrillón's header from a left-winger corner gave Colombia some hope, but Milito sealed a 4–2 win with a deflected shot in injury time. A much-changed Argentina ensured they went through top of the group with a 1–0 win over Paraguay.

In the quarter-final, Argentina met Peru, and if anything the soccer got even better, as Messi and Riquelme produced mesmerizing performances, one full of *gambetas*, the other forever pausing time to lacerate Peru with his passing. Somehow it was goalless at halftime, when Basile took off Milito for Tévez. The substitution had an almost immediate impact: two minutes into the second half, Riquelme took a pass from Tévez, gave it back, recovered it again, and curved a finish just inside the post from twenty yards. Tévez headed against the bar from a Zanetti cross, but just after the hour Messi made it two with a goal that was the essence of Riquelme, who had taken a pass from Verón in space before turning, waiting, and providing Messi with the perfect through-ball. Then it was Tévez and Messi playing a double one-two: Messi's shot was saved, but Mascherano banged in the rebound. Tévez charged fifty yards on the break to lay on a fourth for Riquelme. True, it was only Peru, but the second half had been an exhibition of the sort of soccer of which Argentinian traditionalists dreamed.

As Messi left the field, there came perhaps the first real sign of how hysterical the worship of him had become. He saw at the front of the second tier of the stand a young woman poised to jump down to him. He urged her not to, but she jumped anyway, managed to avoid injury, and kissed him twice before security bundled her away.

In the semifinal Argentina met Mexico, which had already beaten Brazil in the group stage before hammering Paraguay 6–0 in the quarter-final. Mexico began well. Andrés Guardado struck the post in the first half, and Nery Castillo hit the bar early on the second, but eventually they too succumbed. A leaping Gabriel Heinze had nudged in a Riquelme free kick with the outside of his left foot to give Argentina the lead just before halftime, before a moment of Messi brilliance the equal of anything he had done previously. A long ball from Heinze found Tévez in space, and he slipped a diagonal pass outside him to Messi, cutting in from the right. Messi was just inside the box, perhaps five yards to the right of the right-hand post, when the ball reached him, at which he flicked at it with his left foot, scooping a first-time chip high over the Mexico goalkeeper Oswaldo Sánchez. It arced six feet above the line of the bar and then dropped so sharply that it only just hit the back of the net before bouncing. A Riquelme penalty completed a 3–0 win, but it was Messi's goal that dominated the evening, seeming, at least to Basile, to call into question the whole future of soccer. "Shall we pack up and leave?" he asked. "What more do we need? Should we continue after seeing that goal?"

But a goal, however brilliant, is not a trophy, and before Argentina could take home a fifteenth Copa América, they had to beat Dunga's Brazil. After the defeat to Mexico in their first game, they had proved themselves just as dogged as their manager, thrashing Chile in the quarter-final before beating Uruguay on penalties in the semi. Four minutes in a long pass from Elano found Julio Baptista, who cut onto his right foot and lashed a shot into the top corner. When Ayala turned a Dani Alves cross into his own net five minutes before halftime, the game was gone. The right-back surged onto a Vágner Love pass after sixty-nine minutes to wrap up a 3–0 win. Again, Argentina had produced some scintillating soccer at a major tournament, and, again, it hadn't been enough.

The following season, Barcelona was struggling. Ronaldinho was in decline and, perceived as a bad influence, was sold to AC Milan at the end of the season. Frank Rijkaard also left and, to widespread surprise, was replaced by the inexperienced Pep Guardiola. One of Guardiola's first major decisions was, against club advice, to allow Messi go to the Olympics in Beijing to try to ease some of the hurt of Venezuela. It was controversial, but it proved manifestly the right decision, not only for Messi and for Argentina, but also in terms of securing the player's loyalty.

Argentina's Olympic squad was extremely strong, featuring many from the side that had won the 2005 Under-20 World Cup, including Messi, plus Riquelme, by then back at Boca, as one of three overage players.[1] The Riquelme-Messi combination unlocked the Côte d'Ivoire defense for the opening goal in a 2–1 victory in the first group game, and wins over Australia and Serbia took Argentina through to a quarter-final against the Netherlands. Messi seized on a defensive lapse to put Argentina ahead, and, after Otman Bakkal had leveled, it was his exquisite pass that laid in Ángel Di María for the winner in extra-time.

In the semifinal Brazil put up none of the fight the senior side had the previous year. A flowing passing move seven minutes after halftime created space for Di María, and his cross was turned in by Sergio Agüero, who soon added a second before Riquelme's penalty ensured the scoreline at least canceled what had happened in Maracaibo. The gold-medal game was a rematch of the 1996 final, when Argentina had twice led against Nigeria only to lose 3–2; this time, though, once Di María had put Argentina ahead with a run and deft chip, there were no slip-ups, and a 1–0 win retained the Olympic title.

That was the beginning of Messi's golden period. Under Guardiola Barcelona enjoyed the most successful spell in their history, with Messi the key figure, adding a dash of individuality and unpredictability to the occasionally staid perfection of *tiki-taka*. Messi played centrally, as a false nine, for the first time in the 6–2 Champions League quarter-final demolition of Bayern Munich in 2009. He would soon come to define the position. Against Manchester United in the final in Rome that season, he began on the right and moved into the middle after ten minutes so as to confuse United's planning. He got the second goal in Barça's 2–0 win with an uncharacteristic header; as he sent the ball looping back past Edwin van der Sar, his boot came off, almost as though the sheer muscular effort had shaken it loose. There were other brilliant displays, including the 5–0 victory over Real Madrid in José Mourinho's first *clásico* in November 2010 and the five goals in a 7–1 win over Bayer Leverkusen as part of a run of twenty-one goals in nine games in 2011–2012, a season in which he scored fifty league goals. The following season he banged in forty-six. With him the extraordinary soon came to seem quotidian, but whatever heights Messi achieved at club level, there was always the nagging question back at home: Could he do it for his national team? Could he do it away from Barcelona, an environment that made him and has come to seem as though it has essentially been constructed for him?

62

THE END OF THE AFFAIR

The partnership that had once made Boca great, that had once defined their combination of power, pragmatism, and courage, on the one hand, with unapologetic artistry, on the other, ended up tearing the club apart. By the end Juan Román Riquelme and Martín Palermo couldn't stand each other. "The only thing that unites us is defending the colors of Boca," Palermo admitted in 2010 in the midst of a run of three barren years in which Boca changed coach six times.

Palermo had returned to Boca in 2004 after three and a half fairly joyless seasons in Spain, forming a fine partnership with Tévez as Boca's success continued with back-to-back Copa Sudamericana victories and the *apertura-clausura* double in 2005–2006. In August 2006 Palermo's newborn son, Stefano, died. The season started four days later, and Palermo insisted on playing, scoring twice in a 3–0 win over Banfield. He left the field weeping, and most of the stands were in tears too. There was no doubt then that Palermo was the hero of the terraces.

Riquelme came back in January 2007. He'd had a disappointing time at Barcelona, sidelined by Van Gaal, who had been appointed for a second term after his transfer had been agreed in 2002; Riquelme always maintained he hadn't wanted to leave but that he'd been told that if he really loved the club, he had to let them collect the $15 million fee. Van Gaal knew immediately that an individual like Riquelme had no place in his team-based philosophy: it's said that when Riquelme met him, Van Gaal handed over a child's Barcelona shirt for his son, saying, "Take it. He'll wear it more than you." At Villarreal, though, Riquelme had blossomed, Manuel Pellegrini building his team around him as they surpassed all expectations and finished third in 2005–2006—yet he also missed a crucial penalty against Arsenal in the Champions League semifinal. A little more than two months later, Lehmann would again break Riquelme's heart in the World Cup quarter-final, although on that occasion he had been substituted before being given his chance from the penalty spot. It was a time when Riquelme, even when it wasn't his fault, always seemed to be the one responsible, whether because he had played or because he hadn't, or because after all those flawless penalties for Boca, he lost his nerve with a vital one for Villarreal.

The following season the magic had gone. Riquelme played only thirteen times in the league and didn't feature in the Copa del Rey, and with the relationship between the player, on the one hand, and the board and Pellegrini, on the other, deteriorating, he was loaned back to Boca.

Riquelme's return coincided with the appointment of Miguel Ángel Russo as manager. The former Estudiantes midfielder had led Lanús and his former club to the Primera B title and taken Vélez to the *clausura*, and, like Bianchi, he was a pragmatist who was prepared to accommodate an old-fashioned number 10. Boca finished as runners-up in the 2007 *clausura*, but the Libertadores again became their stage—and Riquelme's in particular.

Boca could have gone out in the group stage, but, needing a victory in their final game, at home to Bolívar, they won 7–0 to set up an awkward clash against Ricardo La Volpe's Vélez. Riquelme's greatest gift (at least when he wasn't missing penalties) was his ability to remain calm when chaos reigned around him, as though his metabolism simply functioned at a lower rate than everybody else's—a trait that meant that when things went badly, he was always open to the accusation that he wasn't trying. Rodrigo Palacio had just had a goal disallowed when he burst into the box again after nine minutes. There was a shot, an appeal for a penalty for hands, and the ball pinged about until Palermo worked the ball to Riquelme, who had been idling just inside the box, away from the hubbub. He swept it first-time into the top corner. Then with a half hour played, Vélez self-destructed: Palacio halfheartedly followed an up-and-under into the box with little hope of getting there before Gastón Sessa. The goalkeeper did claim it comfortably enough, but ridiculously thrust out his foot, kicking Palacio and leaving him with a cut to the forehead. He was rightly sent off and a penalty awarded. Palermo took the penalty and hit it high over the bar. The striker did add a second with a characteristic header just after the hour, before fullback Clemente Rodríguez charged forward to tuck in a low shot and make it 3–0 in the final minute. It would prove a vital goal, as Vélez won 3–1 back in Liniers.

Clinging on and scrapping were very much the Boca way. They drew the home leg of the quarter-final 1–1 against Libertad, and had withstood an hour of pressure in Asunción, when Riquelme received the ball on halfway, turned, and ran. He kept running, sidestepping three challenges, before depositing a low shot in the bottom corner. Ten minutes later Palacio added a second from close range to take Boca through to the last four.

There they met the Colombian side Cúcuta Deportivo, overcoming a 3–1 first-leg deficit thanks to a Riquelme free kick and goals from Palermo and Sebastián Battaglia. The final against Grêmio was effectively won in the first leg. The opener came through a familiar route: a Riquelme free kick, Palermo—who was marginally offside—knocking the ball across goal, and Palacio, rat's tail bobbing, following it in. Sandro Goiano collected two yellow cards in the space of five minutes early in the second half, and Boca took full advantage. Riquelme swept in a brilliant free kick before a Patrício own goal, heading into his own net under pressure from Ledesma, made it 3–0.

This was Riquelme's consecration. After his difficulties in Europe, he had returned to win the Libertadores, probing and scheming and coaxing Boca forward. His seventh goal in that season's tournament was spectacular, clipped in from the corner of the box midway through the second half of the second leg as most expected a cross. This, in a sense, was the archetypal Riquelme goal, one requiring him to assess the circumstances, the distribution of players on the field, and the space almost instantly and then, as he received the ball, striking his shot firmly and without excessive back lift, creating a shooting opportunity where most would have simply been lifting a cross to the back post. His eighth was more prosaic, a rebound rammed into an empty net, but it confirmed his third, and Boca's fourth, Libertadores title in the space of seven years, an achievement all the more remarkable given he had spent four and a half of those seasons in Europe. Little wonder his teammates celebrated by lifting him on their shoulders. Riquelme soon signed the biggest contract in Argentinian soccer, a deal that stipulated he would play the final season for free.

Yet within a year, Boca were falling apart, rent in two by a falling-out between their two biggest stars. Pinpointing the exact moment at which their relationship soured, charting its decline, isn't easy, and the acrimony probably ebbed and flowed. There is little doubt though that by the time of 2008 Libertadores semifinal against Fluminense, it was beyond repair. Riquelme was brilliant in the first leg at la Bombonera, controlling the game and scoring two goals. Both times, though, Fluminense found equalizers, the second of them a long-range effort from Thiago Neves that went straight through Pablo Migliore. Riquelme raged at the goalkeeper at the final whistle; Palermo felt the dynamics of the team dictated he should have been supportive.

The impact of their differences wasn't felt immediately. Boca won the 2008 *apertura*, which ended in a three-way playoff with San Lorenzo and Tigre. Decline, though, soon set in. They were fourteenth in the *clausura*, defeated in the last sixteen of the 2009 Libertadores and eleventh in the *apertura*. "I love Boca," Riquelme reminded fans as the club slipped into full-blown crisis. "If I didn't, I wouldn't be working here for free. I'm the only idiot who works for free, so I don't think anyone can come and lecture me about my responsibilities."

But the poor form went on, and Boca finished sixteenth in the *clausura* in 2010, although that season did at least see Palermo become Boca's all-time-record goal scorer, as he got two in a 4–0 win over Arsenal de Sarandí. What should have been an iconic moment, though, became emblematic of the problems at the club. Riquelme had played a one-two with Nicolás Gaitán, and then, with just the goalkeeper to beat, he rolled the ball square with the outside of his boot for Palermo to knock in his 219th goal for the club. Palermo, having made history, began to celebrate, only to realize that Riquelme had run off in the other direction. He began to chase him and then gave up, his expression shifting from puzzled to contemptuous. Half the Boca team celebrated with Riquelme, half with Palermo.

"Anyone can score goals like that," Riquelme said afterward in what was presumably intended as a joke, although the comment rang hollow.

"I won't talk about it," Palermo responded in a radio interview. "What happened is out there for all to see I'm not a friend of [Riquelme's]. I have no relationship [with him]." What actually caused the spat remains unclear: perhaps there was no decisive moment but, rather, a slow buildup of two egos of very differing personalities who played together for too long.

Boca's league form remained dismal. They finished twelfth in the 2010–2011 *apertura* and then seventh, which at least lifted the threat of relegation. As it turned out, it also signaled that a squad was coming together under Julio César Falcioni that could challenge for the title.

Falcioni was appointed at Boca in December 2010 and lost four of his first six games in charge. His face seemed to become even more concave, the sharp lines from his nose to the corners of his mouth even deeper and more disapproving. In the last of those six games, he left out Riquelme. He said it was because of an injury rather than anything tactical, but with Riquelme insisting he was fit, there were howls of protest. The decision at least demonstrated that Falcioni was avowedly his own man, somebody prepared to make difficult decisions even when they ran contrary to popular wisdom, but it meant that the slightest slip would bring down the wrath of fans and sections of the media upon him. In the close season, Falcioni made another decision so bold as to seem foolhardy, signing thirty-eight-year-old center-back Rolando Schiavi from Newell's. Between 2001 and 2005, Schiavi had been a legend at Boca, winning seven major titles. Since then, though, his career had drifted, although he had won the Libertadores on a bizarre short-term loan to Estudiantes and earned a first call-up to the national side at the age of thirty-six.[1] Schiavi became the centerpiece of a defense that conceded just six times in nineteen games, as Boca won the title, going unbeaten through the season.

The following year, though, the tensions became unbearable. Boca scrapped their way to the Libertadores final, where, after drawing the home leg 1–1, they were well beaten 2–0 in São Paulo by Corinthians. Riquelme emerged tearfully from the Boca dressing room long after the final whistle and, unusually, stopped to speak to the waiting media. His face somber, tears glistening in otherwise blank eyes, he began: "I have told the president that I will not continue. I love this club. I'll be forever grateful, but I feel empty and I cannot give anymore."

Clearing his throat repeatedly, shuffling from one foot to another, never catching the eye of any journalist, he went on. "The commitment I have is very great. I cannot play at only half-capacity. I've been playing for sixteen years, but I have nothing left to give the club. Now I just want to go home, hug my kids, and eat *asado* with my friends. I apologize to my son for not winning the cup." The glance that Boca's president, Daniel Angelici, gave Riquelme as he spoke suggested anger or irritation rather than sympathy for a parting legend. There was a sense that Riquelme, slower and more divisive than ever, wasn't worth the hassle anymore. Falcioni had threatened to quit after a clash with Riquelme following the goalless draw away to Zamora in the February, and there had been evident tension all season as Riquelme made clear he would have preferred a more attacking style of play. That manifested itself most clearly as a more expansive approach led to a home defeat to Fluminense in the Libertadores and a 5–4 league defeat to Independiente, results that seemed to confirm the wisdom of the Falcioni method. But having gone back to grinding out results, Boca's form collapsed toward the end of the domestic season. By Christmas Falcioni was out; by February 2013 Riquelme had come out of retirement.

He scored a vital goal as Boca edged by Corinthians in the last sixteen of the Libertadores, but Boca went out in the quarter-final on penalties to Newell's. A year later Riquelme left Boca, this time for good, joining Argentinos Juniors, the club he had supported as a boy.

63

MESSI AND THE MESSIAH

M aradona had telephoned Messi during the Under-20 World Cup in 2005 and again after his goal against Albacete the following season. For a long time, their relationship was, if not close, then at least respectful. Something, though, changed in 2008. In September that year, Maradona was highly critical of Messi after a 1–1 draw in a World Cup qualifier away to Peru. "Sometimes," he said, "Messi plays for Messi. It is Messi FC. If he were to play more with Agüero or Riquelme, opposition defenders would have more to worry about. Matches are not won by attacking every time you have the ball, but by knowing how to attack." Maradona followed up that criticism with another, accusing Messi of "lacking character," saying he hadn't fought hard enough to be allowed to join the Olympic squad, even though he'd fought so hard that he had not merely played at the Olympics but won gold.

Even given Maradona's propensity for unexpected eruptions, it seemed a strange fight to pick, and, in retrospect, it seems likely he was deliberately destabilizing Basile's squad with a view to taking the manager's job himself. He may even have been looking to curry favor with Riquelme, whose role as the icon of the team was being undermined by the brilliance Messi was repeatedly showing for Barcelona. If that was his aim, it worked.

Argentina had begun World Cup qualifying with wins over Chile, Venezuela, and Bolivia, but a defeat away to Colombia marked the start of a run of four draws in a row. They did beat Uruguay on October 11, 2008, but three days later they went down 1–0 to Bielsa's Chile. It was only Argentina's sixth defeat against their western neighbor, their first since 1973 and their first in a game anybody actually cared about. Amid the outcry that followed, Basile resigned. Argentina reacted by doing what they tended to do when crisis approached and turned to Maradona. His return to the national side in 1993 had been ill-conceived and had ended in his drug ban, but at least as a player there was some possibility that he might be able to find a spark to energize the side. Given his two previous stints as a manager had yielded a total of three victories, his appointment to lead the country to the 2010

World Cup was an act of blind faith. His politicking, though, had worked, something acknowledged by Riquelme, who claimed Maradona had encouraged a core of key players to undermine Basile. Maradona was soon criticizing Riquelme's physical condition, the tension between them apparent.

His first competitive game in charge, in March 2009, offered false hope. With Messi in the number 10 shirt—Maradona soon started rebuilding those bridges once the job was his—Venezuela were dismissed 4–0 at el Monumental, but it was a shapeless display against opponents who seemed overawed, one rooted in the excellence of individuals. Four days later came a very different view. Playing at altitude in La Paz had always been a challenge for Argentinian sides, but none dealt with it quite as badly as Maradona's. They were a shambles and lost 6–1 to Bolivia—alongside the humiliation of Helsingborg, Argentina's record defeat.

There was a win over Colombia, but there were also defeats to Ecuador, Brazil, and Paraguay. With two rounds of qualifying to go, Brazil, Chile, and Paraguay were clear of the rest, with Ecuador on twenty-three points, Argentina on twenty-two, Uruguay and Venezuela on twenty-one, and Colombia on twenty, all chasing one remaining automatic qualifying slot with one other side to go into a playoff. Argentina had to beat Peru at home.

When Higuaín ran on to Pablo Aimar's clever pass to put Argentina ahead just before halftime, all seemed well, but the game was building to an extraordinary conclusion. By the final minutes, the rain was torrential and the field covered in places with standing water. With a minute to go, Argentina twice failed to clear, the ball was returned to the middle, and Hernán Rengifo was unmarked to level with a close-range header. Argentina's was the last of the four matches that day to kick off, so they knew that if the match had ended at that moment, they would have been level on points with Ecuador and Colombia and one behind Uruguay, whom they faced in their final match. They had to score. Under the circumstances there was only one man ever likely to emerge as the hero: Maradona had faced opposition when he'd brought Martín Palermo back onto the squad a month shy of his thirty-sixth birthday, but, really, who else could conceivably have scored the goal he did, three minutes into injury time, emerging implausibly unmarked in the downpour to stab a ricochet over the line from close range?

The job still had to be completed against Uruguay, but Argentina managed that, Mario Bolatti's close-range effort with six minutes remaining confirming their qualification. On the touchline Maradona, swaddled in a tracksuit, a red bib flapping about him like a cape, bounced up and down and then fell over. He told the press to "suck it and keep on sucking," a bizarrely triumphalist reaction for somebody who had used fifty-five players in thirteen games in charge and had qualified by the skin of his teeth.

Messi, meanwhile, was criticized for not celebrating Bolatti's goal with sufficient gusto, which seemed like a classic instance of people convinced of a truth using any evidence they can find to support it. It could equally have been argued that Messi's comparative lack of emotion was evidence of his determination to keep focused and see the job through.

Still, the doubts about Messi's commitment, however unfounded, were real enough: the website minutouno.com even presented a psychoanalyst who suggested that Messi's uprooting had left him with feelings of resentment toward his home. Maradona, perhaps remembering how Bilardo had visited him as he recovered from hepatitis, went to Barcelona to meet Messi and asked him how he wanted to play. Messi suggested either a 3-4-1-2 or a 4-3-1-2 with him operating behind a front two of Gonzalo Higuaín and Tévez. Agüero, who would become an added complication, was at the time just twenty-one.

With hindsight Argentina's results from the 2010 World Cup don't look too bad, but there was a pervading air of chaos from the start. Argentina began against Nigeria with Messi behind Tévez and Higuaín. That part, and a midfield of Mascherano, Verón, and Di María, made sense. What didn't, although it was made all but inevitable by the lack of fullbacks on the squad (itself the result of a general dearth of high-class Argentinian fullbacks, even if the omission of Javier Zanetti was bizarre), was the use of Jonás Gutiérrez as a right-back in an otherwise cripplingly slow defense of Martín Demichelis, Walter Samuel, and Gabriel Heinze. It was Heinze who got the only goal of the game, with a powerful header from an early corner, but the overriding impression was of sluggishness and a lack of fluidity. A 4–1 win over South Korea was more convincing, before a much-changed side finished off the group with a third win, 2–0 against Greece.

The momentum was maintained in the second round against Mexico. Tévez was offside as he gave Argentina the lead, turning in Messi's follow-up after Mexico goalkeeper Óscar Pérez had blocked at Tévez's feet. Higuaín capitalized on a defensive error to add a second before halftime, and Tévez made sure of the win with a ferocious drive just after the break, although Javier Hernández did pull one back late on.

That set up a quarter-final against Germany, perhaps the worst conceivable opponent for Argentina's clanking back line. Argentinian hopes lasted three minutes: once Thomas Müller had glanced in Bastian Schweinsteiger's free kick, there was no way back, every Argentinian attacking sally only making them more vulnerable to the counterattacks at which Germany were so adept. They lost 4–0. As a player Maradona had been an architect, far more so than Messi, somebody who was constantly cajoling and directing; as a manager he ended up looking hopelessly naive.

In the dressing room after the game, Messi slumped between two benches, leaning against the wall, wailing. "The players," *Clarín* noted, "discovered Father Christmas doesn't exist—Maradona isn't what they thought he was." It wasn't just the players for whom that realization was something of a shock. Yet the reaction was mixed. There were still those who refused to condemn Maradona, and if the old messiah couldn't be blamed, then the fault was deflected inevitably to the new one. "It isn't Messi's fault," novelist Eduardo Sacheri noted, "that we Argentinians are incapable of ending our mourning for Diego."

64

DISTRUST AND
SHORT-TERMISM

Néstor Kirchner decided not to stand at the 2007 presidential election, but after being succeeded by his wife, he played an active role in her government until his death in 2010. In each of the first nine years under the Kirchners, Argentinian GDP rose, while unemployment fell from more than 20 percent to just over 6 percent and the middle class expanded; for large numbers of the working class, life improved. Just how impressive an achievement that is, though, is questionable. Even before the default of 2014, critics pointed out that the base was so low after Menem and the crash that recovery was inevitable, suggested there had been a deliberate devaluation of the peso to boost exports and the risk of inflation, and wondered whether a protectionist economic policy, restricting access to foreign currency, was merely storing up problems for the future, as Perón had done in his first presidency.

For all those who blame Perón and Kirchner and accuse them of short-sightedness, though, there are just as many who see Argentina's continuing financial problems as having been the result of the way the economy was abruptly exposed to world markets after Perón had been overthrown. But the true reasons for a century of economic failure may be far more complicated than that. As academic Rafael di Tella put it, "If a guy has been hit by seven hundred thousand bullets, it's hard to work out which one of them killed him."

In a sense Argentina was simply unlucky, in that it has perpetually been out of step with the rest of the world. Its model of export-driven growth was hammered by three factors: World War I, the Depression, and Britain's decision to sign preferential trade deals with members of the Commonwealth. When other world powers began to recover after World War II by opening global markets with the General Agreement on Tariffs and Trades (1947), Argentina closed its economy. In part, that was a move that resulted from inbuilt inequalities within the Argentinian system. Producing wheat for

export, as would have been demanded by the open market, meant higher profits for landowners but higher prices for the workers who formed Perón's con-
stituency, a problem exacerbated by how much farmland was owned by so few.

Cristina Kirchner maintained high export taxes on wheat, which produced much-needed reserves of foreign capital for the state, while limits on
exports kept local prices low. The restrictions, though, also dissuaded farm-
ers from trying to increase yields or from planting more crops, and the result
was that Argentina slipped from being the world's fourth-largest producer of
wheat in 2006 to the tenth largest in 2013.[1]

And then there is the fact that Argentina's institutions inspire little faith.
Even after thirty years of democracy, corruption remains a major problem. It
only increases the sense of unease that official figures are widely regarded as
unreliable: in March 2015 annual inflation was officially reported at 16.54
percent, but many estimates suggested the true figure could be around double that. Who wants to invest in Argentina when the government is prepared
to force through nationalization projects, as it did in 2011 when expropriat-
ing 51 percent of the shares in YPF held by the Spanish company Repsol?[2]
It hardly helps confidence that Cristina Kirchner's own fortune grew rapidly
since her husband was elected, from $7 million in 2003 to $82 million in
2012 or that she has been implicated in the scandal surrounding the death
of public prosecutor Alberto Nisman, who was either murdered or committed suicide the night before he was due to give testimony to Congress about
the alleged involvement of the Argentinian government in covering up Iranian involvement in a bomb attack on a Jewish center in Buenos Aires in
1994. The result of the lack of trust is a spiral of short-termism.

Soccer is at least as guilty of that as other business, encouraged by the
short-season structure to think only six months ahead: win a title, sell some
players, start again . . . An improved television deal in 2007 did little to
help. By 2009 the clubs were in even worse financial difficulties than usual,
and so many were struggling to pay players that there was a serious threat
of a strike. The AFA approached Televisión Satelital Codificada, which had
held the rights to top-flight games since 1991, broadcasting most of them
on the cable channel TyC, and asked for a 720 million peso advance to
help them bail the clubs out. TSC, a company co-owned by Grupo Clarín,
had already paid 230 million pesos and refused, at which the government
stepped in, making an (index-linked)[3] offer of 600 million pesos—123 percent—more than the existing deal per year. The AFA broke its deal with
TSC, which extended until 2014, and handed the rights to the government,
creating Fútbol para Todos—Soccer for All.

On August 20, with AFA president Julio Grondona standing to one
side of her and Diego Maradona to the other, Cristina Kirchner made the

televised announcement that all top-flight Argentinian matches would from then on be screened live on free-to-air channels. "We will no longer hijack goals," she said, in reference to the fact that the first chance those without access to TyC got to see the weekend's action was in a Sunday-evening highlight package. "You kidnap goals until Sunday, as you hijack the images and words. As they kidnapped thirty thousand Argentinians. I want this to be no more a society of kidnapping. I want this to be a society that is freer every day." The rhetoric was astonishing and in incredibly poor taste: how could a television rights deal of the sort that is common across the world be compared to state-sanctioned torture and murder?

"I have read," Kirchner continued said, "that soccer is going to be subsidized by the state. But those who write that know that soccer is an extraordinary business that does not need to be subsidized, but to live off its own profits." That was an outrageous manipulation of the reality: while there are plenty who would see it as a public good for sport to be shown free on the air, there was no other democratic government that paid for it to happen, no other government that so directly contributed money so soccer could continue. Perhaps it was desirable that soccer should live off its own profits, but that hadn't happened for decades, and the fact it was so desperately in need of subsidy suggested it was incapable of doing so—despite the huge profits that could apparently be made on transfer fees.

The speech was greeted with applause and the policy with approval from the general public. Others were less convinced. "Soccer should be independent from politics," said Mauricio Macri, the Boca chairman who would succeed Kirchner as president, "and it's quite clear that they [the government] are using soccer for propaganda. Somebody should lower the production costs and open up the program to private sponsorship, so money is not thrown away as it is today." That's the business case against Fútbol para Todos, but there is also a moral argument. "If the government is interested in soccer and wants to keep it free, that's perfect for me," said Juan Sebastian Verón after becoming president of Estudiantes. "What I don't agree with is that it's supported no matter the cost. They could easily invest some of that money in schools and hospitals."

From Kirchner's point of view, though, subsidizing soccer was an easy populist move—albeit one of questionable legality—and one that had the happy by-product of striking at Grupo Clarín, the main media opposition to her government. It represented an extraordinary state subsidy for soccer, the biggest since the soft loans given to clubs to build stadiums in the 1930s and 1940s. Before matches and at halftime, ads focus on various investments the government has made in public works, but even as a simple propaganda tool it seems remarkable that soccer should be deemed so essential to the smooth running of the nation that such sums could be invested in underwriting it. Its true value, perhaps, lay in soccer's power as a distraction. As Borges and Bioy Casares had observed in "Esse est percipi" in 1967, it is much safer for a government when "mankind is at home, sitting back with ease, attentive to the screen," than if he is thinking or engaging in political activity.

Wheat prices were kept low and soccer was made available to all: this was the definition of bread-and-circuses politics, but even leaving aside jibes about the base populism of the program, Fútbol para Todos had one effect nobody had foreseen. Soccer may be the universal opiate, but it does not, as Aldous Huxley wrote of soma in *Brave New World*, have "all the advantages of Christianity and alcohol [and] none of their defects." Rather, soccer, across the world but in Argentina particularly acutely, has been blighted by violence. New money brought renewed interest from organized crime.

Some of the established *barras* had begun to move out of soccer because there were limited profits to be made from it. The new television deal in 2007, though, meant there was money again (even if the clubs handled it badly), and Fútbol para Todos multiplied that. The old *barras* were tempted back, only to find that new *barras* had risen up to take their place. Increasingly, as an investigation by *Salvemos al Fútbol* discovered, the inter-*barra* fighting was replaced by intra-*barra* fighting. That, in turn, had three major effects: the number of deaths increased, violence was no longer confined to the stadium and the immediate surrounding area, and the "lungs"—empty spaces on the terraces—the AFA had insisted upon to segregate rival clubs became ineffective. This ceased to be soccer violence in any meaningful sense and became simply gang warfare; it's just that the spoils being fought over were those tied to a particular club.

Investigative journalist Carlos del Frade, for instance, in his 2007 book on the influence of the *barra* in Rosario uncovers a grim world in which a youth coach at Central, former player Aurelio Pascuttini, was forced to flee the city after his house was shot at because he refused to accept that the *barras* should take the profit from the transfer of promising players. A coach at Newell's, meanwhile, admitted that despite the club's proud record of producing talent, parents had begun to take their children elsewhere for fear of involvement with the *barras*.

Even before the broadcast-rights bonanza, transfer fees offered a prize worth fighting for. When Luis Pereyra, the head of the River group los Borrachos del Tablón (the Drunks in the Stands), was jailed for murder, for instance, it was agreed that leadership of the group would be split between Adrian Rousseau and Alan Schlenker. The two soon had a falling-out. On the opening day of the *clausura* in 2007, fighting broke out between rival gangs at los Quinchos, an area near el Monumental where fans meet before games for *asados*. Shots were fired and people stabbed amid general terror. A few months after what became known as the Battle of the Quinchos came the Battle of the Playón before a game against Independiente. That August Gonzalo Acro, Rousseau's right-hand man, was attacked by four gunmen as he left his gym a little before midnight following a kick-boxing class. He was shot first in the leg and then twice in the head and died two days later. Rousseau accused Schlenker of having arranged the killing. He denied it, pointing out he had been away skiing when the shooting took place, but it's widely believed the murder was related to a dispute over the division of revenues resulting from the sale of Gonzalo Higuaín to Real Madrid.

In August 2011 Ernesto Cirino took his pet Pekinese for a walk in Liniers. It urinated against the wall of a house that, unfortunately, belonged to Gustavo Petrinelli, the brother-in-law of Maximiliano Mazzaro, the deputy of Mauro Martín, the leader of la Doce, Boca's largest *barra*. There was an argument that resulted in Cirino being so badly beaten that he died in the hospital two days later. Martín, Petrinelli, and Mazzaro were tried for his murder, and all three were acquitted. The investigation into Cirino's death, though, revealed the links that existed between not only the *barras* and club hierarchies but also the political and judicial establishment. Although there have been plenty of hints as to what those links may consist of, much of the evidence remains under an injunction.

That wasn't the only issue facing Martín. Toward the end of the 2011–2012 *apertura*, Rafael Di Zeo, who had been the leader of la Doce, was released from jail after serving a four-year term and sought to resume control of the group Martín had taken over. Boca's directors, terrified of a major incident a few weeks before club elections, gave a separate terrace to each group from which they hurled insults at each other and supported the team with competing chants.

Away fans were banned from stadiums in 2013, but that is only part of the problem. Violence remains pervasive, a seemingly irresolvable issue.

65

HOME DISCOMFORTS

The smoke from the *chori*[1] stalls mingled with a low mist to cover the approach to Santa Fe's Estadio Brigadier General Estanislao López in a fine haze. The round bulbs on the lamps that line the broad promenade through the park glowed indistinctly. By the wrought-iron railings, hawkers sold knockoff Argentina shirts, some with "Messi 10" on the back, but at least as many with "Tévez 11": the interaction between the two had been the main point of discussion after Argentina had drawn their first game in the Copa América 1–1 against Bolivia. Could they play together? (Or, perhaps more accurately, given they'd played so effectively together in the 2007 Copa América, why could they do so no longer?) Did they keep trying to occupy the other's space? And if one of them had to be dropped, who should it be? In retrospect, or even from the vantage point of Europe, it seemed weird that there should even be a question, but the Argentinian view of soccer is almost invariably bound up with ideological issues.

There was an odd sense at that point that the 2011 Copa América was yet to begin. Argentina was still in shock—in mourning, even—following the relegation of River Plate, and the scratchily insipid display against Bolivia had provoked only grumbling rather than the rage that might have been expected. This, after all, was Argentina's tournament, their chance to end a run without a trophy stretching back eighteen years. They were the hosts, they had a fine array of attacking talent, and there were huge doubts about a Brazil side that seemed to have been selected with half an eye on blooding young players such as Neymar and Ganso for the 2014 World Cup.

But how could anyone think of the Copa América at a time like this, after River had gone down for the first time in their history? Another of the great certainties of life had been demolished, and that fact overshadowed all else, the parochialism Alabarces had noted after the 2002 World Cup eclipsing the possibilities of national glory. Fifteen years to the day after they'd beaten América de Cali to win the Copa Libertadores for the second time, River faced Belgrano in a relegation playoff. They'd already lost the first leg 2–0 in Córdoba, a game in which masked *barras* ran onto the field to berate their own players. Matters didn't improve in the second leg. With moments to go and the score at 1–1, plastic seats began to rain down from the stands. Players took refuge in the center circle, surrounded by police. Riots spilled into the streets around the ground, smashing windows, cars, and other property. As shots were fired, police helicopters swept in. It was all very sad and very predictable.

There were those who blamed coach J. J. López, who had been left impotent in the face of the gathering panic, his team selections inconsistent and probably needlessly cautious. The irony was River actually finished that *clausura* season ninth, having been fourth in the *apertura*. Had the Argentinian league operated as it once did with just one championship per year and everybody playing everybody else twice, River would have been fifth. They ended up being undone by the very system that was designed to spare the *grandes* the shame of relegation, the *promedio*. After winning the *clausura* under Diego Simeone in 2007–2008, River finished last in the *apertura* in 2008–2009. They woke up to their plight only two seasons later, and, when they did, paralysis gripped the club and they won none of their final seven matches.

Santa Fe is about a hundred miles south of Rosario; the game was in Messi's home province and the closest the tournament came to his hometown. Yet even there, the public sympathy seemed to be with Tévez. The field-side announcer read out the teams before the game, announcing "in the 10, the best in the word, Lionel Messi." There was polite applause. "And in the 11, the player of the people, Carlos Tévez." There was a mighty roar.

To say Messi was ever unpopular in Argentina would be an exaggeration, but there was a skepticism about him: he had not played at home; he had not served his time at River or Boca; was he half a Catalan? It was understandable—he had, after all, left Argentina eleven years earlier—but it was also unfair: Messi has never been anything other than Argentinian. It's true he has a tendency to mumble the anthem, but so do a lot of players, particularly those as shy as he is.

But the fascination, really, was less the suspicion surrounding Messi— one experienced by a large number of Argentinians who have made their name abroad, from Che Guevara to Borges—than the overwhelming popularity of Tévez. When Borocotó described the *pibe*, he gave a startlingly accurate portrait of Diego Maradona. But Tévez, with his shock of black hair, the neck scarred by an early accident with a pan of boiling water, the squat physique, and the impoverished background, fits the template just as well: he too is an archetypal *pibe*, and it is that, almost more than anything else, that really seems to stir the Argentinian soccer public. Messi, by contrast, with his more comfortable background and his sensible haircut, despite his lack of height and the slightness of his build, is somehow something else;

he doesn't quite fulfill the *pibe* stereotype, which feeds into suspicions of a player whose teenage development took place abroad. Tévez was on the squad only because of his popularity: Coach Sergio Batista had dropped him after he'd withdrawn from a friendly against Brazil with "muscular problems" only to play for Manchester City soon after, but had recalled him under what he later described as "political pressure" after Daniel Scioli, the governor of Buenos Aires, had called for his selection.

Colombia rarely looked threatened in a 0–0 draw. A few days later, I visited a vineyard in Mendoza and ended up discussing the Messi-Tévez issue with the manager. We agreed they replicated each other's runs and that they couldn't play together. I asked which she would drop. "For games against weak sides," she said, "play Messi. He is more skillful, more creative. But against good sides, against Brazil or Uruguay . . . ," she rapped her knuckles over her heart, "Tévez has *garra*. He has spirit. He will fight." I had wondered whether the issue was particularly class based: was Tévez the hero of "the people" in the sense of the great mass of the poor? But the feeling was pervasive. Tévez was preferred not because his background was more impoverished but because he seemed more authentically Argentinian.

Tévez was dropped for the final-group game, against an understrength Costa Rica, and, with Messi, Agüero, and Di María arrayed behind Gonzalo Higuaín in a 4-2-3-1, Argentina had far better balance, winning 3–0. They finished second in the group as Colombia won 2–0 against Bolivia, meaning that, rather than playing one of the two best third-place teams in the quarter-finals, they faced Uruguay.

Batista selected the same side, but after five minutes Diego Pérez forced the ball over the line after Alvaro Pereira had headed down a Diego Forlán free kick. Things came back on track as Higuaín headed in a scooped cross from the right from Messi twelve minutes later, and the game seemed to take a decisive shift Argentina's way seven minutes before halftime when Pérez, already booked for an early lunge on Javier Mascherano, picked up a second caution for a block on Fernando Gago. Uruguay's manager, Óscar Washington Tabárez, shifted Alvaro Pereira infield, playing a 4-3-2 with nobody on the left side of midfield. It was a counterintuitive move, leaving Messi free, but Tabárez had recognized that, so inflexible was the Argentinian system, he always cut inside. Messi kept doing so and kept running into traffic. Argentina struggled to create chances, while Uruguay twice hit the bar. Tévez came on for Agüero after eighty-three minutes, but cut a disaffected, petulant figure. The hosts became increasingly frustrated, culminating in a second yellow card for Mascherano with four minutes remaining.

The game went to penalties, Tévez's effort was saved by Fernando Muslera, and Uruguay won. Argentina were out, and the people had begun to turn on Tévez. It wasn't a simple case of blaming him for missing the penalty; rather, it was that the miss came as a symptom of something wider, a sense that Tévez, having been left out, didn't return desperate to regain his place, but sulked. That wasn't part of the *pibe* appeal; that wasn't the tenacity the kid from the *potreros* was supposed to demonstrate. Four years later, Tévez admitted he should never have been selected. "I wasn't prepared in 2011," he said, "and should have been left out of the Copa, but they called me at the last second and I joined the team."

That autumn, during a Champions League game at Bayern Munich, Tévez refused to warm up when asked to do so by Manchester City manager Roberto Mancini. He was dropped and suspended by the club and returned to Argentina, where he played a lot of golf and even caddied for Andrés Romero during the final round of the Open at Royal Lytham & St. Annes. That gave Alejandro Sabella, who succeeded Batista after the Copa América, an excuse not to pick him. By the time Tévez was playing again, Argentina had a system that worked and had taken them to top of the World Cup qualifying group. It wasn't until 2015 that he was selected for the national side again, by which time Gerardo Martino had replaced Sabella.

66

THE LITTLE WITCH, THE POPE, AND THE GLEEFUL CHICKENS

Perhaps the strangest aspect of modern Argentinian soccer is that it continues, despite everything, to be so successful at a continental level. Whatever else is wrong, the Libertadores victories keep coming, but what is noticeable now is how little pattern there is. Nobody establishes a dynasty anymore; the thought of a club doing what Independiente had done in the seventies and winning four in a row is preposterous. The rapaciousness of European clubs and the need of Argentinian clubs for quick cash are too great, the throughput of players too fast. Short-termism reigns.

Take, for instance, Estudiantes. After a decade in Europe, Juan Sebastián Verón returned to the club in 2006. "I want to help the club get back to winning international titles," he said. The club was on the up, and he was still industrious and capable of splitting defenses with precise through-passes, but that seemed a hugely ambitious goal. Then Diego Simeone was appointed coach. Taking the foundations that had been left by Carlos Bilardo, who had promoted a number of young players before departing in 2004, he fashioned a side in the best traditions of the club, conceding only twelve goals in nineteen games in the 2006–2007 *apertura*, winning the club's first title for twenty-three years in a playoff.

Improbably successful as Simeone subsequently was at Atlético, it was that Estudiantes side that embodied his ideal of soccer. "Don't forget Estudiantes," he said. "They remain the team that captured best what I think of soccer, with which I felt most identified: practicality, commitment, collective effort, talent, simplicity." Nonetheless, he soon left for River.

That was the beginning, but it was the surprise appointment in 2009 of Alejandro Sabella that took things to a new level. He was a former Estudiantes player (he had been nicknamed "Pachorra" [Sloth] for his perceived lack of pace), but at fifty-four he had no experience as a head coach, having spent most of his career working as an assistant to Daniel Passarella. Surprise or not, in his two years at the club, Sabella proved more successful than any Estudiantes coach since Zubeldía.

Defensive solidity—five goals conceded in twelve games—saw Estudiantes through to a final against Cruzeiro. The first leg, in La Plata, finished goalless, and Cruzeiro took the lead in Belo Horizonte with a deflected Henrique shot seven minutes into the second half. But five minutes later Verón advanced from deep and spread the ball wide to the overlapping fullback Christian Cellay. He crossed low, and when Fabio, the goalkeeper, flapped and missed, Gastón Fernández nudged the ball in from close range. Sixteen minutes later Mauro Boselli powered in a header from a Verón corner. Verón had made good his vow and followed his father in helping Estudiantes to the Libertadores. "My son came back in 2006 with a simple but seemingly impossible objective—to help the team to win an international tournament again," said Juan Ramón Verón. "He had several offers, but chose to play for his club, the one that he never forgot. The dream that every fan has, he fulfilled it."

The *apertura* followed in 2010, but soon the sell-off began. There could be no sustained success. It would be five years before another Argentinian side lifted the trophy.

Pope Francis is a San Lorenzo fan, of course. He was born in December 1936 in Flores, the barrio immediately to the west of Almagro, where Father Lorenzo had founded the club three decades earlier. His father played for San Lorenzo's basketball team, and as a child he would go with his mother to watch matches. There's always a suspicion with public figures that their professed support for soccer clubs is skin deep, but not with Francis. If he sees somebody wearing a San Lorenzo shirt or carrying San Lorenzo colors in the crowds in Saint Peter's Square, he makes a point of acknowledging them. If San Lorenzo have won their previous game, he will usually signal the score with his fingers. At his public audiences, there are always groups draped in Argentinian flags, looking less like pilgrims than a soccer crowd. Those who work regularly with Francis roll their eyes when asked about his love of the game; apparently, he talks incessantly about soccer.[1]

When Francis was elected pope in 2013, San Lorenzo had won nothing since lifting the *clausura* in 2007. They promptly won the *apertura*,[2] a particularly notable achievement given that the previous year they had avoided relegation only in a playoff while struggling under the weight of a debt of more than $22 million. A new chairman, Matías Lammens, stabilized the club financially, while coach Juan Antonio Pizzi found a way to play.

Pizzi moved to Valencia soon after winning the title, leaving Edgardo Bauza, who had led Liga de Quito to the title in 2008, to take charge of a Libertadores campaign that perhaps meant more to San Lorenzo than it does to most clubs. Winning the Libertadores had taken on the nature of a quest for San Lorenzo, whose supporters had become sick of the jibe made by fans of other clubs that the letters on their badge stood not for Club Atlético San Lorenzo de Almagro but for Club Atlético Sin Libertadores de América.

The first sense that something special was happening came with the final matches in the group stage. The Chilean side Unión Española had already qualified for the last sixteen, while Botafogo were two points clear of San Lorenzo and the Ecuadorian side Independiente del Valle. That meant that if San Lorenzo beat Botafogo at home, they went through in second place, unless Independiente won in Chile, in which case they had to win by two goals more than the Ecuadorians.

At halftime San Lorenzo were in control. They led through Héctor Villalba's goal, while Unión and Independiente were drawing 1–1. Ignacio Piatti scored twice as San Lorenzo won 3–0, but the game in Chile had plenty of twists still to come. Having done their bit, San Lorenzo's players were left waiting on the field for the other match to finish: when it did Independiente had won 5–4, and the Argentinians were through. "They all thought that we were dead, but they forgot to kill us," Piatti said. "This squad has been through a lot but we showed that we are warriors. We might not play well but we will never stop fighting."

Grêmio were beaten on penalties in the last sixteen and Cruzeiro 2–1 on aggregate in the quarter-final. The semifinal draw was kind, matching San Lorenzo with Bolívar, which had a terrible away record but thrived at altitude at home in La Paz. San Lorenzo made sure that advantage wouldn't be a factor, winning 5–0 at home in the first leg. A 1–0 defeat in Bolivia hardly mattered: San Lorenzo had reached the final for the first time.

It wasn't, though, the San Lorenzo that had begun the tournament. Ángel Correa, the highly promising young forward, had been sold to Atlético Madrid—where his medical turned up a heart defect that required surgery— while Piatti, the hero of the group stage, was sold to Montreal Impact and had to leave between the two legs of the final. That is the sad reality of modern Argentinian soccer: no club can ever hold on to players of talent for long.

They drew 1–1 away to Nacional of Paraguay in the first leg of the final. The second leg was nervy and riddled with errors, but the only goal went San Lorenzo's way, as the rotund figure of Néstor Ortigoza converted a penalty. It was a night when the spectacle mattered less than the achievement, when the competition settled its sixty-year debt to San Lorenzo.

Nobody, perhaps, savored the victory quite as keenly as Leandro Romagnoli. He is an old-fashioned kind of player, a dribbler who awakes in Argentinians a nostalgia for the golden age; San Lorenzo in general, in fact, seemed to represent an older school of soccer, less vertical, less frenetic than the *bielsista* school that had begun to dominate the Argentinian game. Romagnoli had been a San Lorenzo fan as a boy, had promised his mother he would make history for the club, and made his debut for them at seventeen.

After fifteen league titles, San Lorenzo at last became the eighth Argentinian winners of the Libertadores; they are no longer defined by an absence. "I think of the joy of the fans," Romagnoli said. "Of what it means to the club to win the cup. They'd never played in a final, but we were able to give that to them. Many of the fans are eighty or ninety years old: they waited a lifetime for this."

The day after the victory, a delegation of players flew to Rome with the trophy and met the pope, as they had after winning the league the previous December. "I am very happy about it, but, no, it is not a miracle," Francis said, as he clutched the trophy with obvious pride. The following month it was announced that when, in 2018, the club moves to its new stadium back home in Boedo, having agreed a deal with Carrefour to share the land they were forced to give up in 1979, it will be named after the pope.

Intense as San Lorenzo's joy was, and hugely important as the Libertadores success was in helping restore to the club a self-esteem that had been diminished by the loss of its home, there was also a wider point: despite all the gloom around Argentinian soccer, despite the obvious economic decline, their clubs could still win continental tournaments. "After a five-year drought, an Argentinian side has won the Libertadores," exulted *La Gaceta de Tucumán* under the headline "National Pride."

Proud they may have been, but an indication of the true level of Argentinian—and by extension South American—soccer was given by the performances of Estudiantes and San Lorenzo in the Club World Cup. Estudiantes at least took Barcelona to extra time before losing in the final in 2009, but San Lorenzo needed extra time to see off Auckland City in their semifinal in 2014 and were well beaten in the final by Real Madrid.

Nonetheless, there'd be another Argentinian Libertadores winner the following season.

At el Monumental grown men wept. At the Obelisco they cavorted in the rain. Nineteen years after Enzo Francescoli had inspired their second victory, River Plate won a third Libertadores and became the first side to hold the Sudamericana, the Recopa, and the Libertadores simultaneously. In the end, after all the trauma River had been through in the competition, it felt almost anticlimactically easy, victory effectively secured by a 0–0 draw in the first leg of the final, away to the Mexican side Tigres UANL, and confirmed by a 3–0 win at home. The joy and the emotion were real enough, even if the sense was that the hard work had been done in coming from a goal down after the home leg to beat Cruzeiro 3–1 in the quarter-final.

Although Marcelo Gallardo's side had played well in patches over the previous year, River had made it through the group stage with the worst record of any of the qualifiers, winning just one game and finishing seven points behind UANL. The draw paired them with Boca, and, after winning 1–0 at home, they'd gone through after the second leg at la Bombonera was abandoned when home fans squirted pepper spray into the tunnel as the players came in for the start of the second half, an unsatisfactory way to win a derby. "The history of this club is about fighting for these kind of competitions," said midfielder Leonardo Ponzio, but the truth is that it isn't. This wasn't a win in the proudest traditions of the club; it wasn't rooted in stylish attacking play; it was a victory for tenacity. Only the most fundamentalist fan would care, but the nature of the success said much about the Libertadores soccer in the modern age. "This," wrote Tim Vickery, the doyen of Europeans covering South American soccer, "was a game of depressingly low quality, a festival of misplaced passes (over seventy in the first half alone) and rough tackles. As a showpiece occasion, the difference between this and the Champions League final is a sad illustration of the chasm which currently exists between soccer in Europe and South America."

River celebrated as San Lorenzo and Estudiantes had, but nobody could pretend these victories were the equal of what Estudiantes had achieved in the sixties, or Boca and Independiente had achieved in the seventies, or a host of Argentinian clubs, including River, had achieved in the eighties, back when the Libertadores and the European Cup had an equal status. This was modern soccer for clubs outside the European elite: a spark of success that advertised the talents of players and managers, who then departed, prompting an inevitable slippage back into mediocrity. There's no pattern, no shape, no sense of structure being built for the future.

In essence, what these recent triumphs demonstrate is little more than the fact that Argentinian soccer, for all its faults, isn't as badly mismanaged as Brazilian soccer.

67

THE ONGOING DROUGHT

All along the Copacabana beachfront they lined up, cars, minibuses, and campers parked nose to tail along the coast road, blue-and-white flags and ribbons everywhere. In the mornings, as the sun rose over the Atlantic, there was a great communal awakening, hundreds of Argentinian fans stirring, boiling the water for *mate* on small Primus stoves. Some slept on the beach, some on benches, displacing the local homeless. The Fan Fest, that dreaded center of FIFA corporatism, where face painting costs $13.50 and a bottle of official wine $215, stood at one end of the beach, but this still felt like the true heart of the tournament, the anarchic hub where fans met and drank, watched games on the big screens, flirted, and argued—fans of all nations, but mainly Argentinian. And with them came the inevitable song, sung to the tune of "Bad Moon Rising," that became, to the horror of Brazilians whose worst nightmare was their bitterest rivals winning the tournament in the Maracanã, the anthem of the tournament.

The year 2014 had been marked out as Messi's World Cup for almost a decade; the Maradona paradigm was laid out for him. In autumn 2005 he negotiated his first contract as an adult with Barcelona. He was eighteen and in his first full season with the first team. Both parties wanted a long-term deal, but they differed on one key detail. Whereas the club wanted Messi to sign until 2014—and ultimately got their way (there have been countless extensions and renegotiations since)—Messi's father wanted a deal that expired in 2013. His thinking was that if anything went wrong at Barcelona, if Messi suffered an injury or had a falling-out with a coach, he wanted his son to have the freedom to leave a year before the World Cup so he would have a season to play himself into form. As it turned out, Argentina's squad for the 2014 World Cup included six players who had played in the 2005 Under-20 final (while defender Gabriel Paletta was on the Italy squad).

But Messi never seized the tournament as Maradona had in 1986, never looked physically capable of doing so. What he offered instead were a series of decisive cameos, as though again and again he realized nobody else was going to turn the game, got "his face on" (to use Grighini's phrase), and made a decisive intervention, just as he had done in youth-team games years earlier.

Argentina had qualified in impressive style, finishing top of the Conmebol group, losing just two of sixteen games (and one of them the final match against Uruguay, long after qualification had been secured) and scoring thirty-five goals. Most important, though, they had seemingly found in Alejandro Sabella a coach who was pragmatic enough and tough enough to ignore political considerations or the popularity of individuals to pick a team structure that worked. Most significantly, he never called up Tévez, who did little to help his own cause by commenting sourly, "Playing for Argentina takes away prestige," a phrase that offered a reminder that, in 2003, as he'd celebrated Boca winning the title at Racing, he'd joined fans in abusive chants about *la selección*.

Sabella had set out with a 4-4-1-1 with Messi behind Higuaín before switching to a 4-3-3, with Messi to the right of Higuaín, but cutting infield and switching with him, and Agüero to left. It was rumored that the change had come at Messi's instigation, that he had wanted his old roommate back on the side, but whatever the reason, the outcome was a team with great balance. Di María shuttled forward from the left side of midfield, protected by a defensive left-back in Marcos Rojo, while Javier Mascherano sat in front of the two central defenders and, on the right of midfield, Fernando Gago sat deep, offering cover as Pablo Zabaleta raided from right-back.

Those plans, though, were disrupted by injury. Gago succumbed to a knee problem, and while he was back for the tournament, he was far from his best (although his form for Boca had been indifferent even before he broke down). Agüero suffered repeated calf and hamstring problems, while Higuaín was struggling to overcome an ankle injury in the days before Argentina's opening game, against Bosnia-Herzegovina at the Maracanã. Even so, Sabella's team selection was mysterious, so baffling as to prompt a series of conspiracy theories: out went the 4-3-3, and in its place came a 5-3-2 that he'd used only three times in qualifying—the games away to Venezuela, Bolivia, and Ecuador that had yielded a defeat and two draws.

In the end, it turned out, this wasn't about Messi demanding to play in a front two or any of the other wilder allegations, but about Sabella, troubled by the injury issues, deciding not to risk all three of his fit forwards at once (and even that tally included Agüero, who was far from his peak). Messi played behind Agüero, with Mascherano flanked in midfield by Di María and Maxi Rodríguez. Argentina took a fortunate third-minute lead as Messi's free kick glanced off Rojo and cannoned in off Sead Kolašinac, but thereafter they were flat and spent most of the rest of the first half defending deep, holding Bosnia at arm's length, but never threatening to increase their lead.

Messi, it's said, asked at halftime for a return to 4-3-3, although he can't have been the only one who realized a change of shape was needed if Argentina weren't to spend the rest of the game clinging on, hoping neither Miralem Pjanić nor Zvjezdan Misimović found a killer pass. Gago and Higuaín were introduced, and Argentina immediately looked far more comfortable. Messi remained quiet, but with sixty-five minutes played there came the linkup that had been a feature of Argentina's play throughout qualifying, Higuaín pulling left to create space for Messi to dart infield, leaving two defenders in a heap before clipping a neat shot low inside the left-hand post. Vedad Ibišević pulled one back late on, but Argentina won 2–1.

At the time, it seemed like little more than a stuttering start, and the assumption was that, with the 4-3-3 reestablished and players returning to fitness, Argentina would find their rhythm. As it was their whole tournament followed the pattern of the Bosnia game. Iran defended almost impeccably, frustrating Argentina and even having a couple of chances of their own—they probably should have had a penalty—before, in injury time, Messi picked up the ball ten yards outside the box to the right of goal. All ten Iranian outfielders were between him and the target, but he looked up, shifted the ball out onto his left foot, and whipped a shot around Reza Ghoochannejhad, over Amir Sadeghi, and between the dive of the goalkeeper and the post. It would, in any context, have been a stunning goal, but to do it then, with the doubts so manifest that Maradona had already left the stadium in irritation, was even more special: this was a player taking responsibility, saying that if nobody else was going to win the game, he would.

That meant that Argentina qualified and the final-group game, against Nigeria, was simply about securing the top spot, which they would have achieved with a draw. As it was, they won 3–2, with Messi scoring twice, the first a fearsome first-time shot into the roof of the net after Di María's effort had come back off a combination of goalkeeper and post, the second a stunning free kick.

That set up a last-sixteen clash with Switzerland in São Paulo. The Swiss sat deep, their whole game plan being to deny Messi room: "This can only be done if we're all together," coach Ottmar Hitzfeld said, "if we have three or four players around Messi, close to Messi." They achieved that. Messi spent the whole game with red shirts buzzing around him. Argentina labored. Agüero, having suffered a recurrence of his hamstring problem, was out and replaced by Ezequiel Lavezzi. Messi made little pretense of starting out to the right, sitting in the classic *enganche* role behind the two strikers, which perhaps made it easier for Switzerland to thwart him. But by that stage it felt as though the usual parameters had changed. This was no longer about

Argentina or about progress through the tournament; it was on some level about Messi trying to fulfill his destiny.

The talk of balance and integration in qualifying had been replaced by a very old-fashioned view of soccer. As journalist Ken Early observed, at Barcelona, Messi would receive a pass, give a pass, and move into space to gather the ball again. For Argentina, he received a pass, and everybody stood and waited for him to do something. It was as though there were three teams: Switzerland on one side and the loose alliance of Messi and Argentina on the other.

There was a moment with a couple of minutes of normal time remaining when Messi received the ball out on the left touchline. He looked up and almost visibly steeled himself, setting off on a *gambeta*. It came to nothing, but the sense was there: here he was, yet again, trying to work out a way of winning the game on his own. At ninety minutes it was 0–0. The two teams huddled in front of their respective benches. Messi was the Argentina captain, an appointment made perhaps for sentimental reasons, so he could replicate Maradona's 1986 as closely as possible, but he was one of the last to join the group. He stood at the back, tipping a bottle of water over his head. Sabella spoke first, then Mascherano. Messi said nothing. Was this the quiet leadership his early teachers and coaches had spoken of? Or was he simply the captain in name only, a silent genius?

There was something fascinating about his minimalism, which had long been apparent in his more general play; although he was capable of extraordinary virtuosity, he had a great capacity to choose the easiest possible action to achieve his desired ends; there was nothing brash or flamboyant about him. This lack of movement, though, was something new. He ran less than any other outfielder on the field—just six and a half miles in the 120 minutes—and spent less time in what FIFA deems medium- and high-intensity activity than any other outfielder. He made just thirty-one sprints, fewer than any other outfielder in the game apart from central defenders Federico Fernández and Fabian Schär. When Brazil beat Chile on penalties in the same round, Neymar ran almost two miles more than Messi and completed 21 minutes in medium- to high-intensity activity as opposed to Messi's 9, while completing fifty-seven sprints. Yet Messi still won Argentina the game. With three minutes remaining, Switzerland's concentration at last slipped at a throw-in. Messi suddenly had space. He accelerated at 17 mph, the fastest he had moved all game, according to FIFA.[1] Defenders, in a panic, converged on him, at which Messi, in a moment reminiscent of Maradona's pass against Brazil in 1990 for the Caniggia goal the Argentina fans were so set on celebrating, pushed the ball into the path of Di María. His first-time finish didn't quite have the flamboyance of Caniggia, but his goal was no less decisive. Having taken the lead, Argentina were in chaos, and Blerim Džemaili very nearly equalized, his close-range header hitting the post, bouncing back against his knee, and cannoning wide, but they held on and reached the quarter-final.

Still there was time for Messi to explode into his version of 1986; after all, it had only really been in the last eight that Maradona had caught fire then. But that explosion never came. Argentina beat Belgium in the quarter-final thanks to an early goal from Higuaín, but Messi was peripheral and, worse, Di María damaged a thigh muscle. Without him in the semifinal, against the Netherlands, they looked a far less dangerous side going forward.

It was a game played under a cloud of sadness. Argentina's players wore black armbands in memory of Alfredo Di Stéfano, who had died the previous week, but the symbols took on extra significance early on the morning of the game when journalist Jorge "el Topo" López was killed when the taxi he had been traveling in was hit by a stolen car being chased by police. His wife, who was also a journalist covering the tournament, learned of his death when she saw a Tweet from Diego Simeone expressing his horror and sadness at the news.

Messi, who had been close to López, sparkled only intermittently, although one run and cross in the closing seconds almost produced a winner. Argentina won on penalties—a victory Messi immediately dedicated to the journalist—and few doubted that the star had been Mascherano, a controlled and combative figure at the back of midfield who, late on, had made a staggering burst and sliding challenge to deny Arjen Robben, a effort that, he said, caused him to "split [his] anus."

With a great performance in the final against Germany, it could still have been remembered as Messi's tournament. Even a goal in a winning display might, in conjunction with the memories of his four group-stage goals and the pass to Di María against Switzerland, have been sufficient to generate the narrative of this being Messi's tournament. And he had his chance, squeezing a shot a fraction wide just after halftime. Argentina, more generally, had their opportunities: Higuaín fluffed a one-on-one dreadfully and had a goal—rightly—ruled out for a tight offside, and Germany goalkeeper Manuel Neuer might have been sent off for hitting the striker with a clumsy head-high clearance.

Sabella probably surrendered the initiative when he withdrew Lavezzi for Agüero at halftime, a gamble on the Manchester City forward's fitness that didn't pay off. The game, in the end, was settled by a 113th-minute volley from Mario Götze. Over the tournament as a whole, Germany had probably deserved it, but Argentina had come desperately close. Messi's final notable act came as Argentina were awarded a free kick just outside the box in the final minute. The best option might have been for Messi to swing it into the box for Ezequiel Garay to attack: the Switzerland game had offered a reminder of how defenders' minds can be scrambled with the prize in reach; making Germany clear the ball would at least have tested character and temperament. Instead, Messi shot, and blasted his effort high and wide. Of course, it's easy to criticize in retrospect, and, of course, had he scored, the incident would have been hailed as another example of him getting "the face," taking responsibility, and sorting the problem out himself. As it was, it simply felt as though he had gotten caught up in the narrative that he had to win the World Cup single-handedly. And so passed the greatest opportunity for the Under-20 champions of 2005, beaten by a Germany side that included five of their 2009 Under-21 European champions.[2]

After the final whistle, as Germany waited to be presented with the trophy, Messi was named player of the tournament. He could hardly have looked glummer as the Golden Ball was thrust into his hands. Nobody blamed him, there was no sense of him having let anybody down, but there were concerns. In the week before the final, quotes attributed to his father—but quickly denied—suggested he felt as though his legs "weighed a ton each." Was it connected to the habit he had developed over the previous couple of years of vomiting on the field? When he then produced another sparkling season at Barcelona, it seemed even more clear there had been something amiss, but exactly what was never satisfactorily explained, even if Messi did eventually acknowledge that he had felt out of sorts for most of 2014.

To speak of failure when a side has just reached a World Cup final, when it has had chances moreover to win that final, would be dreadfully harsh, and most in Argentina seemed grateful to Sabella and his team for reaching a final and shaking off that nagging statistic that, since 1990, the only team Argentina had beaten in a knockout game at the World Cup—without recourse to penalties—was Mexico. So Messi got to wear his mournful face at a number of public receptions, moping in the background as Cristina Kirchner praised the squad, leaving few in any doubt that he was deeply hurt by the fact that Argentina hadn't won his designated World Cup, that the Under-20 team of 2005 hadn't delivered on its promise, that another grand Argentinian dream had melted into the air.

68

THE ETERNAL LAURELS

Eighteen days after the 2014 World Cup final, Julio Grondona died at the age of eighty-two; he had been president of the AFA for thirty-five years. By the end, he was an isolated figure, but his influence was indisputable. With his passing an era had definitely come to an end, one in which the level of Argentinian domestic soccer declined dramatically. Perhaps, like so many Argentinian leaders, he found himself helpless in the face of wider socioeconomic forces; as Menotti noted, Grondona was surely right in his recognition that the national team was where the money lay—even if there was widespread concern about the deal that sold the rights to its matches to Traffic, a company whose dealings in soccer fell under investigation by the US Federal Bureau of Investigation that brought the arrests of seven FIFA executives in Zurich in May 2015. But however corrupt Grondona is accused of having been—and given how many other Conmebol leaders were indicted as part of that investigation, it seems reasonable to assume that death spared him scrutiny—the fact remains that Argentinian soccer cannot escape the basic problems of the Argentinian economy. The day after Grondona died, Argentina defaulted again.

The long postcrash recovery eventually turned sour. The ongoing repercussions of the global downturn hit the exports on which Argentina is heavily reliant, and the country suffered recessions in 2012 and 2014. Inflation rose, as was inevitable given the artificially low rate of the peso: official figures in July 2014 had it at 10.9 percent, although it was widely believed the true figure could be almost three times that. The crisis point was reached on July 31, when Argentina was unable to meet a $539 million interest repayment on bonds issued before the 2001 crash. They'd been picked up cheaply by US hedge funds—Kirchner called them "vultures"—which refused a restructuring program agreed by the majority of bondholders. It was, perhaps, as the government argued, "a technical default" rather than an event as calamitous as 2001—it was more a case of not being willing to pay than not being able—and the effects were nowhere near as dramatic. There was no run on the banks, no street protests, and, for most, life went on as it had before, but, still, the default was a sign of the weakness of Argentina's economy. For many investors, the belligerence of the government and the feeling the default was a deliberate tactic to force renegotiation only heightened the sense that Kirchner was not to be trusted.

Nobody could deny that Grondona was the AFA president in difficult times, but for the general sense of chaos and decay that he left and his failure to stem the violence and the collapse of infrastructure, he must bear responsibility. Such was the aura of corruption that even as he was buried in Avellaneda, in the cemetery his bedroom had overlooked, financial investigators were raiding the AFA's offices. Most culpably of all, perhaps, the second half of Grondona's reign must be regarded as a series of wasted opportunities.

Success at the youth level—five Under-20 World Cups in twelve years—never translated into success at the senior level. The Copa América in Chile in 2015 brought further disappointment. After throwing away a 2–0 lead against Paraguay in their opening game, 1–0 wins over Uruguay and Jamaica were enough to carry Argentina into the last eight, where they met Colombia. They dominated the game, but couldn't score, drew 0–0, and went through only on penalties.

Finally, in the semifinal in Concepción, Argentina caught light. Messi, whose return to form had helped Barcelona to another Champions League, was brilliant, and so too was Javier Pastore. Argentina won 6–1, and although Messi didn't score, he set up three goals directly, playing the penultimate pass for two and the antepenultimate pass for the other. In the buildup to the fourth goal, his *gambeta* was so mesmerizing that he left two Paraguayan defenders neatly stacked on top of each other. Just as significantly, he stopped his side as they left the tunnel for the start of the second half to offer his own team talk. Paraguay had pulled it back to 2–1 just before the interval, and the message was clear: don't let it slip again. This was Messi the vocal leader, taking more responsibility than he had as a largely silent captain at the World Cup.

Including the Confederations Cup in 2005, when they lost to Brazil in the final, it was Argentina's fifth final in eight tournaments. It went the same way as the previous four. Chile, the hosts, fired by a sense that it was their destiny, at home, to win the Copa América for the first time after ninety-nine years of trying, were dogged and well organized. Di María went off injured after a half hour, and gradually Argentina's early menace dissipated. By the end, Messi was a frustrated, disconsolate figure, yet, in injury time, he almost conjured a winner, sliding a pass through for Ezequiel Lavezzi. His cross was a little too far ahead of Gonzalo Higuaín, but the Napoli striker still might have done better than slicing his shot into the side netting.

Penalties had an air of inevitability about them. Higuaín and Ever Banega missed, and Chile were the champions. As the rest of the team gathered in a disconsolate huddle, Messi stood alone, set apart by his genius, set apart by the expectations upon him, his face a mask of devastation. Back in the dressing room, he wept; he was still weeping when the bus arrived back at the hotel. The barrage of criticism and abuse he received was as predictable as it was misguided. It's true he hadn't played especially well in either the World Cup final or the Copa América final, but when the opposition sets up almost entirely to stop one player, sometimes somebody else has to pick up the baton. And for all that, if Higuaín had converted two perfectly presentable chances, Argentina would have been world and continental champions and Messi would have been the key figure in those triumphs.

So what remains? Proud old stadiums crumble, the ghosts of former glories haunting the far-inferior product that remains. Perhaps those immersed in the Argentinian game, those for whom the decline has been a gradual process, have over time become desensitized to the decay, but an outsider cannot but be struck by the contrast between what was and what is. The threat of violence is always present, the ranks of overzealous police in riot gear offering little sense of comfort or security. Players taking corners have to be protected from missiles being hurled at them. At Vélez I once saw fans chase an officer down a stairwell, returning a few minutes later brandishing his shield as a trophy. At a *superclásico* at el Monumental, I saw Boca fans set on stewards, dragging them to the top of the steps and then hurling them down, before laying into them with fists and boots as they sprawled at the bottom, the horror apparently provoked by one steward clenching his fist as River scored. Anybody who's been to games in Argentina will have similar stories and far worse. Measures to counter the possibility of trouble make the experience even less pleasant: for a while home fans were kept back in the stadium until the away fans had dispersed, and then away fans were banned altogether.

Soccer's economics mean that the best players do not play in Argentina. Messi, the all-time great who has never played at home, is just the most eye-catching example of that. Promising young talent is swiftly whisked away to leagues where it can earn more money. That's a process that has been going on since the seventies, but at least then it was only a handful of players and they were moving to the elite leagues of western Europe. Now, every year, dozens of players follow the money to Russia, Ukraine, the Middle East, Japan, China, even Brazil, to return a decade later, their fortunes made, for a sentimental final couple of seasons at home. Teams win a title, and inevitably their best players move on to wealthier clubs: that's simply how the financial system works now. Argentinian clubs need the money, and foreign clubs can afford their assets. Both clubs benefit, the player benefits from the larger salary he will earn abroad, and the agents benefit. Only those who watch the game in Argentina lose out.

The sales work as a sort of reverse of the draft system in US sports: rather than the weakest side getting first pick of the young talent to strengthen for the next season, the strongest teams lose their best players. The result is a very even, very competitive league. The eleven championships between Banfield's success in the 2009–2010 *apertura* and River Plate's in the 2014 Campeonato yielded ten different champions, a remarkable contrast to the way the five *grandes* between them won every title in the first thirty-six seasons of professionalism. Competitiveness, generally speaking, is a positive, and fans in some European leagues won every year by the same one or two sides perhaps even feel a sense of envy, but it's hard not to feel that the process has gone too far, diminishing the value of a title. In the whirl of sales, in which the tallest poppies soon have their heads lopped off and quality is extremely limited, it's almost as though if a side hangs around for long enough, eventually it will enjoy the sort of run of luck and form that will win a title.

At the beginning of 2015, there were a staggering 1,869 Argentinians playing professionally abroad. That creates what's known as the "talent doughnut": there are teenagers with potential and thirtysomethings who once were great, but a player in his twenties who is playing in Argentina either isn't very good or has a specific reason to stay at home.

There is also the sense that what had been a great strength has become a weakness. The legacy of Bielsa is not so straightforward as it might have been. His hard-pressing, vertical style, his reinterpretation of the understanding of space on the field, was radical and produced extraordinary results—at least in the short term. He inspired a generation of coaches, from overt disciples such as Jorge Sampaoli, who took Universidad de Chile to the Copa Sudamericana and three successive league titles before becoming Chile national coach and leading them to victory over Argentina in the 2015 Copa América final, to those such as Pep Guardiola and Mauricio Pochettino, who have taken his ideas and amended or refined them, but there are those within the AFA who wonder whether his impact on domestic Argentinian soccer has been negative. Soccer played with *bielsista* intensity is fine for those who are technically gifted, they argue, but when lesser players look to play at that pace, the result is a mess of poor first touches and misplaced passes, too many balls thumped aimlessly forward: verticality without a purpose. It was little consolation to Argentina at the 2015 Copa América that five of the eight quarter-finalists and all the semifinalists were coached by

Argentinians; the philosophical wrangling goes on, but Argentina remains the intellectual heart of the South American game.

And for all the poverty of the play, for all the danger, for all the discomfort, the Argentinian top division has the seventh-highest attendance figures in the world,[1] behind only Germany's Bundesliga, the Premier League, the Spanish Liga, the Indian Super League, Italy's Serie A, and Mexico's Liga MX (and it trails the Mexican league by only an average of two people per game). What it does have is spectacle.

The *barras bravas* are one of the great problems of Argentinian soccer, but they are also a great draw. The displays of banners and streamers, the blizzards of ripped paper, the constant chanting, the surges to the front of the *popular* when a goal is scored are part of the reason so many tourists go to watch Argentinian games. At times, when a man with a megaphone is hanging from a fence trying to whip a couple of dozen fans into a frenzy as they huddle together on a terrace that is far too big for them, there is something poignant, even pathetic, about the determination to enact the ritual, but the biggest *clásicos* are extraordinary events, viscerally stirring even to a neutral. If Argentinian soccer ever manages to reduce the influence of the *barras*, one of the questions it must answer is whether it's possible to sustain the color and passion they bring without them. And, even then, what is the spectacle but a fur coat draped over the decaying body of Argentinian soccer, sustained by a rickety framework of government subsidy?

The same basic dilemma underlies other debates. El Monumental is a magnificent old stadium that invests even meaningless league games with a sense of grandeur. It's been painted a couple of times since the 1978 World Cup and the advertisements have changed, but it doesn't take much effort to visualize Passarella, Luque, and Kempes striding about the field. "Foreigners always like it," an Argentinian journalist commented, "but they don't have to work there every week." And he was right, of course: many of the great grounds of Buenos Aires are essentially theme parks dedicated to a previous age. But then the same could be said of much of the city; that's part of the appeal.

That's what draws outsiders—so many that at a recent election for the Boca presidency, the main policy of one of the candidates was to reduce the number of tourists at games because of the damage they were doing to the atmosphere (nothing, perhaps, so attests to the victory of Macri and his global vision as that). His supporters would hand out flyers printed with the slogan "¡Socios sí, turistas no!"—which were soon ripped up to be thrown in the air as confetti, thus becoming part of the spectacle, the appeal of which created the problem the flyers were aimed at addressing.

The draw for locals is rather harder to identify, but the prevalence of soccer is undeniable. Even if attendance at the stadiums has dropped since the early fifties' heyday, it is more than made up for by the millions who watch on television. The Fútbol para Todos program, whether regarded as a charitable act to ensure as many as possible could watch games or as a cynical move to anesthetize the population, is evidence of the sport's importance.

In 2015 there came a new indignity. The relegation of River in 2011 horrified Argentinian soccer. Boca fans taunted, but they must have also recognized their rival's downfall as a recognition of their own mortality. If it could happen to River, it could happen to anybody. For San Lorenzo or Racing to go down was one thing, but for River to go down was something else: they were the *millonarios*, the most successful side in Argentinian history. They were also responsible for a significant portion of what little money still trickled through Argentinian soccer. River won promotion at the first attempt, a 2–0 win at home to Almirante Brown, securing the second-division title on the final day of the season (although even that achievement was tainted by the fact that one stand at el Monumental had been closed as punishment for an incident during a game against Boca Unidos two weeks earlier that had left a fan dead), but Argentinian soccer was united in deciding this couldn't be allowed to happen again.

An initial review of the structure of the league arrived at much the same format that it already had: the words *apertura* and *clausura* were substituted with *inicial* and *final*, and, in 2012–2013, a third championship was awarded as the winners of each, Vélez and Newell's, played off, Vélez winning 1–0. The following season, 2013–2014, did away with the playoff before the 2014–2015 *inicial* was replaced with an interim Campeonato, a half-season championship designed to move the Argentinian season back to running from February to December rather than from August to May.

The first season under the new calendar began in February 2015 with perhaps the most ludicrous structure in Argentinian soccer history—no mean achievement. The preposterous championship was named after Julio Grondona, a fitting tribute to his twenty-five-year reign. Faced with a league low on quality and desperately short of money, the AFA increased the size of the league by ten teams to thirty, diluting whatever quality there was further, and reduced the number of games they played over the course of the season from thirty-eight to thirty, with obvious ramifications for match-day revenues.

Even more ludicrously, whatever sporting integrity the new format may have had was done away with when it was decided that each team should play each other side once but their biggest rivals twice, essentially to ensure there would be two *superclásicos*, the only game guaranteed a mass audience, each season. Quite aside from the fact that some sides were disadvantaged by having a stronger *clásico* rival than others, there was the issue of teams without a natural rival who had to be allocated one. Most absurdly, perhaps, fans of Aldovisi in Mar del Plata, 250 miles down the coast from Buenos Aires, were told that their bitterest enemies are Crucero del Norte, a club based in Garupá in Misiones province, 720 miles to the north. This was Grondona's legacy: an unwieldy structure designed to protect vested interests and invoke memories of the past. The *grandes* have to be there because they've always been there.

Perhaps Alexander Watson Hutton, who had founded the body that would become the AFA 122 years later, would have been shocked by the way the game he introduced to Argentina still dominates everyday discourse, but by the time he died in 1936 he had already seen the coming of professionalism and the vast crowds and the enormous radio audiences that brought, the fans clinging to the backs of streetcars as they crossed the city.

He had seen also the first of the coups that have so damaged the country. With decades of hindsight, the parallels are striking: 1912 marked the last general election without universal male suffrage and the last time an Anglo club won the Argentinian championship; 1930 marked both the first decisive blow against democracy and the final championship before the coming of professionalism. The relationship is neither simple nor direct, and is tangled in irony and compromise, but social changes were reflected in soccer just as much as politics.

If soccer plays anything like the role now it did a century ago in the formation of national identity, if it has anything like as much to say about the state of the nation, this is a troubling vision. While the young, the old, and the mediocre play out their baffling league in front of bafflingly large crowds in dilapidated arenas, the cream of Argentina plays its soccer in other leagues in other countries. Argentina is a nation founded on immigration and the immigrant vision of a better world, and soccer has played a central role in the creation of its image and its identity, yet now its best players—even its quite good players—are emigrants, forced to abandon the land of silver for the Old World. Soccer is another Argentinian dream that has slipped away. For Argentinians to see the best their country can produce, they must look either to the past or abroad. Argentinian soccer has become something that is played elsewhere.

ACKNOWLEDGMENTS

No nonfiction book is ever anything but a collaborative effort. Once again, I have been humbled by the amount of time and effort people have offered in the writing of this book.

Particular thanks are due to Martín Mazur, who, despite extremely trying personal circumstances, was a huge help in setting up interviews, translation, and archival research. It's not an exaggeration to say that this book couldn't have been written without him. Thanks also to Alejandra Altamirano Halle.

Kat Petersen again turned her stern eye and sterner eyebrows to correcting the text. I hope immersion in the curiously fey world of *El Gráfico* covers made it worthwhile. Thanks are also due to Rodrigo Orihuelo, who cast his expert eye over sections of the manuscript and made valuable suggestions. I'm grateful also to copyeditor John English for his work cleaning up my words.

At Orion I'm especially grateful to Alan Samson for his patience, his suggestions in streamlining the narrative, and his acceptance that the occasional tangent into the history of barbed wire and headgear in early Argentinian cinema adds depth. Thanks also to Ian Preece, Paul Murphy, and my agent, David Luxton, for their support and advice. At Nation Books I would like to thank my editor, Alessandra Bastagli, and the US production team, Melissa Raymond, Katie Haigler, Shena Redmond, Annette Wenda, Jack Lenzo, and Bill Warhop.

I know that a lot of Argentinians spend most of their days sitting in cafés reminiscing about the old days, but they didn't have to do it for me, so thanks are due to all those who agreed to be interviewed, particularly the ones who didn't try to strangle me to make a point.

The impetus to write this book came from Araceli Alemán, and I'm grateful to her for that, for all her wisdom, support, and generosity over the years, and for lending me numerous books.

So many people helped with logistics, suggestions, and advice that it's almost inevitable I've missed somebody (sorry), but thanks for their help in various ways and at various times to Marcela Mora y Araujo, Roberto Assaf, Philippe Auclair, Guillem Balagué, Esteban Bekerman, Andrès Campomar, Neil Clack, Dan Colasimone, Miguel Delaney, Dan Edwards, Ezequiel

Fernández Moores, Alex Galarza, Klaus Gallo, Seba García, Rick Glanvill, Cassiano Gobbet, Ian Hawkey, Henrik Hedegűs, Sam Kelly, Sándor Laczkó, Sid Lowe, Ed Malyon, Féderico Mayol, Scott Oliver, Gunnar Persson, Joel Richards, Miguel Ryan, Robert Shaw, Rory Smith, Ivan Soter, Tim Vickery, and Pablo Vignone.

Your receipt
Virginia Tutt Branch
2223 Miami St
South Bend, IN 46613
574-282-4637

Renew your books and music at
www.libraryforlife.org
(Movies may not be renewed.)

Items that you checked out

Title:
Angels with dirty faces : how Argentinian
soccer defined a nation and changed the
game forever / Jon
ID: 31986056625836
Due: Monday, January 02, 2017

Title:
Soccer skills for young players / Ted
Buxton with Alex Leith and Jim Drewitt ;
foreword by Gordon Ja
ID: 31986025387468
Due: Monday, January 02, 2017

Total items: 2
Account balance: $0.00
12/12/2016 3:14 PM
Checked out: 2
Overdue: 0
Hold requests: 0
Ready for pickup: 0

Brighten your holiday spirit with carols, hot
cocoa & crafts.
Specials guests from The Music Village
Main Library Plaza
Friday, December 2, 6:00 p.m.

Thanks for using the Virginia Tutt Branch!

APPENDIXES

ARGENTINIAN LEAGUE CHAMPIONS

Year		Champion	Year		Champion
1891		Saint Andrew's	1923	AAF	Boca Juniors
1893		Lomas Athletic		Ama	San Lorenzo
1894		Lomas Athletic	1924	AAF	Boca Juniors
1895		Lomas Athletic		Ama	San Lorenzo
1896		Lomas Academy	1925	AAF	Huracán
1897		Lomas Athletic		Ama	Racing
1898		Lomas Athletic	1926	AAF	Boca Juniors
1899		Belgrano Athletic		Ama	Independiente
1900		English High School AC	1927		San Lorenzo
		(later renamed Alumni)	1928		Huracán
1901		Alumni	1929		Gimnasia y Esgrima
1902		Alumni			La Plata
1903		Alumni	1930		Boca Juniors
1904		Belgrano Athletic	1931	AAF	Estudiantil Porteño
1905		Alumni		Pro	Boca Juniors
1906		Alumni	1932	AAF	Sportivo Barracas
1907		Alumni		Pro	River Plate
1908		Belgrano Athletic	1933	AAF	Sportivo Dock Sud
1909		Alumni		Pro	San Lorenzo
1910		Alumni	1934	AAF	Estudiantil Porteño
1911		Alumni		Pro	Boca Juniors
1912	AAF	Quilmes	1935		Boca Juniors
	FAF	Porteño	1936	CdH	San Lorenzo
1913	AAF	Racing		Cam	River Plate
	FAF	Estudiantes de		CdO	River Plate
		La Plata	1937		River Plate
1914	AAF	Racing	1938		Independiente
	FAF	Porteño	1939		Independiente
1915		Racing	1940		Boca Juniors
1916		Racing	1941		River Plate
1917		Racing	1942		River Plate
1918		Racing	1943		Boca Juniors
1919	AAF	Boca Juniors	1944		Boca Juniors
	Ama	Racing	1945		River Plate
1920	AAF	Boca Juniors	1946		San Lorenzo
	Ama	Racing	1947		River Plate
1921	AAF	Huracán	1948		Independiente
	Ama	River Plate	1949		Racing
1922	AAF	Huracán	1950		Racing
	Ama	Independiente	1951		Racing

1952		River Plate	1987–1988		Newell's Old Boys
1953		River Plate	1988–1989		Independiente
1954		Boca Juniors	1989–1990		River Plate
1955		River Plate	1990–1991		Newell's Old Boys
1956		River Plate	1991–1992	Ap	River Plate
1957		River Plate		Cl	Newell's Old Boys
1958		Racing	1992–1993	Ap	Boca Juniors
1959		San Lorenzo		Cl	Vélez Sarsfield
1960		Independiente	1993–1994	Ap	River Plate
1961		Racing Club		Cl	Independiente
1962		Boca Juniors	1994–1995	Ap	River Plate
1963		Independiente		Cl	San Lorenzo
1964		Boca Juniors	1995–1996	Ap	Vélez Sarsfield
1965		Boca Juniors		Cl	Vélez Sarsfield
1966		Racing	1996–1997	Ap	River Plate
1967	Met	Estudiantes de La Plata		Cl	River Plate
	Nac	Independiente	1997–1998	Ap	River Plate
1968	Met	San Lorenzo		Cl	Vélez Sarsfield
	Nac	Vélez Sarsfield	1998–1999	Ap	Boca Juniors
1969	Met	Chacarita Juniors		Cl	Boca Juniors
	Nac	Boca Juniors	1999–2000	Ap	River Plate
1970	Met	Independiente		Cl	River Plate
	Nac	Boca Juniors	2000–2001	Ap	Boca Juniors
1971	Met	Independiente		Cl	San Lorenzo
	Nac	Rosario Central	2001–2002	Ap	Boca Juniors
1972	Met	San Lorenzo		Cl	River Plate
	Nac	San Lorenzo	2002–2003	Ap	Independiente
1973	Met	Huracán		Cl	River Plate
	Nac	Rosario Central	2003–2004	Ap	Boca Juniors
1974	Met	Newell's Old Boys		Cl	River Plate
	Nac	San Lorenzo	2004–2005	Ap	Newell's Old Boys
1975	Met	River Plate		Cl	Vélez Sarsfield
	Nac	River Plate	2005–2006	Ap	Boca Juniors
1976	Met	Boca Juniors		Cl	Boca Juniors
	Nac	Boca Juniors	2006–2007	Ap	Estudiantes de La Plata
1977	Met	River Plate		Cl	San Lorenzo
	Nac	Independiente	2007–2008	Ap	Lanús
1978	Met	Quilmes		Cl	River Plate
	Nac	Independiente	2008–2009	Ap	Boca Juniors
1979	Met	River Plate		Cl	Vélez Sarsfield
	Nac	River Plate	2009–2010	Ap	Banfield
1980	Cam	River Plate		Cl	Argentinos Juniors
	Nac	Rosario Central	2010–2011	Ap	Estudiantes de La Plata
1981	Cam	Boca Juniors		Cl	Vélez Sarsfield
	Nac	River Plate	2011–2012	Ap	Boca Juniors
1982	Nac	Ferro Carril Oeste		Cl	Arsenal
	Cam	Estudiantes de La Plata	2012–2013	In	Vélez Sarsfield
1983	Nac	Estudiantes de La Plata		Fi	Newell's Old Boys
	Cam	Independiente		Cam	Vélez Sarsfield
1984	Nac	Ferro Carril Oeste	2013–2014	In	San Lorenzo
	Cam	Argentinos Juniors		Fi	River Plate
1985–1986		River Plate	2014		Racing
1986–1987		Rosario Central	2015		Boca Juniors

Notes

Between 1912 and 1914, there were two Argentinian championships run by the Asociación Argentina de Football (AAF) and the Federación Argentina de Football (FAF).

There was a further schism between 1919 and 1926 between the AAF and Asociación Amateurs de Football (Ama).

A professional league (pro) was established in 1931 and for four years ran alongside the amateur AAF league.

In 1936 three championships were awarded: the Copa de Honor (CdH), played between champions of the Copa Municipalidad de la Ciudad de Buenos Aires; the traditional championship (Cam); and the Copa de Oro (CdO), played between the traditional champions and the winners of the Copa de Honor.

Between 1967 and 1979 two championships were awarded, the Metropolitano (Met), for teams in or near Buenos Aires, and the Nacional (Nac), which also included teams from the provinces. Talleres of Córdoba were invited to join the Metropolitano in 1980, after which it became known simply as the Campeonato (Cam) until the return to a one-championship season in 1985–1986.

In 1990–1991 the season was split into two halves, Apertura (Ap) and Clausura (Cl). Initially, the winners of each played off for the championship, but from 1991 to 1992 two championships were awarded.

In 2012–2013 the Apertura and the Clausura were renamed the Inicial (In) and the Final (Fi), with the winners playing off for a third championship (Cam).

The playoff was abandoned in 2013–2014 and the structure changed again to produce a single champion each year.

COPA AMÉRICA

Year	Host	Winner	Runner-up
*1916	Argentina	**Uruguay**	Argentina
1917	Uruguay	**Uruguay**	Argentina
1919	Brazil	**Brazil**	Uruguay
1920	Chile	**Uruguay**	Argentina
1921	Argentina	**Argentina**	Brazil
1922	Brazil	**Brazil**	Paraguay
1923	Uruguay	**Uruguay**	Argentina
1924	Uruguay	**Uruguay**	Argentina
1925	Argentina	**Argentina**	Brazil
1926	Chile	**Uruguay**	Argentina
1927	Peru	**Argentina**	Uruguay
1929	Argentina	**Argentina**	Paraguay
*1935	Peru	**Uruguay**	Argentina
1937	Argentina	**Argentina**	Brazil
1939	Peru	**Peru**	Uruguay
*1941	Chile	**Argentina**	Uruguay
1942	Uruguay	**Uruguay**	Argentina
*1945	Chile	**Argentina**	Brazil
*1946	Argentina	**Argentina**	Brazil
1947	Ecuador	**Argentina**	Paraguay
1949	Brazil	**Brazil**	Paraguay
1953	Peru	**Paraguay**	Brazil
1955	Chile	**Argentina**	Chile
*1956	Uruguay	**Uruguay**	Chile
1957	Peru	**Argentina**	Brazil
1959	Argentina	**Argentina**	Brazil
*1959	Ecuador	**Uruguay**	Argentina
1963	Bolivia	**Bolivia**	Paraguay
1967	Uruguay	**Uruguay**	Argentina
1975	—	**Peru**	Colombia
1979	—	**Paraguay**	Chile
1983	—	**Uruguay**	Brazil
1987	Argentina	**Uruguay**	Chile
1989	Brazil	**Brazil**	Uruguay
1991	Chile	**Argentina**	Brazil
1993	Ecuador	**Argentina**	Mexico
1995	Uruguay	**Uruguay**	Brazil
1997	Bolivia	**Brazil**	Bolivia
1999	Paraguay	**Brazil**	Uruguay
2001	Colombia	**Colombia**	Mexico
2004	Peru	**Brazil**	Argentina
2007	Venezuela	**Brazil**	Argentina
2011	Argentina	**Uruguay**	Paraguay
2015	Chile	**Chile**	Argentina

Notes

Between 1975 and 1983, the tournament was played on a home-and-away basis with no fixed host.

*These tournaments are regarded as somehow "unofficial."

COPA LIBERTADORES WINNERS

1960	Peñarol		1988	Nacional
1961	Peñarol		1989	Atlético Nacional
1962	Santos		1990	Olimpia
1963	Santos		1991	Colo-Colo
1964	Independiente		1992	São Paulo
1965	Independiente		1993	São Paulo
1966	Peñarol		1994	Vélez Sarsfield
1967	Racing		1995	Grêmio
1968	Estudiantes de La Plata		1996	River Plate
1969	Estudiantes de La Plata		1997	Cruzeiro
1970	Estudiantes de La Plata		1998	Vasco da Gama
1971	Nacional		1999	Palmeiras
1972	Independiente		2000	Boca Juniors
1973	Independiente		2001	Boca Juniors
1974	Independiente		2002	Olimpia
1975	Independiente		2003	Boca Juniors
1976	Cruzeiro		2004	Once Caldas
1977	Boca Juniors		2005	São Paulo
1978	Boca Juniors		2006	Internacional
1979	Olimpia		2007	Boca Juniors
1980	Nacional		2008	LDU Quito
1981	Flamengo		2009	Estudiantes de La Plata
1982	Peñarol		2010	Internacional
1983	Grêmio		2011	Santos
1984	Independiente		2012	Corinthians
1985	Argentinos Juniors		2013	Atlético Mineiro
1986	River Plate		2014	San Lorenzo
1987	Peñarol		2015	River Plate

NOTES

Prologue: Utopias and Their Discontents, 1535–2016

1. Literally, "to these dirty faces, to these five shameless ones."

2. Argentinian grounds are generally divided into two sections: the *platea*, the seated area, which normally runs along the long sides, and the cheaper *popular*, a standing terrace usually located behind the goals.

3. The Argentinian league structure is forever being changed and is endlessly confusing, but between 1990–1991 and 2011–2012 each season was split into two championships—each team playing everybody else one time—the *apertura* (opening) and the *clausura* (closing). In that first season, the winners of the *apertura* and *clausura* played off for the title; thereafter, two championships were awarded each season.

4. The most farcical I witnessed were the clashes between police and waiters, all dressed in white shirts and black aprons, which had the air of a *Monty Python* sketch.

5. Bruce Chatwin's 1974 book *In Patagonia* is the encapsulation of that: traveling through the Argentinian South, he describes encounters with a series of misfits, dreamers, and eccentrics, many of whom made significant adjustments to their backstories to create a new life for themselves. The book marked Chatwin's own reinvention, as he abandoned his job at the *Sunday Times* to write it, and itself represented the reinvention of the whole notion of travel writing. It subsequently emerged that many of the episodes Chatwin recounts were themselves in some ways reinventions of his subjects' recollections.

6. I'm grateful to Guillem Balague for bringing Udenio's work to my attention.

Chapter 1: This English Game

1. Cited in Andres Campomar, *Golazo! A History of Latin American Football.*

2. This is something explored in detail by David Winner in *Those Feet*, but to take just one example, the Reverend Edward Thring, headmaster of Uppingham, insisted in a celebrated sermon that masturbation would lead to "early and dishonoured graves."

3. It's a line often attributed to Henry Kissinger, although I've found no evidence of his ever having said or written it.

4. Avellaneda is technically a separate city from Buenos Aires on the south side of the Riachuelo, although in practice it is these days effectively just another industrial district of the capital.

5. Since the home side included nine players from the Albion club, it is often said that it was not a true Uruguayan national team; if that argument is accepted, the first Argentina international took place in Montevideo on September 13 when they beat Uruguay 6–0.

Chapter 2: A Second Birth

1. A pseudonym for Ricardo Lorenzo Rodríguez.

Chapter 4: Argentinidad

1. Yrigoyen followed the teachings of German philosopher Karl Christian Friedrich Krause, who believed that God was the universe and that knowledge was to be attained through the inner self and its contact with God, which in part explains Yrigoyen's severe introversion.

2. The *bombacho* was a baggy-kneed trouser similar to the knickerbocker traditionally worn for horse riding.

3. *Asados* remain hugely popular in Argentina. They're barbecues, but the English term gives only the slightest indication of the social importance attached to the grilling of meat.

4. Wilson, a center-forward who joined Chelsea from Dunfermline in 1921, always wore a glove to protect his hand, which had been shattered by shrapnel during the war.

5. *Mate* is caffeine-rich drink prepared by steeping dried leaves in hot water. Like the *asado*, the significance of *mate* lies in its social role. It's traditionally drunk through a metal straw from a calabash that is passed around those sharing the drink.

Chapter 6: The *Rioplatense* Supremacy

1. This was published in Spanish as *Fútbol y patria*, but all citations in this text are taken from his PhD thesis, "Football and *Patria*: Sport, National Narratives and Identities in Argentina, 1920–98."

2. Gardel had been born to an unmarried laundress, Berthe Gardes, in Toulouse in 1890. Fearing the stigma of bringing up a child born out of wedlock, she fled to Buenos Aires, living in Abasto while her son went to school in Almagro. His talent soon emerged as he sang at bars and private parties. In 1920 he applied for Uruguayan citizenship, claiming at the consulate in Buenos Aires that he'd been born in Tacuarembó in 1887. His precise motive remains unclear, but the most persuasive theory is that he was looking to avoid any difficulties with the authorities in France, where he was about to tour, having failed to fulfill his legal obligation to register with the French military during the First World War. He was issued with an Argentinian identity card that listed him as a Uruguayan national, and only in 1923 did he become an Argentinian citizen. When he was killed in a plane crash in 1935, Gardel was probably the biggest celebrity Argentina had ever known. Given the nature of the emerging nation and its search for *argentinidad*, there seems something appropriate about the fact that he had been an Argentinian for only the final quarter of his life.

3. Such a problem were café-owning players that the Belgian federation had detailed regulations about them, stipulating that players could run cafés only if their parents had owned one for more than five years. Braine had opened a café in December 1929, shortly before the rules were brought in and, rather than sell, chose to move to Sparta Prague, his proposed transfer to Clapton Orient having fallen through for the lack of a work permit.

4. There were two: Francisco Olazar, a defender in the great Racing side of the second decade of the century, and Juan José Tramutola, who, as the official technical director, remains the youngest-ever World Cup coach, 27 years and 267 days old when Argentina played their first game against France.

Chapter 7: Days of Glory

1. The team known as la Máquina was often at the time referred by its diminutive "la Máquinita." Subsequently "la Máquinita"—the Little Machine—came to refer to the River side of a decade later that played in a similar style to la Máquina without ever quite hitting the same heights.

Chapter 8: The Coming of Professionalism

1. The governing body had resumed the name Asociación del Fútbol Argentino in 1936.

Chapter 9: The Rise of River

1. Against a Facultad de Medicina side featuring Bernardo Houssay, who would go on to win a Nobel Prize in 1947 for his discovery of the role of pituitary hormones in regulating blood sugar in mammals.

Chapter 10: Modernity and the Budapest Butcher

1. In *Régi gólok, edzősorsok* (Goals of the past, fate of coaches), the memoirs of György Orth and Béla Guttmann compiled by Tibor Hámori.

2. The fates of Hirschl's first wife and child are far from clear. Gabriela believes they died from tuberculosis, probably before Hirschl left Hungary, although it's possible Hirschl and his first wife had effectively separated before she died.

3. Banfield's stadium is named after him.

4. His middle name, inappropriately enough, was Inocencio.

5. Former Boca Juniors center-forward Domingo Tarasconi, a legend of the amateur era, was another.

Chapter 11: The Knights of Anguish

1. Boca players of the early sixties seem to have a strange hang-up about fishing, as though they saw it as an activity that was somehow beneath them. "I have a yacht and like sailing," Antonio Rattin said. "You know, go out for a couple of days, then come back. Mind you, just sailing, not fishing. But if I stay overnight, I'll throw some bait over the side, and the next morning I'll see if I've caught anything." This perhaps—it's only a tentative theory—is linked to the oddity of Argentinian cuisine being almost entirely focused on beef, despite its having a vast coastline and abundant supply of fish. Many of the Italian immigrants who settled there, from which Boca drew the bulk of their support, had been fishermen at home, and so there was a latent association of fish with poverty. In the New World, beef, the rich man's food, was plentiful, so why go back to fish?

2. Xeneizes is a nickname for Boca derived from the Genoese dialect for the Ligurian word *zeneize*, meaning "Genoese"; many of the club's early fan base were immigrants from Genoa.

3. The term literally means "ours"; its precise derivation is disputed, but it's understood to mean a style of play based on individual skill and self-expression.

Chapter 12: The Rise of Juan Perón

1. The other two books were Plutarch's *Lives* and Lord Chesterfield's letters to his son.

2. The term has been the subject of much debate. It originates from Victor Hugo's 1861 novel *Les Miserables*, where it is used pejoratively by French Bourbons of Spanish social revolutionaries, comparing them unfavorably to the Sans Culottes of the French Revolution. In Argentina it was initially used as a sneer by the middle class, but was soon appropriated. There is no agreement on whether those in the Plaza de Mayo on October 17, 1945, removed their shirts because it was so hot or whether they were too poor to own shirts. Perón named the train he used for his subsequent election campaign *El Decamisado*.

3. Robert D. Crassweller, *Perón and the Enigmas of Argentina*.

4. Heleno was arguably the greatest forward of his age, but World War II denied him a chance to prove himself at World Cups in 1942 and 1946, and by 1950 his lifestyle had begun to sap his talents. He drank; smoked and gambled heavily; was addicted to ether, which he would inhale from a soaked handkerchief; and was an inveterate womanizer, even, it was improbably rumored, having an affair with Eva Perón during an ill-starred stint at Boca. Having succumbed to syphilis, he died in an asylum at the age of thirty-nine.

5. Méndez was one of the three subjects of the 1949 film *Con los mismos colores* (With the same colors), which details the careers of Méndez, Mario Boyé, and Alfredo Di Stéfano from the barrio to the first division. It's tempting to read significance into the fact that when the three heroes are reunited to play for the national team, their opponent is never specified: in the isolated world of Argentinian soccer, it didn't matter—there was simply Argentina and the rest.

6. Argentina's bid was scuppered by the Chilean delegation, who voted for Melbourne because, legend has it, they'd been to Buenos Aires many times before and wanted to visit somewhere new.

7. Sergio Levinsky, "The Cult of the *Pibe*."

8. Evita was Perón's second wife. He had married his first, Aurelia Tizón, nicknamed "Potota," in 1929, two months after the death of his father. She died of cancer of the uterus in 1938, at the age of thirty-six. Remarkably, Enrique Pavón Pereyra's 1952 biography of

Perón, which became the standard work, makes no reference to her, presumably because it was felt that Potota's existence somehow diminished the myth of Evita.

Chapter 13: El Dorado
1. Carl Worswick, "The Ball and the Gun."

Chapter 15: Our Way
1. Argentina is obsessed with dedicating a day to various professions. Those who work in pizza and pasta restaurants, for instance, are celebrated on January 12, brewers on January 19, airport security police on February 22, decorators and window dressers on April 12, journalists on June 7, cartographers on June 26, historians on July 1, hairdressers on August 25, and referees and auctioneers on October 11. In total there are more than 150 officially recognized days.

Chapter 16: The Zenith and Beyond
1. Although he insisted he was Catholic and said he believed in "the words of Christ," Perón also said that he rejected the "rites" of the church because they had been "made by men"—an argument he used to try to weaken the political power of the church while apparently oblivious to the fact that he was essentially defining himself as a Protestant.
2. Crassweller notes that Perón's relationship with Rivas was "more fatherly than concupiscent," and he seems generally in his relations with women to have sought companionship rather than eroticism, but still it cannot be denied that "Perón . . . took advantage of an inexperienced young adolescent . . . and there was certainly a carnal element in the liaison."
3. The Casa Rosada—literally, Pink House—is the executive mansion and office (but not the residence) of the president of Argentina. Located at the east end of the Plaza de Mayo, it was officially inaugurated in 1898 under the presidency of Julio Roca.
4. The term originally referred to local warlords but by the twentieth century had come to mean any strongman leader.

Chapter 17: The Last of the Angels
1. From the forties onward, Argentinian clubs would gather their players in *concentraciós* (either training camps or hotels) on the evening before games to try to ensure they were focused on soccer.

Chapter 20: The Mouse's Nest
1. Sanfilippo is far from alone among his generation of Argentinians in having a touching faith in the reliability of English institutions.

Chapter 22: The Consecration of Pragmatism
1. *Catenaccio* was a style of play developed in Italy in the fifties and sixties that featured a sweeper operating behind the defensive line. Building on the *verrou* first practiced by Karl Rappan at Servette of Geneva, it was pioneered by Gipo Viani at Salernitana—supposedly after he saw fishing boats using a reserve net to catch the fish that had slipped by the main net—and taken to new levels of sophistication, first by Nereo Rocco at AC Milan and then by Helenio Herrera at Inter.
2. The stadium, just a couple of hundred yards down the road from Racing's el Cilindro in Avellaneda, was originally constructed in 1928 and was the first in South America built of cement. The name Doble Visera relates to the "double visor" of the twin roofs.

Chapter 24: El Caudillo
1. He was six foot one. Rattin was two inches taller.
2. The Hindú Club was founded in 1919 by alumni of the La Salle college, whose drama club was known as the "Hindustánicos." It's now a general sporting club best known for its rugby division.

Chapter 26: A Peculiar Glory

1. A traditional South American confectionery, usually a sandwich of two biscuits joined by a sweet paste. They were supposedly introduced to Spain by Arab general Musa ibn Nusair in 712.

2. A musical form found across South America (and influential on tango) but characteristic of Uruguay. Based around rhythmic drumming, it originated with African slaves and is central to the carnival held annually in Montevideo.

Chapter 27: Scorning the Path of Roses

1. An obscure term translating as "inspector" that was used for a time for the de facto president of the federation.

Chapter 30: The Little Pigeon

1. Estudiantes, of course, had won the league four years earlier, but La Plata, thirty-five miles southeast of the city of Buenos Aires, is the capital of Buenos Aires Province.

2. The Organización Canalla Anti-Lepra, founded in September 1966, is a secretive Central fan organization that—jokingly—compares itself to the Masons.

Chapter 32: The Return of Perón

1. That said, some of his arguments about the macho nature of Argentinian society, in particular his observations on the obsession with anal sex, read very strangely now.

2. As Naipaul details, the occult enjoyed a surge in popularity in the seventies. In May 1972, for instance, a Buenos Aires church advertised a special mass against *el mal de ojo*, the evil eye, and attracted a congregation of more than five thousand. "The country," Naipaul wrote, "is being swept by the new enthusiastic cult of *espiritismo*, a purely native affair of mediums and mass trances and miraculous cures, which claims the patronage of Jesus Christ and Mahatma Gandhi." In an increasingly violent world, perhaps the appeal of a pacifist movement is understandable: the *espiritistas* preached reincarnation and the perfectibility of the spirit and believed purgatory and hell were being lived on earth at that moment, the only possible escape being rebirth on a more evolved planet.

3. *Dulce de leche* is a sweet spread popular across Latin America prepared by slowly heating sweetened milk. It's said that it was invented in Cañuelas in 1829, when General Lavalle arrived at the camp of General Manuel de Rosas to negotiate a treaty to try to end the civil war in Buenos Aires Province. Finding Rosas absent, the exhausted Lavalle lay down in a tent to sleep. While he was there, he was discovered by a woman who had been heating milk and sugar for men in the camp. She didn't know Lavalle had been invited and, startled to find the enemy, ran off to summon soldiers. At that Rosas arrived, and, in the confusion, the woman forgot about the milk and sugar being heated over a fire. When she finally went back to it, she found the milk had congealed into a rich brown paste: *dulce de leche*.

Chapter 33: Of Heroes and Chickens

1. Five times in the seven years before the championship split into Metropolitano and Nacional in 1967 and six times afterward.

2. So-called because of his bright-yellow ("mustard-colored") hair.

3. Taverna was the first player to be suspended in Argentina for drug use. The second, in 1980, was the great Independiente and Boca defender Pancho Sá, banned for three months after testing positive for ephedrine.

Chapter 34: The Age of the Devils

1. Pastoriza, the player Rattín had punched on the tour of Italy in 1966, was such a legend at the club that, after his death from a heart condition in 2004, his name was woven into the team jersey just underneath the Umbro logo because forward Jairo Castillo kept getting booked for celebrating goals by removing his top to reveal a T-shirt paying tribute.

2. Veiga was a noted youth coach who had been part of the Independiente side that won the 1948 championship during the players' strike.

3. The Brazilian was a highly respected official who took charge of the 1986 World Cup final.

4. It's a skill at which Juan Román Riquelme excelled, but the most famous example, gallingly for Argentinians, is probably by a Brazilian, Pelé waiting for Carlos Alberto's overlap before laying the ball off for him to score Brazil's fourth in the 1970 World Cup final.

5. The father of Diego Forlán. Pablo's father-in-law, Diego's grandfather, Juan Carlos Corazzo, was also a Uruguay international: all three generations played on sides that won the Copa América.

Chapter 35: Lorenzo and the Boca Fulfillment

1. Zanabria probably meant the term in its modern, pejorative sense of an "act of witchcraft," but it was initially used in the nineteenth century to refer to any non-Abrahamic religion in Brazil.

Chapter 37: Glory in a Time of Terror

1. That said, the mean temperature of Neuquén in March is sixty-five degrees, only seven degrees cooler than Buenos Aires.

2. Sirloin steak.

Chapter 38: The Nativity

1. Weirdly, when I went there in March 2012 for a Copa Libertadores game against Emelec, the pedestrianized main street from the station to the stadium was dominated by a cutout perhaps thirty or forty feet high not of Maradona, or even another Lanús-born Argentina international such as Hector Enrique or Gustavo López, but of Glen Johnson, surely one of the most implausible advertising campaigns Adidas has ever come up with.

2. During a rally at Haymarket Square in Chicago on May 4, 1886, calling for the introduction of an eight-hour workday and in support of demonstrators killed by police at protests the previous day, a dynamite bomb was thrown at police, who returned fire. Seven police officers and at least four civilians were killed. Eight anarchists were convicted of conspiracy, and despite there being no evidence any had actually thrown the bomb, seven were sentenced to death. Four were hanged in November 1887, two had their sentences commuted, and one committed suicide in jail, setting off a blasting cap in his mouth that blew off half his face; it took him six hours to die. Six years later, the new governor of Illinois, John Peter Altgeld, pardoned the three surviving defendants and criticized the trial. The incident is regarded as having led to the celebration of May 1 as an international day of workers' rights.

3. A record subsequently taken by Sergio Agüero, who was fifteen years and thirty-five days when he made his Independiente debut in July 2003.

4. Taken at face value, the church is perhaps best described as a syncretic merging of Catholicism with celebrity worship, although there is an air of parody about it ("Our Diego, who is on field, / Hallowed be thy left hand . . . ") that suggests the church is intended more as a lighthearted tribute than anything else, however seriously its leaders insist they should be taken. "I have a rational religion, and that's the Catholic Church," said one of its founders, Alejandro Verón, "and I have a religion passed on through my heart, passion, and that's Diego Maradona." What the church makes clear is how readily the veneration of the *pibe* fits with preexisting Catholic doctrine and iconography.

Chapter 39: The Unlikeliest Champions

1. There were twenty-one teams in the Metropolitano that year, so each team played forty matches, with two weeks when they would sit out a round of fixtures.

Chapter 40: The Pride of the Nation

1. Escudero left Chacarita for Vélez in 1979, but his senior career was relatively modest. He played more than one hundred games for Unión de Santa Fe and Rosario Central, but was never capped by the senior national team.

2. The "*barra brava*" are Argentina's organized fan groups.

3. The Argentinian name for the Falklands.

4. The *Belgrano* was bought by Argentina from the United States in 1951. It had previously been known as the USS *Phoenix* and had survived the attack on Pearl Harbor in 1941. Its sinking prompted huge controversy, with many critics in both Argentina and the United Kingdom pointing out that the ship was outside the two-hundred-mile exclusion zone around the Falklands. The Argentinian Navy, though, acknowledged that following a warning cabled by the British government to the Argentinian Embassy in Switzerland on April 23, nine days before the sinking, the whole South Atlantic had been regarded by both sides as a theater of war. The *Belgrano*'s captain, Héctor Bonzo, always accepted the attack as a legitimate act, saying he was traveling west to head to a more tactically advantageous position to the south. It's true that a peace plan had been proposed by the Peruvian president fourteen hours before the sinking, but the Thatcher government always maintained it was not aware of that until after the attack.

5. The difficulty of checking precisely what each channel broadcast and when makes it impossible to be absolutely certain he was actually the first, but certainly one of the first people to offer his opinion on the cease-fire was Southampton manager and former guardsman Lawrie McMenemy, improvising awkwardly from his position as a pundit when the BBC cut from the live action to go back to the studio to deliver the breaking news.

6. His maternal grandmother, who had married a Welsh immigrant, was a Falkland Islander.

Chapter 42: Maradona in Europe

1. Showing an utter lack of contrition, Goikoetxea reveled in his "Butcher of Bilbao" nickname and kept the boot with which he'd inflicted the injury in a display case in his living room.

2. Although hours of film were shot, the reels disappeared and have never been found.

Chapter 43: Optimism and the Libertadores

1. Soriano regularly referred to soccer in his work. His short story "El penal más largo del mundo" (The longest penalty in the world), published in 1995, two years before his death, tells the story of a long-deferred penalty that settled a championship in 1958. I discuss it at length in *The Outsider*.

Chapter 44: His Finest Hour

1. Ruggeri didn't actually move to Real Madrid until 1989; in the buildup to 1986 he was still at River Plate. By the time of the 1990 World Cup, fourteen of Argentina's twenty-two-man squad were based overseas.

2. Quite aside from the specifics of that game, Valdano had been named overseas player of the year in Spain that season after helping Real Madrid to the title.

Chapter 45: Burying the Chicken

1. They would go on to lose in the final the following year as well, going down in a playoff to Peñarol. Maybe what the *gallinas* had needed all along was to play another team that were even bigger chokers than they were.

2. Funes had joined earlier that year from the Bogotá side Millonarios, where he became such a favorite in his two seasons at the club that one of their ultra groups is known as the *Barra del Búfalo*. After River he played for Olympiacos and Vélez before being forced to retire because of ill health in 1990. He died of a heart attack in January 1992, at just twenty-eight. The stadium in his hometown of San Luis is named after him.

Chapter 47: Moral Champions Again

1. López Rega died from diabetes while in prison awaiting trial in 1989. Suárez Mason was convicted of forty-three murders and twenty-three kidnappings (including of babies) but was pardoned in 1990 by Carlos Menem. He fled to California but was extradited again in

1995 to face charges of kidnapping minors. He was placed under house arrest—as is usual in Argentina for prisoners over the age of seventy—but was reimprisoned in 2004 for breaking the terms of his detention. He died the following year, at eighty-one, having been sentenced in absentia to life imprisonment by Italian courts for the murder of eight Italian Argentinians and facing further charges in Argentina relating to two hundred kidnappings, thirty murders, and the sale of babies of political prisoners.

2. At times Menem seemed to use the presidency as a form of wish fulfillment. In 1998, for instance, he played in a five-a-side match featuring British sports minister Tony Banks and Bobby Charlton. "I found him to be quite useful on the ball," Charlton noted in his autobiography.

3. Supposedly because the number written in Roman numerals, xvii, could be rearranged to read vixi—I have lived—which, by analogy with Cicero's announcement of the execution of the Catiline conspirators, "Vixerunt," could be taken to mean, "My life is over." So seriously is the superstition taken that Renault's R17 model was released in Italy as R177.

Chapter 49: Tabárez and the Boca Revival

1. Clubs who won them always proudly list the Supercopas and the Recopas among their international titles, but it's debatable how much they were really worth. The Supercopa was organized by Conmebol and ran between 1988 and 1997 before being discontinued for the Copa Mercosur, a forerunner of the Copa Sudamericana. It featured past winners of the Libertadores and was dominated by Argentinian clubs who won six of the ten editions. The Recopa is a one-off tie that was played between the winners of that season's Libertadores and Supercopa, sometimes over two legs, sometimes over one in a neutral venue (Boca's 1990 win over the Colombian side Atlético Nacional, for instance, was played in Miami). It was contested between 1988 and 1998 and reinstituted in 2003 as a fixture between the winners of the Libertadores and the Sudamericana.

2. Jozić had been the coach of the Yugoslavia side that won the Under-20 World Cup in Chile in 1987. With captain Aleksandar Đorđević suspended, five key players injured, Boban Babunski omitted because of a contract dispute, and Siniša Mihajlović, Alen Boksić, and Vladimir Jugović retained by their clubs, almost nobody gave them a chance, but a side featuring Igor Štimac, Robert Jarni, Robert Prosinečki, Zvonimir Boban, and Predrag Mijatović won the tournament playing scintillating soccer. With a large Yugoslav expat community in Santiago, there was also plenty of fun to be had off the field, Štimac meeting the reigning Miss Chile, herself of Yugoslav descent, early in the tournament and refusing Jozić's demands to curtail his social life. Jozić ended up enjoying himself so much that he returned in 1989 when his contract with the Yugoslav youth setup came to an end and led Colo-Colo to a hat trick of Chilean titles.

Chapter 50: The Fatal Urine of Foxborough

1. The fake penis was displayed in a museum in Buenos Aires but went missing during a nationwide tour in December 2003 and has never been recovered.

2. The other occasion was in 1985, when France beat Uruguay 2–0.

3. "Cholo" itself is a much-debated term referring to somebody of mixed indigenous and European blood.

4. He never would have fitted in at Boca.

5. An early indication of the sartorial flamboyance that has developed to the point that he now regularly appears as a pundit on Argentinian television wearing a silk cravat.

Chapter 54: The Lure of the Past

1. Roa was a Seventh-Day Adventist and a vegetarian, which earned him the nickname "Lechuga" (Lettuce). In 1999, at the age of thirty, he left soccer to go on a religious retreat, refusing to discuss a new contract with his club, Mallorca, because he believed the end of the world was imminent. "The year 2000 is going to be difficult," he said. "In the world, there is

war, hunger, plague, much poverty, floods. I can assure you that those people who don't have a spiritual connection with God and the type of life that he wants will be in trouble." A little under a year later, he returned to Mallorca, but never recaptured his earlier form.

Chapter 56: The Crash
1. Although that is still a remarkable proportion of the electorate, it should be noted that voting is compulsory in Argentina.

Chapter 57: The Second Coming
1. So heavy on cheese, in fact, that the few "Italian-style" pizzerias, such as the Piola chain, tend to be full of western European expats and tourists nodding sagely and insisting, "*This* is pizza."

Chapter 58: The Ascent from the Abyss
1. Five months later, their coach Fernando Montoya was left paralyzed after being shot in an armed robbery and was forced to give up coaching to work as a journalist.

Chapter 59: The Growth of the Legend
1. Their fortunes could hardly have been more contrasting. While Alcántara went on to become the club's record goal scorer, Babangida never played a competitive game for Barcelona, won only one international cap for Nigeria, and ended up drifting through Metalurh Donetsk, Olympiakos, Apollon Limassol, Kuban Krasnodar, Mainz 05, Vitesse, and the Austrian second-flight side Kapfenberger SV before retiring in 2012.

Chapter 61: The Ecstasy of Gold
1. The other two were Mascherano and the Anderlecht defender Nicolás Pareja, who were only a year too old anyway.

Chapter 62: The End of the Affair
1. Rumors he'd had a fling with Sandra Bullock turned out to have been a joke cooked up by Schiavi and a friend, apparently to expose the gullibility of a media that eagerly reported the story as fact.

Chapter 64: Distrust and Short-Termism
1. Figures from the US Department of Agriculture cited in the *Economist*.
2. After a two-year legal battle, agreement was finally reached in February 2014 when the Argentinian government issued Repsol, which was backed by the United States and the European Union, with an issue of bonds worth $5 billion.
3. According to *La Nación*, the annual payment was supposed to be increased annually by an amount based on the average cost of cable subscription, but, despite rampant inflation, it appears that happened only once, so by mid-2015 the government was paying 823 million pesos per year.

Chapter 65: Home Discomforts
1. *Chori*, short for *chorizo*, is used in Argentina to refer to any coarse meat sausage, usually pork. It is commonly grilled outside of stadiums and served in bread—a *choripán*.

Chapter 66: The Little Witch, the Pope, and the Gleeful Chickens
1. He has a love of sport in general, encouraging the Vatican cricket team and accepting a cap from the team I play for before we played the Vatican side in Rome in 2015.
2. Francis didn't just have a positive effect over San Lorenzo's results. At the end of October 2013, Sunderland, having failed to win a league match in six months, sent their club chaplain to Rome with a team shirt to seek Francis's blessing for their next match, the derby

NOTES | 395

against Newcastle. He gave it and Sunderland won 2–1, the winner being scored late by Fabio Borini, who, appropriately enough, had moved to England from Roma.

Chapter 67: The Ongoing Drought
1. All figures are taken from Ken Early's piece on Slate.com.
2. It would have been six had Sami Khedira not injured himself in the warm-up. That Germany Under-21 squad also included Ashkan Dejagah and Fabian Johnson, who played, respectively, for Iran and the United States at the 2014 World Cup, and the Poland international Sebastian Boenisch. It seems telling of the respective fortunes of the two nations that while six of Germany's squad went on to win the World Cup, seven of the England squad they beat in the final went on to play for Sunderland.

Chapter 68: The Eternal Laurels
1. Figures are taken from 2013.

BIBLIOGRAPHY

Alabarces, Pablo. "Football and *Patria*: Sports, National Narratives and Identities in Argentina, 1920–1998." PhD diss., University of Brighton, 2001.

Alabarces, Pablo, Ramiro Coelho, and Juan Sanguinetti. "Treacheries and Traditions in Argentinian Football Styles: The Story of Estudiantes de la Plata." In *Fear and Loathing in World Football*, edited by Gary Armstrong and Richard Giulanotti. Berg, 2001.

Alberdi, Juan Bautista. *Bases y puntos de partida para la oragnización polítca de la república Argentina*. La Cultura Argentine, 1915.

Amez de Paz, Eduardo. *La vida por el fútbol*. Self-published, 2002.

Archetti, Eduardo. *Masculinities: Football, Polo, and the Tango in Argentina*. Global Issues, 1999.

———. "Masculinity and Football: The Formation of National Identity in Argentina." In *Game Without Frontiers: Football, Identity and Modernity*, edited by Richard Giulianotti and John Williams. Arena, 1994.

Ardiles, Ossie. *Ossie's Dream*. Bantam, 2009.

Arlt, Roberto. *Nuevas aguafuertes porteñas*. Librería Hachette, 1960.

Armstrong, Gary, and Richard Giulanotti, eds. *Entering the Field: New Perspectives on World Football*. Berg, 1997.

———. *Fear and Loathing in World Football*. Berg, 2001.

Assaf, Roberto, and Clóvis Martins. *Almanaque do Flamengo*. Abril, 2001.

———. *Campeonato Carioca: 96 anos de história, 1902–1997*. Irradiação Cultural, 1997.

Auyero, Javier. *Poor People's Politics: Peronist Survival Networks and the Legacy of Evita*. Duke University Press, 2001.

Balagué, Guillem. *Messi*. Orion, 2013.

Barnade, Oscar, and Waldemar Iglesias. *Mitos y creencias del fútbol Argentino*. Al Arco, 2006.

Bayer, Osvaldo. *Fútbol Argentino*. Editorial Sudamericana, 1990.

Ben-Ghiat, Ruth. *Fascist Modernities: Italy, 1922–45*. University of California Press, 2001.

Bionda, Miguel. *Historia del fútbol platense*. Laboratorio Pincharrata, 1944.

Borges, Jorge Luís. *Labyrinths*. Penguin, 1970.

———. *On Argentina*. Penguin, 2010.

Borges, Jorge Luís, with Adolfo Bioy-Casares. *Crónicas de Bustis Domecq*. Editorial Losada, 1967.

Borges, Jorge Luís, with Margarita Guerrero. *El "Martín Fierro."* Editorial Columba, 1965.

Bottenburg, Maarten van, and Beverley Jackson. *Global Games*. University of Illinois Press, 2001.

Bowler, Dave. *Winning Isn't Everything: A Biography of Sir Alf Ramsey*. Victor Gollancz, 1998.

Brera, Gianni. *Herrera e Moratti*. Limina, 1997.

———. *Storia critica del calico Italiano*. Tascaballi Bompiani, 1978.

Brest, Enrique C. Romero, Alberto R. Dallo, and Simón Silvestrini. "Los deportes y la educación fisica en la república Argentina." In *Geschichte der Leibesübungen*, edited by Horst Überhorst, 6:847–848. Bartels & Wernitz, 1971–1989.

Burns, Jimmy. *Barça: A People's Passion*. Bloomsbury, 1999.

———. *Hand of God: The Life of Diego Maradona*. Bloomsbury, 1996.

———. *The Land That Lost Its Heroes*. Bloomsbury, 1987.

Campomar, Andreas. *Golazo! A History of Latin American Football*. Quercus, 2014.

Castro, Ruy. *Garrincha: The Triumph and Tragedy of Brazil's Forgotten Footballing Hero*. Yellow Jersey, 2005.

Chaine, Federico. *Matador: Biografía de Mario Alberto Kempes*. Carena, 2003.

Charlton, Bobby. *The Autobiography: My England Years*. Headline, 2008.

Chatwin, Bruce. *In Patagonia*. Vintage, 1998.

Ciria, Alberto. "From Soccer to War in Argentina: Preliminary Notes on Sport-as-Politics Under a Military Regime (1976–82)." In *Latin America and the Caribbean: Geopolitics, Development and Culture*, edited by Arch R. M. Ritter. Canadian Association of Latin American and Caribbean Studies, 1984.

Colasimone, Dan. "The Grand Griguol." *Blizzard*, no. 9 (June 2013).

Collier, Simon. *Tango! The Dance, the Song, the Story*. Thames and Hudson, 1997.

Cortázar, Julio. *End of the Game, and Other Stories*. Pantheon, 1963.

Craig, Jim. *A Lion Looks Back*. John Donald, 1998.

Crassweller, Robert D. *Perón and the Enigmas of Argentina*. W. W. Norton, 1987.

Crawley, Eduardo. *A House Divided: Argentina, 1880–1980*. St. Martin's Press, 1985.

Crerand, Paddy. *Never Turn the Other Cheek*. HarperSport, 2007.

Crow, John A. *The Epic of Latin America*. University of California Press, 1992.

Csaknády, Jenő. *Die Béla Guttmann Story: Hinter den Kulissen des Weltfussballs*. Verlag Blintz-Dohány, 1964.

Darío, Ruben. *Prosa política*. Mundo Latino, 1911.

De Bonafini, Hebe, and Matilde Sánchez. *Historias de vida*. Fraterna, 1985.

Del Frade, Carlos. *Central, Ñuls, la ciudad goleada, fútbol y lavado de dinero*. Self-published, 2005.

Dénes, Tamás, Pál Peterdi, Zoltán Rochy, and József Selmeci, eds. *Kalandozó magyar labdarúgók*. Aréna, 1999.

Diéguez, Luis, and Ariel Scher. *El libro de oro del mundial*. Clarín, 1998.

Di Giano, Roberto. *Fútbol y cultura política en la Argentina: Identidades en crisis*. Leviatán, 2005.

———. *El fútbol y transformaciones del Peronismo*. Leviatán, 2006.

Di Salvo, Alfred Luis. *Anécdotas del superclásico*. Proa Amerian, 2011.

Downing, David. *England v. Argentina: World Cups and Other Small Wars*. Portrait, 2003.

Fabbri, Alejandro. *El nacimiento de una passion: Historia de los clubes de fútbol*. Capital Intelectual, 2006.

———. *Nuevas historias negras del fútbol Argentino, 1*. Capital Intelectual, 2008.

———. *Nuevas historias negras del fútbol Argentino, 2*. Capital Intelectual, 2010.

Feitlowitz, Marguerite. *A Lexicon of Terror: Argentina and the Legacies of Torture*. Oxford University Press, 1998.

Ferns, H. S. *The Argentine Republic, 1516–1971*. Barnes & Noble, 1973.

Foot, John. *Calcio: A History of Italian Football*. Fourth Estate, 2006.

Foster, Kevin. *Lost Worlds: Latin America and the Imagining of the West*. Pluto, 2009.

Freddi, Cris. *Complete Book of the World Cup 2002*. CollinsWillow, 2002.

Frydenberg, Julio. *Historia social del fútbol: Del amateurismo a la profesionalización*. Siglo XXI, 2011.

Galeano, Eduardo. *Football in Sun and Shadow*. Fourth Estate, 1997.

Gillespie, Richard. *Soldiers of Perón: Argentina's Montoneros*. Oxford University Press, 1982.

Giulianotti, Richard. *Football: A Sociology of the Global Game*. Polity, 1999.

Giulianotti, Richard, and John Williams, eds. *Game Without Frontiers: Football, Identity and Modernity*. Arena, 1994.

Glanville, Brian. *The Story of the World Cup*. Faber and Faber, 2001.

Goldblatt, David. *The Ball Is Round: A Global History of Football*. Viking, 2006.

Güiraldes, Ricardo. *Don Segundo Sombra*. 1926. Reprint, Letras Hispanicas, 1988.

Hennessy, Alistair, and John King, eds. *The Land the England Lost: Argentina and Britain, a Special Relationship*. British Academic Press, 1992.

Hernández, José. *Martín Fierro*. Clasicos Universales, 2001. First published as *El gaucho Martín Fierro* (1872) and *La vuelta de Martín Fierro* (1879).

Herrera, Helenio. *La mia vita*. Mondo Sport, 1964.

Hunter, Graham. *Barça: The Making of the Greatest Team in the World*. BackPage Press, 2011.

Iwanczuk, Jorge. *Historia del fútbol amateur en la Argentina*. Autores Editores, 1995.

Jones, Charles A. "British Capital in Argentina History: Structures, Rhetoric and Change." In *The Land That England Lost: Argentina and Britain, a Special Relationship*, edited by Alistair Hennessy and John King. British Academic Press, 1992.

Kelly, David. *The Ruling Few: The Human Background to Diplomacy*. Hollis & Carter, 1952.

Kelly, Sir Robert. *Celtic*. Hay, Nisbet, and Miller, 1971.

Knoll, Guillermo. *Historias seleccionadas*. Al Arco, 2006.

Kuper, Simon. *Football Against the Enemy*. Orion, 1994.

Kuper, Simon, and Marcela Mora y Araujo, eds. *Perfect Pitch: Dirt*. Headline, 1999.

Levinsky, Sergio. "The Cult of the *Pibe*." *Blizzard*, no. 12 (March 2014).

Lorente, Rafael. *Di Stefano: Cuenta di su vida*. Imprenta Sáez, 1954.

Lorenzo, Ricardo (Borocotó). *25 años en el deporte*. Atlántida, 1946.

Lowenthal, Abraham F., and J. Samuel Fitch. *Armies and Politics in Latin America*. Holmes and Meier, 1986.

Lugones, Leopoldo. *El payador*. Otero, 1916.

Lynch, John. *Argentina Dictator: Juan Manuel de Rosas, 1829–51*. Oxford University Press, 1981.

Mangan, J. A. *Athleticism in the Victorian and Edwardian School: The Emergence and Consolidation of an Educational Ideology*. Cambridge University Press, 1981.

Maradona, Diego, with Daniel Arcucci and Ernesto Cherquis Bialo. *El Diego*. Translated by Marcela Mora y Araujo. Yellow Jersey, 2005.

Martin, Simon. *Football and Fascism: The National Game Under Mussolini*. Berg, 2004.

Martínez, Tomás Eloy. *Santa Evita*. Alfred A. Knopf, 1996.

Martínez Estrada, Ezequiel. *X-ray of the Pampa*. University of Texas Press, 1977.

Mason, Tony. *Passion of the People? Football in South America*. Verso, 1995.

Mazzoni, Tomás. *História do futebol no Brasil, 1894–1950*. Leia, 1950.

McKinstry, Leo. *Sir Alf*. HarperSport, 2006.

Melhuus, Marit, and Kristi Anne Stolen, eds. *Machos, Mistresses, Madonnas*. Verso, 1996.

Mendelevich, Pablo. *El final*. Ediciones B, 2010.

Menéndez, Eugenio. *Almirante Lacoste: ¿Quién mató al General Actis?* El Cid, 1984.

Menotti, César Luis. *Como ganamos la Copa del Mundo*. El Gráfico, 1978.

Menotti, César Luis, and Ángel Cappa. *Fútbol sin trampa*. Muchnik, 1986.

Mill, John Stuart. *On Liberty*. 1859. Reprint, Longman, 2007.

Miller, Rory, and Liz Crolley, eds. *Football in the Americas: Fútbol, Futebol, Soccer*. Institute for the Study of the Americas, 2007.

Moores, Ezequiel Fernández. *Breve historia del deporte Argentino*. El Ateneo, 2010.

Morales, Víctor Hugo, and Roberto Perfumo. *Hablemos de fútbol*. Booket, Planeta, 2007.

Mosse, G. L. *The Image of Man: The Creation of Modern Masculinity*. Oxford University Press, 1996.

Newton, Ronald C. *German Buenos Aires, 1900–1932*. University of Texas Press, 1977.

Nohlen, Dieter. *Elections in the Americas*. Oxford University Press, 2005.

O'Donnell, Guillermo. "Modernisation and Military Coups." In *Armies and Politics in Latin America*, edited by Abraham F. Lowenthal and J. Samuel Fitch. Holmes and Meier, 1986.

Oliveira Santos, Newton César de. *Brasil x Argentina*. Scortecci, 2009.

Oliver, Scott. "The Other Rival, Another Way." *Blizzard*, no. 4 (March 2012).

Olivera, Eduardo A. *Origenes de los deportes Britanicos en el Rió de la Plata*. L. J. Rosso, 1932.

Pagani, Horacio. *El fútbol que le gusta a la gente*. Al Arco, 2006.

Page, Joseph A. *Perón: A Biography*. Random House, 1988.

Palermo, Vicente, and Marcos Novaro. *Política y poder en el gobierno de Menem*. Editorial Normal, 1996.

Panzeri, Dante. *Burguesía y gangsters en el deporte*. Libera, 1974.

———. *Fútbol, dinámica de lo impensado*. Paidós, 1967.

Papa, Antonio, and Guido Panico. *Storia sociale del calcio in Italia*. Il Mulino, 2002.

Perdigão, Paulo. *Anatomia de una derrota*. L&PM, 1986.

Peucelle, Carlos. *Fútbol todotiempo e gistoria de la Máquina*. Axioma, 1975.

Potash, Robert. *The Army and Politics in Argentina*. Stanford University Press, 1996.

Raffo, Víctor. *El origen Británico del deporte Argentino*. Gráfica MPS, 2004.

Ritter, Arch R. M., ed. *Latin America and the Caribbean: Geopolitics, Development and Culture*. Canadian Association of Latin American and Caribbean Studies, 1984.

Rock, David. *Argentina, 1516–1982*. University of California Press, 1987.

———. *Politics in Argentina, 1870–1930: The Rise and Fall of Radicalism*. Cambridge University Press, 1975.

Romero, Amílcar. "Muerte en la cancha." *Todo es Historia* 209 (September 1984).

Romero, José Luis. *Argentina: Imágenes y perspectivas*. Editorial Raigal, 1956.

Sábato, Ernesto. *Sobre héroes y tumbas*. Sudamericana, 1961.

Sasturain, Juan. *La paatria transpirada: Argentina en los Mundiales, 1930–2010*. Sudamericana, 2010.

Scher, Ariel. *La passion según Valdano*. Capital intellectual, 2006.

Scher, Ariel, and Héctor Palomino. *Fútbol: Pasión de multitudes y de elites*. CISEA, 1988.

Scobie, James. *Buenos Aires: Plaza to Suburb, 1870–1919*. Oxford University Press, 1978.

Sebreli, Juan José. *La era del fútbol*. Debolsillo, 2005.

Sharpe, Ivan. *40 Years in Football*. Hutchinson, 1952.

Simpson, John, and Jana Bennett. *The Disappeared*. Robson, 1985.

Smith, B. L. "The Argentinian Junta and the Press in the Run-up to the 1978 World Cup." *Soccer and Society* 3, no. 1 (2002): 69–78.

Smith, Joseph. *Illusions of Conflict: Anglo-American Diplomacy Toward Latin America, 1865–1896*. University of Pittsburgh, 2009.

Smith, William C. *Authoritarianism and the Crisis of the Argentina Political Economy*. Stanford University Press, 1989.

Überhorst, Horst, ed. *Geschichte der Leibesübungen*. Bartels & Wernitz, 1971–1989.

Udenio. *La hipocresía Argentina*. Ensayo, 2007.

Varela, Mirta. *Los hombres ilustres del Billiken: Heroes de los mediosy la escuela*. Colihue, 1994.

Vargas, Walter. *Fútbol delivery*. Al Arco, 2007.

Vickery, Tim. "The Rise of the Technocrats." *Blizzard*, no. 6 (September 2012).

Viñas, David. *Indios, ejército y frontera*. Siglo XXI, 1982.

Wagg, Stephen. *The Football World*. Harvester, 1984.

Walsh, Rodolfo. *Operación masacre*. Ediciones de la Flor, 1972.

Wilson, Jason. *Buenos Aires: A Cultural History*. Interlink, 2012.

Wilson, Jonathan. *The Anatomy of England: A History in Ten Matches*. Orion, 2011.

———. *Inverting the Pyramid: The History of Football Tactics*. Orion, 2013.

———. *The Outsider: A History of the Goalkeeper*. Orion, 2012.

Winner, David. *Those Feet: A Sensual History of English Football*. Bloomsbury, 2005.

Wirth, John. *The Oil Business in Latin America: The Early Years*. Beard, 2001.

Worswick, Carl. "The Ball and the Gun." *Blizzard*, no. 7 (December 2012).

Zubeldía, Osvaldo, and Geronazzo, Argentino. *Tácticas y estrategia del fútbol*. Jorge Álvarez, 1965.

Newspapers and Magazines
Buenos Aires Herald
La Capital

Clarín
Corriere della Sera
Daily Chronicle
Daily Mail
Daily Record
El Diario
Efdeportes
La Época
Evening Standard
La Gaceta de Tucumán
El Gráfico
Guardian
Herald
Independent
Manchester Evening News
Mirror
La Nación
Pagina/12
Perfil
La Razón
Scotsman
Sporting Chronicle
Standard
Sunday Times
Tiempo
World Soccer

INDEX

Actis, Omar, 193
Agüero, Sergio, 333, 341, 348, 350, 359, 367–368, 370
alcohol abuse, 50, 168, 240; by players, 91, 95–97
Aldabe, Carlos "Cacho," 82
Alfonsín, Raúl, 230, 242–243, 252, 260–262, 323
Alonso, Norberto "Beto," 168–172, 211, 253, 255
Alumni, 8–11, 13
Alzamendi, Antonio, 254–255
amnesty programs, 165, 284
Andrade, José, 21
Angelillo, Antonio, xi, 90–92, 95, 97–98
anti-fútbol, 105–107, 111–112, 120, 143–144, 156, 171, 204, 231–232, 234
Aparicio, Salvador Ricardo, 323
apertura/clausura, 339, 377; Boca under Bianchi, 311–312, 315; Boca's 2002 finish, 329; Newell's under Bielsa, 274–275, 277; River Plate under Passarella, 297–298; River Plate's relegation, 358; split, 274, 286; 2005–2006 Boca win, 343–345; 2008 Boca win, 345–346; Vélez under Bianchi, 296
Ardiles, Osvaldo, 182, 199, 202, 225–226, 229–230, 247, 249
Argentine Association Football League (AAFL), 6–8, 12, 16–17, 31
Argentine Football Association (AFA), 372; AAF schism, 31; corruption allegations, 372–373; *criollisation* of the game, 12–15; first Campeonatos Sudamericanos, 16–17; investigating sporting immorality, 70; league expansion in 2015, 377–378; political figures' involvement in clubs, 35, 55; referee issues, 84; restructuring the championship, 137; short-termism, 353–354; soccer broadcasting rights, 353–354; stadium regulation, 59; violence against referees, 68

Argentinos Juniors, 163, 171, 208–213, 219, 222–227, 243–245
Arispe, Héctor, 54
Arispe, Pedro, 39
Arregui, Carlos, 234
Arsenal, 31
Artemio Franchi Trophy, 286
Asociación Amateurs de Football (AAmF), 16
Asociación Argentina de Football (AAF), 12
attendance at games, 376–377; attracting new viewers, 112; decline after 1958 Olympic Games, 104; decline under junta rule, 233; Evita championship, 78–79; Ferreyra's impact on ticket prices, 61; inaugural World Cup, 42; 1928 Olympic Games, 38–39; 1950s golden age, 51–52; post–World War I growth of, 35; reducing taxes to attract fans, 319

Babington, Carlos, xiv, 162–164, 180–181, 297–298
Bagnato, Luis, 85
Ball of Rags (film), 78
ball size and weight, 57, 61, 66
Balza, Martín, 263
Banega, Ever, 374
Banfield, 8, 70, 85, 169, 171, 183, 319–320, 375
bank fraud, 261
Barcelona, 219, 227, 236–239, 326–327, 331–334, 338, 341, 366–367
Barge, H. J., 5
Barisio, Carlos, 233
Basile, Alfio "Coco," xiv, 282, 286, 290, 305–306, 339, 348–349
Batistuta, Gabriel, 274, 280, 282, 287, 290–292, 305–308, 318
Battaglia, Sebastián, 313–314, 345
Battle of the Quinchos, 356
Beckham, David, 307–308, 318
Belgium, 30, 228, 246–247, 250, 370
Belo Horizonte, 185–186, 362

Jonathan Wilson's *Inverting the Pyramid* won the National Sporting Club Football Book of the Year award and was short-listed for the William Hill Sports Book of the Year award. His other books include *Behind the Curtain: Travels in Eastern European Football*; *Sunderland: A Club Transformed*; *The Anatomy of England: A History in Ten Matches*; *Nobody Ever Says Thank You*, a critically acclaimed biography of Brian Clough; *The Outsider: A History of the Goalkeeper*; and *The Anatomy of Liverpool*. He writes for the *Guardian*, *Sports Illustrated*, and *World Soccer*, and he is the editor of the *Blizzard*.

 **The Nation Institute**

NATION
BOOKS

Founded in 2000, **Nation Books** has become a leading voice in American independent publishing. The imprint's mission is to tell stories that inform and empower just as they inspire or entertain readers. We publish award-winning and bestselling journalists, thought leaders, whistleblowers, and truthtellers, and we are also committed to seeking out a new generation of emerging writers, particularly voices from underrepresented communities and writers from diverse backgrounds. As a publisher with a focused list, we work closely with all our authors to ensure that their books have broad and lasting impact. With each of our books we aim to constructively affect and amplify cultural and political discourse and to engender positive social change.

Nation Books is a project of The Nation Institute, a nonprofit media center established to extend the reach of democratic ideals and strengthen the independent press. The Nation Institute is home to a dynamic range of programs: the award-winning Investigative Fund, which supports groundbreaking investigative journalism; the widely read and syndicated website TomDispatch; journalism fellowships that support and cultivate over twenty-five emerging and high-profile reporters each year; and the Victor S. Navasky Internship Program.

For more information on Nation Books and The Nation Institute, please visit:

www.nationbooks.org
www.nationinstitute.org
www.facebook.com/nationbooks.ny
Twitter: @nationbooks